OUTSIDERS

MEDIEVAL INSTITUTE
UNIVERSITY OF NOTRE DAME

The Conway Lectures in Medieval Studies
2012

The Medieval Institute gratefully acknowledges the generosity of Robert M. Conway and his support for the lecture series and publications resulting from it.

PREVIOUS TITLES PUBLISHED IN THIS SERIES:

Paul Strohm
Politique: Languages of Statecraft between Chaucer and Shakespeare (2005)

Ulrich Horst, O.P.
The Dominicans and the Pope: Papal Teaching Authority in the Medieval and Early Modern Thomist Tradition (2006)

Rosamond McKitterick
Perceptions of the Past in the Early Middle Ages (2006)

Jonathan Riley-Smith
Templars and Hospitallers as Professed Religious in the Holy Land (2009)

A. C. Spearing
Medieval Autographies: The "I" of the Text (2012)

Barbara Newman
Medieval Crossover: Reading the Secular against the Sacred (2013)

John Marenbon
Abelard in Four Dimensions: A Twelfth-Century Philosopher in His Context and Ours (2013)

OUTSIDERS

*The Humanity and Inhumanity of Giants
in Medieval French Prose Romance*

SYLVIA HUOT

*University of Notre Dame Press
Notre Dame, Indiana*

University of Notre Dame Press
Notre Dame, Indiana 46556
www.undpress.nd.edu

Copyright © 2016 by the University of Notre Dame

All Rights Reserved

Published in the United States of America

Library of Congress Cataloging-in-Publication Data

Names: Huot, Sylvia, author.
Title: Outsiders : the humanity and inhumanity of giants in medieval French prose / Sylvia Huot.
Other titles: Giants in medieval French prose
Description: Notre Dame, Indiana : University of Notre Dame Press, 2016. | Series: The Conway Lectures in Medieval Studies | Includes bibliographical references and index.
Identifiers: LCCN 2016007506 (print) | LCCN 2016016930 (ebook) | ISBN 9780268031121 (paperback) | ISBN 0268031126 (paper) | ISBN 9780268081812 (pdf) | ISBN 9780268081836 (epub)
Subjects: LCSH: Romances—History and criticism. | French literature—To 1500—History and criticism. | Giants in literature. | Outsiders in literature. | Civilization, Medieval, in literature. | Arthurian romances—History and criticism. | BISAC: LITERARY CRITICISM / Medieval.
Classification: LCC PQ221 .H86 2016 (print) | LCC PQ221 (ebook) | DDC 840.9/375—dc23
LC record available at https://lccn.loc.gov/2016007506

∞ *This paper meets the requirements of ANSI/NISO Z39.48-1992 (Permanence of Paper).*

CONTENTS

Acknowledgments		vii
List of Illustrations		ix
	Introduction	1
Chapter 1	Inhuman Men and Knightly Fiends: The Vexed Humanity of Giants	27
Chapter 2	An Alien Presence: Giants as Markers of Race, Class, and Culture	69
Chapter 3	Touching the Absolute: Violence, Death, and Love	105
Chapter 4	Giants and Saracens in the Prose *Tristan*: Rival Narratives, Hostile Desires, and the Struggle to (Re)write History	155
Chapter 5	Outsiders in the Story: Galehot, Palamedes, and Saladin	197
Chapter 6	Desire, Subjectivity, and the Humanity of Giants	237
	Conclusion	293
	Notes	305
	Bibliography	331
	Index	345

ACKNOWLEDGMENTS

This book contains material, in revised form, that was originally published in the following locations: "Unspeakable Horror, Ineffable Bliss: Riddles and Marvels in the Prose *Tristan*," *Medium Aevum* 71 (2002): 47–65; and "Love, Race, and Gender in Medieval Romance: Lancelot and the Son of the Giantess," *Journal of Medieval and Early Modern Studies* 37 (2007): 373–91.

I am grateful to the editors of *Medium Aevum* and the Society for the Study of Medieval Languages and Literature and to the editors of the *Journal of Medieval and Early Modern Studies* and Duke University Press, respectively, for permission to reprint this material. I would also like to thank the Bibliothèque de Génève, the Bibliothèque Nationale de France, and Firestone Library at Princeton University for permission to publish photographs of medieval manuscripts in their collections. Finally, my thanks go to Pembroke College, Cambridge, for grants from the Fellows' Research Fund in support of this study.

Many thanks to the Medieval Institute at the University of Notre Dame for inviting me to deliver the 2012 Conway Lectures. The impetus this gave me to shape my thoughts about giants into something more cohesive, and the useful feedback from students and faculty members who attended the lectures, were invaluable in the evolution of this project. I am also grateful to the colleagues and students who contributed so much to my thinking on this subject; particular thanks go to Bill Burgwinkle, Miranda Griffin, and Tim Atkin, as well as others too numerous to mention. And as always, deep thanks to my husband and to my entire family for their loving support throughout my long interaction with the giants.

ILLUSTRATIONS

Figure 1. Guiron fights two giants. Paris, Bibliothèque de l'Arsenal, MS 3477, fol. 327v.   90

Figure 2. Bohort fights Maudit. Paris, Bibliothèque Nationale de France, fr. 119, fol. 424v.   95

Figure 3. The giant rescues Luce from the royal guards. Geneva, Bibliothèque de Genève, fr. 189, fol. 9r.   191

Figure 4. Yvain fights Harpin de la Montagne. Garrett MS 125, fol. 56v, Manuscripts Division, Department of Rare Books and Special Collections, Princeton University Library.   248

Figure 5. Yvain fights Harpin de la Montagne (upper register); Yvain defends Lunete against the wicked seneschal and his supporters (lower register). Paris, Bibliothèque Nationale de France, fr. 1433, fol. 90r.   249

Introduction

The study that follows is an examination of giants and their complex role in medieval French literature: principally prose romance set in the Arthurian or pre-Arthurian world, but sometimes also touching on other genres in both verse and prose. At the outset, I wish to clarify a point of terminology. My discussion of giants in these texts is sometimes cast in terms of relations and oppositions between "giants" and "humans." I make this distinction not to deny the humanity of giants but to distinguish them from "ordinary" people. Medieval texts typically refer to giants as "homme" and giantesses as "dame" or "pucelle," and there is no question that they are fundamentally human beings—however degraded or marginalized this humanity may at times be. In some ways, the category of "giant" is comparable to other racial or ethnic categories found in medieval literature, such as Saxon, Norman, Welsh, or Saracen; and it will be an important aspect of this study to examine the ways in which giants are a fantasy race, yet another of the diverse ethnic groups inhabiting Arthurian Britain, and a vehicle for reflection on the nature of both racial and cultural differences. Still, the common use of *geant* and *geante* clearly marks these men, women, and girls as set apart from the other human subjects of the Arthurian world.

Even when giants form alliances with pagan lords, they are likely to assume a high-handed attitude, exacting tribute and brooking no interference with their affairs, or any challenge to their supremacy. It thus seems important to distinguish between giants of all kinds, wherever they may live, and the other characters with whom they interact. Since *ordinary human knight, nongiant,* or *regular-sized person* is too cumbersome to use on a regular basis, I will also use the terms *giant* and *human* to clarify this distinction.

It is further worth noting that medieval literature as a whole presents two very different kinds of giants: those who are descended from a fully giant lineage and those who are giants only through some accident of birth or exotic upbringing. Most giants in Arthurian romance are of the former type, with varying combinations and degrees of human potential for cultural refinement and ethical behavior on the one hand, or bestial savagery on the other. Giants of the other kind are most commonly found among the Saracens that populate the *chanson de geste*, a genre whose giants tend to inhabit the two extremes of assimilable humanity and monstrous or demonic inhumanity.[1] A third category that we will encounter is that of half-blood giants, whose identity may be somewhat ambiguous: they are likely to be assimilable into chivalric life, but generally not entirely, and not without conflict. In all cases, however, giants are a focal point for racial, social, cultural, and ideological clashes; and there are three principal contexts in which these issues will be examined.

Species, Race, and Culture: Defining Human Identity

Le discours sur le monstre est, en réalité, un discours sur l'homme.
[Discourse about monsters is, in reality, a discourse about man.]
— Annie Cazenave, "Monstres et merveilles"

In speaking of racist and sexist stereotypes, Kobena Mercer states that "we are dealing not with persons, but with the imaginary and symbolic positions through which the contingent, historical and psychic construction of personhood is spoken."[2] Mercer's comment pertains to the discourse of modern colonial and postcolonial societies, but the same can certainly be said of both the giants and the other characters populating medieval art and literature. Giants, no more a cultural fantasy than the shifting stereotypes of race, class, and gender embodied by Arthurian knights and ladies, are one of the means by which medieval Europeans imagined the limits of personhood.

Robert Bartlett's influential work on medieval concepts of race and ethnicity draws on the much-quoted formulation by the early medieval writer Regino de Prüm (d. 915): "Diversae nationes populorum inter se discrepant genere, moribus, lingua, legibus" (The different human nations are distinguished from one another by descent, customs, language, and laws).[3] Giants speak the same language as anyone else, but they do have their own distinctive bloodlines, as well as their typical forms of behavior—and while giants might not be seen as operating according to a rule of law, they could be described as adhering to customary practices, some of which at times do take on a legal dimension within the giant's realm. Bartlett and others have argued that custom, law, and language are all acquired behaviors, and as such subject to change, so that blood descent is the only racial feature that is inherited and inalterable.[4] This may be true of actual, real-life people—though in practice, of course, the imposition of a new language, legal system, religion, or other code of behavior often meets with fierce resistance—and is sometimes also true of the Saracens, pagans, and other exotic people who populate medieval literature. But it is much less clear that it holds true for giants. Certain behaviors—violence, arrogance, intransigence, a free or even obsessive indulgence in libidinous drives—characterize giants regardless of their circumstances and appear to be as essential to their nature as their prodigious size and strength. Medieval literature offers countless examples of people who backslide into moral laziness or depravity, only to repent and atone for their transgressions; of those who lack an ethical sense or a grasp of courtly refinements, but who better themselves through religious instruction and penance, or through a formative experience such as love or warfare; of pagans who convert to Christianity, perhaps even becoming saints, as well as those who resist to the end. The concept of foreign races as assimilable, and of humans as capable of radical change, lies at the core of evangelical Christianity. But giants represent an alternate racial fantasy, one more essentialist in the way that it combines moral character—or lack thereof—and a propensity for irrational violence with the physical characteristics and bloodlines of giants. As an imagined race, giants offer a view of racial and cultural alterity, and thus of human nature overall, somewhat different from that embodied in the admirable pagans, rogue knights, and isolated kingdoms that figure in narratives of moral or religious conversion, the abolition of evil customs, and overall cultural assimilation.

However important differences of custom, law, and religion may be in medieval discourses of human difference, it is equally important to consider the role attributed to climate and geography. As is well documented, a tradition reaching from antiquity through the Middle Ages emphasized the extent to which bodily humors—and thus such features as hair type, skin color, and temperament—are affected by conditions in the earth's climactic zones, with their varying degrees of heat or cold, wetness or dryness.[5] Cultural and environmental models of human diversity interact in medieval texts in ways that are not entirely consistent. Saracens, for example, are first and foremost marked by differences of custom and law. Their little-understood religion defines them as enemies of the Christian faith; they are portrayed as engaging in alien practices such as idolatry and polygamy, as well as indulging a taste for lavish and exotic architecture, clothing, and other accouterments. Only sometimes, however, are they also marked as racially other. Saracens may have black or impenetrable skin, spiky hair, or other features ranging from the merely different to the outright demonic, and this is especially likely to be the case when they hail from more southerly realms, their bodies shaped by a harsh desert environment. Even within the same text, however, they may also be indistinguishable in appearance from their Christian European counterparts. And as is well documented, Saracens are also far from homogeneous in their degree of cultural alterity. Most are implacably hostile to Christianity, but some readily embrace religious conversion in their eagerness to join forces with the heroic Christian warriors at their doorstep. Cultural alterity may at times be identified with physiological difference, and it may be portrayed as intrinsic to a person's very nature; it may also be almost inconsequential, as easily shed as an item of exotic dress.

Considerable variation may obtain even among members of the same Saracen family, in accordance with their narrative role. In the Guillaume d'Orange cycle, for example, the Saracen queen Orable is a white-skinned, impeccably mannered beauty who readily falls in love with Guillaume, converts to Christianity in order to marry him (taking on the baptismal name Guiborc), and becomes an unflinching supporter of the Christian cause. Her brother Rainouart is a giant, complete with a violent temper, a prodigious appetite for food and drink, unruly behavior, and a fanatical devotion to his enormous cudgel. King Louis, who bought him at a slave market, clearly views a Saracen giant as one who is beyond redemption, commenting, "Por sa grandor nel poi onques amer, / . . . Onc nel voil fere bautizier ne lever" (I could never love him because of his size . . . I don't ever want to have him baptised and raised from the font).[6] This attitude is shown to be an unfounded and indeed pernicious prejudice, however, as Rainouart literally begs to be baptized and to be allowed to fight alongside Guillaume, to whom he is fiercely loyal. Guiborc's strong-willed, uncompromising personality may derive in part from the stereotypical intensity of Saracens as depicted in *chansons de geste*, but it also makes her the perfect match for the equally impulsive and irascible Guillaume; Rainouart, his slapstick caricature, is the perfect sidekick. Their father Desramez, however, a king in Spain and possibly also a giant, is the sworn enemy of Guillaume and of Christendom in general; and whereas Rainouart is "biax" (v. 3595; handsome), Desramez's appearance reflects his sinister character:

Desramez fu fort et grant et corssuz,
Long ot le col, noirs ert et toz chenus;
En tote Espaigne n'ot paien si membruz.
                          (vv. 6113–15)

[Desramez was strong and big and muscular, he had a long neck, he was black and completely white-haired; in all of Spain there was no pagan so powerfully built.]

The Saracen armies fought by Guillaume and Rainouart in the aftermath of Guillaume's marriage to Guiborc—the allies of Desramez and his brother, to whom Guiborc was originally married—run the full gamut from ordinary human knights and richly armored kings to grotesque and monstrous figures: Agrapart, a three-foot-tall dwarf who bites and claws his victims (vv. 6256–611); Rainouart's cousin Aenré, said to have devoured many a Frenchman (vv. 6028–42); Grishart, a knight whose hunchback daughter Guinehart eats raw human flesh (vv. 6675–77); and Grishart's fifteen-foot-tall sister Flohart, whose smoky breath has a toxic effect on the Frankish troops (vv. 6716–81).

This degree of variation is possible partly because medieval culture did not have a fully consistent, canonical theory of race, and partly because the entertainment value, ideological import, and narrative intrigue of literary texts could all take precedence over any pretense to historically or scientifically accurate depictions of real or imagined people and places. As Lynn Tarte Ramey has commented, any reading of the Saracen in medieval French literature "must take into account the personal or collective ends for which the Other was introduced in the first place."[7] "Saracens" were used to support a wide range of erotic, doctrinal, and military fantasies, in which an exotic foreign woman might be either alluring or horrific; adherents to an alien religion might acknowledge the universal appeal of Christian doctrine in their ready conversion or might embody the intransigence and wickedness of the infidel in their benighted resistance; a sophisticated foreign culture might be a source of human and material resources from which much good could be salvaged and assimilated or a demonized anticulture just waiting to be crushed by the superior forces of European Christendom.[8]

Independently of the occasional giant-sized member of an otherwise normal family, giants are imagined by medieval writers as existing throughout the known world; they tend to share the religious practices of the pagan or pseudo-Muslim peoples of the region in which they live, sometimes even joining with Saxons or other pagans in battles against Arthur and his Christian predecessors, or with Muslim armies in fighting European crusaders. In terms of physiognomy, giants are also likely to resemble their neighbors in certain respects. African or Near Eastern giants, for example, often have the dark complexion supposedly caused by the intense heat and sunlight of southerly latitudes, while the Norwegian Gueant aux Cheveulx Dorez in *Perceforest* is a Nordic blond. Giants' most essential features, however—large size and violent temperaments—seem unaffected by factors of climate and geography. In any given location, giants exist as a people both similar to, but also differentiated from, the other inhabitants of that area; and whereas giants may be in league with Saracens or other peoples regarded as enemies by Western Christendom, they are also often in conflict with the nongiant population, particularly in the Arthurian world. If a giant is the ruler of an island, a feudal manor, or a kingdom, his subjects are generally ordinary people, chafing under his despotic rule; if he dwells apart, isolated in his castle or lair, he is likely to be a menace to the surrounding population on whom he preys. Giants, subject to the influences of climate and geography, exhibit the same spectrum of bodily diversity as other human beings, and they follow many of the same cultural practices; but they are also always a separate presence. In a sense, giants are a parallel form of humanity, a larger-than-life doubling of the human race with their own distinct bloodlines, their characteristically extreme behavior, and their unmistakable bodily proportions.

As Abdul JanMohamed notes, colonialist discourse depends on "a transformation of racial difference into moral and even metaphysical difference."[9] Such ideas have a long history; David M. Goldenberg, for example, has traced the characterization of people inhabiting the extreme northern and southern latitudes—particularly black Africans—as occupying a position higher than that of animals but nonetheless subhuman in their savagery. From an initial formulation by classical writers such as Aristotle, these stereotypes were perpetuated throughout the Middle Ages in both Islamic and Christian traditions.[10] In a similar vein Steven F. Kruger comments that, in medieval thought, sexual difference was sometimes cast in ethnic or racial terms—as in the use of the term *sodomite* both for the residents of the cursed city of Sodom and for practitioners of a loosely defined sexual deviancy—while "religious difference . . . and racial or ethnic difference are often associated with sexual 'crimes.'"[11] Kruger further notes that the blend of moral character and blood descent in medieval concepts of race results in a double focus, whereby racial identity is at once changeable and immutable: "For the Middle Ages, sexuality, race, and religion are all constructed at least partly in moral terms—as choices that might be changed—and partly as biological difference, which would suggest perhaps a more determinate and unchangeable (sexual, racial, or religious) 'nature.'"[12] As strongly stereotyped embodiments of the racial and cultural other, giants are a classic instance of the moralization of race. The qualities so often attributed to conquered, enslaved, or colonized races in the modern era—cannibalism, brute lust, senseless violence, inability to grasp abstract concepts, and even the eroticization of the sensual native woman—are already present in medieval depictions of giants, vividly constructed stereotypes of a hostile race resisting subjugation by those bringing the blessings of civilization. The Arthurian giants are an imaginative reconstruction of exotic aliens in a setting closer to home—distant not in space but in time. The distinctive bodily features of giants, along with their predictable behavior, crystallize into a stereotype of racial identity that combines both moral and physical deviance from the idealized norms of European Christians.

Tales of barbaric, uncultured giants, then, were a place in which fears and desires aroused by cultural and racial alterity could be freely explored. As such, these narratives both mirror and shape the lurid accounts of religious, racial, or ethnic groups targeted for conquest, subjugation, or expulsion by historical or fictional monarchs—be they Saxon or Celtic, Jewish or Muslim, European, African, or Asian.[13] The racial and cultural other could thus be imagined in contrasting modes that support slightly different fantasies and political ideologies. On the one hand, the willing Saracen converts to Christianity—gallant knights or beautiful princesses—as well as the virtuous Indian ascetics or the uncouth Welsh lad who turns out to be the Grail knight Perceval, offer a model of assimilation, of difference that is not so different after all: a comforting promise that aristocratic refinement, feudal homage and loyalty, and Christian ideology are universal values that can indeed be a means of uniting disparate peoples, both within Europe and throughout the world at large.[14] At the same time, savage giants and other racial fantasies—from the sodomite Welshmen and the Irish with their proclivity for bestiality, as described by Gerald of Wales, to demonic Saracen warriors and the monstrous races—counter this with a model of intractable otherness and depravity that fully justifies conquest, subjugation, and extermination.

As background to a study of giants as figures of aberrant humanity, foils for the idealized heroes and heroines of epic and romance, we may consider various analogies in modern cultural, scientific, and political discourses. First, medieval giants might be seen as occupying a position somewhat similar to that of Neanderthals in nineteenth- and twentieth-century thought. *Homo neanderthalensis* was identified as a distinct species in 1856, just three years before Darwin published *On the Origin of*

Species. Neanderthals were recognized as clearly human in at least some sense, but they were also constructed as irretrievably different from us. Hulking, brutish, and dim-witted, they lacked the cognitive skills, technological sophistication, and strategies of social cooperation that allowed our ancestors, *Homo sapiens*, to spread through the world and make it theirs. Largely through extermination, though perhaps also to some small extent through absorption by interbreeding, these creatures gave way and vanished before the onward march of modern humans, the natural inheritors and rulers of the land. Such is the story that, for the past century and a half, has defined the human species that inhabited large parts of Europe and Asia before the arrival of our distant ancestors. This view has been challenged to some extent in recent years; ongoing archaeological discoveries along with the use of newly developed techniques, such as DNA analysis, continue to refine and expand the scientific understanding of humanity's cultural and biological prehistory. In the popular imagination, however, the club-wielding Neanderthal is an icon of all that our superior human intelligence has enabled us to overcome. An evolutionary dead end, more ape than man, our Neanderthal predecessors are imagined as a kind of hinge that linked us to a dark, bestial past while also highlighting the extent to which we, endowed as we always already were with language, culture, and a spirit of innovation, occupy a unique and privileged position distinct from all other animal species. At the same time, the recent revisionist view of Neanderthals as capable of cultural and technological sophistication is a reflection of contemporary aversion to racial stereotyping of any sort, and thus itself an effort to realize an inclusive sense of human diversity, hallmark of what we now see as our better nature. For better and for worse, Neanderthals continue to occupy a privileged place in discourses of race, culture, and humanity.[15]

Similarly, in medieval legend, giants are the indigenous inhabitants of Britain and other parts of Europe, encountered when "our ancestors" arrived—not from Africa in this telling of history, but from Troy and, later, the Holy Land—and began to settle and cultivate the land. Medieval thought could not imagine either humans or giants as descended from animals, but giants were again a hinge linking humans to a much darker past, sometimes seen as demonic and other times as the cursed lineages of Cain and Ham. And like Neanderthals, they were portrayed as humans of a kind, while nonetheless usually lacking the refinement and rational discretion needed for true assimilation into a courtly, chivalric community.[16] The very way that both giants and Neanderthals were depicted confirmed not only their status as a race doomed to extinction but also ours as one destined to a position of stewardship. As caricatures of savagery and voracity, bereft of the most important features that define human preeminence in the natural order, giants, like Neanderthals, function in the cultural imagination as a means of defining both the errors and excesses that threaten our frail humanity, and the means that we uniquely have at our disposal to regulate our lives and rise above mere animal instinct. As generations of nineteenth- and twentieth-century thinkers grappled with the implications of the evolutionary model, it was perhaps a consolation to believe that if humans really were descended from apes, still it was in the failed lineage of Neanderthals that this apishness was fully channeled, while *Homo sapiens*—as the name implies—are defined above all by their uniquely human intellect. And from the medieval perspective, though humans are marked by Original Sin and share with giants a common origin in those first parents beguiled by the serpent, it was reassuring to imagine an alternate line of descent—in a sense, a race of scapegoats. David Lewis-Williams comments that "the Neanderthal debate is not merely an esoteric dispute among inhabitants of an ivory tower: it has major implications for the way in which we see life today."[17] Similarly, medieval tales of giants are not just fanciful entertainment; they are a vehicle for reflections about the nature of culture, power, and human identity.

Neanderthals are not the only modern analogy for giants; we may also read them more generally through the lens of racial and ethnic difference, particularly as these differences have been constructed in the violent conflicts of colonial and postcolonial subjugation and resistance. Again, giants are the primal aboriginals at the origins of British history, who had to be cleared from the land along with wild animals and impenetrable forests to make way for conquest and settlement by successive waves of Trojans, Romans, and others. In the Arthurian era, they may be the inhabitants of island or mountain kingdoms to which access is needed as stopping points for traveling merchants and knights on quests or diplomatic missions. They are also frequently found in the Saracen kingdoms targeted in *chansons de geste*, ostensibly in the name of spreading Christianity, but clearly also for their opulent cities and lucrative trade networks. Whether at home or abroad, giants consistently obstruct the exploitation of natural resources, the establishment of commercial and diplomatic networks, the process of royal conquest and expansionism, and the spread of Christianity. As such, their cultural image is analogous not only to that of Neanderthals in modern archaeological discourse but also to Native Americans, Africans, Asians, or Australians as these people have figured in the imagination of Euro-American warriors, explorers, settlers, and entrepreneurs. I do not, of course, mean to imply that all of these peoples were ever perceived or imagined in exactly the same way, that interactions between incomers and natives always took the same form, or that they were stereotyped in support of the same ideological agendas in all times and places.[18] Nor can we expect that fictional giants will occupy precisely the same position in the cultural imagination as did any of the peoples who really were encountered by Europeans as they spread throughout the world. Nonetheless, the analogy is a useful one in unpacking the complex and sometimes contradictory treatment of giants in medieval texts.

In particular, if we think of giants as figures for colonized people resisting the incursions of an incoming race, their behavior can be understood as evoking a fear comparable to that of the modern obsession with guerrilla warfare and terrorism. The intransigence of giants, who may systematically kill anyone who enters their territory, and who generally fight to the death with no concept of compromise or truce, constructs this enemy in remarkably similar terms to those used in our own times for the "fundamentalist" and "militant" enemies of the West. The giants' obsessive behavior and the rigidity of their customs, which typically allow no option but violence unto death, is implicitly contrasted with that of Arthurian chivalry, in which knights are expected to have internalized a moral compass enabling them to assess individual encounters on their own terms and to negotiate a suitable outcome of absolute victory, compromise, or truce, and of vengeance and punishment or forgiveness and reconciliation. And while I do not mean to identify medieval cultural ideology with that of post-Enlightenment liberalism, this conception of "us" as flexible in our application of violence and vengeance, and "them" as inflexibly determined by received laws and customs, does reflect Wendy Brown's characterization of the modern liberal subject as one presumed to be guided, not by blind obedience to cultural and religious imperatives, but by a rational sense of universalizable morality. As Brown puts it, "The liberal formulation of the individuated subject as constituted by rationality and will figures a nonindividuated opposite who is so *because of* the underdevelopment of both rationality and will."[19] Giants, overall, tend to be constructed along lines that recall the two models developed by Freud and other post-Enlightenment thinkers for premodern humans: in Brown's words, the "lone savage" or the "primitive tribalist."[20] The imagined "culture wars" of knight and giant, in more ways than one, can be seen as the distant foundations of the conflicts and self-justifications currently at play in Western civilization.

The War on Giants

> *Et certes, se ilz savoient ore a Taraquin la verité de la mort a cest jayant, ilz acourroient tuit ça maintenant, car ilz ne desiroient rien du monde autant comme ilz faisoient sa mort. [And if the people in Taraquin knew that truly this giant is dead, they would all come running right away, for there is nothing they desired so much in all the world as his death.]*
> —Suite du roman de Merlin

Terrorism, in modern political discourse, is the fear that haunts the political landscape, constantly being eradicated as terrorists are arrested or killed, yet never disappearing.[21] And in the Arthurian world giants, though constantly eradicated by generations of knights and saints, are similarly always present, a fantasy that serves a powerful purpose too important to be given up. Slavoj Žižek has suggested that "authentic community is possible only in conditions of permanent threat."[22] And giants in medieval romance, by providing a permanent threat against which the Arthurian court defines itself, perpetuate the idea of an Arthurian hegemony preyed on by giants but always resisting them: a glorious foundation and mirror of the feudal society and court culture of medieval Europe. Like terrorists, giants evoke the specter of cultural decline and divergence, the fear of an entirely unknowable future that is not continuous with or generated by our law, our narrative trajectory.

And killing them not only ensures the continuation of a particular historical narrative but also reiterates its very existence. As Samira Kawash states, in the postcolonial world the ubiquitous specter of terrorism is a way of configuring "the possibility and the immanence of an epochal collapse of the law that constitutes this history and this reality, and an opening onto some otherwise and elsewhere."[23] In the eyes of the colonial power, decolonization and terrorism threaten to destroy prevailing concepts of law and right, and the identities thereby formed, leading—in Kawash's words—to "a future that cannot be known, that has not been given in advance by the narrative trajectory of history."[24] As we will see, the giants of medieval romance resist the cultural work of Brutus and his descendants down through Uterpendragon and Arthur, sometimes to the point of setting different and alien terms, as if in an effort to reorient the master narrative of history onto a trajectory incompatible with the one established by those Trojan settlers and their successors. As such, they can never be allowed to succeed, but for all that they never stop trying. And just as the "war on terrorism" has become central to contemporary constructions of Western cultural identity, similarly the "war on giants" and the battle to control the narrative are defining features of Arthurian culture and civilization, and one of the ways in which it is constantly reaffirmed as Civilization in an absolute sense. Roediger's comment about white Americans' fear and hatred of Native Americans, even in areas from which the native population had long since been removed or exterminated, are relevant to a reading of giants as they figure in the world of Arthurian romance: "'Civilization' continued to define itself as a negation of 'savagery'—indeed, to invent savagery in order to define itself."[25] Fear and loathing of giants, desire for their death, and adulation of their killers are potent ingredients in the construction of a collective past: a shared history that, however fictional or fanciful, can tell its readers who they are, how they came to be, and where they might be headed.

The notion of a "War on Giants," and the related conflicts over past and future trajectories, lead to another important thread of the study to follow, one focused on the struggle to produce the narrative of history; and I will turn to this topic shortly. First, however, I want to dwell just a little longer on the violence that characterizes any encounter between humans and giants. Violence can assume many forms.

Among other possibilities, it can be perfunctory, as in the simple elimination of vermin or pests; utilitarian, as in the killing of animals for food; righteous, as in the execution of criminals or the blood vengeance taken against those seen as having wronged one's family or social unit; ideological, as in battles undertaken against those who abuse or debase feudal power, or resist the expansionist supremacy of the king; or militantly pious, as in Holy War against the infidel. There is equally a spectrum of recreational violence—athletic matches, tournaments, the aristocratic hunt—comprising varying elements of rivalry, ritualistic self-staging, and playful enjoyment. Violence may imply a relationship of hostility, mutual respect, or simple disregard; the deaths that result may be viewed as tragic, as necessary and proper, as a sign of divine judgment, as glorious, or even as utterly inconsequential. As Karl Steel notes, the question of whether a life is to be mourned is crucial in the definition of humanity as an ethical category, to which some men and women are admitted while others, such as giants or other "enemy combatants," are not. In Steel's words: "Fields of representability divide grievable lives, whose injuries and losses are accorded merit and commemoration, from lives outside the frame, not understood as significantly vulnerable and whose deaths do not matter; thus it might be said that the frames divide life from nonlife."[26] Defining the nature of human-giant violence, its emotional, political, and spiritual currency, and its larger implications is one way of approaching the question of who and what, exactly, giants actually are, and how they contribute to medieval reflections on culture and humanity.

Like the modern War on Terrorism, the "war on giants" is not usually warfare strictly speaking, since it is more likely to involve single combat, often in isolated locations. Nonetheless, as we will see, it may have elements both of political power struggles and of Holy War for the glory of God; and when giants are encountered in the context of pitched battle between armies, it is nearly always in the context of crusading against a pagan or Saracen enemy. Outside the context of the Crusades, battles with giants take various forms. They may be hunted down and killed by a knight determined to put an end to their violent marauding, or to rescue a lady or fellow knight that the giant has abducted; or they may be encountered by chance as knights errant inadvertently pass through giant territory and come into conflict with giants who bar their way, demand tribute, or simply react with hostility to anyone entering their domain.

At its origin, in a Britain just discovered by Brutus and his band of Trojan refugees, the struggle against giants is inscribed in the context of colonization, within which the work of "ethnic cleansing" is analogous to that of hunting down dangerous carnivores, clearing the land for cultivation, and generally eliminating the natural and elemental obstacles to farming and urbanization. This is clear not only in Geoffrey of Monmouth's *Historia Regum Brittanie* and its vernacular adaptations but also in the corpus of Arthurian romance. Giants may be men, but not men who are worthy of populating the new Trojan kingdom or its Christian successor. Like hunting, extermination of giants has a recreational dimension. Brutus's companion Corineus in particular enjoyed the sport of wrestling giants and established himself in Cornwall because there were more giants there than elsewhere.[27] Later in the *Historia*, Arthur himself laughs with pleasure upon defeating the Giant of Mont-St-Michel;[28] similar bravado and thrill characterize numerous other chivalric battles with giants throughout the romance tradition. The pleasure taken in the violent struggle for dominance, whether it ends in slaughter or subjugation, is different from the righteous indignation with which a knight attacks a rampaging giant on a spree of rape and destruction. It is also different from acts of simple extermination, where the rumor of a giant will cause a knight to make a brief detour in order to kill him.

The violence of giant against knight is similarly varied, and it is important to bear in mind that most Arthurian giants are not as demonic and irrational as those featured in the Old Testament or in the fourteenth-century poem *Des grantz geanz*. Sometimes giants enjoy sporting with humans, whom they assume they can easily defeat in matches of wrestling, racing, or fencing. Some even take pleasure in collecting humans to keep as companions, or perhaps more properly as pets or playthings. But although the mix of fascination, hostility, contempt, respect, and desire that giants manifest for the knights they capture can be intensely focused and powerfully expressed, it is unlikely to result in anything that we might call a relationship of equals. As we will see, such situations ultimately bring out the impossibility of any mutually beneficial relationship between giant and knight, turning instead on a kind of mutual dehumanization that entails its own dimension of violent coercion and resistance. In other cases still, giants are portrayed as attacking knights on sight, as if in their eyes the knight occupied the same position of pest or vermin that giants often do for knights. And of course giants also prey on humans as a food source, reinforcing the lack of empathy that characterizes human-giant encounters.

Still, if the preceding examples highlight the incomprehensible, inhuman aspect of giants, we must not forget that they can also attack knights out of a very human sense of justice, seeking redress for wrongs that the knights have committed against them or their families. Giants may even exhibit a chivalric concern for "fair play" in agreeing to a set of terms—for example, a prescribed area within which the combat will take place—or allowing the knight an opportunity to regain his footing if he is knocked down, rather than killing him when he is unarmed or off his guard. Similarly, a giant's capture of human beings as food may take a stark and animalistic form in which the stronger predator snatches and devours the weaker prey. But it may also involve a recreational element analogous to the pleasure of the hunt, as with a giant in the prose *Tristan* who uses riddles to catch his prey, or the Golden-Haired Giant in *Perceforest* who prolongs his enjoyment of the battle by toying with the knight Lyonnel "ainsi que le jenne chat fait de la soris" (as the young cat does with the mouse).[29] Giants are portrayed as having a capacity for inventive play and the pleasure of competition, however grisly the context within which this is displayed, and however reluctant they may be to accept defeat. And whatever the lack of human dignity accorded by knights to their giant adversaries, giants do value and grieve for one another. Though some giants live alone in a state of permanent hostility with the outside world, others live in family groups. And medieval French literature is replete with examples of giants seeking vengeance for the death of a family member killed by some enterprising chivalric hero. Xenophobic and intensely territorial, giants are permanently at odds with the knights; but they do inhabit an internally coherent world.

There is thus a double focus for the slaying of giants, as human and giant perspectives present irreconcilably different visions of the same act. Meili Steele's comments about contemporary society apply equally to Arthurian knights, ladies, and giants: "Living in gendered, raced bodies means that one will be subject to certain discourses and have access to certain discourses in a way that those who are gendered and raced differently will not."³⁰ Humans and giants alike mourn their respective allies and kin, but the reader is never invited to sympathize with giants seeking vengeance, for in the discourse of Arthurian romance the killing of a giant is always justified and can never be read as murder. Parallel behaviors exhibited by giants and knights respectively—attacks on rival lords, territorial expansionism, the acquisition of a wife as a reward for military service, vengeance taken for family members slain by an enemy—are coded very differently. Clashes between knights and giants are certainly violent on both sides, but the behavior of giants is portrayed as embodying a deeper level of violence, one that strikes at the heart of social order, class structures, and codes of honor. The focus on the horrific violence of giants, then, becomes a way of sanitizing and valorizing the violence that pervades aristocratic warrior society. Richard Kaueper has analyzed the ways in which the regulation, channeling, and ideological coding of violence in the warrior society of medieval Europe was both an object of fascination and essential to public order. In his words, violence was recognized as "a power akin to fire: if noble, necessary, and useful, such violence requires much care and control."³¹ Medieval literature is much concerned with the exploration of violence and the identification of its honorable and dishonorable manifestations, a process in which giants are useful scapegoats. As Slavoj Žižek has noted, "When we perceive something as an act of violence, we measure it by a presupposed standard of what the 'normal' non-violent situation is—and the highest form of violence is the imposition of this standard with reference to which some events appear as 'violent.'"³²

Whether they are portrayed as racial inferiors, insolent ruffians, marauding bandits, pagan tyrants, or man-eating carnivores, giants are not, in Steel's words, "grievable lives," any more than knights and ladies are to them. And the abyss that separates the knights and giants who interact so closely in romance texts means that every narrative of giants rests on a possible, silenced or thwarted counternarrative. Might there be an alternative narrative trajectory in which the giant would have a legitimate place in the human world—a castle, a fiefdom, a right to marry, to ally with feudal lords, or to collect his own taxes and tolls? Can the giant be fully accounted for within the terms of chivalric narrative, and could there be a "giant narrative" that offered a different, but still coherent, perspective? Despite the strict parameters within which giants are portrayed in Arthurian romance, we can glimpse other story lines at work—or at least potential story lines, shadow stories foreclosed by the chivalric narrative framework. Most fundamentally, we might ask: Is the giant an authentic subject? Can the giant speak?

The Discourse of the Giant

Or oi merveilles, dit rois Pelias, com tu ta desonor et ta honte et ta deleauté me raconte. ["Now I hear a marvel," said King Pelias, "how you tell me your dishonor and your shame and your treachery."]
—*Tristan en prose*

Giants do, of course, speak in medieval literature, engaging both knights and one another in dialogue. Perhaps the most extended instance of a full-blooded giant dialoguing with knights occurs near the beginning of the prose *Tristan*, where a giant waylays passing knights with riddles, some of which are autobiographical accounts, in metaphorical language, of his own acts of rape, murder, incest, and cannibalism: the stuff of a giant's life. On occasion he also attempts to solve riddles posed by the knights. This episode, which I will examine in detail in chapters 4 and 6, is illuminating for its implicit message that communication across the human-giant divide is always a riddle of sorts, and in the fullest sense of that word. Giants are perplexing and irrational, they challenge the chivalric worldview; and yet for the truly discerning they are also relatively simple to read and to "solve," as a knight's store of experience and received wisdom actually tells him exactly what giants are. This paradoxical mixture of shock and incomprehension coupled with easy recognition is expressed by the knights to whom the Riddler speaks. On the one hand, the narrator explains that the giant has stumped—and beheaded—a good many people, "car totes les devinailles estoient si oscures qu'a poines pooient eles estre seües" (for all his riddles were so obscure that they could scarcely be solved).[33] And yet if the chivalric protagonists of the romance feign amazement at the scabrous content of the riddles—King Pelias terms the giant's riddles "merveilles ... les greignors que je onques mes oïsse" (*PT*[C], 1:80; the greatest marvels I ever heard)—somehow they always know the solution. If the riddles really lie so far beyond anything Pelias has previously experienced, how then is he able to decode them without missing a beat? The giant in fact embodies a well-defined stereotype of racial and cultural difference, to which Edward Said's characterization of European perceptions of the "Orient" is remarkably apt: "One tends to stop judging things either as completely novel or as completely well-known; a new median category emerges, a category that allows one to see new things, things seen for the first time, as versions of a previously known thing. . . . The threat is muted, familiar values impose themselves."[34] In their reading of the giant's riddles, the knights—to quote Homi Bhabha—"individualize otherness as the discovery of their own assumptions."[35] There is no need to understand the giant on his own terms—to discover a place from which his behavior and the pleasure he takes in boasting of it might make a kind of sense—because the knight already understands the giant completely from within his own frame of reference. The giant, seemingly so exotic, is in fact rather mundane, a blasphemer in the grip of demonic temptation: "Se tu tenisses riens des diex, ja n'en parlasses. Mes je sai bien que tu as les anemis en toi" (*PT*[C], 1:79; If you respected the gods at all, you wouldn't speak of that. But I know very well that you have demons in you). As Jeffrey Jerome Cohen has argued, the medieval giant "conjoined absolute otherness with reassuring familiarity" in what Cohen terms "intimate alterity."[36]

The Riddler is not the only giant to tell a story outlining his sense of a personal past or future. In *Des grantz geanz*, the tale of the demonic origins of British giants is attributed to Gogmagog himself, who first related it to Brutus. In *Perceforest*, the Golden-Haired Giant speaks of his plans to marry his own daughter as soon as she is old enough. And in the *Chevalier du Papegau*, the Chevalier Jayant, having been mortally wounded by Arthur, makes a full confession at the point of death. All of these stories, however, are appropriated by the human interlocutors and turned to their own advantage as a means of amplifying the heroic or kingly aura of the giant killers. Giants also establish customs within their own lands, sometimes working to keep the outside world at bay, while at other times incorporating aristocratic knights and ladies into a parody or debasement of feudal governance. In such cases the giant may be reacting to events, seeking to right what he has experienced as a wrong or to set history on a course more advantageous to himself or his people.

But these constructions of "giant discourse" or "giant culture" are inevitably overturned as they come into conflict with the larger Arthurian narrative in which they are—perhaps unwillingly, perhaps unwittingly—contained.

Giants, then, operate on fixed narrative trajectories and aim to rewrite or restructure the chivalric and Christian history that has overtaken them; knights in turn aim to reimpose their narrative onto giants. When the two trajectories collide, both are distorted. And this contributes to the sense we often have that the narrative cannot entirely account for the giants within it, as it presents conflicting and contradictory versions of their stories. A giant may enter and seemingly conform to aristocratic culture, while simultaneously also corrupting and debasing it, and ultimately being destroyed by it. In the *Chevalier du Papegau*, the Chevalier Jayant is the half-blood son of a giant and the woman he abducted into marriage; and in his deathbed confession he portrays his father as *both* a violent rapist *and* a pious man who imparted sound moral and spiritual principles to his son. The Chevalier Jayant himself attacks Arthur without provocation, in hopes of severing his right hand and thereby winning a lucrative marriage by proving his own supremacy; yet in the end he dies in Arthur's arms, in a state of piety and remorse. As we will see, in the course of the narrative a given giant may be termed both "monstre" and "homme"; different characters may remember him as a savage tyrant or as a valiant knight who governed his realm in peace and prosperity. Cohen makes a similar point in stating that to conceptualize the giant "either through an exterior (gigantic) or interior (human, all too human) frame of knowledge is to fail to capture both categories in all their fullness. Only in the constant movement between these two hermeneutics can the monster's nature be glimpsed."[37]

Giants originate, and often continue to operate, outside and alongside the "master narrative" of Arthurian history, and the process of incorporating them into this master narrative is one of violence: to the giants and to their versions of history and culture, but also to the chivalric history and culture that subsumes them. Human societies are unified around collective participation in a given narrative, informed by a common body of cultural knowledge and by a shared desire for the same end point. This is not, of course, to say that human society as depicted in Arthurian romance operates smoothly and without internal conflicts;

on the contrary, these texts are marked by rival plots and competing narrative perspectives.[38] Nonetheless, the texts and cycles overall tend to work toward a resolution, whereby what had seemed disruptive elements and invasive story lines turn out to be the support for future episodes in the grand sweep of Arthurian history. Tortured and undead bodies, portals allowing for passage of demons and damned souls from hell, disabling spells and toxic waters, malevolent fairies and predatory giants or monsters, all ultimately play their role in the rise of a chivalric hero and the consolidation of Christian and Arthurian power. Even the disastrous final battle of *La mort le roi Artu* does at least provide a narrative framework that attempts to tie up the various "loose ends" left over after the climactic finish of the Grail Quest: Lancelot's paradoxical combination of adulterous passion for Guenevere and unwavering loyalty to Arthur, the implacable enmity of Morgan, the wrath of Gawain, the sinister Mordred, the malaise pervading a Britain that has been abandoned by the Grail. Mutually assured destruction is, in its way, a resolution to the many strands of Arthurian history, in which each character plays out his or her role to the fullest extent, and each is equally vital to the final outcome.

Whatever the conflict, intrigue, symmetries, and rivalries generated by the influx of new characters into the Arthurian narrative, and the complex interlacing and entanglement of their story lines, the Arthurian kingdom provides a matrix within which these competing narratives can coexist as they rise, multiply, and eventually subside into the final dénouement. As Trachsler notes, the story elaborated around the triad of Tristan, Palamedes, and Dinadan is very different from that defined by Galahad, Perceval, and Boort. Yet Lancelot, for one, is able to intersect with both, and both exemplify and embody core values of the Arthurian world. If they seem in conflict, it is because the Arthurian world itself is riven by conflicting codes, such that both erotic passion and virginal piety, for example, can be lauded as supreme values. Giants, in contrast, are a more troubling form of deviance, as the "master narratives" of giants exceed the capacity of Arthurian romance. As we will see, the half-blood giant Galehot imagines his own triad of himself, Lancelot, and Tristan in a novel recasting of feudal lordship, love, and chivalric bonding. But his vision, distorting Arthurian norms beyond recognition, cannot be realized. Accounting for the behavior of giants entails a need to express the unspeakable, threatening to reveal just how well a knight understands this unspeakable truth, and how close it may come to reflecting on aspects of his own behavior, his own unspoken fears or desires. The giants' close interaction with human settlements and kingdoms—a mix of violent predation, aggressive desire, political conflict or truce, and intermarriage—results in trauma that unsettles narrative coherence and language itself. This trauma is dispelled, not by listening to the giants' voices and understanding their alterity, but through their rapid degradation and death. Once safely objectified and removed from action, the giant passes into legend, where he may be commemorated in monuments or oral histories. In this posthumous guise he can split into different personae—lurid monster, worthy patriarch, valiant knight, cruel tyrant—serving different cultural purposes, each independent, never needing to be integrated in a single human subject that, if ever fully acknowledged as such, might challenge cherished cultural ideals of human subjectivity. The giant speaks; but in the end he is silenced, becoming a figure to be spoken about by others.

In the study that follows, I have drawn on a range of theoretical approaches. Given my focus on giants as figures of racial and cultural otherness, implicated in narratives of conquest and cultural expansionism, it has been fruitful to borrow ideas and formulations from a broad spectrum of critics working in the related fields of postcolonial theory, colonial politics, and the construction of race and ethnicity in different times and places: Homi Bhabha, Frantz Fanon, Abdul JanMohamed, Samira Kawash, and numerous others. I have also made occasional use of critics writing from other theoretical perspectives, such as René Girard, Slavoj Žižek, and Julia Kristeva, insofar as their work touches on topics such as violence or ethnic alterity that are germane to my own work. I have not chosen to privilege any one theoretical "school" or any particular critic as the key to unlocking medieval depictions of giants. It is not my intent to account for the theoretical framework of, say, Bhabha or Fanon as an integrated whole, and then to apply it as such to a reading of Old French texts. Most of the theoretical texts in question were formulated with regard to modern or early modern societies; some are focused largely or even exclusively on

Asia, Africa, or the Americas. One could not expect that the structures they unpack, and the cultural strategies they reveal, would correspond precisely to those of medieval French romance. It often happens, however, that the principles that such writers articulate can illuminate the constructions of cultural and racial difference that medieval texts present, or that the insights proposed by these writers offer useful analogies in understanding the medieval history of race and ethnicity as cultural concepts.

This book is divided into six chapters, each of which looks at giants from a particular perspective. The first chapter begins with origins: biblical stories about the emergence of giants, both in the aftermath of the Fall and in the wake of Noah's Flood, and the application of similar ideas of demonic insemination in the fourteenth-century Anglo-Norman poem *Des grantz geanz*. The latter poem is somewhat unusual among francophone vernacular texts in explicitly attributing demonic parentage to giants, and thus in excluding them definitively from true humanity. Still, many other texts do use giants to explore the limits of the human, the boundaries between the human and the animal, and the construction of human subjectivity. Unlike demons, humans belong to the realm of nature and are subject to natural law; but unlike animals, they are also capable of violating nature with various forms of behavior viewed as perverse and unnatural. Humans also differ from both demons and animals in having moral responsibility, and thus the possibility of either damnation or salvation. Though giants often seem to lack the capacity for true penance and redemption, there are indications that they are not absolutely excluded from that process either; and while they are frequently associated with animalistic violence and amorality, the very perversity of their crimes, in the end, associates them more with human sin than with animal instinct. The figure of the giant thus becomes a vehicle for an implicit meditation on the nature of human identity as a moral construction.

The second chapter moves away from the question of the human and the nonhuman to focus on distinctions of class, race, and gender. Giants are sometimes portrayed as low-class ruffians challenging the privileges and authority of the aristocracy, or of aspiring improperly to aristocratic status themselves. They frequently act as knights and feudal lords, but generally in a skewed, parodic, or debased version of that role. They are also often merged with Saracens—whether pagan or pseudo-Muslim—as a culturally distinct population permanently at war with the Christian rulers of Britain. Examining the racial and ethnic associations surrounding giants, both in literary accounts and in manuscript illuminations depicting them, will allow for some initial conclusions about the different ways that race and class are configured in terms of moral status and culturally coded behaviors.

Chapter 3 looks at the role of desire in tales of giants. Combat with giants is a means by which a knight achieves objects of absolute desire—chivalric honor, and sometimes also love or marriage—but it is also an object of desire in and of itself; as a bodily experience, it rivals the extremes of love or sexuality. I will examine examples of interactions with giants, and the behavior of the giants themselves, in terms of the powerful motifs of desire and sublimation, the erotics of battling with giants, and way that it affords access to the Absolute of violence, death, or amorous fulfillment. I will also examine examples in which these motifs are treated in a more lighthearted, skeptical, or parodic vein.

Chapters 4 and 5 look more closely at the ongoing struggle between knights and giants to manipulate and control the trajectories of history. Chapter 4 examines four episodes from the prose *Tristan*, three involving giants and one involving "Saracens" (i.e., British pagans), in which we see the efforts of an outsider race to take control of history by constructing their own master narrative, which they seek to impose on the knights and ladies of the surrounding kingdoms. These attempts to write or rewrite history always fail when the giant or Saracen world is invaded by a powerful story line like that of Tristan; the master narrative will inevitably dominate and reduce the giant's own story to a mere subplot, one of the many interlacing threads of Arthurian legend. Chapter 5 continues in this vein with a close reading of the half-blood giant Galehot and his attempts to reconfigure the Arthurian world. A comparison of Galehot and Palamedes again allows contrasting views of the giant and the Saracen outsider respectively. This chapter is rounded out with a brief reading of Saladin and the fascination he exhibited for his putative French ancestry in the fifteenth-century *Saladin*, where his depiction draws heavily on the two iconic figures of Galehot and Palamedes.

Chapter 6 returns to the various texts already analyzed to investigate the question of chivalric subjectivity and the objectification of the giant as a racial and cultural alien. In narratives of chivalric identity formation, giants, fellow knights, and ladies play distinct and contrasting roles that allow the chivalric hero to be defined both in terms of participation in an intersubjective network, and by narcissistic relationships of aggression or desire with figures who are either desirable or threatening in their marvelous or uncanny similarity. Overall, I hope to have shown the myriad ways in which giants serve both to elaborate fantasies of racial and cultural alterity and to explore the traumas and desires that shape Christian chivalric subjectivity.

CHAPTER I

Inhuman Men and Knightly Fiends

The Vexed Humanity of Giants

The giants of Arthurian legend, for all their exotic alterity and their distinctive designation as *jaiant*, are neither a supernatural race nor an alien species. Francis Dubost stresses the troublingly ambiguous nature of the giant's difference, noting that "les différences que l'on renie comme inhumaines s'inscrivent cependant sur un fond de ressemblance avec l'humaine nature."[1] Jeffrey Jerome Cohen makes a similar point in his forceful assertion: "The giant's body figures not an alien corporeality but an intimate strangeness that *is* human embodiment."[2] Though they may carry associations with both the bestial and the demonic, giants must ultimately be seen as people in varying states of assimilation or resistance to both pagan and Christian societies. If some live rough in forest lairs and mountain caves, others are knights and lords with strongly fortified castles, however problematic this identity may always be. Tales of giants are set in that difficult borderland between peoples and cultures, and they explore the problems of human difference: just how much difference can be tolerated, to what extent it can be neutralized, when conversion or assimilation are possible and when they are not. In beginning this extended study of giants and the cultural ideologies they both question and confirm, we will start with the most fundamental of questions: How can we evaluate the humanity of giants? And whatever the answer, just what does it tell us? How is the category of "human" defined, and given meaning and substance, by tales of giants, knights, and ladies?

Giant, Man or Monster?

A giant is not simply a human being of above-average size. And the subtle but crucial difference between a giant and an oversized knight is already apparent at the beginning of the Old French Arthurian tradition, in Chrétien's *Erec et Enide*. Erec fights two giants who have abducted the knight Cadoc de Cabruel and are beating him savagely as they carry him off to their lair. Like Harpin de la Montaigne in *Le Chevalier au lion*, the giants are ruffians, armed only with huge clubs and whips. Though Erec does initially ask them to relinquish their prisoner peacefully, it is clear that this is only a formality, and once they have refused he is quick to kill first one and then the other. Though they are formidable, and one delivers a blow that nearly stuns him, Erec is able to take advantage of their lack of armor to stab one in the eye and slice through the other one's head. Later, in the "Joy of the Court" episode, Erec also faces a large and powerful adversary in the person of Maboagrain. In fact, Maboagrain's massive size is portrayed as a defect that prevents him from embodying the true ideal of masculine beauty:

> . . . s'il ne fust granz a enui
> soz ciel n'eüst plus bel de lui,
> mes il estoit un pié plus granz,
> a tesmoing de totes les genz,
> que chevaliers que l'an seüst.[3]

> [If he hadn't been excessively tall, there would be no one under the heavens more handsome than he, but he was a foot taller, according to what everyone said, than any knight known.]

As a profoundly isolationist figure who kills any knight that enters his domain and displays his head on a pike, and who is jealously guarding a beautiful maiden from contact with any knight who might aim to return her to the world of the court, Maboagrain has much in common with the typical Arthurian giant. When the giant-sized enemy appears, shouting his challenge, the reader might well suppose that Erec is about to face yet another giant—and that his death, in liberating the damsel, is the event that will trigger the anticipated Joy.

Yet the word *jaiant*—consistently used to designate the two bullies from whom Erec liberates Cadoc—is never applied to Maboagrain, who instead is termed "li granz chevaliers" (the big knight).[4] And in fact, his behavior turns out to be far from giantesque.[5] He accepts defeat graciously, explains the reasons for his behavior, and is delighted to learn that Erec is the son of a king at whose court he once served; and it turns out that far from holding the lady prisoner, he is the one being held by her, in a sinister parody of the "prison of love." In attacking anyone who enters their garden, he is acting under constraints imposed by the lady herself rather than expressing an unbridled libidinous aggression motivated by the sheer joy of lethal violence. He and his beloved do form a skewed paradigm of chivalric prowess and courtly love service, which must be dismantled and righted before they can rejoin court society. But since it operates on the fundamental principles of channeling chivalric combat into a form of service to a lady, protecting her from other knights in accordance with her wishes, and remaining true to one's word at all cost, it is possible for their relationship to be reconfigured in such a way as to bring heterosexual love into harmony with the male homosocial world of the court and the chivalric community. Just as Erec has recovered the proper balance between love and chivalry in his own marriage, now he enables Maboagrain as well to assume his place as both knight and lover—something that would be unthinkable if he actually was a giant.

If a giant is something other than a very large man, then, does that make him a monster? The example of Holland, giant ruler of a small island in the late medieval prose romance *Perceforest*, offers an interesting perspective on the question of the giant's simultaneous humanity and monstrosity.[6] Holland is described as being two feet taller than ordinary men, and this alone justifies the term *geant* that is frequently applied to him. He is also deformed in body, having an extra head and extra pairs of arms and legs. None of these superfluous members are functional; they simply "pendent aval comme mors" (hang down as if dead) and "ne lui font que empescement" (are nothing but an obstruction to him).[7] Finally, when angry he exhales toxic fumes that kill all living things. This bodily freakishness earns him the further epithets of "monstre" and "creature defformee." Holland's character, finally, is one of unmitigated barbarism; he is repeatedly designated "cruel" and "tyrans." He imprisons Hollandin, his twenty-year-old nephew and stepson, to prevent him from establishing an amorous relationship with a maiden on the neighboring island; he terrorizes his subjects; he kills and eats any outsider who strays onto, or even too close to, his island.

Holland, then, is characterized both by bodily deformity and by the savage behavior so typical of giants. Earlier, he killed his brother and kidnapped his pregnant sister-in-law, whom he loved for her beauty. He respected her wish that the forced marriage not be consummated until she had given birth; but in her dread of a liaison with the giant, she died immediately after the child was born. He embodies tyrannical rule, such that his subjects are overjoyed at his death and praise the knight "qui nous a delivré d'un tant pesant encombrier" (1:121; who delivered us from such an oppressive burden). Both his violence and his toxicity force sailors to give his island a wide berth. Sador—usually identified by his cognomen of "Dieu des Desirriers" or "Chevalier au Delphin"—asks to be taken there so that he can confront the giant, but the sailor to whom he appeals replies: "Je n'y puis aller, car mieulx ayme que par inobedience me fachiés morir que estre occis par la puanteur de celle inhumaine creature" (1:109; I cannot go there, for I would rather that you killed me for my disobedience than be killed by the stench of that inhuman creature). The giant is thus an obstruction to commerce, and his death not only liberates his people from tyranny but also opens the island to travel, diplomacy, and trade. The Chevalier vows that Holland will be slain and "toute la contree delivree de lui, tellement que toutes personnes privees et estranges pourront illecq frequenter et marchander" (1:108; the entire land liberated from him, so that residents as well as foreigners can come and go, and engage in commerce). The giant's imprisonment of Hollandin was an effort to maintain his isolationism, in resistance to chivalric culture, marriage, and political alliances. After

Holland's death, however, both his stepson and the island itself are absorbed into the larger world of feudal Britain: "Hollandin receut l'ordre de chevalerie, puis espousa Marse la pucelle qu'il aymoit tant, parquoy les deux isles furent par l'acord de l'une partie et de l'autre adjoustees a une seignourie" (1:127; Hollandin received the order of knighthood, then married Marse, the maiden whom he so loved, whereby the two islands were, by mutual accord, united into one estate).

Is this giant human or monster? On the one hand, his grotesque bodily doubling and the dragonlike toxicity of his smoky breath place him truly beyond the pale; and the Chevalier au Delphin targets precisely this monstrosity in the battle, systematically amputating the giant's extra limbs. These excessive and useless members are a blight on nature itself: of the two heads, for example, "L'une estoit naturele et l'autre contre nature" (1:113; One was natural and the other counter to nature), while at another point the knight cuts off "la jambe dont nature estoit blamee" (1:116; the leg that was a reproach to nature). Indeed, the narrator explains that the giant's aversion to visitors derives from "la vergoigne qu'il avoit de luy meisme" (1:111; the shame he felt at his own person). Once all such limbs have been severed, the Chevalier taunts Holland, exclaiming: "Vous avez perdu le nom de monstre, ou lieu duquel on vous puet bien nommer geant a cause de vostre haulteur" (1:117; You have lost the name of "monster," instead of which you can appropriately be called "giant," because of your height). Even as a "mere" giant, however, Holland is beyond redemption. Indeed, despite having been purged of his monstrous limbs, in the final moments of the battle "Il sambloit mieulx demoniacque que autrement" (1:119; He seemed more truly demoniacal than ever) in his rage at being unable to harm his attacker. Holland's human status flickers in and out of focus, depending on the perspective from which he is viewed. The Chevalier au Delphin, when he first sees his adversary approaching, is momentarily transfixed to see "la maniere de ce inhumain deable" (1:112; the manner of this inhuman devil). But as the giant puzzles over his enemy's ability to withstand his fumes, concerned to have encountered the first opponent able to stand and fight him, the narrator terms him a "pervers et inhumain homme" (1:113; perverse and inhuman man)—perhaps the first sign of his human vulnerability, as he suddenly faces man-to-man combat with an opponent who is not merely a victim but an aggressive threat. In the eyes of his subjects, in turn, Holland is a "pervers et inhumain tyrant" (1:127; perverse and inhuman tyrant). Finally, it must be noted that Holland apparently came from a normal family: as far as one can tell, neither his brother nor his nephew is gigantic, deformed, or rapacious. Demonic in battle, hideous in form; tyrannical and isolationist as a ruler; envious of his brother's successful marriage and showing both brutality and an odd respect to the woman he desires; cruelly jealous in his paternal love; ferociously aggressive but also ashamed in the eyes of the world—the giant is a contradictory and lethal mix of human emotions, flaws, and excesses and of inhuman grotesquerie. This simultaneous presence of the alien and the all too human is, perhaps, what is most truly expressed in the designation of *geant*. Whether it is applied to the monstrous offspring of otherwise normal parents or to an aberrant people endowed with their own, quite separate lineage and history, the term *geant* naturalizes this notion of the "inhuman man." Rather than expanding the definition of natural humanity, the giant is the aberration that helps define the more limited norm. The Orwellian implications of the text are perhaps that all men are human but that some are more human than others.

I will return to Holland toward the end of this study. Along the way, we will see that in medieval literature overall there is no one way that giants are portrayed. One can certainly identify features that very commonly adhere to giants, such as violence, intemperance, and a resistance to organized political and commercial networks. But along this spectrum of more or less typical giant behaviors, the individual giants that figure in medieval literature have a shifting profile that gives them slightly different status in different texts. Examining these variations will shed light on the question of just how giants are used, and in service of what sorts of narrative and ideological agendas; how they figure in an implicit discourse of personal, racial, and cultural identity; and how their presence can warp the very fabric of culture and the coherence of historical narratives.

Monstrous Origins: The Biblical Background

The book of Genesis famously identifies giants as the result of sinful miscegenation, though of what sort exactly is not entirely clear: either a mingling of incompatible human bloodlines or an even more sinister mix of human and demonic. The Vulgate describes the advent and immediate aftermath of the giants as follows:

> Cumque coepissent homines multiplicari super terram, et filias procreassent, videntes filii Dei filias hominum quod essent pulchrae, acceperunt sibi uxores ex omnibus, quas elegerant. . . . Gigantes autem erat super terram in diebus illis: postquam enim ingressi sunt filii Dei ad filias hominum, illaeque genuerunt, isti sunt potentes a saeculo viri famosi. Videns autem Deus quod multa malitia hominum esset in terra, et cuncta cogitatio cordis intenta esset ad malum omni tempore, poenituit eum quod hominem fecisset in terra.

> [When men began to multiply on the face of the ground, and daughters were born to them, the sons of God saw that the daughters of men were fair; and they took to wife such of them as they chose. . . . The Nephilim [giants] were on the earth in those days, and also afterward, when the sons of God came in to the daughters of men, and they bore children to them. These were the mighty men that were of old, the men of renown. The Lord saw that the wickedness of man was great in the earth, and that every imagination of the thoughts of his heart was only evil continually. And the Lord was sorry that he had made man on the earth, and it grieved him to his heart.][8]

Exegetical tradition was split on the identity of the "sons of God and daughters of men," which were alternatively seen as referring to demons—that is, fallen angels—impregnating human women or as the male descendants of Seth consorting with the female descendants of Cain.[9] Augustine examines this question in the *City of God*, acknowledging that the former interpretation is often put forward. He likewise admits that the stories of women having sexual relations with incubi are so widespread that one cannot really deny the existence of such things, while holding back from any definitive conclusion as to whether spirits "possint hanc etiam pati libidinem ut, quo modo possunt, sentientibus feminis misceantur" (are also able to experience such lust and so have intercourse in such a way with women who feel the sensation of it).[10] For all that, however, Augustine sees the giants not as demonic but as the result of lustful miscegenation between the lineage of Seth and that of Cain. The opening emphasis on male attraction to female beauty, as well as the detail in the Septuagint version of Genesis that these men "generabant sibi" (engendered progeny for themselves), indicated that the women of the cursed line of Cain were corrupting the virtuous lineage of the "good" son given to Adam as replacement for Abel, that "antequam sic caderent filii Dei, Deo generabant, non sibi, id est non dominante libidine coeundi, sed serviente officio propagandi, non familiam fastus sui, sed cives civitatis Dei" (before the sons of God fell as they did, they engendered children for God, not for themselves, that is, that sexual lust was not their master but the servant of their reproductive function, and that they did not engender a family for their own pride but citizens for the City of God).[11] Whereas Original Sin occurred because the first man listened to his wife and valued her word above that of God, the birth of giants results from a further descent, in which libidinous pleasure is valued as an end in itself rather than a means to procreation, and in which procreation becomes an extension of personal power and pride rather than a means of serving God.

Giants, in Augustine's reading, are a sign of the moral depravity of their parents: their maternal lines are tainted by descent from Cain, who first introduced violent aggression into the world, while their fathers' lustful desires caused them to take wives from a cursed and taboo people. Fratricide, wrath, arrogant pride, and sexual transgression mark their very being. The size and strength of the giants, in turn, encode a further moral lesson into their bodies: God created them, Augustine explains, "ut etiam hinc ostenderetur non solum pulchritudines verum etiam magnitudines et fortitudines corporum non magni pendendas esse sapienti" (in order to make it known in this way too that the wise man should attach little importance not only to physical beauty but to physical size and strength as well).[12] In support of this point Augustine cites the book of Baruch, in which the giants are also held up as examples of irrational violence. As the Vulgate states: "Ibi fuerunt gigantes nominati illi, qui ab initio fuerunt, statura magna, scientes bellum. Non hos elegit Dominus, neque viam disciplinae invenerunt, propterea perierunt; et quoniam non habuerunt sapientiam, interierunt propter suam insipientiam" (In it were born the giants, famous to us from antiquity, immensely tall, expert in war; God's choice did not fall on these, he did not reveal the way to knowledge to them; they perished for lack of wisdom, perished in their own folly).[13]

Giants relied entirely on brute force to accomplish anything, for they were incapable of social organization, negotiation, or rule of law. Their propensity for violence led them into constant conflict; their lack of rational wisdom deprived them of any means by which this violence might be mitigated or suspended through truces or alliances. They were a people uninformed by any ethical framework and utterly lacking the human capacity for self-knowledge or remorse. And as a result they were a race doomed to extinction—by God's hand in the Flood, but also at one another's hands.

Rather than a tale of supernatural parentage resulting in fantastic offspring, then, the giants are glossed by Augustine as a moral allegory for the effects of sin and the failure of spiritual community. Despite the influential role of Augustine's writings, however, the alternative interpretation of demonic engendering never entirely disappeared, kept alive perhaps in part by the very fact that Augustine considers it at all. It appears, for example, as a secondary, but still plausible, interpretation of the passage in Peter Comestor's influential *Historia scholastica*.[14] The enigmatic biblical text thus ensured that giants would retain at least a hint of the demonic about them. Either way, of course, giants are the product of a forbidden mingling of peoples. Augustine notes in *The City of God* that in separately recounting the descendants of Cain and those of Seth the Bible intended "has duas societates suis diversis generationibus primitus digerere atque distinguere" (to arrange and distinguish from the beginning these two societies in their respective generations);[15] Peter Comestor comments that "mortuo Adam, Seth separavit cognationem suam a cognatione Cain. . . . Nam et pater vivens prohibuerat ne commiscerentur" (when Adam died, Seth separated his lineage from that of Cain. . . . For while their father was alive, he had forbidden them to mix).[16] And they represent a wickedness so absolute that God himself saw no solution other than mass extermination. David Williams sums up the lessons expressed in the biblical giants by noting that, as an individual of excessive size and appetites, "The giant shows us what would be possible if the body were not a container and if being were not limited" and that, as a contaminated lineage, the giant race "signifies the breaking of the confines of genus as container of being and the transgression of the separating limits of animal, human, and divine."[17]

As would be later reflected in the medieval legends of British giants, who survived first the mass slaughter carried out by Brutus and his Trojans and then the relentless depredations sponsored by Uterpendragon and Arthur, giants are a race targeted for extermination, yet never fully exterminated. Of the most famous postdiluvian biblical giants, Nimrod and Goliath, the former makes his appearance just three generations after Noah as the son of Cush and the grandson of Noah's son Ham. Of Nimrod, the Vulgate says only that "ipse coepit esse potens in terra, et erat robustus venator coram Deum" (He was the first on earth to be a mighty man. He was a mighty hunter before the Lord).[18] Augustine, however, argues for a slightly different reading in *The City of God*: "Hic coepit esse gigans super terram. Hic erat gigans venator contra Dominum Deum" (He began to be a giant upon the earth. He was a giant hunter against the Lord God).[19] Consistently referring to Nimrod as "gigans," Augustine glosses this "hunter against the Lord" as "animalium terrigenarum deceptor oppressor extinctor" (the deceiver, oppressor, and destroyer of earthborn creatures).[20] Augustine also confirms that Nimrod was responsible for the Tower of Babel, an interpretation that remained current throughout the Middle Ages. Again the giant is a figure of transgression, rebelling against God in lawless mayhem while imposing his own tyrannical law on his hapless subjects. And as the architect of Babel, Nimrod is further associated with the corruption of language. Formerly a universal medium of communication that fostered the unity of all humankind in a single cooperative community, language now becomes a principle of division. The giant is a site of rupture, violating natural and sacred boundaries, and a site of fragmentation, as communal unity of purpose disintegrates into mutual incomprehension and discord, and what were once one people are scattered across the earth. At the same time, in his very marking of boundaries and in his generation of linguistic, cultural, and racial diversity, the giant might also be seen as the instigator of human history in all its complexity. I will return many times to this crucial, if paradoxical, aspect of the giant as both the ultimate threat to rule of law and cultural hegemony and the point of resistance around which that very law and hegemonic order can define itself.

On the Margins of Nature: Giants and Demons

Medieval exegetes debated the question of whether any giants had survived the Flood.[21] Giants feature in postdiluvian Old Testament history not only as individuals such as Nimrod or Goliath, whose descent from Noah's family can be explained, but also as the gigantic race encountered by the scouting party sent by Moses to investigate the Promised Land: "Populus, quem aspeximus, procerae staturae est. Ibi vidimus monstra quaedam filiorum Enac de genere giganteo: quibus comparati, quasi locustae videbamur" (All the people that we saw in it are men of great stature. And there we saw the Nephilim . . . and we seemed to ourselves like grasshoppers, and so we seemed to them).[22] The relationship between this monstrous people and those born before the Flood is never clarified, leaving exegetes to ponder inconclusively whether some giants might have been tall enough to keep their heads above water. The actual link (if any) between the biblical giants born of potentially demonic miscegenation, or those found in the Promised Land, and the British giants of medieval legend is equally unclear. But if nothing else, the Bible establishes a framework for conceptualizing giants as products of transgressive sexual liaisons, possibly demonic in origin, and associated with an extreme form of sinfulness that allows for no redemption but calls only for extermination. It identifies giants with an aboriginal population that, however terrifying, must with God's help be cleansed from the land targeted for occupation by a favored race.

In particular, scholars have noted the parallel between the giants inhabiting the Promised Land and Geoffrey of Monmouth's tale of the giants found in Britain, the "promised land" for Brutus and his Trojan refugees. As Cohen notes, the British giants are "the remnant of a race encountered in its twilight, living artifacts of a prehistory ready to cede to a heroic era. As in the foundational narrative of the Book of Genesis, a time of giants is yielding to empire."[23] And just as the arrival of the Israelites in Palestine would create the conditions allowing for the eventual advent of Christianity, so the establishment of the Trojans in Britain founded the culture that would later be worthy of receiving the Holy Grail and would lead ultimately to the glorious Christian kingdom of Arthur. The elimination of giants, in short, is essential to the process of establishing civilization and furthering God's plan, whether in the Holy Land or in Britain. Whereas Britain under the giants remained in a state of wilderness, Brutus and his men divide it up according to a system of feudal government, build cities, and "improve" the land through agricultural management. Tellingly, neither Geoffrey of Monmouth nor Wace addressed the question of where the British giants came from or how they might have lived before the arrival of the Trojan settlers. The history of Britain, as presented by these writers and those who followed them, is not the history of the giants who first inhabited it; it is the history of the race that settled and civilized it, and it begins accordingly with the fall of Troy and Brutus's rebellion against his Greek rulers. Other Arthurian "histories," such as the prose *Tristan* and the Lancelot-Grail cycle, may posit a starting point in the Holy Land with the departure of Joseph of Arimathea and his entourage on the voyage that would bring the Grail to Britain. In these texts, British history is framed by the spread of Christianity and serves in a sense as a continuation of the Gospel narrative. In both cases, giants are secondary players, subsumed within the more important stories of Greco-Trojan and Christian history, the two master narratives whose fusion made Arthur's kingdom possible. In effect, giants do not make history; if anything, history is made and advanced through the extermination of giants.

Positioning giants in this manner is another means by which their humanity is degraded. As Pramod K. Nayar notes, a human being "is traditionally taken to be a subject... marked by rational thinking/intelligence, who is able to plot his/her own course of action depending on his/her needs, desires, and wishes, and, as a result of his/her actions, produces history."[24] And the systematic silencing and thwarting of any attempt on the part of a giant to produce a giant-centered, giant-driven history is also a way in which Arthurian giants are portrayed in a manner analogous to the various peoples colonized by European powers. As Frantz Fanon has noted: "Le colon fait l'histoire et sait qu'il la fait. Et parce qu'il se réfère constamment à l'histoire de sa métropole, il indique en clair qu'il est ici le prolongement de cette métropole. L'histoire qu'il écrit n'est donc pas l'histoire du pays qu'il dépouille mais l'histoire de sa nation.... L'immobilité à laquelle est condamné le colonisé ne peut être remise en question que si le colonisé décide de mettre un terme à l'histoire de la colonisation... pour faire exister l'histoire de la nation."[25] The "epistemological revolution" of decolonization, as Edward Said terms it—the reorientation of history away from the incoming race, to place the native people at its center—is one to which giants are frequently portrayed as aspiring, but never with lasting success.²⁶ In this way too, the cultural ideologies that underpinned European colonial expansion and the development of modern racial theory can already be glimpsed in the medieval fantasies of traumatic contact between peoples in the deep British past.

The origins of British giants went unexplained until the fourteenth century, when the topic was addressed by the Anglo-Norman poem *Des grantz geanz*: a tale of postdiluvian giants that parallels the biblical account of lustful—and in this case explicitly demonic—miscegenation.²⁷ In *Des grantz geanz*, giants are born of virgin mothers and incubi. Their mothers are not virtuous virgins, however; rather, they are haughty princesses—daughters of a Greek king identified as reigning 3,970 years before the writing of the poem—who resisted marriage because they could not bear the thought of losing their independence through subjection to a husband. After their betrothal, the sisters, thirty in number, hold a secret meeting:

> E coyment se conselerent,
> E si unt entre eux ordiné
> Qe nule ne soit si assoté
> De suffrir en nule guise
> De estre en autri danger mise,
> Ne de seignur, ne de veisin,
> Ne de frere, ne de cosin,
> Ne nomément de sun barun.
> (vv. 44–51)

> [And secretly they conferred together, and they decided among themselves that none of them would be so foolish as to put up in any way with being under the domination of another; not of a lord, not of a neighbor, not of a brother or cousin, and certainly not of her husband.]

The princesses make a pact to murder their husbands if the men do not accept total subjection and obedience to their wives; the plot is foiled when the youngest sister reveals it to her father. Set adrift at sea, they eventually make landfall in Britain, at that time completely uninhabited; the eldest, Albina, bestows her name on the island, calling it Albion. Finding the land rich in game, the sisters lead a comfortable life and are soon overcome by lust—a need readily met by "li malfee / Qe sunt apellez Incubi" (vv. 406–7; demons who are called Incubi). Though invisible, these demon lovers are capable both of producing sexual sensations in their female partners and of inseminating them:

> E la furent engendré
> Enfaunz qi geaunz devindrent,
> E aprés la terre tindrent.
> Tut lur delit acumplirent;
> Mes les dames rien ne virent
> Ceux qi pargieu les avoient,
> Mes qe soulement sentoient
> Come femme deit home fere
> Quant s'entremet de tiel afere.
>   (vv. 424–32)

[And thus were engendered sons who became giants and afterwards held the land. They had all their pleasure; but the ladies saw nothing of those who lay with them, but only felt them, as a woman should feel a man when they come together for such a purpose.]

The giants born to the Greek sisters reproduced through incestuous couplings, both mother-son and brother-sister; and their lives, like those of the biblical Nephilim, were marked by murderous internecine strife, as "chescun a sun poer / Voleit autre sourmounter" (vv. 501–2; each according to his power wanted to conquer the others). So violent were they, in fact, that only twenty-four of them were still alive by the time Brutus arrived in Britain.

In *Des grantz geanz* as in the biblical tradition on which it is clearly based, giants thus lack any viable father figure. At best, their paternal line is tainted by the corruption of once righteous men by the daughters of Cain, and at worst there are no human forefathers at all, while ensuing generations are contaminated by repeated incest.[28] With fathers also filling the role of half-brother, uncle, or cousin to their offspring, no patriarchal order or clear lineage is possible. The human-demon liaisons that founded the race of giants are the product of their mothers' depravity: a desire for sexual pleasure, coupled with an absolute resistance to patriarchy and marriage. This sexual reproduction that evades any actual sexual relationship is more allied with autoeroticism than with the miscegenation that Augustine saw in the biblical account. It is almost as though the giants simply sprang, fully formed, from their mothers' lustful but fiercely defiant bodies. The giants as described in *Des grantz geanz* are sometimes interpreted by modern critics as representing the wildness of nature in opposition to culture. Cohen, for example, characterizes Albion as "a realm of pure, undifferentiated nature."[29] I would argue, however, that the race described in *Des grantz geanz* is anything but natural. The giants are monstrous, "A regarder hidous . . . / Car malfez les engendrerent" (vv. 457–58; hideous to behold . . . for demons engendered them); unlike even the most savage beasts, they kill one another to the very edge of extinction. The giants of *Des grantz geanz* are portrayed not as a reversion to nature but as a deformation of culture that violates the boundaries of nature itself.

The giants of *Des grantz geanz* thus define the very borderline of humanity, where the natural shades into the perverse and the demonic. They blur the distinction between self and other, between kin and non-kin. They form a single extended family, linked through their mothers, who are joined by blood and by their homicidal pact. Definitively severed from their Greek homeland and lineage, these founding mothers make up a kind of primal horde. From this maternal band, there is no escape; within it, there is aggression, lust, and an all-consuming struggle for power. This account of monstrous origins is an attempt to identify the giants of vernacular romance with those of biblical tradition, producing an overdetermined image of an enemy race doomed to failure. As a prehistory of Britain, the poem contributes to the sense of Britain as a Promised Land—indeed a second Holy Land, rising from violent and gigantesque origins to foster a glorious Christian civilization and provide a suitable home for the Grail. And in attributing Greek ancestry to the giants, the poet may have intended to strengthen their status as outsiders to British history. It was after all to escape subjugation by the Greek destroyers of Troy that Brutus and his men fled their Mediterranean homeland and made their way to these islands at the western edge of the known world.

Des grantz geanz thus presents us with a double vision of giants as both human and inhuman enemies of culture. On the one hand they are "gent de faerie" (v. 467; fairy folk) and the spawn of demons; like the Old Testament giants, they massacre one another in an endless process of irrational and unstoppable violence. And on the other hand, they are a criminal offshoot of a people both illustrious and suspect: ancient enemies of the Trojan ancestors claimed by Britons and Normans alike, and medieval perpetrators of both a church and an empire that stood in an uneasy mix of alliance and rivalry with Roman Catholicism and the feudal houses of western Europe. This ambiguous status of giants as both human and nonhuman is reflected in the ambiguity surrounding the habitation of Britain before Brutus's arrival. In the *Historia regum Britanniae* and the vernacular works that draw on it, the Britain to which Brutus sails is characterized both as uninhabited and as inhabited by giants, while the giants themselves are both acknowledged as a presence encountered by the Trojans upon arrival and relegated to the past, as though their very existence is merely the relic of an era that is always already over.[30] In Geoffrey of Monmouth's account, the oracle of Diana urges Brutus to sail for a Britain that is simply waiting for his people to inhabit it: "insula in occeano est habitata gigantibus olim, / nunc deserta quidem, gentibus apta tuis" (an island of the ocean, where giants once lived, but now it is deserted and waiting for your people).[31] Upon arrival, the Trojans find that the land "a nemine, exceptis paucis gigantibus, inhabitabatur" (had no inhabitants save for a few giants).[32] Wace's Diana similarly states that "Gaiant i soelent abiter" (giants used to live there),[33] while the oracle in *Perceforest* specifies that "habitee / fu de tresgrans geanz jadiz. / Ore est gaste et habilitee / pour ta gent" (it was inhabited long ago by enormous giants. Now it is a wilderness suitable for your people).[34] When the Trojans reach Britain, Wace notes that "En cele ille gaianz aveit, / Nule gent altre n'i maneit" (vv. 1063–64; in this island there were giants, and no other people lived there); *Perceforest* tells us that "Albion . . . n'estoit habitee de nullui fors d'un pou de geans" (Albion . . . was uninhabited except for a few giants) (*Perce/I*, 1:26–27).

As the indigenous inhabitants of an island that is nonetheless uninhabited and ready for settlement, giants illustrate Samira Kawash's characterization of the native as "non-existent" in the eyes of the colonizer, for whom the indigene fades into the background as merely part of the landscape awaiting management and rule: the "thing that has been excluded as the condition for the colonizer's view of the 'empty landscape.'"[35] And just as that excluded native resurges in the colonial imagination as "a monstrous apparition that threatens the order of the landscape and the colonizer who rules it," so also the landscape of medieval romance is ever haunted by the sudden appearance of terrifying giants inimical to social and cultural order.[36] Lesley Johnson has noted that *Des grantz geanz* attributes the knowledge of the giants' origins to a tale told by Gogmagog to Brutus, commenting that "Gogmagog's ability to produce a coherent narrative of his own origins works against the projection of the giant community as one of non-civilized aliens."[37] But if this ability to narrate one's own history may indeed identify the giants as human, it does not make them civilized in the eyes of either medieval writers or the fictional knights of ancient and Arthurian Britain; nor does it place them on an equal footing with the newly arrived Trojans, self-appointed rulers and guardians of the land. Instead, it links them to a long tradition of colonial subjects whose internal history and cultural norms serve only to confirm their lack of civilized refinement and their need to be ruled by a more "advanced" people. Homi Bhabha characterizes the colonial encounter in these terms: "From the point of view of the colonizer, passionate for unbounded, unpeopled possession, the problem of truth turns into the troubled political and psychic question of boundary and territory: *Tell us why you, the native, are there*. . . . The colonialist demand for narrative carries, within it, the threatening reversal: *Tell us why we are here*."[38] The giant's account of himself and his people is, in fact, a justification of the Trojan—and later Arthurian—mission to exterminate them, ridding the land of a troublesome presence that has kept it locked in a barbaric past, blocking the forward movement of history. The demonization of giants and their designation as *gent de faerie*, in other words, serve less to mark them as magical than to relegate them to subhuman status, doubly outsiders to a British kingdom that knows itself to be at once Trojan and Christian. Their characterization in medieval French romance carries features that we might think of as "racial"—their distinctive size, perhaps also their exaggerated facial features—as well as those that might be termed "cultural" or "ethnic": a resistance to centralized monarchy, an adherence to behavioral patterns stigmatized as primitive and barbaric. In short, as noted above, the term *geant* carries within it an implicit identification of racial alterity with cultural deviance and thus allows for the elaboration of a subclass of failed humanity requiring governance, reformation, and ultimately extermination by the bearers of civilization.

On the Margins of Humanity: Giants, Men, and Beasts

It is not only on the border between the human and the demonic that giants are located. They are also associated with the border between humanity and bestiality; and this can be illustrated with a brief survey of the fifteenth-century *Conte du Papegau*, together with examples drawn from other texts that offer analogous points. The *Papegau* narrates the adventures of the newly crowned Arthur, who, disguised as the Chevalier du Papegau, embarks on a journey throughout his lands. In the course of his travels he encounters three figures in whom the boundary between the human and the animal—in particular, the close relationship between a knight and his horse—is particularly troubled. The first of these, known as the Poisson Chevalier (Knight Fish), is a monstrous creature incorporating human and animal traits in a hybrid body. The Chevalier Jayant (Giant Knight), born of the marriage between a giant and a human woman, is characterized by a mixture of violence, courtly pretension, and chivalric honor that plays on his hybrid human-giant identity. And the Jayant sans Nom (Giant without a Name), finally, is a forest-dwelling simpleton for whom the very distinction between human and animal has no real meaning.

The Poisson Chevalier is certainly the least human of these three figures, but when he first appears he is assumed by all to be a giant, armed as a knight, and riding an equally gigantic horse: "Et ne demoura guerez qu'il virent de loing venir chevauchant le plus ydeux et le plus orrible chevalier par semblant qui mais fust veu . . . car le cheval estoit bien aussi grant comme ung olifant et le chevalier aussi grant comme il convenoit au cheval" (And it wasn't long before they saw, riding up from afar, the most hideous and horrible-looking knight that had ever been seen . . . for the horse was as big as an elephant, and the knight of a size appropriate to the horse).[39] The first sign that this knight in armor may not be quite what he appears comes when Arthur strikes his opponent's shield and is surprised to see that the blow draws blood, even though "il ne luy estoit mie advis que son espee touchast ne fust ne fer" (104; it didn't seem to him that his sword had touched anything other than wood and iron). Once the enemy is slain, Arthur examines his armor, attempting to remove it, and discovers that it is actually part of his body. And on further investigation, it emerges that the same applies to the knight's weapons and even to his horse: "Le chevalier et le destrier et le haubert et le heaulme et l'escu et l'espee et la lance fut tout une chose" (106; the knight and the steed and the hauberk and the helmet and the shield and the sword and the lance were all of one piece). The gigantic knight, in fact, was human only in appearance; in reality, as the narrator explains, he was "ung monstre qui en mer a sa conversion que l'en clame Poisson Chevalier" (118; a monster that lives in the sea, called the Knight Fish). When the local residents follow his tracks back to the shore, they find the sea in tremendous agitation and hear a terrifying din of "cryer et braire et plourer" (120; crying and roaring and weeping), interpreted by some as demons and by others as "la generation du Poisson Chevalier" (120; the relatives of the Knight Fish). That the Chevalier Poisson would have a family capable of mourning his death is an interesting detail, suggesting that, however inhuman they may be, these "monsters" do nonetheless mirror humanity in certain respects—not only in their ability to mimic chivalric combat but also in their capacity for communal bonding with one another. Nonetheless, the lack of differentiation between equipment, animal mount, and warrior clearly places this creature beyond the bounds of humanity. A knight is a wonderfully effective example of the ways that technological expertise and the domestication of animals can enhance human stature and power. His close bond with the horse that serves him stages both the capacity of humans to interact with animals, by mastering the skilled maneuvers that can be performed in collaboration with equine strength and prowess, and also the rational superiority of humans over the animals that they train and deploy.[40] His armor and weaponry, in turn, bear witness to human artifice and ingenuity in exploiting the raw materials of nature. No such skill or mastery of the natural world, no capacity for mutual cooperation between species, is evident in the

Chevalier Poisson: he is simply a sea monster, acting as his instincts drive him to behave, and incapable of any other form of behavior.

The Chevalier Jayant, in turn, challenges the Chevalier du Papegau to combat in an effort to win the hand of the Duchess of Estregalles by defeating the champion widely regarded as the best knight in the kingdom. He intends, in fact, to bring her Arthur's right hand as proof of victory—a ploy that backfires, as he is killed in the ensuing skirmish. I will return below to the burlesque aspects of his disastrous attempt at love service. What concerns us here is the unorthodox manner in which the Chevalier Jayant travels: not on horseback but on foot. Though his suit of armor is impressive—so much so, in fact, that at the point of death he gives his hauberk to Arthur, in recognition of the latter's chivalric supremacy—the giant does not wear the iron shoes that are normally part of the equipment. These would make walking difficult, and as the narrator explains, "Il estoit si grant qu'il ne trouvoit chevaul que pourter le peust puis qu'il fust armé, et mieulx va a pié et plus tost que nulle beste sauvage" (162; He was so big that he couldn't find a horse that could carry him when he was armed, and he moved better on foot, and more swiftly, than any wild animal). Where the Chevalier Poisson combined knight and horse in a single hybrid body, the Chevalier Jayant embodies, as knight, human skills and prowess along with equine agility and speed. His behavior, moreover, resembles that of a beast tracking its prey: "Tout ainsi com le lion familleux et irez va suyvant sa proye quant il a faim, tout ainsi va le chevalier cerchant le Chevalier du Papegau. . . . Il ala ainsi courant comme le lion familleux va suyvant la beste ou la brebis" (162; Just as the famished and wrathful lion tracks its prey when it is hungry, so the knight goes in search of the Knight of the Parrot. . . . He was running like the famished lion tracking game or sheep). It is not uncommon to compare the fury of a knight in combat to that of wild animals; but these epithets do seem particularly apt in the case of one who has, as it were, absorbed the role of the chivalric animal partner into himself.[41] The comparison with a beast of prey also reminds us of the giant's gruesome plan—the dismemberment of Arthur's body and the use of his hand as a trophy—while subtly associating this behavior with the man-eating habits common to both lions and traditional giants.

And yet the Chevalier Jayant is hardly a cave-dwelling savage, but a count with fourteen castles and, most importantly of all, a pious man whose beliefs, insofar as we hear of them, are compatible with Christianity. With his dying breath, he informs the Chevalier du Papegau that his father—the giant who raped and forcibly married his mother—taught him that one must know three things: one's Savior, the distinction between good and evil, and oneself. He then acknowledges the folly of his behavior, makes his confession, and commends his soul to God. Further details of the giant's background are not provided; possibly we are meant to assume that his father converted to Christianity as a condition for the marriage, much like a Saracen prince who falls in love with a Christian woman—though perhaps with less happy results. The intricate interplay between human and animal characteristics makes the Chevalier Jayant a particularly complex figure. His gigantism excludes him from riding a steed, presumably the sine qua non of any aristocratic warrior, and seemingly reduces him to the lowly status of foot soldier. That same gigantism also renders the horse unnecessary by endowing him with size, strength, and speed equal to that of any mounted knight; but that very fact means that the Chevalier Jayant's own body blurs the boundary separating the human warrior from his animal servant or partner. In some ways he is simply a more humanized version of a hybrid creature like the Poisson Chevalier—or a more aristocratic version of a rustic giant like Harpin de la Montagne in Chrétien de Troyes's *Chevalier au lion*, who not only fights on foot but also eschews both armor and a sword and who aims not to marry the maiden he is fighting for but to make her the sexual plaything of his lowliest servants.[42] For all his castles and his aristocratic title, his pretensions to advantageous marriage and his martial skills, ethical insight, and spiritual faith, the Chevalier Jayant is also little better than a ruffian, governed by bestial passions of lust, pride, greed, and murderous rage. Only in death, it would seem, does he finally achieve true aristocratic virtue and, in his spiritual contrition, true humanity. His behavior troubles the parameters of chivalric masculinity—and the sharp contrasts within his character make this loss of distinction even more disturbing than in the case of an actual monster like the Poisson Chevalier or a simple brute like Harpin.

Various other medieval French giants also travel and fight on foot. Lack of a horse contributes to the degradation of the Saracen giant Ferragu, for example, in *Valentin et Orson*. Initially, Ferragu appears to be a typical, if giant-sized, Saracen king: though capable of treachery and cruelty, and hostile to Christianity, he is nonetheless a wealthy and powerful ruler, able to command a formidable army. At his first appearance, in fact, Ferragu seems fairly benign, offering asylum to the falsely accused and exiled Queen Bellissant, sister of Pepin. Though it is mentioned at this point that he is too large to ride a horse, the fact seems inconsequential as the giant king peacefully goes about the business of inspecting the ships that pass through his port and collecting taxes from them. Struck by the beauty of the queen, who is on board one of the ships and has nowhere else to go, he ushers her back to his castle "en grant honneur et sans luy vouloir faire villennie" (with great respect, without wanting to cause her any harm).[43] There, rather than raping her as one might expect from a giant, Ferragu "commanda a sa femme que Bellissant fust chierement gardee comme son corps" (ordered his wife to watch over Bellissant as she would her own self); and whenever Bellissant is overcome by grief at the loss of her children, "tousjours la resconfortoit la femme du geant et dessus toutes personnes au plus pres d'elle la tenoit" (the giant's wife always comforted her and was close to her more than anyone else).[44] Both the giant's brother, the Green Knight, and his sister, Esclarmonde, prove capable of assimilation into Western court culture. Esclarmonde, a damsel endowed with wisdom, impeccable manners, and dazzling beauty, marries Bellissant's son Valentin; the Green Knight, though initially savage in his predatory designs on the daughter of the Duke of Aquitaine, accepts defeat at the hands of Valentin's brother Orson and converts to Christianity, becoming a model knight and loyal companion to the Franks. Ferragu, however, cannot countenance his sister's marriage to a Christian and imprisons both Valentin and Orson in the same castle where he is already keeping their mother. When all three escape, Ferragu flies into a rage; and as he leads his army in pursuit of the fugitives, the allusion to his horseless condition triggers a description of the giant in lurid terms:

> Lors a prins une massue moult grande et pesante et devant tous les aultres est sailly hors des portes sans cheval, car tant est grant et pesant que a peine pouoit il trouver cheval qui le peust porter. La teste avoit grosse et les cheveulx noirs et roides ainsi que pors sauvaiges, et les bras gros et ossus, et les espaules larges; de jambes et de corps portoit estature longue de treze pieds de long.

[Then he took hold of a massive, heavy club and, before them all, burst out of the gates without a horse, for he was so big and heavy that he could hardly find a horse able to carry him. His head was huge, his hair black and stiff like that of a wild boar, his arms large and bony and his shoulders wide; his legs and his body carried a height of thirteen feet.][45]

Explicitly excluded from the privileged chivalric status of mounted warrior, Ferragu now assumes the guise of a giant combatant, in whom the qualities of aristocratic knight and low-class ruffian are incongruously fused. As his giantesque anger consumes him, Ferragu's aristocratic facade abruptly crumbles, revealing the familiar racialized caricature of a monstrous, bestial man.

In scenes of combat between a knight and a giant, the partnership of knight and horse can also be used to highlight the nonchivalric status of the giant. In the *Suite du roman de Merlin*, for example, Gawain's brother Gaheriet makes full use of his horse in killing the giant Aupatris. Whereas there is no mention of the giant having a horse—one assumes that he is on foot, being of a stature that allows him to fight head-on with a mounted knight—Gaheriet's horse is repeatedly mentioned as an active and vital partner in combat. In his initial joust, Gaheriet "vient si grant oirre comme il pouoit du cheval traire" (came at him with as much speed as his horse could muster), and, after wounding Aupatris with his lance, "met la main a l'espee et li court sus tout a cheval" (laid his hand on his sword and ran at him, still mounted on horseback).[46] When he sees that the giant is about to regain his footing, Gaheriet employs the horse even more directly: "Il le fiert si du pis du cheval qu'il le fait revoler a la terre et li met le cheval tantes fois par dessus le corps que tout le debrise" (He struck him so hard with the breast of the horse that he caused him to fall back to the ground, and he ran the horse over him so many times that his body was completely shattered).[47] Gaheriet delivers the final coup de grâce on foot, beheading the now unconscious giant as he lies helpless on the ground. Still, the battle is very much a process of collaboration between man and steed, and as it descends momentarily into a violent confrontation of horse against giant, the adversaries are clearly distinguished. One masters and works with the animal partner that he has expertly trained, while the other—facing off against the force of a charging beast and its ruthless hooves—is little better than an animal himself, undeserving of the chivalrous respect that knights ordinarily accord one another.

It must be said that giants are not always distinguished by the lack of a horse. The giant Caradoc is riding an equally giant horse when he abducts Gawain.[48] Another giant, Maudit, rides a horse when he embarks on his wild killing sprees across the countryside (*PLanc*, 4:257–59). Unlike the club-wielding giants who dwell in forest thickets or mountain caves, these giants are feudal lords, albeit cruel and tyrannical in their uncouth behavior. As noted, Arthurian giants occupy a spectrum that encompasses differences of class and culture. Despite his horse, though, Maudit resembles both Ferragu and the Chevalier Jayant in his brutality. In his wild rides, we are told, he would strike terror in anyone "qui li veist les ieulz rooillier et les danz estraindre et croler la teste" (4:258; who might see him roll his eyes and gnash his teeth and shake his head); as he searches for victims, "si s'areste ausi com .I. lions, quant il a les bisches occises" (4:258; he stops like a lion, when he has killed the does). Mounted or not, a giant on the warpath is a frightening specter who combines the martial skills of human knights with the ferocity and indiscriminate aggression of a wild carnivore. As Cohen has remarked in reference to medieval discourses of racial and ethnic difference, the "racialized body" is imagined as combining human and animal traits, "a monster on whose body unresolved differences in species stood in for inassimilable differences of culture."[49] And of course one consequence of the association of racial or cultural others with mere animals is the reservation of full humanity, with all its rights and privileges, for those of aristocratic lineage, Christian faith, and Western chivalric culture. Cary Wolfe notes that "the full transcendence of the 'human' requires the sacrifice of the 'animal' and the animalistic, which in turn makes possible a symbolic economy in which we can engage in a 'noncriminal putting to death' . . . not only of animals, but of other *humans* as well by marking *them* as animal."[50] What giants offer, again, is the fantasy of a people who, though human, are nonetheless animalistic in both behavior and appearance—and who thus do not merit the dignity and respect normally accorded to fellow knights.

My final example from the *Conte du Papegau*, Jayant sans Nom, is the son of a dwarf and an ordinary woman who were stranded on a remote island at the time of his birth. His mother died in childbirth, leaving the infant and his father to fend for themselves; luckily, the father located a unicorn who consented to nourish the child with her milk, while also bringing back game until the boy was old enough to hunt for himself. It was because of this marvelous food that he grew up to be a giant in size and strength. Because of the wilderness setting, the child was never baptized and therefore has no official name; and he lacks any understanding of knighthood or of other social conventions. When he first appears, he is carrying a recently killed bear in one hand and a massive club in the other—an iconic image of the savage giant. And he shows his confusion about the human-animal boundary in his inability to distinguish a knight from his horse: his immediate reaction upon seeing the Chevalier du Papegau is to assume that this creature—an armor-clad man mounted on a horse—is some kind of fantastic beast, and he is about to attack him with his club when his father intervenes. Whereas aristocratic lords and ladies originally mistook the monstrous Poisson Chevalier for an armed knight on horseback, the giant "wild child" mistakes an actual mounted knight for a monster. The text thus moves full circle through a series of figures that problematize the humanity of the knight—a human figure encased in iron, intimately bonded to the animal with whom he moves as one, and endowed with a capacity for lethal violence—while always reaffirming the crucial boundaries separating knight from monster or beast. In reality, of course, it is the giant himself who embodies, in caricatured form, the anxieties surrounding knightly identity. As we have seen, the Chevalier Jayant combines animalistic behavior with an inability to grasp the refinements of chivalric competition and love service, whereas the Jayant sans Nom was nursed by a unicorn and raised in the forest wilds. Though his father was attached to a knight as court dwarf and personal valet, and longs for a return to civilized life, Jayant sans Nom is a rustic creature for whom civilization and courtly refinements are utterly alien. He hunts and devours his prey on the basis of an animal instinct that knows nothing of culinary arts, cultural taboos, or a hierarchy of beings.

 The Jayant sans Nom manifests the same prodigious appetite as that other comic giant Rainouart, companion and brother-in-law of Guillaume d'Orange. At dinner he devours half a stag, astonishing Arthur to such an extent that he is unable to eat anything at all. The act of killing and consuming his prey, in fact, appears to be the young giant's principal pastime; and this behavior provides a context within which the question of human identity can be further addressed. His father admits to Arthur that his son has never quite learned to distinguish between humans and animals: whatever he encounters in the forest, he kills and brings to his father, who has to tell him whether it is to be eaten (animals) or consigned to an ever-growing mass grave (humans). Though his lawless behavior derives from a kind of innocence and can still be controlled by the intervention of his father, the Jayant sans Nom clearly has the potential to fall into the anthropophagic habits sometimes found in more ferocious giants.[51] The devouring of human flesh blurs the human-animal boundary in two different ways. On the one hand, it compromises the humanity of giants and other exotic races accused of this practice by identifying them with carnivorous beasts—bears, lions, wolves—who might also target humans as prey. And on the other hand, it compromises the very category of humanity itself by collapsing people into the same category of "game" or "food" normally reserved for animals. This motif, frequently associated with giants, bears closer examination.

Cannibalism and the Category of the Human

Karl Steel has noted that the human position at the top of the food chain is a crucial feature in the definition of humanity in both medieval and modern discourses and that the prohibition on cannibalism is aimed less at protecting select individuals from meeting a culinary death, than "as a defense . . . of the human itself."[52] Steel's argument is based in part on his reading of Jacques Derrida, who maintains that the designation of animals as a category of beings that can be killed outside any structures of law or justice is "fondamental, dominant . . . essentiel à la structure de la subjectivité, c'est-à-dire aussi au fondement du sujet intentionnel."[53] Allowing people to be subsumed into the category of food would threaten both the cultural integrity of the human body and the basis of human subjectivity, at least as this is constituted in the Judeo-Christian tradition. Humans strive constantly to demonstrate their ability to kill even the most savage of carnivores—though often only as game, not necessarily as food—and consider themselves off limits as food for any species. And giants, as is well attested in medieval literary traditions, are the most formidable carnivores of all. It is no accident that the "mighty hunter" Nimrod came to be seen as a giant, whose hunting emblematically expressed the ruthless domination he imposed on people and animals alike. For Peter Comestor, Nimrod was a "Gigas decem cubitorum" (giant ten cubits in height) and a "robustus venator hominum" (mighty hunter of men) whose ruthless subjugations not only hinted at the reduction of human beings to the status of prey but also compromised the rational soul itself by imposing the irrational practice of idolatry: "id est exstinctor, et oppressor amore dominandi, et cogebat homines ignem adorare" (that is, exterminator, and oppressor for the love of domination, and he forced men to worship fire).[54]

The Bible does not explicitly address the issue of cannibalism, but the book of Genesis does trace a clear distinction between man and beast as targets of violence. The first act of violence in human history is Cain's murder of Abel in the aftermath of their rival sacrifices to God; and while Cain offers a vegetarian sacrifice—"de fructibus terrae munera" (an offering of the fruit of the ground)—Abel sacrifices "de primogenitis gregis sui" (of the firstlings of his flock).[55] As René Girard has noted, the outcome of this event is that Cain is a murderer; and that the murderer is "celui qui ne dispose pas de ce trompe-violence que constitue le sacrifice animal."[56] Girard's interest is specifically in ritual sacrifice, but the story does also establish an even more fundamental distinction between legitimate and illegitimate violence; and history's first criminal—primeval ancestor to giants—is one who spares animals while killing his fellow man. The use of animals as creatures whose death implicitly renews the primacy of human life and its sacred bond with God—despite their presumed scarcity at this particular moment in biblical history—is repeated in Noah's first act after the Flood: "Aedificavit autem Noe altare Domino: at tollens de cunctis pecoribus et volucribus mundis, obtulit holocausta super altare" (Then Noah built an altar to the Lord, and took of every clean animal and of every clean bird, and offered burnt offerings on the altar)."[57] It is also at this point that animals are confirmed, by divine mandate, as a natural food source: "Et terror vester ac tremor sit super cuncta animalia terrae, et super omnes volucres caeli, cum universis quae moventur super terram; omnes pisces maris manui vestrae traditi sunt. Et omne, quod movetur et vivit, erit vobis in cibum" (The fear of you and the dread of you shall be upon every beast of the earth, and upon every bird of the air, upon everything that creeps on the ground and all the fish of the sea; into your hand they are delivered. Every moving thing that lives shall be food for you).[58] An unspoken (and perhaps unspeakable) prohibition of cannibalism is implied in the greater taboo associated in this passage with human blood. Even the blood of animals is not to be eaten; but, God tells Noah, "Quicumque effuderit humanum sanguinem, fundetur sanguis illius; ad imaginem quippe Dei factus est homo" (Whoever sheds the blood of man, his blood will be shed; for God made man in his own image) (Gen. 9:6).[59] According to the Bible, the very category of the human is founded on the notion of a human resemblance to divinity—understood by medieval theologians as possession of a rational and immortal soul—and the resulting status of people as creatures who are free to subdue, kill, or eat all other living things; while people themselves are the one species who cannot be subjugated or killed outside strictly defined legal structures and limitations and are absolutely not to be eaten.

The Bible does not, of course, attribute cannibalistic behavior to Cain, though it does later prohibit the practice of human sacrifice while instituting animal sacrifice as a sacred obligation. Cain was, however, frequently identified as the ancestor of giants; and he is explicitly identified with a cannibalistic giant in the prose *Tristan*. This figure, whom I will discuss more fully in subsequent chapters, uses riddles to entrap his prey, and the narrator makes quite a point of his anthropophagic proclivities: "Il estoit acostumez de mangier char d'ome, ne d'autre chose ne vivoit, ne il ne se delitoit autant en nule chair come en chair humaine" (He was in the habit of eating human flesh, nor did he live on anything other than that, or delight so much in any kind of meat as he did in human flesh).[60] In addition to local knights, the giant has also eaten some of his own family members; and in a riddle recounting his murder and consumption of his mother, he figuratively identifies her as "Abel" and himself as "Cain." (*PT*[C], 1:79–80). This designation has the immediate effect of underscoring both the innocence of the maternal victim and the depravity of the giant aggressor. But it is also telling that a medieval author would make an association between the wicked brother who spared animals while murdering his fellow man, and the giant who similarly disdains animals as food while enthusiastically dining on humans.

Cain can be seen as the first "outsider": his primeval act of murder caused a separation between his lineage and that of Seth, just as Nimrod's later arrogance and violence generated the ethnic and linguistic diversity that marks the world as we know it. The rivalry between humans and giants as predators both reflects and perpetuates this stigmatization of the alien race, identifying racial and cultural alterity with the animalistic enemies of civilization. Like lions and wolves, who compete with humans for hunting grounds and in the consumption of livestock—and who are feared for their real or imagined predations on humanity itself—the indigenous population known as "giants" are marked as a dangerous foe. And unlike Cain, but like animals, giants are legitimate targets of violence: to kill them is not merely permitted but encouraged. An episode near the beginning of the prose *Tristan* even exploits the anthropophagic reputation of giants as a means of identifying their extermination with divine grace and the spread of Christianity. "At that time," we are told—that is, not long after the arrival in Britain of Joseph of Arimathea—Cornwall and the Leonois were infested with giants who lived on human flesh. Word of this reached St. Denis, himself recently arrived to establish Christianity in France:

> Mais quant Sainz Denis sanz faille fu venuz en France, et il oï dire que en ces deus reaumes avoit genz qui manjoient chair humaine, il le tint a grant merveille, si pria adonc a Nostre Seignor qu'il ne sofrist des ores mes qu'il avenist en cele terre si grant delealté com de char humaine que manjast l'autre. Celi soir meïsmes qu'il fist cele priere a Nostre Seignor avint que tuit le jaiant de Cornoaille morurent. (*PT*[C], 1:77)
>
> ―――
>
> [But when the infallible St. Denis had come to France, and he heard that in these two realms there were people who ate human flesh, he considered it a great marvel, so he prayed to Our Lord that he not allow, from then on, that there should exist on earth any treachery so great as human flesh eaten by another human. The very night that he made that prayer to Our Lord, it came to pass that all the giants of Cornwall died.]

The saintly missionary, viewed within medieval culture as a disciple of St. Paul himself, accomplishes through his prayers a feat even greater than that of the most valiant knight: whereas they were limited to killing giants one at a time, or at best in small groups of three or four, St. Denis succeeds in having the entire giant population of Cornwall eliminated in a single night. This divine act of vengeance, like that perpetrated in the Deluge that exterminated the giants of old, is motivated by a sinfulness that places the giants beyond the boundaries of ordinary human failings.

Interestingly, however, this passage that dispatches giants so swiftly in the name of advancing Christendom does also grant them humanity of at least some sort. Animals, after all, can be known to devour humans; but while saints sometimes triumph over individual carnivores, they do not normally seek the genocidal massacre of entire species.[61] Though the narrator informs us that the giants were known as "mostres" (monsters) for their size and strength (*PT*[C], 1:77), he also refers to them as "genz"—a "people" or "race"—whose man-eating proclivities are not simply animalistic. Instead, we are told that "il estoient acostumé de mangier chair humaine, ne plus ne se gardoient que feïssent bestes mues" (1:77; they were accustomed to eat human flesh, and worried no more about that than would dumb animals). If giants can be said to behave "as would dumb animals," this can only be because they are not, themselves, animals; and St. Denis's own formulation—"char humaine que manjast l'autre"—clearly implies the devouring of human flesh by another human. Giants are subject to punishment for their actions, not only in this example but also in another episode from the *Tristan*, where the riddling giant is struck by celestial fire for killing and eating his mother. However "animalistic" they may be, as we have seen above, they are nonetheless situated in an ethical framework that identifies their behavior less with the natural violence of animals than with the perversity of human sin. Paradoxically, it is as humans that giants threaten the very concept of humanity: an enemy at once alien and at the heart of human subjectivity.

The stigmatization of giants as anthropophagic savages, though not a universal feature of their character, runs throughout Arthurian romance, and we can recognize the motif even in instances that do not involve actual cannibalism. We have seen that both the Chevalier Jayant in *Papegau* and Maudit in *Lancelot* resemble hungry carnivores as they track their human prey. The motif of rival or aberrant hunts is more subtly evoked in the episode of the prose *Tristan* concerning the giant

Taulas de la Montagne.⁶² Taulas disports himself by hunting and killing Cornish knights in the forest of the Morois; because of this, members of the court avoid passing through the forest if at all possible. Taulas is seeking vengeance for the death of his father, who was killed by Cornish knights, and does not appear to eat his victims; but the systematic way in which he scours the Morois in search of knights, hiding behind trees and ambushing any that come his way, is reminiscent of a hunt. When King Mark learns that the giant has finally been killed and that he can once again freely use this territory, he celebrates by going deer hunting with a large party of knights and barons. The king thus reasserts his control of hunting rights, an important prerogative of royal power that had temporarily been superseded by the giant, while also implicitly contrasting the ceremonial deer hunt—a staging ground for aristocratic power, splendor, and refinement—with the terroristic hunting of humans perpetrated by Taulas. If giants are the one race or species that is eaten by no one other than themselves, while reducing humans and all other animals alike to the status of prey—creatures that can be killed with impunity, as a kind of sport, and sometimes even eaten—then the human privilege of stewardship and dominion within the natural order is undermined.

In the *Conte du Papegau*, Jayant sans Nom illustrates this problematic in a darkly humorous way, as his exasperated father shakes his head over his son's stubborn habit of confusing men and women with legitimate prey. Like the Chevalier Jayant, however, Jayant sans Nom has encountered not just any knight but the great King Arthur. And just as he has spent the entire romance dispatching or reforming capricious and villainous characters of various kinds, so now Arthur brings the dwarf and his giant son back to Windsor, where Jayant sans Nom is baptized, knighted, and integrated into chivalric society. No longer, as far as one can tell, does he attempt to eat people or confuse them with wild game. Recovering one's own human identity through social integration—acquiring a name, a social rank, and membership in a community—is the key to recognizing the distinctive human qualities in others. This particular point, in fact, is stressed in modern psychoanalytic theories of subjectivity. In the words of Judith Butler: "To have a name is to be positioned within the Symbolic, the idealized domain of kinship, a set of relationships structured through sanction and taboo which is governed by the law of the father and the prohibition against incest."[63] In this particular case the crucial prohibition is against cannibalism rather than incest, but the principle is much the same: both prohibitions entail the demarcation of a particular grouping with which one is identified, and within which certain behaviors are forbidden. Conforming to ethical law as incarnated in the person of the king, the no longer nameless giant can learn to channel his aggression in a socially constructive manner, for the distinction between knight and giant depends on this crucial circumscription of acceptable uses of violence. Arthur's very presence, it would seem, suffices to convert a potentially anthropophagic giant into a civilized knight, or to bring out the capacity for Christian penance and mutual chivalric respect in a giant combatant. Whether the changes wrought are merely a shift of perspective—a courtly veneer over what is still a culture of primal drives and violent power struggles—or whether it is a genuine passage from benighted savagery to Christian refinement is a matter for readerly reflection.

Bestial Depravity and Human Sin

I have focused here on the ways that a giant's violent behavior compromises his humanity and associates him with the bestial: his preternatural speed and strength, his treatment of humans as a food source, his propensity for acts of aggression that lie outside legal structures. Though a giant's behavior offers parallels to that of ordinary tyrants or outlaws, an incapacity for surrender, submission, contrition, or reform nearly always sets him apart from all but the most hardened of chivalric villains. On the one hand, his violent behavior seems, like that of animals, to be essential to his nature, and thereby something less to be punished or rehabilitated than to be deplored and, if possible, exterminated. Medieval theologians interpreted the biblical statement of human dominion over animals as a figurative expression of a divine mandate for those in whom human rationality is most perfectly developed, to regulate and govern those whose sinful behavior has in effect placed them on a par with irrational beasts: it is not might that makes right, but reason.[64] In this sense the stigmatization of giants, or any other enemy people, as "bestial" is itself a justification for their subordination, enslavement, or eradication. At the same time, the "unnatural" quality of a giant's acts—expressed in the epithet *pervers* with which they are sometimes described—and the obsessive delight he often takes in rape, murder, and torture as ends in themselves identify him more with human sin and depravity than with the natural instinct of the animal world. As was commonly repeated by medieval writers, the rational mind endows humans with not only the possibility but also the obligation for self-knowledge and the moral consciousness that this implies—a quality inaccessible to animals—and thereby also with the possibility for sinful behavior that exceeds the mere brutishness of animals in its violation of nature itself. An early and formative statement of this obligation for moral self-knowledge appears in the *Consolation of Philosophy*: "Humanae quippe naturae ista condicio est ut tum tantum ceteris rebus cum se cognoscit excellat, eadem tamen infra bestias redigatur, si se nosse desierit. Nam ceteris animantibus sese ignorare naturae est; hominibus vitio venit" (For the nature of man is such that he is better than other things only when he knows himself, and yet if he ceases to know himself he is made lower than the brutes. For it is natural for other animals not to have this self-knowledge; in man it is a fault).[65] Medieval moralists and theologians often note that whereas animals dutifully follow the law of nature, it is humans—despite or perhaps because of their greater rational faculty—who resist and corrupt nature with their endless indulgence in sin.[66] Alexander of Hales, in fact, states categorically that "solummodo enim inter res corporales homo deordinat se per peccatum, quod non faciunt bruta animalia" (for among bodily creatures, man alone disorders himself through sin, something that brute animals do not do).[67] Humankind's only hope is that through contrition and penance born of self-knowledge they can purge their sinful souls and achieve the spiritual salvation to which humans, uniquely, have access. As Susan Crane succinctly states, "Augustine, Ambrose, and further church fathers agree that only humans possess the reason and free will that allow for both sinning and repenting. Other animals are driven by instinct."[68] If we apply this model of the human/animal dichotomy to giants as they are constructed across a range of texts, the results are ambiguous. With few exceptions—and those most likely half-blood giants, or giants by accident of birth rather than genealogical descent—a giant engages willfully in human sins of a sort that medieval writers often saw animals as being incapable of, such as rape, incest, and cannibalism, while lacking the human capacity for self-scrutiny and self-discipline.

It is in fact striking that the two Arthurian giants most devoted to cannibalism—the Riddler in the prose *Tristan* and the Golden-Haired Giant in *Perceforest*—are also both implicated in incestuous intrigue. I do not, of course, mean to imply that these two traits necessarily coincide; one can find examples throughout medieval literature of giants or other villains, as well as foreign or monstrous races, who perpetrate either one without the other. Still, it is interesting that the riddling giant, who is said to live exclusively on human flesh, admits to having raped his daughter, as well as to having eaten both her and his mother; while Golden-Hair, whose preferred diet is humans, intends to marry his daughter. All giants are violent, but many engage in relatively "normal" crimes: the rape of local women and the incarceration, subjugation, mutilation, or murder of local men. These acts, in themselves, do not really set giants apart from other people and are found often enough in the renegade knights and outlaws that are regularly confronted by chivalric heroes; what is distinctive to giants is the consistency and enthusiasm with which they pursue these behaviors, as if constitutionally unable to resist them. Giants have the capacity, however, to cross the line between ordinary violence and the more spectacular forms to which chivalric society considers itself immune—and they do so without the slightest sign of shame. The giant's riddle of father-daughter incest and cannibalism, in fact, implies a view of the daughter as naturally subject to her father's appetites. Using the metaphor of a tree to represent his wife, the Riddler states that he first picked its flower, then ate its fruit:

> La biauté del fruit m'enorta
> A ce que je la flor en pris.
> Aprés le fruit tant en mespris
> Que le fruit manjai sanz refu.
>   (*PT* [C], 1:76)

> [The beauty of the fruit excited me so much that I took the flower. Later, I so scorned the fruit that I ate it without hesitation.]

Just as the flower naturally matures into fruit, so the sexual vulnerability and erotic attractions of the young daughter develop, as she matures, into the culinary appeal of a bite to eat. The rhyming pair *pris/mespris* underscores the simultaneous presence of desire—the sexual "taking" of the love object—and disregard: the movement from paternal love through sexual arousal culminates in the denigration of the daughter and sexual partner as nothing more than food. The giant's riddle encapsulates Maggie Kilgour's characterization of cannibalism as "the place where desire and dread, love and aggression meet"—an assessment that would certainly apply to incestuous rape as well.[69] Incest and cannibalism are both actions that not only violate but actively rewrite fundamental categories of identity, defining immediate kin as sexual partners and fellow humans (or giants) as inert matter to be eaten, their deaths unmourned.

As such both incest and cannibalism are so threatening to cultural constructions of self and other that they tend to be construed as embedded not in culture itself but in nature. In modern psychoanalytic discourses—most notably Freud, with his foundational myth of the primal horde—as well as colonial discourses of alien races ripe for enslavement or exploitation, these behaviors are associated with an imagined "state of nature."[70] The medieval theological distinction between animal instinct and human sin, however, taught that animals, for all their violence and brute lust, would not devour members of their own species or mate with their immediate family.[71] As Gaunt has shown in his recent study of Marco Polo's *Devisement du monde*, cannibalism is not necessarily imbued with horror in medieval thought; as portrayed among certain peoples of the Far East, it can be a practice that forms part of a well-organized society, governed by laws of kinship and social justice.[72] But when they are located among people identified as enemies of the Christian West, both incest and cannibalism tend to be markers of extreme and disturbing alterity. Forming a closed circle with their incestuous couplings and possibly even devouring the outsiders who come their way, such people can only remain an unknowable enigma and an inassimilable kernel of traumatic difference; as with the cannibalistic giants of Cornwall, mass extermination may be the only solution to their violation of both nature and culture. The concentration of both crimes in the person of the giant underscores the extent to which he represents a sinful deformation of human character, corresponding to his racially aberrant body. The giant becomes a means of naturalizing cultural prohibitions that are almost too traumatic even to voice, by locating such behaviors in an enemy associated with the two cursed lineages of the Bible—Cain and Ham—and therefore doomed to destruction. At the same time, paradoxically, the very perversity of his wickedness also underscores his separation from nature: his all-too-human susceptibility to sin.

I will explore this aspect of giants more fully in subsequent chapters. For now, we might simply consider that what giants ultimately represent may be the fantasy of a race of humans corrupted by Original Sin, yet resistant by their very nature to any concept of Christian redemption: a people who are not only uncivilized but quite uncivilizable. It is not wholly impossible, of course, for a giant to convert to Christianity; the salvific benefits of Christ's passion can only be understood as universally accessible to all descendants of Adam and Eve. St. Christopher was a giant, after all, and Arthurian romance also provides rare examples of giants who are receptive to moral or spiritual instruction.[73] These are very much the exception, however, serving more through their very novelty to highlight the intransigence and perversity of the giant race overall. Still, such examples do remind us that giants are at least potentially invited to accept Christian salvation, even if they may be constitutionally disinclined to do so; and this resistance again marks them as more truly depraved than animals, who are excluded—one might even say excused—from the dynamic of sin, penance, salvation, and redemption. If at times they seem to merge with the animalistic world of brute nature or with the demonic supernatural, giants nonetheless belong more fully to the human world than to anything that lies outside it.

Bearing this in mind can help us understand the way that giants interact with the world of *faerie*. *Des grantz geanz* is not the only text to associate giants with this inhuman realm. In the *Mélusine* of both Jean d'Arras and Coudrette, Presine, Mélusine's fairy mother, sets a giant as guard on the tomb of her husband Elinas, apparently without concern for the fact that she has thereby unleashed terror onto generations of local inhabitants.[74] For the fairy, a giant is a powerful guarantor of security, rather than a scourge of civilization to be eliminated at all cost. Both giants and fairies are aboriginal or alternative inhabitants of the land, living a kind of parallel life that intersects with human civilization but also lies well outside it. Of these, however, fairies are by far the most alien, with their immortality, their magic powers, and their association with places that humans simply cannot access, or even discern at all, unless the fairy permits it. Where fairies use magic to incapacitate or bedazzle their human victims, giants rely on sheer physical violence. Emerging from their lairs, they prey on society through recognizably human forms of terrorism and guerilla warfare, resisting the new regime that threatens to displace them completely. And, importantly, giants are not absolutely excluded from human society—distinguishing them once again from the animals who live closely with people but only in the form of domesticated creatures used for labor, entertainment, or food; from the fairies who pass through human society and may even join it for a time but never remain there permanently; and from the demons whose sole participation in human life is as tempters and troublemakers from another realm. As we saw with the Chevalier Jayant, giants may assimilate to at least some extent into the world of feudal politics; and these stories allow for more complex reflections on the racial and cultural other and the problems that arise in any effort toward intermarriage, alliance, and assimilation. This topic will be a recurring theme throughout the study to follow.

The Need for Giants

Giants, in sum, are a people who are always disappearing, yet somehow never quite fully disappeared, for the world of medieval romance requires their presence. As Susan Stewart has noted, they exist in a kind of permanent twilight: "Giants, like dinosaurs, in their anonymous singularity always seem to be the last of their race . . . usually described as both archaic and on the verge of extinction."[75] From the biblical Flood to the divine massacre of Cornish giants, from the victories of the Israelites to the wholesale slaughter carried out by Brutus and his men and the concerted giant killing of Arthurian knights, giants represent that which must be eliminated or reconfigured in the forward march of human history. Yet this very process is so vital to the construction of Christian chivalric culture that it can never be allowed to end. Even

God himself, having rid the world of giants with the Flood, allows more giants to spring up among the descendants of Ham—and possibly, according to some commentators, inexplicably even allowed some of the original giants to survive. Similarly, after cleansing Cornwall and the Leonois of giants, he apparently makes no move to prevent other giants from repopulating the region: "Et sachiez qu'il n'ot puis en ces deus reaumes jaianz s'il n'i vindrent d'autre terre" (*PT*[C], 1:77; And indeed there were never again giants in those two realms unless they went there from some other land). There are always more giants lurking in the mountains, forests, and fens; the giant heritage absorbed through the marriage of a knight with a giantess persists in the most illustrious of lineages, ever capable of producing just one more ferocious descendant whose defiant behavior serves as the crucible in which new heroes are formed. Combat between a giant and a knight is one of the most familiar motifs of medieval literature, appearing in both romance and epic; and these encounters are colored by a mixture of fear and rage, desire and enjoyment, desperation and the thrill of danger. Killing a giant is the ultimate chivalric adventure, separating true superheroes from mere knights. In the words of the damsel seeking to dissuade the Bel Inconnu from attacking a pair of giants: "Ocis serra, n'i pues faillir, / Se tu te conbas as jaians; / Tant les sai fels e conbatans" (You will be killed, you can't avoid it, if you fight the giants; so much do I know them to be evil and belligerent).[76] It is often in combat that knights first encounter one another, and by means of combat that they develop the mutual respect that allows for a cessation of hostilities and the establishment of friendship. A similar note of admiration can occur in combat with giants; as Cohen states, in the giant's body "prohibition is always entwined with enjoyment, otherness with intimacy."[77] In fighting the giant Maudit, Bohort "sant que il est de la greignor force que chevaliers que il onques trouvast" (*PLanc*, 5:22; feels that he is more powerful than any knight he ever encountered)—a perception that carries a hint of both fear and desire. The stories of Galehot in *Lancelot* and *Tristan*, and of the Chevalier Jayant and his brother in *Papegau*, show that half-blood giants are capable of reconciliation and even friendship with their human adversaries, though always with somewhat problematic results. The transition from enmity to companionship cannot be made with a truly savage giant; but the conventions of knightly combat establish a context in which that possibility is subtly evoked.

Geoffrey of Monmouth, though couching his narrative in an overall framework that promotes the eradication of giants, does not shy from acknowledging the element of enjoyment that the Trojans found in their interactions with Britain's indigenous inhabitants. Brutus's companion Corineus, for example, selects Cornwall as his portion because of the abundance of giants there: "Delectabat enim eum contra gigantes dimicare . . . cum talibus congredi ultra modum aestuabat" (He loved to fight giants . . . [He] was always most eager to fight giants).[78] Given his almost excessive pleasure ("ultra modum") in wrestling giant bodies, it is no surprise that, when asked to fight Gogmagog, Corineus is "maximo gaudio fluctuans" (overjoyed).[79] The adaptation of Geoffrey's text at the beginning of *Perceforest* reiterates Corineus's attraction to giants, explaining that he chose Cornwall as his portion because "il luy plaisoit moult combatre contre les geans, desquelz la copie habondoit plus illecques que en nulles des provinces qui eussent esté distribuees a ses compaignons" (*Perce/I*, 1:27–28; he greatly enjoyed fighting the giants, of whom there was a greater abundance there than in any of the provinces given to his companions). For the author of *Perceforest*, in fact, it is Corineus's own desire that motivates his combat with Gogmagog, for "oultre maniere desiroit a celuy a assembler" (1:28; he had an overwhelming desire to grapple with him).

In the Arthurian portion of the *Historia regum Britanniae*, it is not merely the excitement of the fight that is stressed but also a titillating process of simultaneous identification with, and condemnation of, the giant's rapacity. Though Arthur was "acri ignescens ira" (blazing with fierce rage) while fighting the Giant of Mont-St-Michel—itself a means of sharing in the giant's savage fury as he assails any and all knights to come within view—his ultimate reaction after killing the giant is one of pleasure and excitement at the giant himself as an exotic object:[80] "Rex ilico in risum solutus praecepit Beduero amputare ei caput et dare uni armigerorum ad deferendum ad castra, ut spectaculum intuentibus fieret. . . . In secundae noctis diluculo ad tentoria sua cum capite remeauerunt, ad quod ammirandum cateruatim concurrebant." (Immediately the king laughed, telling Beduerus to cut off his head and give it to one of the squires to take back to the camp as a sight for his men to gaze upon.... At the dawn of the third day they returned to their tents with the head, which the soldiers rushed in crowds to see).[81]

Though the head is merely admired and not eaten, this collective enjoyment of the rival's dismembered body does come uncomfortably close to replicating the giant's dismemberment and gluttonous consumption of knights defeated by him. And after his battle with Ritho, Arthur not only claims the giant's cloak of beards—constructed, in true giant fashion, of beards flayed from the faces of defeated kings—but even takes Ritho's beard as well to improve his trophy.[82] The giant's fascination with his rivals and his desire to clothe his body in theirs, it would seem, is equally shared by the great Christian king. And while Arthur could never embark on a project of wholesale conquest aimed at amassing a collection of human beards, the mediating presence of the giant, who created the grisly cloak and from whom Arthur wins it in a fair fight, allows him to possess an item that would otherwise be taboo. In Arthur's hands the cloak takes on a double meaning. It reifies the excessively potent masculinity of the giant, too unseemly for explicit aspiration but seductive nonetheless, and symbolically present in the combat trophy that Arthur does not hesitate to keep. But in commemorating his victory over Ritho, the cloak simultaneously signals Arthur's distance from the giant's barbarism and his rejection of a masculinity based purely on brute force. If, as Wace asserts, the battle affords Arthur the greatest fear he has ever known, it may be not only because his opponent pushes him so close to death but also because of the forbidden desires embodied by this particular enemy, the ultimate warrior's fantasy.[83]

The boundary separating giants from other humans, in short, is marked by an emotional intensity unrivaled in medieval literature. The giants killed by the heroes of medieval romance embody the ideals of a warrior society—virility, single-minded determination, ferocity in battle, a powerful physique—but in an absolute form that clashes with the other side of courtly chivalric culture: courtesy, humility, moderation, deferral of desire. In Cohen's words, the giant is "the site where everything that exceeds containment in the chivalric matrix becomes possible again," making him at once a powerful temptation and an enemy to be destroyed at all cost.[84] The giant, as a fantasy construct, embodies pathologies of racial antagonism similar to those that have been identified in analyses of race relations in modern British and American societies. With no moral constraints on his behavior, the giant is free to indulge the libidinous drives that the knight is forced to restrain and deny. As such, he is a racial construct analogous to—and in many ways no less fictional than—the early modern construction of "blackness" as described by David Roediger: "Racism grew so strongly among the Anglo-American bourgeoisie during the years America was colonized because blackness came to symbolize that which the accumulating capitalist had given up, but still longed for. Increasingly adopting an ethos that . . . postponed gratification, profit-minded Englishmen and Americans cast blacks as their former selves."[85] In the literary depictions of giants and their interactions with the knights and ladies of the court, we can discern a fraught mixture of emotions similar to that characterizing the ideology of white supremacy: in Jerry Phillips's words, a blend of "desire and hate, envy and enmity, nostalgia and estrangement."[86]

Aboriginals from whom land, women, and power must be wrested by the new ruling order, giants embody what Bhabha has described as "those terrifying stereotypes of savagery, cannibalism, lust and anarchy which are the signal points of identification and alienation, scenes of fear and desire, in colonial texts."[87] Conversely, giants are often portrayed as driven by a powerful fascination toward the humans who are alien intruders into what had always been giant territory, but also fellow beings with what is ultimately a shared human history. As was finally made explicit in *Des grantz geanz*, the giant's very self is marked by the traumatic encounter of human and nonhuman, and this inner conflict implicitly plays itself out in the giants' combined tendencies to isolationism—the simultaneous absorption and destruction of intimate kin through incest, cannibalism, and the murder of family members—and obsessive attraction for knights and ladies, whether as targets of violence, objects of incarceration, or even companions and lovers. Murderous antagonism between giants and humans goes hand in hand with passionate desire, leading to opposing movements of eradication and assimilation. The giantess bride may emerge as a remnant of "giantism" carried over into human life; and a need to cast the giant as monstrous may be combined with an implicit acknowledgment that he has more in common with the knights than anyone cares to admit. More savage and more fearsome than the Saracens with whom they are frequently aligned, giants are also more intimately a part of chivalric culture. Indigenous to the British landscape, they are the foreigner who is also a local, exotic yet very close to home. As terrorists operating with confident bravado out of strongholds in the very heartlands of Arthurian Britain, they threaten the integrity of a chivalric culture founded on the paradoxical ethos that power and prowess are enhanced through a process of renunciation. To absorb giants is to risk a return to that state of ferocity that the Arthurian knight abhors; but to fight them requires an unleashing of violence that again threatens the boundary between knight and giant, until the moment when the giant is safely dead. The giant embodies a fundamental fear of both social and psychological degradation, similar in many ways to that inspired by the terrorist in modern imagination: the realization that, in Kawash's words, "the outside that terrorizes is always already at the heart of the inside that demands to be secured . . . and thus threatens the claim to difference that guarantees the identity of the inside as such."[88]

Whether they are killed in the name of God, of the king, or of personal honor or love service, finally, Arthurian giants are targeted as degenerate or culturally deviant men. Though their capacity for sheer evil may cause them to be taunted and denigrated as *deable* or *monstre*, they are not identified, like those in *Huon de Bordeaux*, as the descendants of demons and sea monsters; indeed, the Poisson Chevalier of the *Conte du Papegau* is as much a foil for the Chevalier Jayant as he is for Arthur himself. In the end it is their human status—ambiguous, bestialized, degraded, but also essential to their character—that gives giants their particular place in the medieval literary imagination and shapes both the horror and the fascination that they elicit. Abject beings, giants live on the borderlines where civilization blends into deviance and heresy, culture into nature, the natural into perversity and otherworldly demonism, and humanity into inhumanity. And as such they underwrite the very concepts of nature, culture, and human identity.

CHAPTER 2

An Alien Presence

*Giants as Markers of Race,
Class, and Culture*

It is hardly necessary to dwell on the fabled violence of giants; by most accounts, wrath and homicide characterize their very being. Examples of giants who kill or imprison anyone who comes within their domain, ravage the countryside, extort a heavy ransom from their human victims, and rape or abduct women are well known and too numerous to catalog. Some are simply hostile to any contact with the outside world. In the *Estoire del Saint Graal*, for example, Nascien and his son are lost at sea and attempt to land on a small island endowed with a beautiful castle. But no sooner does the ship pull into port when a giant bursts from the castle; without even waiting to find out who the visitors are, he cries out: "Mar i arivastes en mon isle sanz mon congié! A morir vos en covient!" (Woe that you came to my island without my permission! You must die for this!).[1] Giants are not always such extreme isolationists, however. They can also be participants in aristocratic court life and feudal lords in their own right, members of the pagan culture that was imagined to have dominated Britain in the distant past and whose vestiges still last into the Arthurian era. We have already seen the example of the Chevalier Jayant, a wealthy count hoping to promote himself to duke through an advantageous marriage, and in the pages that follow we will see other giants who are an integral part of the feudal society of pagan Britain. In examining these stories of giants as actors within aristocratic and feudal power structures we can come closer to understanding the political and cultural ideologies that they support.

The Beard-Collecting Rion: Giant or Enemy King?

Even when they have taken on chivalric status or aristocratic titles, giants' behavior tends to the extreme, distinguishing them from more ordinary rebel barons or outlaw knights; and they are rarely, if ever, willing to accept negotiated settlements or to submit to a higher authority. The beard collector variously known as Retto, Ritho, Rithon, or Rion is an interesting example of a character whose identity shifts between giant and ordinary human king from one text to another, and with it the overall trajectory of his story.[2] Geoffrey of Monmouth is unequivocal in alluding to the adventure in which Arthur "Rithonem gigantem in Arauio monte interfecit" (had killed upon Mount Aravius the giant Ritho).[3] Wace similarly identifies Rithon as "gaiant."[4] In both of these accounts, the focus is on single combat between Arthur and his challenger, with no mention of an army on either side. In *Brut*, Rithon's demand for Arthur's beard is couched in the following terms:

> E si Artur cuntrediseit
> Ço que Rithon li requereit,
> Cors a cors ensemble venissent
> E cors a cors se combatissent.
>
> [And if Arthur refused what Rithon was asking of him, they would meet face to face and fight in single combat.][5]

Details are sketchy, but at this stage Rithon appears to be a typical lone giant, vanquishing kings in single combat and "scalping" their beards, until he is finally killed by the greatest king of all.

The situation is different, however, in the *Premiers faits du roi Arthur*, a series of adventures sometimes found in manuscripts of the Vulgate Cycle between *Merlin* and *Lancelot*, and corresponding roughly to what is also known as the Vulgate *Suite du Merlin*.[6] Here, Rion wages an extensive war against Arthur and his allies in which he is described as a ferocious giant equipped, rather unusually, with an army composed of giants as well as Saxons and other pagans. When forced to surrender, he harbors resentment and soon reappears with a new army seeking vengeance — indeed, it is apparently his bitterness at the earlier defeat, and his need for an unmistakable sign of supremacy, that prompts his request for Arthur's beard in this second challenge. Only after this second round of fighting does Arthur finally succeed in killing his adversary. It is clear that by this point in the evolving Arthurian tradition Rion is no rustic savage. He is king of Ireland, with his own army and a number of pagan vassals willing to muster extensive troops on his behalf. And as befits a king, he has an ancient lineage, being descended from none other than the great Hercules. Finally, although Rion does wield a club on the battlefield — so often a giant's weapon of choice — he also has a sword of surpassing strength and beauty forged by the god Vulcan, presented by Hercules to Jason when he went in quest of the Golden Fleece, and passed down within the lineage of Hercules to Rion himself. Arthur wins this sword from Rion in the first battle and ultimately manages to kill the giant with it. Perhaps in recognition of Rion's status as a powerful king, there is no mention of Arthur appropriating (much less adding to) the cloak of beards; instead, his trophy is the more conventional one of a superlative weapon.

In this account, Rion takes on a somewhat ambiguous character as both giant and king. His description during his first single combat with Arthur emphasizes the grotesque and bestial qualities for which giants are known:

> Et quant cil se sent navré si estraint les dens et roulle les ex de mautalent qu'il ot gros et enflés et rouges. . . . Et il estoit grans et fors a merveilles sor tous les homes que on seüst et avoit bien, ce dist li contes, .XIV. piés de lonc, des piés qui adont estoient. Et si avoit entre .II. ex plus de plaine paume mesuree et estoit maigres et plains de vainnes et de ners et figurés de tous menbres que trop faisoit a redouter. (1106)

[And when he feels himself wounded, he gnashes his teeth and rolls his eyes, large and swollen and red, with ill will. . . . And he was large and marvelously strong, more so than any other man known, and according to the tale he was fourteen feet tall, as measured in the feet then in use. And there was more than a full palm-width between his eyes, and he was thin and marked with veins and tendons, and his limbs formed in such a manner that he was terrifying to behold.]

His heritage is illustrious, to be sure, but it also carries an implicit marker of alterity. As in the later poem *Des grantz geanz*, the giant is of Greek descent and is thus a natural enemy of the Trojan Britons—a hostility that can be imaginatively transferred to the aristocratic classes of medieval England and France, who also considered themselves of Trojan descent. In the first round of battles, his troops are repeatedly referred to as "gaians" (giants), while the war itself is termed "la bataille des Saisnes" (the battle with the Saxons), and Rion is both "gaians" and "roi d'Irlande" (king of Ireland). The different terms are also applied interchangeably to individual warriors, such as King Jonap, whom Arthur fights, and who is first described as "un grant gaiant et fort et merveillous" (1084; a huge, wondrously powerful giant) and then, only a few lines later, as "li Saisnes" (1085; the Saxon). The defensive side in the war, on the other hand—an alliance including such notable figures as Arthur, Bademagu, Ban of Benwic, Bohort of Gaunes, and Léodegan of Carmélide—is collectively termed "li Crestien" (the Christians). By the time of the second war, Arthur has defeated the Saxons and driven them from the land; this time Rion calls upon his vassals from the islands, so that his army is "l'ost des Yrois et des Illois" (1549; the army of the Irish and the Islanders). For whatever reason, there is no further use of the term *gaians*; Rion is simply "le roi." Overall, in this extended episode the category of "giant" merges with that of the various renegade races—Irish, Saxons, rebellious Islanders—imagined by medieval readers as the enemies both of Arthur and of his Norman successors. And in pitting "li gaiant" against "li Crestien," the text further identifies these races as the enemies not only of specific political dynasties but also of Christendom itself. Geographic, ethnic, and cultural differences fuse in the emerging portrait of the giant king.

Finally, when Rion appears in the slightly later *Suite du roman de Merlin*, he is no longer identified as a giant at all.[7] Rion is now the king of Norgales, making him British rather than Irish; and he is described by one of Arthur's knights as "uns des biaus chevaliers dou monde" (56; one of the handsome knights of this world),[8] although he is still seen as an extremely powerful adversary who is thus far undefeated in battle, and his demand for Arthur's beard is an obvious outrage. And rather than being killed by Arthur, in the *Suite du Roman de Merlin* Rion is ambushed and captured on his way to an adulterous love tryst by two knights under the guidance of Merlin, after which his army is defeated; the affair is settled when Rion surrenders and agrees to hold his lands in homage from Arthur. The possibility of settling the dispute through conventional warfare and feudal vassalage presumably arises only because the adversary has shifted from a giant to a fully human, if nonetheless arrogant, king. Giants are normally confronted in single combat with a hero, most commonly as an isolated event; though Arthur's two single combats with Rion in the *Premiers faits* take place in the context of a larger war, they still adhere to this customary way of resolving disputes with giants. And in all cases these encounters are lethal; the giants' beards or indeed their heads can be freely taken as trophies. Rival kings, however brutal they may be, are more likely to be implicated in narratives of love, intrigue, and stealth; to be endowed with armies that must still be defeated in pitched battle even if the king himself is captured; and to be people from whom surrender and negotiated settlement are a viable alternative to mortal combat.

In many ways, Arthurian giants form a kind of shadow society that is both a mirror and a deformation of the dominant ruling structure. As lords their lineage may be either tainted or lacking in nobility; as knights they have prodigious prowess but may also lack a sense of chivalric honor or refinement. In varied ways, they corrupt and confuse the very concept of the aristocracy as a distinct social class defined by both superior behavior and aristocratic genealogy. The giants' distortion of aristocratic knighthood is reinforced by their status as a separate people, so that the designation *giant* subsumes within itself differences of race, class, and culture, while also implicitly confirming the imagined equivalence of these categories. The giant can thus be merged in the literary imagination with the chaotic violence of peasants and wildmen, with an overly ambitious middle class attempting to buy or force its way into aristocratic power, and with the real or imagined enemy races that lay outside the familiar world of Christian Europe.

On the Margins of Civilization: Giants in Feudal Society

It is true that the giants usually lack genuine principles of social cohesion and cooperation on a large scale; the Rion of *Les premiers faits* is, in this sense, a rare exception. Still, belying the chaotic origins posited in *Des grantz geanz*, the giants of medieval romance often live in family groups and operate a government of sorts, albeit generally one on the model of brute tyranny, aimed at the exploitation of humans rather than the cultivation of a society of giants. The networks of kinship and alliance that they form often motivate narrative developments. In the *Tristan* of Thomas d'Angleterre, the nephew of Rion—here called "l'Orguillos Grant," but clearly identified as a giant who collected royal beards until he was killed by Arthur—continues his uncle's practice; he is killed by Tristan when he demands the beard of the Spanish emperor that Tristan is then serving.[9] In *Guiron le courtois*, Uterpendragon kills the giant Brun because the latter has usurped the king's authority, seeking constantly to enlarge the domain in which he is, perforce, accepted as the absolute ruler. His aspirations are of an imperial scale, though based entirely on a concept of bodily strength rather than on any pretension to civilizing mission, cultural refinement, or aristocratic birthright: "Il baaoit a avoir la segnourie toute de la Grant Bretaingne, par la force de son cors et pour ce qu'il ne pooit trover home ki conquester li peüst" (He aimed to have lordship over all of Great Britain, through the force of his body and because he could not find any man who could conquer him).[10] And after Uterpendragon kills him, Brun's sons "descendirent... de la montaingne et tant firent que un gentill home de ceste contree les fist chevaliers" (came down... from the mountain and accomplished so much that a nobleman of that country knighted them).[11] Having earned their knighthood through legitimate means, the young giants then seek to avenge their father by continuing to terrorize the population he once ruled over; they also take up his custom of guarding a strategic bridge controlling passage between Ireland, North Wales, Sorelois, and Northumbria, killing all who attempt to cross it.[12] Barbaric though these customs are, the sons' behavior reflects their sense of family traditions, of a paternal legacy that they are honor bound to carry forward. The same text also features four giant brothers bent on blood vengeance: "Il voloient adont courre en la fin de ceste roialme sour .I. chevalier qui a celui tens lour avoit ochis . I. lour parent" (They intended to launch an attack at the edge of the kingdom on a knight who at that time had killed one of their relatives).[13] Bonds of kinship may loom larger for giants than those of feudal or marital alliance; they value the personal power of individual bodily force above the symbolic authority of kingship or noble lineage and seem completely unconcerned with any question of competing religions or other ideological belief systems. Still, giants are to some extent civilized beings shaped by a culturally determined code of conduct, one not entirely unlike the Christian chivalric culture of Uterpendragon and Arthur with which the romance audience identifies.[14]

Medieval texts lack consensus on the living conditions of giants and the degree of savagery or sophistication reflected in their dwellings, clothing, and weaponry. Some rush into battle armed with cudgels, clad only in simple tunics or rough hides, while others wear highly crafted armor and wield impressive swords; some live in caves or rustic shelters while others command elaborately fortified castles. A particularly rapacious giant in the prose *Tristan*, who "ochioit tous chiaus k'il trouvoit" (killed everyone that he found) until he is killed by Boorz of Gaunes, apparently lives a nomadic existence in the forest, much like that of a wild beast.[15] As explained by the squire of a knight that the giant killed, "je ne quit pas k'il demeurt adés en un lieu" (*PT*[M], 1:149; I don't think he lives all the time in any one place). The giant in question is eventually found sleeping near a fountain, under a screen of foliage that permits him to lie in wait for his victims; whether he has any more formal home than that is unclear. Sometimes giants live in mountain caves, like the four brothers killed by Febus in *Guiron le courtois*. Yet even the demonic giants of *Des grantz geanz* do build defensive structures to fortify their otherwise primitive homes:

> Par la terre se partirent
> E caves en terre firent;

Grant murs entour funt lever
E des fossés environer.¹⁶

[They dispersed across the land, and made caves in the earth; they raised great walls around them, and surrounding moats.]

And many giants, finally, inhabit impressive castles that are described in terms no different from those used for the castles inhabited by human knights and lords. Taulas de la Montagne, for example, lives in an impregnable castle that has stood for two hundred years; in *Perceforest* both Holland and the Golden-Haired Giant also live in castles and are the acknowledged lords of their respective islands. In Jean d'Arras's *Mélusine*, when Gieffroy goes to fight the giant Grimaut, he finds him living in a fully fortified castle featuring "une grosse tour quarree, bien guerlandee et carnelee" (a massive square tower, well crenulated).¹⁷ Grimaut's cousin Gardon de Guerrande, another giant slain by Gieffroy, lives in an even more elaborately described complex that is certainly worthy of any aristocratic lord; as Gieffroy and his men advance,

Ilz virent en une montaigne une grosse tour qui sourveoit .v. lieues de paÿs autour de lui. Et fu la tour bien fossoye et les fosséz bien curéz, et bonnes, fortes, et haultes brayes; et autour, dehors les fosséz, bons murs, et fu la tour bien guerlandee et y ot deux paires de bons, fors pons leveiz. Et y ot basse court, forte et bien muree, bons fosséz, fors portes et bon pont leveiz, et furent les murs druz de bonnes tours.¹⁸

[They saw on a mountain a massive tower that dominated five leagues of countryside around it. And the tower had a good moat, and the moats were well maintained, and good, strong, with high sides; and around that, beyond the moats, good walls, and the tower was well crenulated and there were two pairs of good, strong drawbridges. And there was a lower court, strong and well fortified, with good moats, strong doors, and a good drawbridge, and the walls were furnished with good towers.]

Despite their working relationship with a fairy—their lineage is tasked with guarding the tomb of Elinas, mortal husband of the fairy Presine—these giants are not magical beings, nor are they rustic wildmen. Rather, they can be seen as vestigial relics of a dying race, former rulers who continue to wield power in their ever-dwindling pockets of land, staunch in their resistance to the ever-expanding power of the Christian aristocracy.

A more complicated example of the giant as feudal lord, involving both extermination and assimilation, is found in *Perceforest*, with the episode of the Golden-Haired Giant and its aftermath.[19] The giant is killed by Lyonnel as a task imposed during his courtship of Blanchete, the Scottish princess that he eventually marries; and when Lyonnel arrives at the distant island ruled by the giant, he discovers a ferocious enemy indeed. The giant's favorite food, he learns, is human flesh; moreover, he regularly rapes and murders the women of the island and intends to kill his own wife and marry their daughter Galotine as soon as the young giantess is a little older (she is then just nine years old). Lyonnel learns this in a conversation with the giant's wife, whom he encounters almost immediately upon disembarking at the island; and the conversation itself is a classic illustration of Bhabha's characterization of the colonial encounter in which the ruling people's interrogation of native history and culture is in reality a search for self-justification. Lyonnel begins by asking the giantess to explain why she is so distraught: "Sy vous prie que vous me vueillez dire l'occasion de vostre doeuil et aprés vous diray quelle est l'occasion de ma venue" (1:347; I beg you to please tell me why you're grieving, and after that I'll tell you why I've come). The giantess replies by narrating the entire story of herself and her golden-haired husband: how they fell in love in their native Denmark and eloped to establish themselves on this little island, which they have now ruled for fifty years; how her husband, once a peaceful and competent lord, has recently turned savage and conceived his murderous, incestuous plan. And once the giantess has explained all this, Lyonnel's explanation of his own mission is inevitably colored: her personal history becomes a gloss on his, revealing why the Scottish queen set this particular task for her daughter's suitor. Although Lyonnel states only that he has come to take the giant's head because it has been requested by "la pucelle que j'ay enamouree" (1:349; the girl that I love) as the means by which he can earn the right "de la veoir a mon vouloir" (1:349; to see her as I wish), his statement of purpose is now implicitly a promise to the giantess to save her and her daughter by slaying their tormentor. After killing the giant, Lyonnel brings his head back to Scotland, where it is displayed it the

Temple de la Franche Garde along with wall paintings that chronicle Lyonnel's exploits in minute detail. Its features accentuated by the artful application of paint, the head becomes a monument to savage barbarity vanquished by chivalric nobility in the name of love. What might have seemed a purely personal quest on Lyonnel's part, motivated by erotic desire and dreams of glory, has taken on the aspect of a cultural mission.

At this stage there is little scope for sympathy with the giant; but the affair is not yet over. In part 3 of *Perceforest*, Blanchete's brother Nestor kills the giant Brancq, a feat he undertakes initially in defense of the lord to whom he is serving as squire.[20] It transpires, however, that Brancq is a cousin of the Golden-Haired Giant. Upon learning that Nestor is British, Brancq at once proclaims his hatred for all British knights "pour l'amour de Lyonnel du Glat, qui a mis a mort mon cousin germain, qui en son temps estoit le plus bel et le plus puissant de corps et le plus preu du monde" (for love of Lyonnel du Glat, who killed my cousin, who in his day was the most handsome and the most physically powerful and most valiant man in the world); he adds that "le desleal Lyonnel l'occist par traïson" (2:260; the disloyal Lyonnel killed him treacherously). In vanquishing Brancq, then, Nestor not only saves his lord but also forces the giant to recant his slanderous accusations against Nestor's future brother-in-law: "Si le fist desdire de ce qu'il avoit blasmé Lyonnel du Glat, et gehist qu'il avoit occis de bel fait le Geant aux Crins Dorez" (2:261; Thus he made him take back his blame of Lyonnel du Glat, and he admitted that he had killed the Golden-Haired Giant in a fair fight). The genteel prince and the brutal giant share a common concern with the public reputation of their companions and family members. And as oral histories take shape, the Golden-Haired Giant's reputation splits between valiant lord—paragon of masculine beauty and might—and monstrous enemy of civilization, whose face strikes terror into the hearts of all who behold it.

Nestor focuses only on the question of whether the giant met his death through treachery or through proper chivalric custom; the issue of whether he deserved to die at all is left unresolved. And since his daughter Galotine marries Lyonnel's squire Clamidés, the giant becomes the patriarch of a feudal house whose sons win fame as valiant knights of the realm and whose daughters intermarry with the feudal houses of Europe. When Galotine's youngest daughter, Clamidette, is betrothed to the king of Sicambria, the Sicambrian prince Thorax paints a glowing portrait of the girl's grandfather as "ung gentil homme" (a noble man) and "chevalier . . . sy grans, sy puissant, sy hardy et sy chevalereux que son pareil ne avoit ou païs" (a knight . . . so large, so powerful, so bold, and so chivalrous that he was peerless in the land); having taken charge of his island, "Il se fist seigneur de la terre . . . et en joÿ grant temps paisiblement avecq sa dame" (He established himself as lord of the realm . . . and ruled it peacefully for a long time with his lady).[21] Of the giant's death, Thorax states only that "ce geant fut mis a mort par ung vaillant chevalier" (1:166; this giant was killed by a valiant knight). Thus, while Lyonnel's actions are not impugned—of necessity, since his squire is Clamidette's father—neither are those of Golden-Hair himself. If his head remains enshrined in Scotland, sign of the victorious march of civilization against unspeakable savagery, he is celebrated elsewhere as the illustrious and heroic ancestor of aristocratic knights and ladies—indeed, as the forefather of both Gawain and Galehot.[22] Yet even these heroic descendants are not without ambiguity. Galehot is a deeply problematic figure, whom I will examine in chapter 4. As for the sons of King Lot, they are among the most prominent members of Arthur's court. And yet it could hardly be said that the brothers are beyond reproach. Gawain alone kills eighteen knights of the Round Table during the Grail Quest, including the eminently worthy King Baudemagu—acts he admits were committed not "par ma chevalerie, mes par mon pechié" (through my knightly prowess, but through my sin), and for which he is severely chastised by Arthur.[23] Gawain's violent behavior, as well as the brothers' murder of their mother in the prose *Tristan* and Gawain's implacable blood feud with Lancelot in *La mort le roi Artu*, is implicitly explained in this retrospective attribution of giant origins to their paternal lineage. If their giant forefather ruled his own island wisely and peacefully for several decades before lapsing into violence and depravity—as claimed by his wife in her conversation with Lyonnel—so too his descendant Gawain served the king honorably until overcome by an innate capacity for wrath and vengeance. Such, at least, is the gloss on Gawain's behavior provided by the author of *Perceforest*. The problematic legacy of the giant persists even in that of his most celebrated descendants.

Overall, then, giants are a shifting presence, both within society and also preying on it from the outside. As tyrants and terrorists on the margins of society, they define a limit to culture, to civilization and the rule of law—even as they participate in rituals of knighthood, maintain fortified castles, and form alliances with other (usually pagan) lords. As potentially anthropophagic predators with superhuman size and strength, they threaten the crucial boundary dividing the human from the animal kingdom—even as they, too, may sometimes ride horses and dine on the salted and roasted flesh of wild game, like any other knight.[24] And as the descendants of spouse-murdering virgins and demons, they define a limit to nature itself and to humanity as part of the natural order—even as they also take human husbands or wives, sometimes becoming the ancestors of illustrious Arthurian heroes. Their implacable hostility to the centralized monarchy is shown in stark relief in the challenge with which two giants greet Lancelot: "Chevalier, se tu hes le roi Artu et la roine et la gent de sa maison, si vien seurement, que tu n'as garde de nous; et se tu les aimes, tu es mors" (Knight, if you hate King Arthur and the queen and the people of his household, proceed with assurance that you have nothing to fear from us; and if you love them, you are dead).[25] What giants represent is not raw nature—wild beasts do not discriminate between the adherents of the king and those who defy him—but a resistance to the chivalric culture and courtly refinements of medieval romance. Their powerful identification with savagery and monstrosity, however, allows this distinction to be blurred, as the dominant feudal order is identified, not as one of many possible forms of civilization, but as Civilization itself. Most fundamentally of all, with only rare exceptions, giants resist Christianity. And in this respect they touch not only on beasts or fabulous monsters but also on that rival culture so central to the medieval Christian imagination: the vast body of peoples, both pagan and Muslim, known as Saracens.

On the Margins of Christendom:
Giants and Saracens in Crusade Literature

Giants often turn up among the Saracens of *chanson de geste* tradition, increasing the exotic horror or appeal of an alien race ancestrally linked to Ham and his notorious giant descendants.[26] Many are identified with Saracen nobility and are apparently giants only in the sense of being excessively large, strong, and fierce. Some, like Ferragu, are intractably wicked and prefer death to Christian baptism. Others, like Fierabras, the king of Alexandria defeated and then befriended by Olivier, embrace Christianity and become heroic fighters for the European crusading army. Like Guillaume d'Orange's companion Rainouart, a similar Saracen convert of giant proportions but human ancestry and sensibility, they may retain a touch of the burlesque in their ongoing adventures; but then the same could be said of Guillaume himself. Rainouart, in fact, turns out to be the son of a Saracen king in Spain, and the brother of Guillaume's Saracen wife; he is hardly a demonic savage. *Chanson de geste* also features more purely evil incarnations of the giant, however, at times threatening not only Christians but even Saracens in their relentless attacks on social order and stability. In keeping with the ideological framework of Holy War as pitting Christian good against "pagan" evil, these characters are likely to be explicitly identified with the fearsome giants of the Old Testament. They may even boast of their kinship with devils; evidently a practice of demonic miscegenation has continued in some of the ancestral lines descending from Noah's cursed son. These more demonic Saracen giants are often much larger than the giants of romance, extending to fifteen, twenty, or even thirty feet tall, while the former may only be a head or two taller than ordinary knights; and they tend to have monstrous attributes such as black skin, spiky hair, eyes glowing red like embers, or impenetrable hide. Defiant enemies of God and his people, giants may debate Christian doctrine with the knights they fight, boasting of their diabolical origins while denigrating Jesus as a man who could not even save his own life, and mocking the notion of a god who is both one and three. As the embodiment of evil, these epic giants magnify the dangers that lurk in the non-Christian world, its intimate contact with the unnatural, the inhuman, and the damned.[27]

The Old French translation of the *Pseudo-Turpin Chronicle* identifies the Saracen champion Fernagut as "uns jaianz . . . dou lignage Goulias" (a giant . . . from the lineage of Goliath) brought from Syria by the emir of Babylon.[28] Here, then, is a genuine throwback to the enemy vanquished by the young David, imparting a biblical aura both to Charlemagne's Holy War and to Roland's ultimate victory over the giant.

Ferocious on the battlefield, Fernagut challenges Roland about the Christian faith for which he and the Franks are fighting, asking a few questions about doctrine and dismissing all of Roland's explanations. His battlefield debate with Roland stands in contrast, however, with that held between Charlemagne and the Saracen king Agoulant. Agoulant first mounts an argument grounded in feudal rights of succession, angrily asking Charles "pourcoi tu nos as tolue ceste terre ou tu, ne tes peres, ne tes ayous ne ti ancesseurs n'orent onques riens" (53; why you've taken this land from us, where neither you, nor your father, nor your ancestors ever held anything). When asked by Charles to accept Christianity, he appeals to the sanctity of his own cultural traditions, insisting that his people will never give up the faith revealed to them by God's messenger Mahomet. Ultimately, having been forced through military defeat to agree to baptism, Agoulant changes his mind when he sees the moral corruption and hypocrisy of the Franks, as exposed in their shabby treatment of the poor: "Ta loi que tu diz qui vaut mieulz que la nostre, ci nous moustres tu qu'ele est fausse" (56–57; Your religion that you say is better than ours, is here shown to be false). Even Charlemagne has to agree regretfully that the Saracen's moral sense was at that point stronger than his own, and he mends his ways accordingly. Fernagut, on the other hand, is portrayed as simply baffled by Christian beliefs. He does show some understanding of monotheism, asserting that "li faisierres dou ciel et de la terre est uns Dieus" (63; the creator of heaven and earth is one god); but he manifests a complete inability to grasp theological subtleties. When Roland mentions the Incarnation, Fernagut insists that God could not have been engendered; and he resists all of Roland's efforts to explain the Trinity, stubbornly claiming, "Ne puis pas veoir . . . coment trois choses soient une chose" (64; I cannot see . . . how three things are one thing). While such literal-minded rejection of sacred mysteries can be a feature of medieval depictions of both Saracens and Jews, within this particular text it does set the giant apart from the king: whereas the latter can appeal to both political and moral principles, the former does not even attempt to understand Christian doctrine. As such he is consistent with an overall stereotype of Saracen intransigence, while also demonstrating a notable incapacity for intellectual engagement. If Agoulant allows for a critique of Christian hypocrisy and a reminder of the need to uphold principles of social justice, Fernagut reassures Christian readers of their privileged access to sacred mysteries.

Saracen giants also appear in *Huon de Bordeaux* (1260s), where they are fought and vanquished by the eponymous hero: l'Orgueilleux in Palestine and his brother Agrapart in Babylon. Both giants are explicitly (pseudo-) Muslim, repeatedly invoking "Mahon" or "Mahommet mon dei" (Mohammed my god). In the tradition of the Old Testament giants, Huon's adversaries are demonic creatures. L'Orgueilleux is eighteen feet tall, with eyes as red as hot coals, and boasts of his unnatural lineage:

> Ains m'engerra Beugibus le maufés,
> Dame Murgalle moy portait en cez léz,
> Une joiande qui conversait en mer;
> Deden infeir n'ait diable ne malfez
> Que il ne soit de mon grant parrantez.[29]
>
> ———
>
> [Beelzebub the devil engendered me, Lady Murgalle, a giantess who lives in the sea, carried me in her body; in hell there is no devil or demon who is not related to me.]

Nonetheless, even these relentlessly evil giants have an honor code of sorts. L'Orgueilleux refuses to take advantage of Huon's temporary loss of consciousness when he suffers a particularly heavy blow, waiting for the knight to be back on his feet before resuming the battle. This unexpected concern for military honor mirrors Huon's own refusal to kill the giant in his sleep. Reflecting that even though there were no witnesses and the act would therefore not damage his knightly reputation, Huon nonetheless regards such behavior as a sin in the eyes of God: "Et Dammedieu me puist hui crevanter / Si je lou fier si l'arait deffiet" (vv. 4994–95; And may God strike me dead if I attack him without first challenging him). And so he wakes the giant up for a fair fight. Even with giants, chivalric honor must be respected. Agrapart, though incandescent with rage and spoiling for a fight, similarly allows the emir time to select and arm his champion. Indeed, he is so impressed by Huon's noble lineage and his valor that he twice offers to make a truce if Huon will only renounce his god and become his vassal—offering extensive land grants and even his own sister in marriage—and ultimately surrenders when he realizes that Huon really is capable of killing him. Though he conforms to the biblical model of demonic origin, as would also be picked up in the fourteenth-century *Des grantz geanz*, Agrapart does not manifest the irrational instinct of inevitably fighting to the death that both of those texts describe. What is striking, here and elsewhere, is the extent to which epic giants in particular can display a curious mix of chivalric honor, spiritual intransigence, and otherworldly demonization. Just human enough to allow for chivalric confrontation, they are also monstrous enough to imbue this confrontation with the grandeur of a cosmic clash between Good and Evil: the ultimate Holy War.

Neither of Huon's battles is motivated by religious dogma: he is forced to fight l'Orgueilleux after incautiously entering the giant's castle, and he later agrees to fight Agrapart when the latter storms into court in Babylon—where Huon is being held prisoner—demanding restitution for the death of his brother. Nor is Huon's visit to the Holy Land a Crusade, at least not in the conventional sense of that term: his voyage is in fulfillment of a trial imposed by Charlemagne after Huon killed Charlemagne's son, and it includes a series of objectives aimed primarily at humiliating, rather than conquering, the emir. The ludicrous tasks set by Charlemagne as conditions for Huon's reintegration into the Carolingian feudal alliance—such as kissing the princess, taking the emir's beard, and bringing back four of his teeth—make no allusion to either conquest or religious conversion. Nonetheless, his battles with giants are inscribed in a context of theological debate as Huon and the giants invoke their respective gods and assail that of their adversary. L'Orgueilleux, for example, tauntingly urges Huon to abandon his God:

> Fai une chose, se il vous vient en grey,
> Que tu garpisse Jhesu le rassottez;
> Ja enver moy ne toi porait tancer:
> Comment t'aidroit, quant soy laissait pener
> Ens en la croix et au Jüyf tueir?
> (vv. 5200–5204)

> [Do this, if you will, abandon that foolish Jesus; he can never help you against me: how could he help you, when he let himself be hung on the cross and killed by the Jews?]

Huon, for his part, offers a thirty-six-line prayer to God after being briefly knocked unconscious by the giant, in which he rapidly summarizes Creation and Original Sin, the Annunciation and the life of Christ, Christ's passion, the Harrowing of Hell, and the evangelizing mission of the apostles, before finally imploring God's assistance in overcoming his terrible enemy (vv. 5246–84). Agrapart's oaths, rather like Huon's prayer, elaborate his pseudo-Muslim faith; at one point, for example, he swears "Per Mahomet, qui tant ait potesteit, / Qui fist le ciel et lumiere et clerteit, / Et homme et femme ot de limon formér" (vv. 6763–65; By Mohammed, who has such power that he created heaven and light and brightness, and formed man and woman from clay). And Huon defeats Agrapart in the name of "Jhesu Crist que vous avez blafmér" (v. 6794; Jesus Christ whom you have maligned). In this latter combat, we see the familiar Crusade motif of competition between rival religions on the battlefield, as each warrior hopes that his god will grant him victory.

The confrontation of knight and giant, then, is conflated with that of Christian and Saracen; and while it is not part of a larger crusading effort, it does result not only in the defeat of two diabolical beings but also in the grateful emir's liberation of all Christian prisoners currently held in his lands. Indeed, by the time he returns to France, Huon has forcibly converted a large number of the inhabitants of Babylon and massacred the rest, including the emir himself. What began as a bizarre trial by ordeal to see whether Huon would prove worthy of Charlemagne's pardon has turned into a kind of unintended Crusade after all, in which giants and Saracens alike are dispatched by the ever-victorious French hero and his magical ally Auberon. Luke Sunderland has characterized *Huon de Bordeaux* as a utopian fantasy in which a Western Christian baron is proved to be the agent capable of resolving conflicts not only within the West but also between West and East.[30] Settling disputes with giants and liberating their prisoners is an integral part of this overall picture and shows the crucial place occupied by giants in the medieval French cultural imagination.

Giants and Christian Ideology in Romance

Giants in *chansons de geste* occupy the fringe of Saracen society where the non-Christian human blends into the demonic inhuman, while still retaining the possibility of responding to the Christian message of the crusaders with either conversion or doctrinal argument. Giants in romance are also on a borderline, but one defined more generally by the distinction between the refinements of courtly chivalric culture and the uncivilized hinterlands that lie outside it. Though they are still, of course, pagan and inherently evil, the focus is less on an eschatological clash between the saved and the damned or on an evangelical mission to convert the heathen, and more on the secular values of a feudally organized chivalric culture seeking dominion over its own lands and those on its immediate borders. The tale of Mélusine, which includes elements reminiscent of romance and *chanson de geste*, draws on both traditions in its use of giants. On the one hand, Gieffroy's battle with the giant Grimaut pits him against a pseudo-Muslim enemy and suggests a parallel between his solitary quest and the pan-Mediterranean warfare collectively pursued by the Lusignan brothers, in which Gieffroy also participates fully. In Jean d'Arras's prose *Mélusine*, Grimaut swears by "Mahon" (Mohammed).[31] And in Coudrette's version of the story, when Grimaut is losing his battle with Gieffroy, he reacts much like Saracen warriors who turn against the gods that have failed to protect them from Christian armies:

> Ses dieux maudit, ses dieux renie,
> Se la ne lui donnent aÿe;
> Margot, Appolin, Tervagant
> Et Juppra va moult regretant.[32]

> [He cursed and renounced his gods for not giving him assistance;
> he lamented Margot, Appolin, Tervagant, and Jupiter.]

One manuscript gives the reading "Mahom" in line 4695—a term that makes more sense than the mysterious "Margot." The presence of "Mohammed" in the giant's belief system underscores his identification not only with pagans in general but with Saracens in particular, as he invokes the quartet of Saracen gods identified in both the *Estoire del Saint Graal* and *Lancelot*.[33] The legend of Mélusine develops the familiar tropes of Crusade epic with the victories won by the Lusignan brothers against various Saracen adversaries, including no less an adversary than the sultan of Damascus. Gieffroy, of all the brothers the one most given to individual adventuring, comes closer to the knights errant of medieval romance; but even here he faces off against an adversary who can be considered Saracen in at least some sense of that term.

At the same time that it complements the Lusignan wars in the Near East, Gieffroy's battles with Grimaut and his cousin Gardon also allow for the resolution of narrative threads that come straight out of romance: the struggle between giants and feudal lords for control of territory, and the love affair of Mélusine's parents, Elinas and Presine, abruptly terminated when Elinas violates the conditions laid down by his fairy bride. Gieffroy sets out to fight Gardon because the giant has taken over lands in Guérande that rightfully belong to Gieffroy's father, Reymondin of Lusignan, and has levied a tax on the inhabitants, a shameful affront to the Lusignan rulers. Gardon's move appears to be part of an ongoing feud between the giant's family and that of Reymondin, who tells Gieffroy that "Gardon sera bien paiéz de sa desserte. Ja lui occist Hervieu, mon pere, son ayol en Pointieuvre" (Gardon will get his just deserts. My father Hervé killed his grandfather in Penthièvre).[34] It is on the strength of Gieffroy's established reputation as a giant killer that the people of Northumbria then request his assistance in freeing them from Grimaut, who has depopulated the countryside around his castle with his violent marauding; and it is this venture that leads Gieffroy to his discovery of the story of his maternal grandparents. The insertion of a giant into the story of Elinas and Presine, in fact, allows for an interesting perspective on the difference between a simple fairy tale and a tale of giants. Elinas was destroyed by his marriage to a fairy: he sank into hopeless despair when she abandoned him, and he was subsequently imprisoned inside a mountain by his half-blood fairy daughters. But Presine constructed an opulent and beautiful tomb for her husband in this subterranean prison, provided a plaque telling the whole story, and set a giant to guard it. In so doing she moved Elinas from the narrative of "man driven mad and lost to the world through love for a fairy" to one of "king imprisoned by a giant who is ravaging the countryside"; and this latter scenario is one that the paradigms of chivalric romance will work to resolve. If not for the giant, Gieffroy would have had no reason to explore the mountain crevices in the first place; it is solely because he embarked on a mission against predatory giants that he discovered his grandfather's tomb and the story of his own maternal ancestry. Fairies are immortal and will appear and disappear according to their own whims or as the result of laws that escape the understanding of mortals. But giants are always killed in the end by a chivalric hero. With the establishment of the giant guard on his tomb, Elinas is assured of his eventual reconnection with history. Just as Christian princesses are saved from unwanted marriages with renegade barons and rampaging Saracens, so the king is rescued from the oblivion imposed by the giant who watches over his incarceration. Once Gieffroy has completed his mission, the king is revealed in his public role as royal patriarch to the house of Lusignan, a noble lineage founded by and named for his eldest daughter.

Overall, the Lusignan brothers defeat a wide range of Christian and "pagan" enemies. Rapacious feudal lords, Saracens, and giants—along with the malevolent son Orible, in whom the dangerous potency of fairyhood is most lethally concentrated—all stand in opposition to feudal law, good governance, social order, and Christian faith. The giant can be seen as a kind of hinge, linking the different ideological threads of the story. He is at once a native warrior who violates the liberties and feudal rights of the surrounding population and challenges the new Lusignan rulers in their claim to the land he occupies; an obstruction to historical knowledge, whose presence blocks any understanding of the maternal lineage of the Lusignan dynasty and its links with the royal house of Scotland; and an enemy of the Christian faith. In its juxtaposition of these different kinds of threats, the Mélusine story traces the boundaries and the defining features of Christian feudal order. And, as we have seen before, the concentration of religious heresy and political tyranny in the figure of the giant supports an unspoken identification of feudal governance, aristocratic lineage, and Christian orthodoxy as inseparable parts of civilization itself.

The identification of battles with giants as a kind of Holy War is, in any case, fully compatible with the larger themes and ideology of courtly romance in general.[35] The great prose romance cycles, after all, chronicle the establishment of Christianity in Britain with the arrival of the Grail entourage and the work of subsequent missionaries; and they celebrate the extension and consolidation of royal power by Uterpendragon and Arthur, a power grounded in Christian chivalric institutions. In *Guiron le courtois*, Uterpendragon builds an abbey commemorating his victory over Brun, "pour la grant honour que Dieu li avoit feit a celui point de ce qu'il avoit le jaiant mis a mort et par son cors solement" (for the great honor that God granted him at that time, in that he had killed the giant purely through his own bodily strength).[36] In the prose *Tristan*, Bohort of Gaunes similarly builds an abbey to mark the spot of his victory over a marauding giant who killed one of his relatives: a feat accomplished only by the grace of God and considered "uns grans miracles" (*PT*[M], 1:150; a great miracle) by all who hear of it. What was once a site of pagan terrorism now becomes a center of Christian piety and a refuge where knights errant can seek shelter, receive medical treatment for injuries sustained in battle, or even withdraw from the world for a life of spiritual penance and solace. All of these possibilities are concisely represented when Palamedes and Kahedin arrive at the Abbey of Gaunes; whereas Palamedes merely spends the night and continues on his way, the badly wounded Kahedin stays behind to be healed by "un cevalier ki en la maison estoit rendus pour le sauvement de s'ame, ki de plaies et de bleceüres estoit merveilleusement sages" (1:151; a knight who had taken up residence in the establishment in order to save his soul, who was marvelously knowledgeable about injuries and wounds). Neither of the above altercations with giants was motivated by religious difference. But with the consecration of the ground where the battles took place, a reprisal against a potential usurper and an act of blood vengeance nonetheless both take on the aspect of Holy War.

Medieval manuscript illuminators, in their responses to the texts they illustrated, reveal a range of interpretations of the giant and of underlying ideologies of race, class, and culture that these figures support. And a very interesting aspect of this visualization of giants is the frequency with which the iconography of Near Eastern Saracens is overlaid onto British giants. A mid-fifteenth-century illustration of the two giants slain by Lancelot in an altercation over allegiance to Arthur—as cited above—shows both giants in full suits of armor, whose ornate appearance may in itself be intended to evoke Asiatic opulence; one wears a turban and sports a long, double-pointed beard.[37] In commenting on this passage, I stated that the giants in question, with their political agenda, clearly represent not animalistic nature but a rival, underground

Figure 1. Guiron fights two giants. Paris, Bibliothèque de l'Arsenal, MS 3477, fol. 327v.

culture, engaged in a kind of terrorism or guerrilla warfare against the Arthurian kingdom. And the artist, in portraying one of them as a Saracen warrior, has given visual support to this reading. A combat scene in an early fifteenth-century copy of *Guiron le courtois,* to cite a further example, depicts giants with a mixture of typical giant and Saracen attributes (fig. 1).

The giants do wear armor, of a type very similar to that of Guiron, here traveling under the pseudonym of Le Chevalier a l'escu d'or (the Knight with the Golden Shield); but two of them lack helmets, and one wears the distinctive knotted headband of the Saracen warrior. This garment is a stock feature of medieval Orientalist fantasies; it is common in illustrations of Saracen warriors in Crusade texts, and in images depicting the exotic East in such texts as Mandeville's *Livre des merveilles,* Marco Polo's *Devisement du monde,* and the various versions of the Alexander legend.[38] The decapitated giant lying on the ground was clearly armed with a scimitar—still resting near his head—in another touch of Near Eastern exoticism, while the other wields a huge club. The simultaneous presence of scimitar and club, like the typical giant habit of wearing armor without a helmet, graphically portrays both the giants' pretentions to aristocratic knighthood and the arrogance and rustic savagery that belie their posturing. The implication is not that either giant emigrated from the Near or Far East. But like the term *Saracen* itself, which can apply not only to Moors and Arabs but also to European pagans such as Vikings or unconverted Britons, the exotic garment marks the giant as culturally alien. He is neither a low-class pretender nor a rogue element within the knighthood of Arthurian Britain, but the vestige of a now supplanted people—pre-Arthurian, pre-Christian, pre-Trojan—whose very existence is an obstacle to cultural progress. In beheading the giant, Guiron not only saves the life of the individuals that he was threatening but also rids Britain of a violent predator in whom religious, social, and political menace are fully conflated.

Giants and the Spirit of Chivalry

Saracen knighthood offers the troubling specter of chivalric glory and nobility of spirit in the absence of Christian ideology, allowing the role of Christianity as an essential foundation to knighthood to be questioned even if it is always ultimately confirmed. Outside an explicitly Christian framework, confrontations with giants pose a slightly different conundrum: Can chivalric prowess and feudal lordship exist without the nobility of spirit that comes with aristocratic breeding? Can social privilege be claimed, and political power wielded, on the basis of sheer bodily might?[39] As we saw in chapter 1, medieval political theory posited rational discipline, not bodily strength, as the justification both for human domination over animals and for the political dominion of rulers over a population at large. Giants often use their superior strength not only to resist the authority of kings or other feudal powers but also to secure knighthood, land, and titles for themselves; and this in itself can be the basis for altercations between giants and "genuine" knights. Guiron le courtois, for example, pursues a giant who has just abducted two knights; when the giant sees him he reacts with the bravado of one whose authority is unassailable: "Vous ne faites pas grant sens qui par ma contree chevauchier sans mon congié, car bien sachiés que tout ceste contree est moie" (You don't behave with much sense when you ride through my territory without my permission, for rest assured that this entire territory is mine).[40] Guiron, however, sees no legitimate authority in the giant; indeed, he wrests the giant's club away from him so as to attack him with that, "car li estoit bien avis que l'espee seroit avillie s'il en occioit .i. vilain" (for it seemed to him that his sword would be debased if he used it to kill a *vilain*).[41] In a similar vein, Lancelot encounters two giant brothers who were given a castle and feudal lordship by Duke Conoins, in gratitude for saving the latter from prison. The brothers are typical of giants in extorting a toll from anyone who enters their castle precinct. In Lancelot's case, the gatekeeper attempts to seize his horse, which Lancelot angrily denounces as a crime against the aristocratic class: "Lanceloz dist qu'il . . . ne doit paiage ne coustume, car il est frans, et tuit li chevalier du monde" (*PLanc*, 5:42; Lancelot said that . . . he did not owe any toll or customary payment, for he is free, as are all the knights in the world). They also manifest the usual aggression and arrogance of giants. When the brothers challenge Lancelot for killing their gatekeeper, they are fitted out not as knights in armor, but "an guise de champion qui doivent escremir, car il orent les testes nues et descovertes et portoient bons escuz forz et avoient vestuz bons hauberz doubliers; si tint chascuns une espee bonne" (5:43; like a champion swordfighter, for they had their heads bare and uncovered, and carried good strong shields, and they were wearing good hauberks of doubled chain mail; and each held a good sword). One of the castle knights later explains that "par la force qu'il sentoient en eux ne se voloient il autrement armer que vous veistes" (5:45; because of the strength they felt themselves to possess, they never wanted to arm themselves other than as you saw them). Perhaps because of their nonchivalric garb—or perhaps simply because they are giants—Lancelot sees at once that the brothers "n'estoient mie chevalier; si lor dist que de .II. vilains n'a il garde" (5:43–44; were not knights; and he told them that he wasn't afraid of a couple of churls). And in fact, after Lancelot kills the first giant, the other one "torne an fuie au plus tost qu'il puet" (5:44; turns and flees as quickly as he can) in a state of very unchivalric terror, prompting Lancelot to taunt him as "coarz failliz" (5:44; cowardly loser). Needless to say, this second giant is quickly finished off by our hero with a sword blow to his unprotected head.

The very idea of low-born strongmen occupying a castle and exacting a toll from knights is, in itself, violence against proper social customs and hierarchies, and it calls for the swift and unceremonious elimination of the perpetrators. But the story told here goes beyond merely reinforcing traditional class structures. The designation *jaianz* marks these two feudal lords, like the self-styled smallholder encountered by Guiron, as something other than ordinary Britons, subjects of Arthur or other British kings. They are a different people, rooted in an impossibly distant past predating the arrival of the Britons' Trojan ancestors, survivors of "ethnic cleansing" against giants carried out by British kings and knights from Brutus and Corineus down through Uterpendragon and Arthur—not to mention the occasional divine massacre. But the antiquity of their ancestry does not make it illustrious, any more than possession of a castle makes the giant brothers into bona fide knights. Vilifying nouveaux riches peasants as giants—or giants as nouveaux riches peasants—makes an association between those of a lower class and those of a different race, implying that this racial identity forecloses any possibility that they might legitimately rise above their original condition because they intrinsically lack the qualities of courage, prowess, and nobility of spirit essential to the chivalric identity. Like Bhabha's "mimic man"—"the effect of a flawed colonial mimesis, in which to be Anglicized is *emphatically* not to be English"—a giant who enters into knighthood, feudal lordship, or aristocratic marriage is still a giant, and his status remains ambiguous at best.[42] To be knighted and enfeoffed for services rendered to a duke might seem an acceptable upward trajectory for a low-born but capable and ambitious young warrior. But *Lancelot* shows that this path is not open to giants; for them, chivalric or aristocratic identity is indeed little more than pretentious mimicry.[43]

The insolent but ultimately cowardly giant brothers make an interesting contrast to the giant Maudit, killed by Bohort in the preceding section of *Lancelot*.[44] Officially, at least, Maudit is a genuine knight and lord. His nongiant stepfather, who held the lands in vassalage to Arthur and who married Maudit's giantess mother, took him through the ceremony of knighthood, and he now rules his father's lands, having taken homage from the inhabitants. But whereas the two brothers rely entirely on their ability to maintain power through intimidation and sheer bodily force, crumbling as soon as they face serious opposition, Maudit is the very embodiment of ferocity: he ascended to power in the first place by killing both his stepfather and his mother, and his rule is a reign of terror. Far from shrinking from battle, he puts up a fight that very nearly defeats even a knight as formidable as Bohort. Where the brothers lack any real skill in combat or capacity for sustained military prowess, Maudit has these qualities in excess, lacking any sense of restraint or mercy. All three giants are caricatures of genuine knighthood and aristocratic power, in which, as the Lady of the Lake tells the young Lancelot, both cruelty and compassion must play their part. A knight, she explains, must have two hearts, "l'un dur et serei autresi com aimant et l'autre mol et ploiant autresi comme cyre caude" (*PLanc*, 7:253; one hard and steadfast like a lodestone and the other soft and pliant like hot wax); and he must always ensure that he is absolutely hardhearted and cruel towards evildoers, while showing mercy to the weak and the good, and placing himself at their service. She further stipulates that a knight should never fear death, but only shame. And she approves Lancelot's own insight that a knight must combine "les vertus del cuer et cheles del cors" (7:248; the virtues of the heart and those of the body). Clearly giants, however well endowed in body, fall woefully short of any understanding of the virtues of the heart, and in this they show their distance from true nobility. As Lancelot himself knows well, "Riens ne fait le preudome se li cuers non" (7:248; Only the heart makes a man noble).

Any renegade knight has fallen short of this ideal, of course, but giants, with their spectacular capacity for might and bravado, cast the difference between brute force and chivalric prowess in high relief. Interestingly, Maudit too is depicted with a hint of Saracen exoticism in manuscript Bnf fr. 119, originally made for Jean de Berry and then somewhat reworked for Jacques d'Armagnac when he inherited it (fig. 2).[45]

Maudit's armor and garments are notably more ornate than those of Bohort or Lancelot, who appears in the background at the far left: his tunic and sleeves are fringed and embroidered, with a twisted belt, and his helmet is of a completely different design; his shield, with its threatening face that echoes his own grimacing features, adds a further sinister note. Once again, the category of "giant" designates an identity

Figure 2. Bohort fights Maudit. Paris, Bibliothèque Nationale de France, fr. 119, fol. 424v.

drawing on stereotypes of both race and class, in which true Christian knighthood is not merely absent but somehow impossible—thereby implicitly identifying this all-important combination of physical, moral, and spiritual virtues with both the culture and the lineage of European aristocracy.

Race, Class, and Gender: The Saracen or Giantess Bride

The beautiful giantess of courtly romance who falls in love with a knight or assists in his assault on the giant stronghold parallels the Saracen princess of *chanson de geste* who falls in love with a Christian knight and conspires to betray her kingdom into his hands.[46] Sharon Kinoshita has noted that the Saracen queen Orable, who falls in love with Guillaume Fierebrace and betrays the city of Orange into his hands in the *Prise d'Orange*, "incarnates the very possibility of assimilation through conversion," resulting in "an eroticized representation of Frankish aggression against the Saracens of Spain that, for all its comic inversions, vindicates the military and amatory prowess of a masculinized French feudal society."[47] The Saracen prince or princess who converts out of love for a Christian knight or lady, in other words, serves as a euphemistic trope for the forced Christianization of an enemy people. In texts like *Floire et Blancheflleur* or *La fille du comte de Ponthieu*, the mixed-blood offspring of Franco-Saracen marriages are portrayed as staunch Christians and valiant crusaders, or at the very least as admirable figures. The former text attributes Saracen ancestry to none other than Charlemagne; the latter identifies the Count of Ponthieu as having Saracen ancestry, while attributing French ancestry to the great Saladin. Similarly, the giants and giantesses who desire knights or ladies as companions or lovers support the fantasy of the European aristocracy, and the values and ideologies it embodies, as natural objects of desire, recognized as such even by benighted or enemy races.[48]

The mixed-blood lineage that results from marriage between human and giant, however, is more ambiguous. In some cases, as we will see, the lure of a giantess bride risks blinding a knight to the very real dangers of associating himself with a people who are implacably violent at best, demonic at worst. Even in cases where the marriage is successful, the results are not always wholly positive. We have seen that in *Perceforest* the giantess Galotine falls in love with and marries the knight Clamidés; and her successful assimilation into court culture not only earns her a reputation for beauty and courtly manners but even works toward the rehabilitation of her father's posthumous reputation. Nonetheless, the strong-mindedness of her daughter Clamidette, who ultimately avoids marriage with the king of Sicambria by eloping with her lover Nero, could be seen as a sign of her problematic giant origins. And the distant descendants of this particular "mixed marriage"—Galehot on the one hand, the sons of King Lot on the other—are illustrious knights whose overall reputation is nonetheless somewhat ambivalent. The Saracen prince or princess and the combative or amorous giant all, in different ways, act as vehicles for comic or dramatic irony, for reflections on both the enticements and the dangers of becoming intimate with exotic others, and for frequently playful reflections on the balance (or imbalance) of power in love.

The Saracen world is typically a space of wish fulfillment offering a solution to a crisis arising at court; in the well-known examples of *Le charroi de Nîmes* and *La prise d'Orange*, for example, Guillaume handles the king's failure to reward him by embarking on war against the Saracens, through which he acquires land, wealth, and a bride. While it could be argued that war against the Saracens is an end in itself that needs no further justification, Guillaume's vow as he takes arms against Orange defines the expedition as a kind of exotic tourism, ultimately motivated by erotic desire: "S'avrai veü com Orenge est assise; / Et si verrai icele tor marbrine / Et dame Orable, la courtoise roïne. / La seue amor me destreint et justise" (Indeed I will see how Orange is laid out; and I will see that marble tower, and Lady Orable, the courteous queen. Her love constrains and overwhelms me).[49] That Orable falls in love with Guillaume and chooses to give herself and Orange to him affirms his heroic masculinity; that she converts to Christianity for his sake confers a genuinely holy dimension on Guillaume's adventuring. Now the well-endowed lord of wealthy lands and the head of a major feudal house, he can reattach himself to Louis as a vassal of considerably higher standing than before. Despite the ironic overtones, the different parts of the narrative come together and allow Guillaume to consolidate his place in the Frankish empire and in Christendom itself. As depicted here, Saracen culture is just alien enough to be attractive, with its opulent palaces and lush gardens, its exotic fruits and flowers, its thriving cities that serve as hubs for the lucrative pan-Mediterranean trade in luxury goods. But it is also reassuringly similar to France in its feudal hierarchies and its culture of aristocratic warfare. The only real difference—religious faith—can be effaced in a single moment at the baptismal font, and love—fulfilled in marriage—is the perfect context for a Saracen lady looking to make this move.

A giant's stronghold may lack the sensuality, aesthetic splendor, and opulent luxury of a Saracen court, but it can still be a space of wish fulfillment of a somewhat different sort. And while the alterity of giants cannot be focused in the single, if crucial, area of religion, their savagery does conform to conventional stereotypes. Their behavior may shock, horrify, or titillate, but it is ultimately comprehensible as a hypermasculine transgression of moral and civil codes; their portrayal, like that of Saracens, recalls Homi Bhabha's comment that "colonial discourse produces the colonized as a social reality which is at once an 'other' and yet entirely knowable and visible."[50] Giants, much like Saracens, offer racially caricatured versions of the outlaws, knights, and lords that populate courtly romance. And like the Saracen princess, the giantess can emerge as a racially inflected love object for Christian or proto-Christian knights. Neither conforms perfectly to the model of femininity incarnated by the European Christian aristocratic lady. Both, indeed, manifest a femininity infiltrated by the masculine aura of the rival culture to which they belong: the sheer bodily force and unregulated drives of the giant, and the status of Islam as a rival religion permanently at war with Christendom. This "distortion" of gender is sometimes unsettling for the chivalric protagonist, as he copes with the realization that "their" women are not quite like "ours"; and it certainly allows for comic, ironic, or sinister overtones as the narrative unfolds. Nonetheless, both giantess and Saracen princess remain accessible in their humanity and lend themselves readily to narratives that seek to interrogate the ways that racial and cultural differences inflect desire and shape intimacy, as well as the efficacy of love and marriage as means of overcoming such differences.

Both the savagery of the giant and the sympathetic qualities of the giantess are illustrated in the episode of the Golden-Haired Giant in

Perceforest.⁵¹ Although Lyonnel sets out to kill the giant only because he has been told that he can see his beloved Blanchete as a reward for bringing back the giant's head, it turns out, as we have seen, that this act is justified by the giant's constant perpetration of sexual violence. And this extends not only to the maidens living on his island but also to his own family. When Lyonnel reaches the Isle du Geant, he finds the giantess wife lamenting her fate, grieving at the violence being meted out to the local women, and fearing for her daughter's welfare. In accepting Lyonnel's offer of assistance, she invokes the Sovereign God, object of a proto-Christian, monotheistic cult imagined by the *Perceforest* author as an alternative to paganism in pre-Christian Britain. As she tells Lyonnel, "J'ay espoir en la vengence du Dieu Souverain" (1:349; I have hope in the vengeance of the Sovereign God); and again, "Dieu vous doint pouoir d'achever ce que vous avez emprins" (1:350; God grant you the power to achieve what you have undertaken). As for Galotine, she is described as a child so innocent that she does not shy from exposing her naked body to the male visitors, but also one whose size and great beauty are those of a full-grown "normal" woman. As a result, she arouses the desire of Lyonnel's squire Clamidés, who rapes or seduces her. The giantess is furious at his molestation of her daughter—she clearly has a stronger sense of morality than the noble squire himself—and nearly kills Clamidés on the spot, refraining only because she recognizes that killing the giant is a higher priority. Once Lyonnel has slain her golden-haired husband, she is overwhelmed by gratitude and relief and accepts the newly knighted Clamidés's marriage to Galotine as sufficient compensation. As for Galotine, she has fallen head over heels in love with Clamidés, proclaiming: "Par ma foy, je ne vueil avoir mary fors le beau jone varlet qu'il a amené" (1:361; By my faith, I want no other husband but the handsome young man that (Lyonnel) brought here).

This process of intermarriage does provide a context within which Galotine's giantism can be modified. Clamidés, we are told, takes his child bride firmly in hand: "Mais le gentil chevalier nourry et enseigna en telle maniere sa jenne mariee en l'eaige de josnesse que quant elle vint aux ans de discrecion, elle fist tant qu'elle fut tenue la meilleure, la plus doulce et debonnaire, la plus charitable et de meilleure vie . . . que l'on sceust" (*Perce/II*, 1:363; But the noble knight raised and instructed his young wife during her youth in such a way that when she reached the age of discretion, she behaved in such a way that she was considered to be the best, the sweetest and most well-mannered, the most charitable lady, and the best behaved, that anyone knew). Galotine, indeed, is "tant belle, tant saige et tant bien faitte de son corps que on ne s'en pouoit sauler de le regarder" (so beautiful, so well-behaved, and so well formed in body that one could not tire of looking at her).[52] She is a treasured companion to other young princesses and queens; when she and Clamidés later pay a visit to Lyonnel and Blanchete, "Sy devés sçavoir que la court fut moult esjouye de sa venue" (*Perce/IV*, 1:179; You should know that the court was overjoyed at her arrival). In this respect the giantess conforms to a frequently recurring perception of foreign or exotic women as more readily assimilable than their male counterparts—a form of stereotyping reflected in the "Saracen princess" motif in Crusade literature, and one that sometimes led to the active encouragement of marriages between European male settlers and Asian women during the colonial expansion of the early modern period. As Carmen Nocentelli notes, such policies rested on "the notion of the female body as racially pliable material" and the expectation that native women would "'absorb' the status of their husbands."[53] Nocentelli associates these practices with the early modern construction of "domestic heterosexuality" and the notion of conjugal love as "a uniquely European disciplinary technique" that can serve as "an instrument in the formation of colonized subjectivities."[54] If the colonial expansionism of the early modern period provides a context in which these concepts take on new forms and new cultural significance, it is nonetheless clear that medieval tales of both Saracens and giants already had a place for the "civilizing" role of cross-cultural or interracial love and marriage.

Still, the effacement of racial and cultural difference is never straightforward; Nocentelli's analysis of sixteenth-century accounts of the women in colonial India notes that "desire and appreciation are never too far away from revulsion and derision."[55] And while "revulsion and derision" would be somewhat overstating the case with regard to the exotic brides of medieval epic and romance, the fact remains that even the most alluring giantess can be difficult to assimilate completely. From the start, Galotine is a disorienting figure in her combination of youthful innocence and seemingly adult body:

> Adont regarde Lyonnel la pucelle, qui estoit venue a la grandeur de femme commune et si estoit tresbelle, mais moult estoit innocente et enfant de sens. . . . Clamidés se jouoit a Galentine la pucelle et tant y fut en pou d'heure privé, comme celle qui estoit ignorant et sans discrecion, combien qu'elle eust grandeur de commune femme, que Clamidés fut a ce meu qu'il jeut avecques elle. (*Perce/II*, 1:350)
>
> ---
>
> [Then Lyonnel looked at the girl, who had reached the size of an ordinary woman and was very beautiful, but she was extremely innocent and childish in her understanding. . . . Clamidés amused himself with the girl Galotine and was soon so intimate with her—she who was naive and lacking discretion, even though she was the size of an ordinary woman—that Clamidés was aroused to the point of lying with her.]

And if in adulthood Galotine has been carefully raised and trained in courtly etiquette by her husband, she also retains an air both comical and slightly disturbing because of her size—fully two feet taller than her husband—and strength.[56] Even the narrator's praise of the young giantess is not unqualified: she was, we are told, "la plus belle et la plus plaisant et la plus feminine *selon sa grandeur* que l'on sceust" (*Perce/II*, 1:363, emphasis mine; the most beautiful and the most pleasing and the most feminine lady, *for someone her size*, that anyone knew). Clamidés's sexual exploitation of the naive nine-year-old girl, though viewed as serious enough to require marriage as compensation, is nonetheless treated with a lightheartedness that associates the young giantess more with the ravished shepherdesses of *pastourelle* tradition than with the idealized maidens of courtly romance.[57] When Galotine expresses her desire to marry Clamidés, for example, Lyonnel "commença a rire comme celluy qui bien sçavoit dont celle amour venoit" (*Perce/II*, 1:361; began to laugh, like one who knew very well where that love came from). As befits a giant—largely defined by bodily appearance and appetite—it is Clamidés's sexual prowess that inspires her love and not his chivalric prowess, which, as squire, he has not yet even had occasion to demonstrate. Some time after the marriage, Clamidés assures Perceforest that there is no other woman "plus douce ne plus debonnaire" (sweeter or more genteel) but also admits that she has grown so large as to make him seem a mere child by comparison: "Elle est devenue telle qu'elle me porte sus son bras comme l'en porte ung petit enffant" (*Perce/III*, 3:19; She has reached the point where she carries me on her arm as one carries a little child). And during Galotine's visit to Lyonnel and Blanchete, when the Welsh queen Genyevre is unable to find her husband in the crowded castle hall, the young giantess "fendy la presse comme forte qu'ele estoit oultre mesure, puis print le chevalier parmy les coustez, combien qu'il fust aincoires armé, et en l'eslevant en hault comme se ce fust un anffant de cinq ans commença a dire: 'Madame, vous pouez bien voir le chevalier vostre mary'" (*Perce/IV*, 1:180; cut through the throng, being strong beyond measure, then took hold of the knight, despite the fact that he was still in armor, and lifting him up as though he was a five-year-old child, she began to say: "Madame, you can see the knight your husband"). If Blanchete is "overjoyed" at Galotine's visit, one cannot help wondering if it is not only because the young giantess is beautiful and charming but perhaps also because of the slightly exotic comedy that she provides.

Not only, then, is the giantess just a little more readily available for sexual fantasy and exploitation—and more forthright in voicing her desires—but also her feminine "sweetness" is uneasily coupled with traits that border on masculinity. As her husband notes with regard to her size and strength, "S'elle avoit couraige d'homme, il n'est chevalier au monde qui la ousast envahir" (*Perce/III*, 3:19; If she had the spirit of a man, there is no knight in the world who would dare invade her territory). In this respect too she is comparable to a Saracen convert like Orable/Guiborc of the *Guillaume d'Orange* cycle: beautiful, tender, and devoted to her husband, this woman nonetheless willingly betrays her kingdom, countenancing the slaughter of kin and countrymen. In *Fierabras*, the Saracen princess Floripas, sister of the eponymous hero, also falls in love with a crusading knight and converts to Christianity; and if anything she encompasses even greater extremes of ideal femininity and pagan ferocity. When her father refuses baptism, she resolutely urges Charlemagne to behead him, while asking in the same breath to be married to the Christian knight she has fallen in love with; as Suzanne Conklin Akbari notes, Floripas "is beautiful and delicate, but also aggressive and violent . . . she even kills with her own hands."[58] Like Galotine, eagerly proclaiming her desire to marry the squire whose knight has just killed her once-beloved father, Floripas is a woman unafraid to voice desires both vengeful and amorous. I stated above that the amorous giantess or Saracen princess manifests an exotic difference just pronounced enough to make her interesting, but not enough to place her outside consideration as a possible wife. This statement can also be turned around: though the giantess or Saracen princess embodies courtly femininity in most respects—physical beauty, courtly manners, devoted obedience to her husband—she nonetheless remains in some sense an outsider. Perhaps more accurately, she is a convert: assimilated to Western aristocratic court culture but not entirely "of" it.

The giant incarnates, in a single being, a threat to the political order of a centralized monarchy supported by feudal ties with powerful but loyal barons; to the cultural values of aristocratic chivalry and courtly refinement, expressed in a construction of masculinity that values both aggressive virility and self-regulating discipline; and to the spiritual values of the Christian faith, with its emphasis on self-scrutiny, penance, and humility before God. In his vacillation between the exotic and the intimately familiar, the giant incarnates that sense of alterity described by Michael Uebel as a suspension between defamiliarization and exemplarity.[59] The giant is something of a marvel, inspiring wonder and a grudging respect even in the knight who kills him, for whom the encounter goes above and beyond any prior experience; and a cautionary mirror, caricaturing the failings and excesses into which any knight may fall, and against which he must be constantly on guard. Though he may mimic the outward appearance of aristocratic power, feudal alliance, chivalric combat, love service, and even the self-discipline of atonement for past transgressions, the giant typically lacks the capacity for a genuine realization of any of these ideals. When he appears as a low-born wildman armed only with a cudgel, the giant makes up for his lack of weaponry through sheer brute size and strength; the knight's ability to overcome this primal threat with a combination of martial training and sophisticated armaments is a powerful confirmation of the skill and refinement of the aristocratic warrior. As one whose primeval origins are marked by both the traumatic separation and the taboo conjoining of peoples, the giant embodies the principle of racial and cultural impurity, expressed in outbursts of blasphemy, lawlessness, and unspeakable excess—the very things that courtly ideology and Christian rule of law are designed to contain and suppress. Confrontations with giants allow the multiple discourses of Arthurian culture—gender and sexuality, class and political power, ethics and religious faith—to be merged, supporting the fantasy that one cannot be separated from another as all are interlinked, intrinsic to the essence of civilization itself.

CHAPTER 3

Touching the Absolute

Violence, Death, and Love

The previous chapters have focused on the humanity of giants, their proximity to both the animal and the monstrous, and their place within a human spectrum comprising differences of race, class, and culture. With their problematic mixed bloodlines, they are the hinge joining the human race to the demonic hosts—or, at the very least, the community of the redeemed to that of the damned. Excluded from feudal relations in Christian society, yet vital to the construction of civilized humanity, they are the ever-present threat that is also an opportunity for chivalric self-crafting and the staging of royal authority, as ruler or warrior respectively confronts this most formidable of enemies. When gender difference is introduced into the world of giants, the narrative possibilities become even more varied and complex. A male giant, seemingly by definition, is a dangerous and rapacious rival. A female giant, however, can sometimes (though certainly not always) be beautiful and even vulnerable, in need of chivalric protection. She can be rescued from the sexual predations of a male giant, or married as a prize for conquering a giant stronghold; she can even fall in love with a knight and insist on marrying only him. We have seen that in *Perceforest* the beautiful and innocent Galotine is rescued from the incestuous designs of her golden-haired father—who also showered abuse on his virtuous and long-suffering wife—to be married to a British knight. The prose *Tristan*, in turn, features a giant who, in a series of riddles, boasts not only of having raped his daughter but also of having killed and eaten both his daughter and his mother; while his other daughter, like Galotine, falls in love with a knight. None of the giantesses in the *Tristan* are developed as characters, but they do contribute to the portrayal of the giant world in strongly gendered terms. Overall, the giants' cruel treatment of their own female family members—what might in modern parlance be seen as the oppression of women in giant culture—contributes to their status as a miscreant race: one whose men are to be exterminated, and whose women are to be given the blessings of chivalric civilization. To paraphrase Gayatri Spivak's famous sentence: in the world of medieval romance, human men are saving both human *and* giant women from giant men.[1] Encounters with giants serve to enhance a knight's heroic masculinity, not only by allowing him to defeat a suitably challenging menace to society, but also by enabling him to impress, rescue, or avenge a beautiful damsel—usually an aristocratic lady, but on rare occasions a giant herself.

Tales of giants, then, are not just brutal stories of combat, dismemberment, and ignominious death. René Girard has stressed the need to acknowledge that "d'une manière ou d'une autre, la violence soit toujours mêlée au désir."[2] And as if to illustrate this point, even the most violent encounters between giants and humans are fueled by desire: chivalric desire for combat with the giant or for his death, and for the prizes won by killing a giant—honor, land, wealth, marriage—as well as the appetites that drive giants in their relentless attacks on both knights and ladies: for food, for sexual gratification, for vengeance, for power. But giants also animate tales of love: a knight's love for the lady who either requests or forbids his combat with a giant, or even for a beautiful giantess bride who loves him in return; a giant's love for a lady he attempts to court or marry, and sometimes even for the knights themselves. A closer look at these narratives allows us to explore the different ways that medieval authors construct the sexual and cultural others with whom knightly protagonists interact. And they can help us understand the ways that particular concepts of love, desire, and subjectivity underwrite not only the depiction of intimate personal relations but also the physical and ideological violence of military adventuring, imperial expansionism, and the consolidation of cultural hegemony. In this respect giants again offer parallels to Saracens, who also figure in romance and *chanson de geste* not only as mortal enemies but also as love objects, as converts assimilated into Christian society, and thus as partners in marriage or military adventuring.

Love, Death, and Courtly Subjectivity

The lyric *chanson de croisade* depicts Holy War as an obligation that separates lovers by taking men to exotic, dangerous locations; prolonged desire across vast distances characterizes the bond between the crusading warrior and the lady who comes to embody the homeland. "Ahi! Amours, con dure departie / Me convendra faire de la meillour / Qui onques fust amee ne servie!" (Alas! Love, what a difficult separation I must make from the best lady who was ever loved or served!), laments Conon de Béthune as he sets out on crusade; the Châtelain de Couci similarly regrets his upcoming separation from "cele qui m'ert dame, conpaigne, amie" (the one who was my lady, friend, beloved).[3] At the same time, of course, participation in Holy War is an act both pious and heroic, bringing suitable rewards. As Conon further notes, "La doit on faire chevalerie, / Qu'on i conquiert paradis et honor, / Et pris et los et l'amour de s'amie" (This is where one should perform chivalric exploits, where one wins honor and paradise, and praise and glory and the love of his sweetheart).[4] The enterprise that prolongs desire through enforced separation, then, also creates the possibility for its eventual fulfillment as spiritual, military, and erotic quests converge in a single culmination. In the *chanson de geste*, the distant object of desire is more likely to be directly identified with the Saracen world itself, as the beautiful foreign princess personifies the lucrative cities coveted by adventuring European warriors, and her conversion in the name of love offers an eroticized fantasy of victory over a race of infidels. When Guillaume Fierabras sets off to conquer Orange, for example, he is not leaving any lady love behind; indeed, his thirst for adventure is fueled not only by a desire for the thrill of war but also by a sense of dissatisfaction that he and his men originally left France and conquered Nîmes without remembering to bring along "harpeor ne jugler / Ne damoisele por noz cors deporter" (harpist or performer or young lady to entertain us).[5] His conquest of Orange is motivated by the riches and sensual attractions of both the city and its beautiful queen; as he exclaims when announcing his plan, "Ja ne quier mes lance n'escu porter / Se ge ne voi la dame et la cité" (I wish no longer to bear a lance and a shield if I do not see the lady and the city).[6] *Chanson de geste* differs from lyric in that the crusading knight's desires, both military and erotic, are likely to be fulfilled in a narrative resolution. But the model of exotic foreign love can certainly be found in the lyric tradition. One need only think of Jaufre Rudel, for example, whose *vida* tells us that his songs expressed his love for the distant Countess of Tripoli, and that when he finally made the journey to find her, he lived just long enough to die in her arms. As is also implied by numerous other lyric poets, it is as though the gratification of desire—whether for chivalric honor, erotic love, or the spiritual bliss of heaven—can be experienced only through bodily death.[7] In fact, the *chanson de croisade* suspends the warrior-lover between two geographically separate love objects, the lady and the Holy Land. While these might seem mutually exclusive, they function more as complementary representations of one and the same desire for the Absolute and can thus be fused not only with each other but also with the spiritual fulfillment of the afterlife, in the yearning of *amour de loin*.

Combat with giants similarly offers an opportunity for adventure that brings honor and prestige in the eyes of society, while also allowing for the catharsis of ultimate, all-out combat as it brings the hero face to face with death. In separating the knight from his lady at risk of his life—particularly when it entails a lengthy quest to find the giant in question—it generates anguished fears and yearning, while hope for reunion with the loved one drives him beyond the battle with the giant, which is no longer the end point of his desire. An enterprise so dangerous and all-consuming may be blocked by prohibition from the lady herself, even as it may also be a means of winning her love or her hand in marriage. It may even be a way for a knight to win a giantess bride—who, like the Saracen princesses of epic tradition, is likely to be both alluring and strangely unsettling. Whether it is carried out in the name of law enforcement, personal honor, or love, the War on Giants is imbued both with the aura of sacred obligation surrounding Holy War and with a dynamic of self-fashioning through engagement with the other. As we will see, Simon Gaunt's characterization of what is sometimes called "courtly love" applies equally to tales of knights and giants: "Love . . . however altruistic it might seem, turns out to be Narcissistic, in that its function seems to be to produce, to ensure and to confirm the self's integrity, not simply to reach out towards the other. . . . What seems to be a desire to encounter difference/otherness is, in fact . . . a means of contemplating the self."[8] Both giants and Saracens are vehicles for the narrative probing of male homosocial violence and heterosexual love as two forms of desire that define the chivalric subject, working sometimes in tandem and sometimes in opposition to each other, and requiring an ostensibly self-sacrificial gesture that is actually one of self-creation. And tales of giant or Saracen lovers allow for the exploration of alternative or skewed constructions of gender and sexuality, and the ways in which desire—whether thwarted, protracted, or fulfilled—is inflected by differences not only of class or gender but also of race and culture.

The Touch of the Giant: Absolute Violence and the Desire unto Death

Combat with a giant allows a knight to realize not only his own, but a universally held, desire for the giant's death. Not only do giants terrorize a local population through their violent predations, but also they block the fulfillment of other desires through their obstruction of marriage, feudal alliances, travel and commerce, and the exploitation of natural resources such as land, timber, and game. We have seen that the death of Holland in *Perceforest*, for example, allowed his stepson to be knighted and to marry the heiress to a neighboring island, so that the two manors were united in a single estate; it also opened the island to trade with the mainland, and the offshore waterways to navigation by sailors. To kill the giant is to cut the Gordian knot in which erotic, feudal, dynastic, political, economic, and commercial desires are intricately bound together and thwarted by a common enemy. The giant's subjects react to his death with unequivocal delight. "Ce poeple esbahy desiroient moult la mort de leur seigneur pour sa cruauté" (The people, all agog, greatly desired the death of their lord because of his cruelty), and when his death is confirmed, "moult furent joyeulx" (they were utterly overjoyed).[9] Similar reactions greet the deaths of other giants throughout romance tradition. When Lyonnel kills the Golden-Haired Giant, the local inhabitants "commencerent . . . a faire grant feste pour la mort desiree du gueant" (began . . . a great celebration for the longed-for death of the giant).[10] And when Gaheriet kills the giant Aupatris in the *Suite du roman de Merlin*, he is assured that the giants' subjects "ne desiroient rien du monde autant comme ilz faisoient sa mort" (desired nothing in the world so much as they did his death).[11]

Yet however much people desire the giant's death, they are often loath to allow a valiant knight to engage in a battle that they assume he cannot win. When the Chevalier au Delphin promises Marse, Hollandin's lover, that he will kill the giant, she feels unable even to accept his offer, exclaiming: "Ha! sire . . . je vous requiers, querez ung autre chemin pour acomplir mon desirier, car ceste voye est trop perilleuse" (*Perce/IV*, 1:108; Oh! Sir, . . . I beg you, seek a different way to fulfill my desire, for this one is too dangerous). Similarly, when Lyonnel informs the wife of the Golden-Haired Giant that he has come to claim the giant's head as a gift for his beloved, she urges him to abandon his foolhardy mission and escape while he can, though she knows the giant intends to murder her. And when Gaheriet ignores the advice of a hermit and insists on fighting the giant Aupatris, his squire bursts into tears "quant il voit que toutesvoies se veult son seigneur combatre encontre cest ennemy" (when he sees that his lord nonetheless intends to fight this fiend).[12] Paradoxically, then, the people who most desire a giant's death may be the very ones who try hardest to prevent the knight from achieving his goal, so that he faces not only the violent resistance of the giant himself but also the verbal discouragement of everyone around him. Such altercations make it very clear that the battle is not merely an obstacle to be overcome in bringing about the desired death of the giant, or even in winning honor and fame. It is also an object of chivalric desire in and of itself, one that requires the knight to overcome other obstacles in his pursuit of the ultimate combat experience.

An interesting case in which giant killing literally becomes a forbidden object of desire occurs in the prose *Tristan*, in the episode of the marauding giant Taulas de la Montagne. Taulas inhabits a fortified castle in the forest of the Morois in Cornwall, and his savagery is such that neither Mark nor any of his knights dare venture into his territory, despite its rich potential for hunting or other aristocratic pleasures. Tristan, of course, is by nature attracted to dangerous adventure, but in this case Iseut herself intervenes:

> Mesire Tristrans . . . i vaut par maintes fois aler pour combatre soi encontre le gaiant. . . . Mais la roïne Yseut, ki maintes fois avoit oï parler de le grant force du gaiant, li avoit tou adés desfendu et bien li avoit dit apertement que tout vraiement seüst il que, s'il i aloit encontre sa desfense, vainquist u ne vainquist, que jamais, a nul jour qu'ele vesquist, a lui ne parleroit. . . . Mesire Tristrans, ki en nule maniere n'alast encontre le conmandement de sa dame, tout fust il ensi k'il eüst mout grant volenté d'esprouver soi encontre le gaiant, si s'en estoit il tenus toutes voies.[13]

> [Sir Tristan wanted many times to go fight the giant. . . . But Queen Iseut, who had often heard talk of the giant's great force, had utterly forbidden it, and had told him explicitly that he must truly know that, if he went against her prohibition, whether he won or not, she would never speak to him again as long as she lived. . . . Sir Tristan, who would never go against his lady's command no matter how badly he wanted to test himself against the giant, had kept from doing so.]

Though the death of the giant would clearly be the ultimate goal in fighting him, what is explicitly mentioned here is not that, but rather Tristan's desire to test himself against an opponent of extreme prowess. It is the combat itself—the intense and passionate experience of two bodies locked together in mortal struggle—that forms the object of his fantasies and his "grant volenté." And while Iseut's most obvious fear is simply for Tristan's death if the giant proves invincible, one might wonder if she is not also threatened by this spectacle of a bodily coupling—violent rather than erotic, but equally all-consuming—that might threaten to displace her as the central focus of Tristan's desire. Iseut is the other through whom Tristan defines himself, the source of both his pleasure and his pain; their every tryst, however ardently desired, also carries the risk of violent and imminent death at the hands of her husband or one of his lackeys. Iseut does not dissuade Tristan from engaging in battles or tournaments with other knights, but combat with a giant is of an entirely different order—so extreme in its bodily and passionate intensity that it might genuinely be seen as a supplement or even a rival to erotic love. For his part, the giant has heard of Tristan's phenomenal prowess and fears that in hand-to-hand combat Tristan might prove more than a match: "Il ne li estoit pas avis k'il peüst encontre lui durer a bataille, s'il en venist a l'espreuve" (1:259; he didn't think he could stand up to him in battle, if put to the test). Thus, while Tristan avoids straying into the Morois for fear of meeting the giant and thereby losing Iseut, the giant himself retreats to the safety of his mountaintop castle, preferring to give up his life of marauding rather than risk an encounter with Cornwall's greatest knight. Tristan, Taulas, and Iseut exist in a complex triangle of fear and desire, in which Taulas, despite his desire for violence, fears the chivalric prowess of Tristan; Tristan, despite his desire to fight the giant, fears the wrath of Iseut; and Iseut, despite her desire to see Tristan's glory augmented, fears the lethal but powerfully alluring force of the giant.

It is Tristan's period of madness that releases both himself and Taulas from the paralysis of Iseut's prohibition. Tristan's erroneous belief that Iseut has betrayed him by accepting an amorous liaison with Kahedin causes him to lose his mind and his memory.[14] In a state of madness, having lost his identity and having been given up for dead by nearly everyone, Tristan has in effect fallen out of his own story line and no longer defines himself either as the lover of Iseut or as a knight desirous of fighting a giant. Taulas, in turn, hears that Tristan is dead and returns to his life of pillage and murder in the Morois. In this space of oblivion—a space outside the story of the fateful love affair—it becomes possible for knight and giant to meet. Neither recognizes the other, but when Taulas attacks a passing knight, the shepherds with whom Tristan is living urge the madman to take up the knight's sword, which has fallen by the wayside, and kill the giant. Tristan duly beheads the giant, and the fit of passion thus sparked threatens to explode out of all control: "Au cevalier meïsement, ki desous le gaiant estoit, eüst il la teste caupee, mais li pastour li escrient k'il ne l'ochie pas" (He would similarly have beheaded the knight, who was underneath the giant, but the shepherds shouted at him not to kill him).[15] In his unformed state, the act of killing a giant nearly causes Tristan to take on the giant's identity for himself, but fortunately he stops short of this crucial turning point. It is the death of the giant, in turn, that inspires Mark to organize a celebratory hunting party in the Morois and to take the entertaining madman back to court; and thus Tristan can eventually be recognized, and cured by Iseut. Killing the giant does, if indirectly, enable him to recover his heroic identity and to reconnect with his beloved—though not in the manner of a more traditional tale of love and combat, such as that enacted by Lyonnel.

Far from being an obligation or a burden, then, combat with a giant is an object of masculine desire—one that may be protracted through a long period of seeking out the giant and surmounting the objections of those who try to dissuade the knight from what they see as a suicide mission; and one that, as we have seen, affords the knight intense excitement, cathartic passion, and ultimately a powerful sense of joy. Though many knights are killed by giants, those few who are able to survive the encounter have tested themselves against an extreme of masculine power. In surviving this brush with the Absolute—with absolute violence, with absolute masculine virility—the knight can fully know himself and reveal himself to others as one who has gone above and beyond the norms of knighthood. The giant is always someone who has caused the deaths of countless previous victims and intends to do the same again; by evading this fate, substituting the giant's death for his own, the knight emerges as a singularity, the one and only being ever able to withstand the giant's fury. The example of Tristan and Taulas does, however, illustrate a potential danger posed by this most intense form of combat: the possibility that the knight, having equaled and indeed exceeded the giant in sheer lethal violence, will be unable to return to the chivalric model in which aggression is regulated, contained, and sublimated into culturally sanctioned activities such as feudal governance, love, and marriage.[16] Killing a giant, after all, should be a way for a knight to demonstrate his difference from this enemy of society—not a means of taking his place. This danger is evoked, not only in the encounter of

Tristan with Taulas, but also in the episode of the Chastel de Plour earlier in the prose *Tristan*. Here any knight who arrives at the giant's island kingdom must fight the lord to the death and, if he wins, replace him as the new lord, with the obligation to kill any further knights who land on the island. I will examine this passage in chapter 4. An example even more closely relevant to the present context is the giant killer Gieffroy in the *Roman de Mélusine*.

Gieffroy a la Grant Dent, probably the fiercest of Mélusine's surviving sons, kills two giants, as I discussed in chapter 2: first Gardon, who has usurped Lusignan power over the Guérande, and then Grimaut, who turns out to have been guarding the tomb of Mélusine's father, King Elinas of Scotland. True to form, Reymondin attempts to keep Gieffroy from finding out about Gardon's actions, "pour doubte qu'il n'alast combatre le jayant, car il le sentoit de si grant cuer qu'il ne lairoit point qu'il n'y alast" (for fear that he would go fight the giant, for he knew him to be so bold of heart that he would never refrain from going there).[17] Equally true to form, Gieffroy is not to be dissuaded and has soon dispatched his enemy and received the invitation from Grimaut's victims to kill that giant as well. It is at this moment—poised midway between two combats with giants—that Gieffroy learns of his brother Fromont's entrance into an abbey. His horrifically violent reaction to that news—burning down the abbey with all of the monks trapped inside, including his own brother—seems difficult behavior to grasp in a knight who has just been a major player in a successful Holy War against Saracens.[18] But it can be explained at least in part by the fact that Gieffroy is at this point in a somewhat altered state. Still riding a high wave from his defeat of Gardon, for which he is feted throughout the land, and having just agreed with alacrity to a repeat performance, he is in a space defined entirely by this most violent and solitary form of combat with the most lethal of adversaries. Given this state of affairs, it may not be altogether surprising that upon hearing of his brother's ascetic avocation, "il fu si doulens que a pour pou qu'il n'yssoit hors de son sens" (680; he was so distressed that he nearly lost his mind). As if temporarily identified with the libidinous *jouissance* of the giant, Gieffroy cannot tolerate his sudden association with the spiritual renunciation of bodily desire and enjoyment of all kinds, and he furiously denounces his brother in the presence of his fellow monks: "Par mon chief . . . si en seréz paiéz avecques les autres, ne il me sera ja reprouvé que j'aye moine a frere!" (682; By my head . . . you will pay for it along with the others, nor will I be reproached for being the brother of a monk!). It is the destruction of the abbey that motivates Reymondin to despair and publicly to denounce Mélusine as a phantom and serpent, resulting in her transformation and disappearance from human life. And when Gieffroy, after killing his second giant, hears this story, he reacts with still more violent rage by murdering his uncle, the Count of Forez, whom he holds responsible for having first turned Reymondin against Mélusine.

At this point, then, Gieffroy has come far too close for comfort to replicating the behavior of the very enemy against whom he has won his fame. He has desecrated a monastery, killed an entire community of monks, murdered his own brother and uncle, and indirectly caused the collapse of his parents' marriage and the disastrous betrayal of his mother's highest hopes: behavior indeed worthy of a giant. But although he is one-quarter fairy—an "ethnic" reality that finds bodily expression in his enormous tusklike tooth, and surely a contributing factor in his temperamental excess—he is also a European Christian and an aristocratic knight of royal descent. And once his rage subsides, Gieffroy shows his true humanity in his sudden move to self-scrutiny, contrition, and penance. Realizing the enormity of his sins, he travels to Rome to make confession to the pope, then goes to visit his father in the hermitage of Montserrat where he has taken refuge. The episode illustrates L. O. Aranye Fradenburg's point that a culture is always constructed around a split between excessive and insufficient enjoyment: "More important even than identifying with one or the other term of the morality/passion dichotomy is maintaining the dichotomy itself, and the artistry required to negotiate it. A culture's 'modes of enjoyment' will present themselves as the "perfect" balance between discipline and pleasure . . . necessary if the distinction between enjoyment and the law is to be broadly sustainable."[19] In constructing himself as a Christian warrior and a powerful but merciful aristocratic lord, Gieffroy must prove himself capable of the "artistry" that will allow him to negotiate his path between the ascetic monk and the rapacious giant. And while he kills both monks and giants, he also shows his ability to partake both of violent warfare and of Christian piety and penance.

Understandably, people now regard Gieffroy with great wariness: for them, he is already taking on the aspect of a giant or other extreme menace to society. In Montserrat, for example, the monks ask their chaplain: "Qui est ce grant deable al la grant dent? Il semble moult crueulx!" (742; Who is that big devil with the large tooth? He looks awfully cruel!). And upon learning that Gieffroy will succeed his father as ruler of Lusignan, the people "moult redoubtoient Gieffroy pour sa fierté" (736; greatly feared Gieffroy for his ferocity). But, as the narrator assures us, "Pour neant le doubtent, car il les gouvernera bien et doucement" (736; They're worried for nothing, for he will govern them with fairness and magnanimity). As we saw in chapter 1, the capacities for moral reflection, self-reformation, and redemption are the hallmarks of human nature: the factors that distinguish fallible and often sinful humans from both beasts and monsters—and often, as well, from giants. Gieffroy has certainly touched the Absolute in more ways than one: in the crucible of combat with giants and in the incandescent rage that led him to set fire to an abbey and to kill his father's brother, but also in the pain of contrition and penance. And in this way he lives up to his promise as Holy Warrior and vanquisher of Saracens to emerge as a true hero—one who rids the world of giants, while managing not to become a new sort of giant himself.

Seeking the Absolute: Combat in the Name of Love

When giant killing is linked to love service, the desire for mortal combat merges with that of erotic love: itself an enterprise that is frequently dismissed as foolhardy by the uninitiated. Both forms of desire entail a trajectory toward an often long-deferred end point of passionate release and cathartic bodily coupling: a narrative matrix for chivalric self-staging and redefinition in which the stakes are literally life or death. As Lyonnel sets off in search of the giant he has been asked to kill, his squire Clamidés derides his "folle emprinse" (*Perce/II*, 1:286; foolish enterprise)—a term that seems to apply equally to desire for battle with a giant that cannot be found anywhere, and to love for an unattainable maiden—as an impossible goal: "Bien sçay que les vies y mectrons, car nous querons ce que oncques ne fut ne jamais ne sera"

(1:286; I know very well that we will spend our lives on this, for we are seeking that which never was nor ever will be). Lyonnel, however, has been told that he can see Blanchete only if he brings back the Golden-Haired Giant's head, and he steadfastly pursues his quest, embracing its many hardships with equanimity: hunger, cold, and ever-more deadly battles with lions, with a flying serpent, and ultimately with the giant himself. All such brushes with death are welcomed as an opportunity to prove his worthiness in love: "Blanche comme fleur de lys, se ne conquiers ceste beste, digne ne suys de vous veoir!" (1:289; Lily-white Blanche, if I don't conquer this beast, I am not worthy of seeing you). Struggling endlessly through uninhabited Scottish wilderness, finding no one who can tell them where the giant might be, Lyonnel and Clamidés suffer extreme deprivations:

> Sy furent depuis tellement menez qu'il leur convenoit mengier par famine les chars des bestes sauvaiges toutes crues. . . . Et furent depuis sy povres de toutes vestures qu'il leur convenoit enveloper leurs piez et leurs jambes de peaulx de cerfz. . . . Et sachiez que Lyonnel fut tellement mené que le poil qui yssoit de sa char par povreté luy passoit parmy les mailles du haubergeon. (1:286)

> [From there on out they were so hard-pressed that, from hunger, they had to eat the raw flesh of wild beasts. . . . And they were so lacking in clothing that they had to wrap their legs and feet in deerskins. . . . And truly Lyonnel had such travail that the hairs growing on his body protruded between the chain links of his hauberk.]

Lyonnel's single-mindedness has brought him to a point where he seems little different from the hermit who originally attempted to dissuade him from the follies of love; this man "avoit une barbe longue et noire et houchue et la cheveleure grande et mal pignie si qu'il n'apparoit de son viaire fors les yeulx et le nez et pou du front et des mascelles" (1:192; had a long, black, shaggy beard and a full head of uncombed hair, such that all you could see of his face was the eyes and the nose, and little of forehead or cheeks). And indeed the quest to kill the giant and thereby win the right to see Blanchete is understood by Lyonnel as a mortification of the flesh that parallels that of the hermit: "Tout en telle maniere que la beaulté de paradiz ne puet estre veue se l'on ne l'achate, en telle maniere la tresgrant beaulté qui est en la pucelle que je quier a veoir ne doit estre veue de moy se je ne l'achate par paine et par travail" (1:193; Just as the beauty of paradise cannot be seen if one doesn't earn it, similarly the great beauty in the maiden that I seek to see should not be seen by me if I don't earn it through pain and travail). The spiritual quest for the joys of another world, the chivalric quest for mortal combat with a mysterious, seemingly unknown giant, and the erotic quest for the aesthetic and amorous pleasures afforded by a beautiful princess all merge as Lyonnel's protracted state of yearning leads him through an elaborate process of self-refashioning.

Fighting a giant, like war with the fearsome Saracens and like love itself, is a form of both bodily and emotional torment, pain, and deprivation. And this pain—like the *dous mal* of erotic desire and the ascetic rigors of spiritual devotion—is also a path to both bodily and spiritual delight. The Châtelain de Couci expresses the paradoxes of love in describing the object of his desire as "Ma bele perte u ma haute richour, / Ne sai lequel, s'en ai joie et paour" (my beautiful loss or my fabulous wealth, I know not which, as I have both joy and fear of her), while subsequent strophes of the same song reiterate his certainty that death is the only possible outcome if the lady does not reciprocate his love.[20] The simultaneous emotions of terror and joy, and the stakes of glorious death or abundant wealth, parallel those of combat, particularly the ultimate combat of the wars on both giants and Saracens. Conon de Béthune, again, states this succinctly in "Ahi! Amours." The crusader not only wins *paradis*, *honor*, and *l'amour de s'amie* but also welcomes combat's opportunity for a glorious death that is really a rebirth:

> Que cele mors est douce et savereuse
> Dont on conquiert le regne precïeus,
> Ne ja de mort nen i morra uns seus,
> Ainz naisteront en vie glorïeuse.[21]

> [For that death is sweet and delicious by which one conquers the precious kingdom (of heaven); nor will anyone actually die there, but rather be reborn into a life of glory.]

In a symbolic passage through death and release into another life, Lyonnel is similarly reborn as a knight single-mindedly devoted to love, which now informs his every act. And the crucial turning point of this trajectory is mortal combat with a giant. The symbolic nature of Lyonnel's "death," however, marks an important difference between the "culture war" of combat with giants and the Holy War of combat with Saracens. Vanquishing the infidel is certainly a desirable goal, but death in Holy War is a form of martyrdom, so that while victory is a glorious achievement, so too is the self-sacrificial gesture of death in battle. A martyr's death is a means of demonstrating absolute love and devotion to God, the ultimate love object; and far from proving him unworthy, it will be this very death that admits the holy warrior into God's presence. In fighting a giant, the knight does show his willingness to face death, but the real goal here is twofold. On the one hand, the knight needs to emerge victorious from that space of absolute violence, in order to prove both his superlative prowess and his ability to reenter the social and political network of feudal friendships and alliances. And on the other hand, the giant targeted in single combat is an enemy that must be defeated, whether for the purpose of rescuing another knight or lady who has fallen into his clutches, of putting an end to his despotic rule or predatory violence, or, as in Lyonnel's case, of acquiring the trophy that will buy him favor with his beloved. In this context, a self-sacrificial "gift of death" is pointless; what is crucial for the knight is to succeed in substituting the giant's death for his own.[22] Staging one's own death as an expression of absolute love works in the spiritual context of the soul's union with God in an afterlife; it can also be the consummation of a lyric trajectory of desire whose end point is itself an absolute, beyond which neither language nor consciousness can reach. But in the chivalric context of feudal warfare and marriage, the knight seeks to stage not his death but precisely his ability to evade death in performing services that strengthen social and political stability.

Because it brings a knight so close to death and dissolution, combat with giants is a prime object of desire in the chivalric quest for heroic self-fashioning; and also for that reason it is seen as a reckless venture by those with a stake in preserving the social order and retaining the services of the knight. Since battle with giants lacks the sacrificial dimension of Holy War, the knight's death will serve no purpose; and no matter how ardently people may long for the death of the giant, the potential loss of a valuable warrior may still seem a risk too great to run. A knight's beloved does not always want him to fight giants at all, as is shown in the example of Iseut; nor is she necessarily the spur to his desire for combat. Bearing this in mind allows us to appreciate just how extreme the task set for Lyonnel really was and to wonder whether there could even be some truth to Golden-Hair's taunt when Lyonnel confronts him and explains his mission: "Par ma foy, sire chevalier, la pucelle amoit mieulx aultruy que vous, qui ce vous demanda, car, a ce que je puis veoir, elle desiroit a estre delivre de vous" (*Perce/II*, 1:354; By my faith, Sir Knight, the maiden who asked you to do that loved someone else more than she did you, for, as far as I can see, she wanted to be rid of you). The giant's interpretation is, of course, a sinister one; but even his wife implies that Lyonnel himself is to blame for taking seriously what could not possibly have been a genuine request: "Ha! chevalier de haulte emprinse, a pou de conquest fors de la mort, dist la dame. Amours vous ont deceu ainsi comme se elle vous eust dit: 'Buvez la mer et puis je vous donneray ce que vous desirez'" (1:349; Oh! Knight, in this lofty enterprise there is little to be conquered other than death, said the lady. Love has deceived you, just as if she had said to you: "Drink the sea dry, and then I'll give you what you want"). In fact, it was Blanchete's mother, Queen Lydoire, who set the terms of Lyonnel's quest; perhaps the girl herself would not have conceived such a thing. However that may be, it is clear that Lydoire has set a very high standard indeed for her daughter's future husband; and she has determined that it would be better for any unworthy suitor to die in a distant land than for him to so much as lay eyes on her daughter for a second time. The suggestion that a request to kill a giant could in fact be a kind of homicide is not entirely unrealistic. And this possibility is realized in a different text, in which a princess sends her would-be lover on a mission to kill giants—but not with the intention of ultimately granting him her love.

The Princess and the Giants: Love and Death in Guiron le courtois

The thirteenth-century prose romance *Guiron le courtois*, set during the latter part of the reign of Uterpendragon and the early part of

Arthur's reign, also contains many flashbacks to still earlier periods of pre-Arthurian British history. Some of these feature close engagement with both giants and pagans, as generations of heroic ancestors prepared the way for the Arthurian world. A particularly interesting intersection of giant and pagan adversaries occurs in the episode recounting the career of Guiron's ancestor Febus, eldest son of King Childeric.[23] Traveling from Christian Gaul to Britain, Febus wages war on three brothers, each the king of a pagan kingdom; in a series of stunning victories, he and his forty retainers decimate a pagan force of fifteen thousand, killing two of the three kings. Eventually, however, he agrees to a truce with the one surviving brother, king of Northumberland, because he is in love with the king's daughter, a maiden celebrated for her beauty. Under pressure from her father, who is desperate for a pause in the destructive warfare, she reluctantly agrees to show some small signs of favor to her admirer, while secretly plotting his demise. She sets him tasks that are proposed under the guise of love service but that are really efforts to send him to his death against ever more formidable adversaries. When Febus proves undefeatable, she sends him to kill a group of four giants, with the added proviso that he cannot leave their lair until she comes to join him—something she intends never to do. Finding himself thus trapped in a remote mountain dwelling on the distant Isle of Orkney, and realizing at last the perfidy of his beloved, Febus suffers a broken heart and languishes at the point of death. Moved by this sign of perfect devotion, the damsel is suddenly gripped with guilt—seeing that her implacable hatred has destroyed a glorious hero and truly dedicated lover—and journeys to his bedside, arriving just in time for him to die in her arms. She vows to spend the rest of her life tending his tomb and thus meets her own death in the same mountain cave.

Febus's spectacular military exploits, his easy victories over giants, and his passionate love for a beautiful pagan princess are stock motifs that could have led to the familiar narrative motif of the Saracen princess who converts to Christianity and assures the final victory of both the individual knight and the religion in whose name he fights. Unfortunately for Febus, however, this particular princess has no interest in conversion. When he asks for her love, she retorts, "Vous n'estes mie de ma loy ne ge de la vostre" (You are not of my religion, nor I of yours) as well as reminding him that he has killed both of her uncles and ravaged her kingdom.[24] Febus persists, however, and when she feigns pleasure at his successful completion of a mission against the pagan king of Orkney—one in which she had, of course, expected him to be killed—he decides to don a disguise and attend a festival of Venus held at her father's court. Here he encounters two giant brothers who are allied with the king of Northumberland; and the role of these giants pays closer scrutiny.

Typical of giants, the brothers inhabit a mountaintop forest and force the inhabitants of Northumberland to pay annual tribute. Though they participate fully in the festivities, it is also to receive their payment from the king that they attend the festival of Venus. Far from feeling shamed at suffering extortion, however, the king is happy with the arrangement, for he views it as just recompense for an unexplained incident in which the giants saved his life. When told that the giants have arrived, he treats them as honored guests, exclaiming, "Bien soient il venus! . . . Nous n'eüsmes onques d'eus fors que honor et courtoisie" (122; They're very welcome! . . . We have never had anything from them other than honor and courtesy). In a single stroke, savage giants are transformed into noble lords, allies of the king. Upon arrival, they converse with the king, listening sympathetically as he laments the deaths of his brothers and his own shame at the hands of a Christian warrior. Though they can do nothing to reverse the damage already done, they promise in eloquent language to take appropriate vengeance: "Or saciés tout certainnement que pour l'amour de vous feriom nous tant que se vous nous poés ensegnier en tout le roialme de Nohoubelande celui qui vos freres ocist, nous somes appareilliés que nous aillom la tout droitement et que nous faiçom de son cors ce que vous en commanderois" (126; Now be assured that out of love for you, if you can tell us who in the entire realm of Northumberland killed your brothers, we are prepared to do our utmost to go there directly, and we will do with his body according to your command). The ambivalent status of the giants, poised at the threshold between monstrous villain and courtly pagan, is equally expressed in the tribute paid by the king: ten robes of crimson silk, six maidens, and six young men. That the giants covet luxury garments associates them with an aristocratic opulence in keeping with their lordly status. That they also exact a human tribute is more troubling, identifying them with the stereotype of giants and other demonic figures as cruel and oppressive tyrants. One thinks, for example, of the giant Aupatris in the *Suite du roman de Merlin*, who demands twelve maidens every year from the castle of Taraquin: it is the need to rescue the maiden he had been escorting that impels Gaheriet to fight Aupatris, for he will lose all honor if she is handed over to a giant. We might also think of the silk workers collected as tribute by the two demon brothers in the "Pesme Aventure" episode of Chrétien de Troyes's *Chevalier au lion*.[25] Even the unheroic King Mark of Cornwall was grateful to be released from his payment of human tribute to the king of Ireland—an arrangement viewed by all as deeply shameful—after Tristan's defeat of the Morholt. In this episode of *Guiron*, giant and pagan meet across a divide that is very thin indeed; and the pagan king is exposed as a weak figure, who views Christian knights as enemies while accepting a dishonorable servitude to giants. And since both the giants and the princess are intent on Febus's death—the former, one assumes, in an openly declared battle, and the latter through deception and subterfuge posing as love—it is difficult to say which, in the end, is the more savage and which the more genteel.

Febus, however, overhears the entire exchange between the king and his giant allies; and he takes advantage of an athletic contest to spark a violent encounter with the brothers. Having first defeated one of the giants in a contest of speed, Febus proceeds to vanquish him in a wrestling match, thereby proving himself both more agile and more powerful than the king's champion. Furious at the shame thereby brought to his brother, the other giant draws his sword and rushes at Febus; needless to say, our hero successfully defeats and kills first the one giant and then, for good measure, the other. In the wake of this disaster, having recognized that this stranger can only be Febus, the king again urges his daughter to love the seemingly omnipotent knight. It is at this point of desperation that she hatches her plan to send him against the four giant brothers, confident that if they do not kill him his promise to remain on the scene until she joins him will at least imprison him for life in a distant location. Unbeknownst to Febus, he is actually living out the grisly scenario imagined by the Golden-Haired Giant in his meeting with Lyonnel.

That this deadly encounter between a Christian hero and a pair of giants takes place in the context of a festival of Venus—thus recalling the Trojan origins of the Britons—is no coincidence. That the presiding deity is Venus subtly underscores the interplay of pagan barbarity and erotic love that runs throughout the story of Febus's life. More importantly, however, the episode recasts the episode in Geoffrey of Monmouth's *Historia regum Britanniae* in which giants launch an attack on a Trojan religious festival in Totnes, culminating in the wrestling match between Gogmagog and Corineus. Of Corineus and Gogmagog, we are told that "alter alterum uinculis brachiorum adnectens crebris afflatibus aera uexant. Nec mora, Goemagog, Cornieum maximis uiribus astringens, fregit ei tres costas" (Corineus and the giant [were] closing in to encircle each other with their arms, whilst their panting breath disturbed the air. Gogmagog swiftly gripped Corineus with all his strength and broke three of his ribs).[26] This contest is echoed in *Guiron le courtois* when the Northumbrian giant "prist Febus a .II. bras par mi les flans" (132; wrapped both arms around Febus). He is unable to budge the young warrior, however; and in response Febus literally pulls the giant off balance: "Le prist adonc as .II. mains par les deus bras et le tira si fort a soi qu'i li fist le visage hurter a terre" (132; Then he took him by the arms with each hand and pulled him forward so hard that he caused him to crash face down on the ground). Though less dramatic than Corineus's response to being nearly crushed by Gogmagog— Febus kills both giants slightly later, in the ensuing brawl—the giant's fall is nonetheless a domesticated version of Gogmagog's violent death as he is hurled off a cliff and dashed to bits on the rocks below.

In these two battles with giants, however, there lies a crucial difference. In the *Historia* the giants are the enemy, targeting a festival that, taking place in pre-Christian times, involves no sacrilege; if anything, it shows the pious adherence of the Trojans to the only religion they have ever known. In *Guiron*, however, the giants are the honored guests of a pagan king resistant to Christianity, with whom they plot to destroy a Christian warrior. It is also in *Guiron* that we encounter the giant Brun, who challenges Uterpendragon and seeks to extend his own rule over the whole of Britain, and whose sons are knighted by a local lord. This reconfiguration of the political landscape of Britain highlights the very real danger that the Trojan "culture wars" may be lost, as a pagan culture integrates humans and giants in a violent stand against Christendom. The "civilizing mission" spearheaded by Brutus and Corineus has led to mixed results. Though giants have assimilated to the extent of embracing feudal alliances and at least some aspects of aristocratic life, the result is not one compatible with the Christian chivalric values of the Arthurian kingdom about to be established—a kingdom that, moreover, must be established as the defining framework for the Grail Quest. Instead, Britain is in danger of following a pagan trajectory in which humans will be dependent on giants and subject to their tyrannical rule. James Simpson's comments regarding the giants in *Erec et Enide* are applicable here as well: the giants' appearance "constitutes an irruptive resurgence of the monstrous depravity of precolonisation Britain ... [and] an attempt to undo chivalric modernity."[27] The precarious balance of civilization must now be saved by a new wave of incomers: from the Holy Land, as Joseph of Arimathea brings Christianity and the Grail to Britain, and from the Christian kingdom of Gaul, with the arrival of a new avenging hero. This second clash of cultures pits Christian knighthood against paganism, rather than pagan civilization against chaotic wilderness; but giants are a focal point in both power struggles.

This tale of warfare and giant killing is also one of passionate and fatal love, and it is noteworthy that a knight who single-handedly slays seven giants is unable to survive his love for a pagan princess. The site of his victory over the final four giants—their grotto dwelling—becomes his deathbed when he realizes that the princess has betrayed him. Febus is employing the methods used in courting Christian maidens: renouncing war and accepting the hand of the princess as a peace offering, slaying giants and performing other exploits to show the strength and inspirational force of his love, and of course resisting any thought of taking his love object by force. But he has entered an alien cultural space, one in which his ever-escalating feats of prowess—one giant, then two, then four—only underscore his enmity to his beloved's family and their allies.[28] And he has fallen in love with a girl less tractable than the dutiful Christian heroines of romance, and less willing to be used in negotiations between men. Febus's story differs from the standard romance model in two important ways. On the one hand, his combats with giants are too easy, lacking the element of exciting danger and suspense that one expects in such encounters. And on the other, the princess is too little impressed by the heroism of her suitor.

Fighting a giant is normally a protracted affair, in which a knight is stretched to the absolute limit of endurance, and in which even the doughtiest of warriors may legitimately experience fear and dread. Arthur's fear, for example, is mentioned in the various texts recounting his battles with both Rion and the Giant of Mont-St-Michel. In the *Estoire del Saint Graal*, Nascien is attacked by a giant; finding himself unarmed, the hero is "si destroiz et si angoisseus que nus plus" (as distressed and anguished as anyone could ever be).[29] He survives only because, in this state of "destrece de mort et peors" (332; fear and panic in the face of death), he commits himself into God's hands and is thereby miraculously provided with an invincible sword. In a later battle with the giant Faran, Nascien fights to the point of utter exhaustion without managing to defeat his adversary: "Nasciens, qui plus estoit foibles que li jaianz, ert ja tant las et tant traveilliez qu'il ne se pooit tenir en estant, ainz ert chaoiz adenz" (395; Nascien, who was weaker than the giant, was so exhausted and so worn out that he could not remain standing, but fell to the ground). On this occasion he is saved only through the intervention of his companion Nabor. In the prose *Tristan*, when Bohort of Gaunes fights the marauding Cornish giant, "La bataille avoit tant ja duré que a poi que li rois Boorth n'estoit mors d'anui et de traveil" (*PT*[M], 1:148; That battle had lasted so long that King Bohort had very nearly died of travail and exhaustion). In *Guiron* itself, Uterpendragon's battle with Brun is so arduous that the king never does fully recover: "De cele bataille fu il si durement navrés qu'il ne fu puis de si grant pooir com il avoit devant esté ne puis ne pot armes porter si esforchiement com il fesoit devant" (58; In this battle he was so severely wounded that he was never as powerful as he had been before, nor could he bear arms with the force that he had previously shown).

In contrast, Febus dispatches giants with a swiftness that seems almost anticlimactic.[30] In the altercation on the athletic field, he is unarmed. But when the first giant draws his sword and charges him he shows no fear at all. Unlike Nascien, who desperately calls upon God to save him from the *maufé* (demon), Febus remains supremely confident. Stepping up to the challenge, he "feri le jaiant sour la temple si durement del puing qu'il l'abati mort a la terre de premier coup" (132; punched the giant so hard in the temple that he fell down dead at the first blow). He is then immediately attacked by the giant's brother, but

"Cil qui trop avoit de pooir si fist de lui tout autrestant a cele espreuve com il avoit feit de son frere" (134; He who had such great power did the same to him as he had done with his brother). Even fighting four giants at once is no problem for this knight: "Quant il ot dit ceste parole, il n'i mist autre demourance, ains se met esroment entr'eus et feri le premier, qu'il ataint si durement qu'il le rua mort a la terre del premier cop. Aprés le premier ocist le secont et puis le tierc et puis le quart" (142–44; When he had spoken thus, he delayed no further, but ran among them and struck the first one, whom he hit so hard that he brought him down dead at the first blow. After the first one, he killed the second and then the third and then the fourth). If giants fall before him with excessive ease, the princess remains completely unmoved until the very end, where the amorous union of the lovers coincides with Febus's death. In fact, this affair follows a model closer to the irresolvable desire of lyric than to romance with its tales of love and dynastic marriage. The lyric poet repeatedly claims to be offering his death as a gift to the lady, when what he really gives her is the indefinite deferral of his death by means of its symbolic representation in an endless series of songs. Febus, for his part, accepts the possibility of death in service to the princess, but his death too is endlessly deferred—though here it is through a series of substitute deaths, as foreign kings and giants fall victim to his ongoing demonstration of love. It is only when he finally literalizes the lyric trope of love-death that the princess embarks in response on a life of unrequitable yearning, devoted to the memory of a beloved whom death has placed beyond all possible reach. Indeed, when the princess arrives at Febus's bedside in the giants' grotto, his words are a powerful expression of the extent to which the consummation of erotic desire has fused with death: "Bien vegniés, dist il, ma douce mors, la chose de cest monde que j'ai plus desirree! Or ne me chaut grantiment desormais quant la mort viegne, car toute ma volentés est acomplie quant ge la voi" (146; Welcome, said he, my sweet death, the thing I have desired most in this world! Now I don't much care when death comes to me, for my desire is completely fulfilled when I see her). Febus's words imply that what he desired was not so much an ongoing physical relationship with the princess as a gesture of acknowledgment: a willingness to grant him her presence, a reciprocal expression of love. As is so often implied in courtly lyric, love and death converge as twin aspects of the end point targeted by desire; but as in so many romances, victorious battle with giants is still the means through which this end point is reached.

Though Febus's heroic stature is a factor in the princess's recognition of her misjudgment, it is ultimately the knight's emotional vulnerability—his decidedly nongiantesque willingness to submit himself to her will even if it means the end of his heroic career or of his very life—that motivates her change of heart. Faced with this absolute devotion, she feels compelled to respond with an equally absolute devotion of her own, and only at this point can she shift her grief from the deaths of her uncles to that of the man who killed them. Ignoring her father's orders to return home, the princess is steadfast: "Se ge muir pour la soie amour aprés ce qu'il morut pour moi, ce n'est mie trop grant merveille" (148; If I die for his love after he died for me, it's no great wonder). Unwilling to be used as payment for services rendered or as tribute to a military conqueror, but ultimately giving the gift of selfless love unto death in return for a similar gift from a knight, the princess incarnates in absolute form the qualities that Sarah Kay identifies with the Saracen princesses of the *chanson de geste*: a determination to "assume control over their own persons rather than subordinating them to the control of their families" and a skepticism concerning "such fundamentally 'epic' notions as heroism, patriarchy, and the 'exchange of women'" that subtly undermines male feudal hegemony.[31] Rather like the giantess, the pagan or Saracen princess preserves a powerful sense of self-determination. This construction of feminine identity as grounded in a resistance to masculine narratives of arranged marriages and homosocial exchange is one of the ways that racial difference, coded as cultural difference, is explored in medieval literature.

Febus's two principal combats with giants—at the Northumbrian festival and in the mountain lair—inscribe giant killing in different contexts that imply, in turn, opposing models of social bonding. The Northumbrian giants, allies of the king, have just agreed to avenge the deaths of his brothers by killing the foreign warrior whose predations threaten not only his family network and political power but also—as representative of a rival religion and "law"—the cultural fabric of pagan Britain. Febus's attack on the giants is a stark reminder of the king's vulnerability as the only monarch to survive the war; in robbing the king of his defenders, he creates a lack that he can easily exploit—or, if he becomes the king's son-in-law, that he can fill. This development has the effect of inciting the king to redouble the pressure on his daughter to acquiesce to Febus's love and allow herself to be used as the commodity with which the king can purchase an alliance with this formidable enemy. Such an outcome would place the princess in a position uncomfortably close to that of the human tribute formerly paid to the giants themselves, and she resists this trajectory with all her might. In fact, it is unlikely that Febus himself really wishes to proceed by negotiating with the king for a forced marriage with his daughter; what he wants is to touch the princess's heart, and he approaches this goal in slightly more roundabout fashion. The four giants that Febus kills in the mountains have no grievance against him, nor does he with them. This is an act carried out solely as service to the princess, and done at her request. In giving her the death of giants as a gift, the hero hopes to implicate her in a reciprocal exchange whereby she will, in turn, give him the gift of love. One model, in other words, posits the primary relationship as being between rival warriors; the other one posits the primary relationship as being between lover and lady.

In both of the above scenarios, giants are an expendable third party. We saw in chapter 1 that giants, racially stigmatized through an association with the animal kingdom as beasts of prey in human form, are absorbed into the "sacrifice carnivore" identified by Derrida as a founding basis for human subjectivity. Though giants are never eaten by humans, their potential capacity to eat human flesh and their generally violent behavior place them, along with fully nonhuman animals, in the category of creatures that must be eliminated in the establishment of human dominion over the natural world. They can also be sacrificial victims of a different sort when they are used as proxies in military or erotic conflicts in which the giants themselves are not even players. On the one hand, the two giant brothers are a surrogate for the king in what is now a kind of "cold war" with Febus, their public deaths a means by which the hero stages both his unstoppable force and his refusal to abandon the fight. And on another level, their deaths are a substitute for Febus's own death: thwarting the king's desire for his demise, Febus aggressively usurps the giants' place as the kingdom's most formidable warrior. Similarly, the four giant brothers are a surrogate adversary in Febus's ongoing erotic sparring with the princess, as though in defeating them he could vanquish her resistance. What Febus fails to realize, however, is that, like her father, the princess never actually wanted to see the giants killed: what she desired was Febus's own death. In refusing her this ultimate gift and offering instead the deaths of giants, Febus thwarts the princess's desire just as surely as he does that of her father. And it is only when he finally does give her the gift of death—his own death— that she is willing to reciprocate by giving him her love.

In mediating these fatal relations of hostile and amorous desire, the giants ultimately serve the fundamental purpose of identifying Febus as one who is truly peerless. As is explained by his son, who appears in the story as an old man tending his father's grave: "Il fu homme de si estrange force que tant com il vesqui, il ne pout onques trouver home qui contre lui peüst durer de force. . . . Celui fu bien hom sans per, car il n'ot nul pareill el monde ne de force ne de chevalerie tant com il vesqui" (90; He was a man of such amazing strength that as long as he lived, he could never find any man who could withstand him. . . . He was indeed a man without peer, for there was no one like him in the world, in terms of strength and chivalry, as long as he lived). In the conventional romance paradigm, combat with giants affords a knight access to the Absolute. Giants, the ultimate enemy, test his bodily prowess and martial skills to the fullest possible extent. They enable a release of violence and passion so extreme that it must be reined in and renounced when the battle is over if the knight is to retain the crucial dimension of chivalric discipline and courtly decorum that distinguishes him from giants, beasts, and brigands. This experience of reciprocal force and the emotions it unleashes—an aspect of what Roland Greene calls "requitedness" in his study of desire in the context of colonial expansion—is something Febus never achieves.[32] The giants that he fights regard him with contempt, irritation, or indifference, but never with the admiration or fear accorded by giants to their opponents in protracted battles: he kills them so quickly that there is no actual battle at all, and often no time even for them to react in any way. Turning again to René Girard, we are reminded of the profound relationship between violence and desire in terms that are strikingly apt to Febus's trajectory: "La violence devient le signifiant du désirable absolu, de l'auto-suffisance divine, de la 'belle totalité' qui ne paraîtrait plus telle si elle cessait d'être impénétrable et inaccessible. Le sujet adore cette violence et il la hait; il cherche à la maîtriser par la violence. . . . Si par hasard il triomphe d'elle, le prestige dont elle jouit va bientôt se dissiper; il lui faudra chercher ailleurs, une violence plus violente encore, un obstacle vraiment infranchissable."[33] As pagan armies and clusters of giants fail to gratify his desire for the Absolute, Febus finally meets his match in the resistance of the princess. Perhaps for this reason alone, her value as an object of desire remains untarnished; but when he is finally trapped in the giants' grotto, unable to pursue either his courtship or his program of military conquest, Febus is left with nowhere to go. His only possible experience of an unconquerable Absolute at this point is death; and, as we have seen, it is this final gesture that elicits a reciprocal gesture on the part of the princess, as though she, too, could love only that which she can never have—and as though she too must ultimately express that love through death. Impervious to exploits, enticements, or pressure of any kind, the princess is as singular as the hero himself in her utter self-possession, manifested in her ability to invest her own death fully with the meaning that she wishes it to have. And it is only as two singularities that she and Febus can realize their relationship. After their fleeting union—"Quant ele l'ot embrachié, il ne demoura puis grantiment que il morut entre les bras de la damoisele" (146; When she had embraced him, it wasn't very long before he died in the damsel's arms)—the lovers are forever divided by the impenetrable barrier of death. Or to put it differently, we might say that they are paradoxically conjoined through a mirrored experience of solitary desire and yearning for an absent and untouchable beloved. Perhaps this is the only form of true requitedness that so peerless an individual as Febus could ever attain. In a distant mountain grotto, the absolutism of giants is supplanted by the absolutism of desire unto death.

The Tables Turned: The Knight as Object of Desire

The Saracen princess and the beautiful giantess allow for the articulation of desire across a seemingly unbridgeable divide, as an exotic foreign culture splits along gender lines. Giantess and Saracen alike are imagined as emotionally volatile, physically powerful, and exotically beautiful creatures whose desire is naturally (if sometimes belatedly) enflamed by European manhood, and who are ultimately willing to sacrifice family, culture, and religion out of love for a foreign knight. The relative success of their adaptation, combined with remaining traces of otherness, marks their role as points of vulnerability in an alien race or culture that must inevitably give way before the spread of Christian or proto-Christian hegemony. Violent warfare with truly formidable male antagonists unfolds in tandem with stories of feminine love, conversion, and assimilation, adding subjective depth and complexity to the clash of Christian and non-Christian, West and East, human and giant. The story of Febus in *Guiron le courtois* presents the other side of the coin: here the almost disappointingly easy conquest of a land whose male defenders put up no genuine resistance whatsoever is balanced by the fierce resistance of a beautiful but unattainable maiden. But exotic love affairs are not always initiated by the knights themselves and thus are not always quite so straightforward in providing a forum for the staging of Western chivalric supremacy. Sometimes the knight is taken by surprise in becoming the object of giant or Saracen desire, and narratives of this kind allow a different perspective on the element of danger and violence that colors "interracial" or cross-cultural love and the mix of desire, antagonism, and anxiety that it entails.

In the prose *Tristan*, the knight Luce, son of the king of Leonois, is abducted by a giant known to live entirely on human flesh; but the giant's interest in Luce has nothing to do with food. Instead, he introduces the knight to his daughter, "une demoiselle de merveilleuse biauté, qui n'avoit plus d'aaige que quinze anz" (*PT*[C], 1:70; a damsel of marvelous beauty, who was no more than fifteen years old). The young giantess, it turns out, is in love with Luce—so much so, in fact, that "se fust ja ocise deus foiz ou trois por ce qu'ele ne vos pooit avoir" (1:70; she already tried to kill herself two or three times because she could not have you). Beautiful and emotionally vulnerable, but also headstrong and highly manipulative, the girl is a pampered and much prized love object; the giant explains that she is "la riens ou monde que je plus aime" (1:70; the thing I love most in all the world) and that he would not consent to give her away were it not for the extremity of her love and its mortal grip on her heart. Even paternal love can have a ferocious dimension in the world of giants; Galotine's father intended to marry her, and the giant in *Tristan* reveals in a later episode that he has already both raped and eaten another of his daughters. The giantess's love for Luce, in other words, has placed the prince in a position of mortal rivalry with her father that he could never have foreseen. Despite his jealous love, however, and despite his fondness for human flesh, the giant guarantees Luce's welfare as long as he accepts the proposal: "Se tu veus ceste prendre a feme, et creanter moi que tant com tu vivras d'autre n'acointeras, je te lerai vivre" (1:70; If you're willing to take her as wife, and swear to me that as long as you live you will take no other woman, I will let you live). In this passage the unstoppable libido of the giant—one who does not stand on ceremony in taking what he wants, and who clearly does plan to kill Luce if he refuses the marriage—coexists in a fascinating way with the more courtly, but still disturbingly potent, longings of the young giantess.

Sarah Kay has outlined the ironies and ambiguities that typically accompany the "Saracen Princess" motif in the *chanson de geste* tradition.[34] The Frankish warriors who marry Saracen princesses do not always do so on their own initiative or even of their own volition; rather, it is the princess's desire that drives the narrative, leading Kay to conclude that "if the Saracen princess is the product of a male fantasy, then, it is as much one of anxiety as of wish-fulfilment."[35] The two unions with giantesses that we have seen—Clamidés and Galotine, Luce and the giant's daughter—do not correspond precisely to the epic model, but the fraught mixture of desire and anxiety is powerful nonetheless. As we have seen, Luce's acceptance of marriage to the giantess is his only means of escaping instant death, and only the death of the giant can release him from this prison. The giant offers his daughter freely as a gift; but as Kay notes, "The ambiguity of the gift is framed by the ever-present threat of violence.... You deal simultaneously in intimacy and rivalry, alliance and oppression."[36] If on the one hand the giant requires nothing in exchange for his daughter—no political alliance, no feudal obligations, no reciprocal gift of a woman from Luce's family—it could also be said that the price he exacts is absolute: Luce's very life as he has known it up to that point. One might even see the arrangement as one in which the giant gives Luce the gift of life—saving him from execution and sparing him from becoming a giant's meal—at the price of agreeing to serve forever after as the husband of a giantess and companion to her father. Severed from all aspects of his identity as knight and prince in the kingdom of Leonois, Luce now exists in a limbo of erotic enjoyment tinged with the ever-present specter of violent death.

As we shall see in chapter 4, it is only when the giant is killed by another adventuring knight that Luce is free to return to his previous life; and like Galotine or Floripas, the giantess soon recovers from the shock of her father's death when Luce's father, King Pelias, assures her that she will be well provided for as his daughter-in-law. The giantess originally chose death by suicide as the means of expressing the absolutism of her love for a knight that she thought could never be hers. Luce might be said to have responded—if not entirely by choice—by giving her his death in symbolic form. Renouncing his life as prince, he agrees to live among giants, with a father-in-law who could still potentially decide to use both him and his bride as a meal; and in the end she reciprocates by renouncing her life as a giantess to live at court, in the company of those for whom a giant is a mortal enemy. As with Febus and his pagan princess, a love so impossible must be consecrated by an absolute desire that does not stop short even of death. Unlike the latter couple, however, Luce and the giantess can be reincorporated into the feudal world as the giant is eliminated and Luce's father regains his authoritative position. A marriage that began with the giant kidnapping Luce and giving him to the giantess is resolved when the king, in effect, authorizes the marriage by accepting the giantess himself and giving her to Luce. And the giantess, who had originally driven the narrative forward with the force of her desire, now acquiesces to the priorities of her husband and father-in-law, adapting to her new role in their world as she ceases grieving for her father. To invoke once again the model of early modern colonial culture, the newly submissive giantess illustrates Nocentelli's model of "domestic heterosexuality as an adequate compensation for powerlessness and objectification."[37]

Clamidés's marriage to Galotine is similarly inscribed in two overlapping but contradictory contexts. On the one hand, the local residents call for their liberator to marry the giant's daughter, heiress to the island, and Lyonnel exercises his feudal rights in bestowing this prize on his faithful squire in compensation for services rendered. On the other hand, however, the marriage is one of coercion, offered to Galotine's mother as compensation for a serious transgression against the family honor;

we must recall that she had been on the point of killing Clamidés for seducing her daughter before Lyonnel intervened. One model empowers Clamidés with an idealized chivalric masculinity as victor, husband, and lord; the other disempowers him as little more than tribute paid by a knight to a wrathful giantess. Clamidés's initial reaction, indeed, suggests the latter interpretation more strongly than the former. When the giantess makes her proposal, "Il baissa le menton et fut tout honteux et ne dist mot" (*Perce/II*, 1:362; He lowered his head and was completely ashamed, and said nothing); and when Lyonnel departs, leaving the newly minted lord with his child bride, "S'en retourna Clamidés tout larmoiant pour le department de son seigneur qu'il amoit de bon amour" (1:364; Clamidés went back weeping because of the departure of his lord, whom he loved truly). Clamidés does make the best of his situation. He attempts to redefine the marriage from the second model described above to the first, stating that he will not marry the giantess unless he is knighted by Lyonnel. With this move, he makes the entire contract contingent on his own consent; and linking the marriage to a knighthood reinforces the idea that Galotine is a reward being given to him, rather the other way around.[38] But the fact remains that for both Clamidés and Luce the close association of love and death is irrevocably skewed away from the model that we find in courtly lyric or in the career of Febus. For the latter, death was the ultimate means of consummating his desire, a desire beyond all other desires—a consummation more perfect and absolute even than the killing of giants, or sexual union with the beloved—and one that he freely accepted. Indeed, it was the only thing he could give his beloved that she truly wanted.

    For Clamidés or Luce, the driving force of desire emanates in a double focus from the giantess and her mother or father—erotic in her case, lethal in theirs—and it is only in acquiescing to the damsel's desire that he can save himself from death. Becoming the object of giant desire and mercy may confer a certain singularity on the chivalric subject thus favored. But it is not quite the same as the singularity won by the hero who sidesteps death by bringing about that of the giant in his place—one whose peerlessness is staged in spectacular exploits that express his uncompromising purity as subject, not object, of desire. Even while boasting to Perceforest of his wife's sterling character, Clamidés cannot help acknowledging the disconcerting infantilization he experiences as the husband of a giantess. The adoring love of the giantess bride cuts both ways, leading her to obey her husband and accept his moral and religious instruction, but also moving her to carry him around like a baby—behavior that might lead one to wonder just who is really obeying whom in this marriage. And yet this entire narrative trajectory was launched because of Clamidés's desire for Galotine and his adult exploitation of her childish innocence. The giantess edges her lover uncomfortably close to a literalization of the courtly trope of the man as humble servant and victim of the all-powerful lady; her power over him is supposed to be a construct serving to enhance his masculine prowess, not a bodily reality. Gender roles begin to blur as love runs up against giants' proclivity for simply taking what they want, with little concept of sublimation or deferral. The question of who is controlling the narrative, and who has power over whom, is complicated anew with each turn of the plot.

Exotic Brides and Intractable Difference: The Problem of Miscegenation

A giantess is never entirely straightforward as a marriage partner; and sometimes she is unsuitable in the extreme. We have seen that the different narrative strategies and ideological focus of *chansons de geste* foster a somewhat different use of giants, and this more explicit framework of militant Christianity enables the giantess and the Saracen princess to be contrasted as potential brides of alien, non-Christian background. In *Huon de Bordeaux*, as noted in chapter 2, the giant Agrapart—blood kin to every devil in hell—offers to give Huon his sister in marriage if Huon renounces the combat and converts to the giant's religion:

> Car lai ton Dieu et a ma loy te prant,
> Je te donrait et terre et chaissement;
> Si en vanrait o moy en Orïant,
> S'avrais la marche de ci qu'an Bocidant,
> Si te donrait ung moult riche presant:
> Ma suer germainne, noir est comme errement.
> Grandre est de moy, si ait ung piet de dant.[39]

[Leave your God and take mine, I will give you land and fiefs; if you come with me to the Orient, you will have the territories all the way to Bocidant, and I will give you a very rich gift: my own sister, who is as black as can be. She is bigger than me, and has teeth a foot long.]

On the one hand, this is a conventional model of feudal marriage, in which two knights develop a mutual admiration through combat and settle into an alliance, sealed by the marriage of one to the sister or daughter of the other. But marriage with the giantess would entail both displacement from France to the non-Christian "Orient" and alliance with a demonic lineage. Huon wants no part of such a marriage, declaring, "Je ne vien mie pour tel mariement" (v. 6740; I didn't come to make a marriage like that). In fact, he has already pledged himself to the Saracen princess Esclarmonde, who adheres to the typical Crusade narrative motif. Having fallen in love with him when he forcibly kissed her three times—one of the tasks imposed by Charlemagne—she converts to Christianity, cares for him in her father's prison, and engineers his release when a champion is needed to fight Agrapart; the two are eventually married. Huon initially resists her advances, protesting that "Sairaisine estez, ne vous poroie amer" (v. 6045; you are a Saracen and I could never love you) and swearing that he would rather spend the rest of his life in prison than "a vous corpz adeser" (v. 6051; to have carnal relations with you). When Esclarmonde responds by starving her prisoner, however, Huon is forced to change his tune: "Se je dobvoie tous lez jour d'ui flambeir / Deden Ynfer en la chartre mortelz, / Si ferait je toute vous vollanteit" (vv. 6085–87; If I had to burn in the mortal prison of hell forever, I would nonetheless do your bidding). Huon finds himself in a position somewhat similar to that of Luce or Clamidés in the giant's lair. The alternatives are love or death, but not because the driving force of his own love will culminate in the Absolute of death; rather, it is the love of the other for him that, if he accepts it, can shield him from an otherwise inevitable death by starvation or execution.

Again, it is often the Saracen princess who takes control of the story line, even in cases where the Christian knight may originally have been the one who sought her out.[40] While acknowledging the argument developed by Kinoshita and others—that the princess's desire is "an ironic cover over the narrator's determination for his hero to achieve sexual as well as military victory over the Saracens"—Kay sees the princess's power as a genuine threat to Frankish male control, concluding that "although the self-interest of the Franks may ironize the desire of the Saracen princess, the derision, autonomy, and narrative authority of the Saracen princesses can also be seen as ironizing the pretensions of male hegemony."[41] Esclarmonde illustrates Kay's argument, as it is definitely she who drives the narrative and sets its terms. But the potentially emasculating qualities of the powerful Saracen woman are to some extent allayed through juxtaposition with the truly horrific prospect of the giantess bride, just as the emir, for all his hostility to Christianity and his autocratic rule, is a less grotesque enemy than the giant. Though the emir must die, his daughter at least emerges as a positive remnant: virtuous, devoted to Huon and to the French cause, and ultimately a Christian convert. The giants, in contrast, have no redeemable potential, and any alliance formed with this family would be founded on a mortal sin: commerce not simply with an infidel but with the spawn of the devil himself. Rather like the *Pseudo-Turpin Chronicle*, with its juxtaposition of the Saracen king and his giant champion, *Huon de Bordeaux* presents Saracen culture as having two faces. One is human, susceptible at least in part to negotiation, conversion, political alliance, love, and marriage; one is giant, with whom no engagement is possible other than aggressive verbal sparring and mortal combat. The opposition here is not between giant and giantess but between giant and human within the Saracen world; but in both cases the contrast provides complementary frames of reference within which Christian chivalric masculinity can be defined.

Writing of the Petrarchan tradition in sixteenth-century Europe and its relationship to the overarching context of global exploration and colonization, Roland Greene sees in these colonizers and explorers an "urge to have it both ways: they want to maintain their privileged, culturally particular standpoints but also to step away from those standpoints and experience otherness, in their lovers or themselves."[42] Similar fantasies are supported by the knights who variously fight, love, and are loved by both giants and Saracens in medieval epic and romance. Febus, for example, consciously makes himself a feared and unwanted other in pagan Britain, and the narrative invites us to see him this way, first through the eyes of the pagan kings and their advisers, then even more explicitly through the eyes of both the surviving king and the princess—even as it also enshrines him as unequaled hero and lover. As the centerpiece in a carefully tended mountaintop shrine, Febus ultimately "lives on" as a timeless icon of Arthurian cultural values and a vehicle for chivalric and courtly ideology. Luce becomes a much-desired other in the world of giants, a place characterized by riddling discourse, erotic pleasures, and the horrific violence of incest and cannibalism; he later returns to court bringing with him a trace of that otherness in the form of a giantess bride. These figures, as well as Lyonnel and others, illustrate Michael Uebel's assertion that "becoming the complete stranger is . . . a process of self-fashioning that involves symbolic death and rebirth."[43] The tale of Galotine allows the other to be absorbed into Arthurian history and genealogy, in a move that simultaneously domesticates the giant while inflecting a figure as familiar as Sir Gawain with a disturbingly alien dimension. But in addition to opening up new possibilities for the reinvention of the self, this flirtatious dance with otherness carries its risks.[44] Foreign brides can never be fully excised from their native cultures and families, which continue in at least some sense to define them even as the bride's assimilation may also redefine those family origins. And sometimes the baggage attached to an exotic bride proves insurmountable; this is the case with a giantess bride in *Lancelot*, mother of the evil giant Maudit.

At the time of Uterpendragon, we are told, there is a region inhabited exclusively by giants who live a bestial existence and kill anyone who strays into their territory. When Arthur comes to power he accordingly sets out to civilize the area and has killed all of the giants when he comes upon "une damoisele reposte, fille d'un jaiant, et estoit de grant biauté et tenoit entre ses braz un petit anfant qui ses filz estoit, et ele . . . n'avoit mie plus de .XV. anz" (a damsel hiding, the daughter of a giant, and she was very beautiful, and was holding in her arms a little baby who was her son, and she . . . was no more than fifteen years old).[45] Arthur is about to kill her as well when a knight appears and pleads for her life. Arthur accordingly grants him the giantess as his wife along with the territory in question and provides settlers to populate it. As far as one can tell, the giantess is committed to her marriage and to maintaining at least some degree of civilized order, attempting to discipline her son's worst offenses; but inevitably, the boy grows up to be a giant. As a teenager he is already more powerful than any knight in his father's lands. When his stepfather one day strikes him in anger, the young giant kills him; and "Quant la mere vit ce, si courut sus a son fil et il trest s'espee, si occist sa mere" (*PLanc*, 4:252; When the mother saw that, she ran at her son and he drew his sword and killed his mother). Taking over his family estates, the giant establishes a reign of terror across the region that earns him the name "Maudit." An aristocratic lady that he abducts imposes as a condition of her love that he must not leave the castle unless it is necessary to protect his territory or defend his honor. But the giant finds a ruse that permits him to escape. Setting up a pavilion in the forest, he hangs his shield on a tree and places his helmet and sword in a bed, with the stipulation that if any passing knight should knock the shield to the ground, the giant's honor is affronted and the perpetrator must be punished. The shield is ultimately dislodged and the helmet and sword are removed by Yvain, who is unaware of their significance and is tricked by a wicked old woman. Thus released from his enforced domesticity, Maudit embarks on a rampage, wreaking a terrible vengeance on anyone he encounters—men, women, and children—until he is finally slain by Bohort. As so often, the giantess is beautiful and blameless, but here she carries with her a fatal relic of her savage origins. We have already seen that the descendants of the courtly Galotine sometimes show signs of rebellious autonomy, arrogance, or brutality, as if reverting to their giant ancestry; here the disaster is far more immediate. Not only, then, can the giantess as romance heroine be compromised by a hint of androgyny that prevents her from conforming seamlessly to courtly femininity; but also, as mother, she is the means by which a new generation of giants can rise again to renew the relentless assault on civilization.

The story of Maudit explores the problem of failed assimilation, resulting in a simultaneous presence of cultural refinement and gratuitous cruelty.[46] And his liaison with the lady frames this question in a particular way. Can a giant also be a lover? Giants are certainly sexual, but are they capable of maintaining an erotic relationship—one characterized by love and the pleasurable pain of desire? And what is the effect on a lady who becomes the object of a giant's attentions? We have seen the complexities of the giant combatant and the giantess bride as points around which masculine chivalric identity is both questioned and constructed. It is equally illuminating to examine the dynamic when this aggressive violence is refocused in the confrontation of giant and courtly lady.

*The Giant and the Lady:
Sexual Violence and the Violence of Love*

As a general rule, a giant's touch is as lethal to ladies as it is to knights. Whereas the latter are killed in a combat of unimaginable fury, the former meet their death through an equally horrific sexual violence. The wife of the Golden-Haired Giant laments her husband's sexual predations against the women of the island, explaining that "il les atourne telles que elles meurent, car elles ne sont pas de grandeur pour le recepvoir" (*Perce/II*, 1:348; he treats them so badly that they die, for they are not big enough to receive him). Contact with this particular giant, at least, literalizes the trope of sexual consummation as death in the most gruesome way possible. Though the giant is unscathed—neither eroticism nor a need for reciprocal love being concepts that apply to him—the lady is given a bodily experience that, combining sexual transport with the deadly violence of combat, takes her beyond all possibility of pleasure or desire, into the Absolute of death. Whether it is the "delictz" that he finds in eating human flesh (1:337) or the "luxure" and "voulentez" that he gratifies in raping women (1:348), the Golden-Haired Giant's appetites are such as to be utterly overpowering for any human adversary other than Lyonnel himself. His homicidal sexuality and the cannibalism that complements it are two parallel forms of behavior through which the giant violates the boundaries of the person and robs his human victims of their very selves.

The Giant of Mont-St-Michel, as depicted by Geoffrey of Monmouth, also combines these two forms of aggression—one directed at women, and one at men—in his ravishment of Helena, his rape of her old nurse, and his practice of devouring the knights who attack him in an effort to rescue the women. Interestingly, the giant does not eat Helena herself, who is given a proper burial by her nurse; these two forms of lethal bodily union are distinctly separated into heterosexual rape and homosocial cannibalism.[47] Helena's death, however, is framed somewhat differently from that of the unfortunate victims of Golden-Hair: her death arose not from being battered and injured by the giant's bodily violence but as a response to the very idea of rape by a giant, and a means of avoiding its trauma. As her nurse explains, "Recepto infra tenerrimum pectus timore dum eam nefandus ille amplecteretur, uitam diuturniori luce dignam finiuit" (She felt in her most tender heart such terror at his wicked embraces that she breathed her last).[48] Lest one think that this fear might have arisen during the experience itself, the nurse specifies that the giant "illam . . . foedo coitu suo deturpare nequiuit" (could not inflict his foul desires on her).[49] A similar fate befalls the woman abducted by Holland in *Perceforest*: confronted with a forced marriage to the giant, she "en print telle paour qu'elle en morut a grant meschief" (*Perce/IV*, 1:122; was so terrified that she died a miserable death). These women are able to preserve their integrity as subjects by choosing death over sexual violation. Like the virgin martyrs, they attain a purity and a singularity that makes them the equal of romance heroes and heroines who die of lost or unrequited love. Indeed, their death is an active, even an aggressive gesture: no less surely than a hero like Lyonnel, Febus, or Arthur, these ladies have put up an absolute resistance to the giant. Though they would not be capable of killing him, they have been capable of ensuring that, at least in their case, his lust was unfulfilled.

On rare occasions, however, the marriage or cohabitation of a giant and a lady may be possible, at least for a time. Maudit's liaison with an aristocratic lady combines violent abduction with the discourse of love: having killed her husband and forcibly taken her to his castle, the giant "moult l'annora et la requist d'amors" (*PLanc*, 4:253; greatly honored her and asked for her love). When the lady retorts that she cannot possibly love someone so cruel, he appears to repent and to submit himself, like a humble courtly lover, to her wishes. In response to her remonstrations, "Il dist que qu'il avoit fait ça arrieres, il l'amanderoit de ci en avant" (4:253; He said that however he had behaved in the past, he would make up for it from then on), and he accepts her prohibition on leaving the castle for any reason other than to avenge his honor with seeming equanimity: "Je ferai ce que vos voldroiz" (4:253; I will do as you wish). The flimsy excuse that Maudit invents to release himself from domesticity, however, and the killing spree on which he then embarks, are hardly in keeping with the spirit of chivalric love service. Maudit interprets the lady's terms in the most literal possible way, transforming what should have been a metaphorical "prison of love" into actual imprisonment inside his own castle. Rather than benefiting from the improving effects of love or "domestic heterosexuality" as a means of perfecting self-discipline and channeling violence into socially useful forms, the giant knows only the two extremes of idle inactivity and all-out mayhem.

What the lady attempts to teach Maudit lies at the very core of chivalric culture—of civilization itself, as it is imagined in Arthurian romance—and might be summed up succinctly as the art of sublimation. In seeking a liaison with a lady, rather than simply raping her, Maudit discovers a concept foreign to what we might think of as "giant culture": in a word, desire, as opposed to unregulated bodily drives. The lady introduces him to the concept of love objects that cannot be taken by brute force because they depend on the willing recognition of an individual or collective other: that elusive quality of "requitedness," expressed in chivalric honor and reciprocal love. As the ultimate object of desire, requitedness cannot be achieved—cannot even be conceived of—without the corresponding experience of unrequitedness; and unrequitedness itself is a state that can be exploited within the confines of courtly culture for both pleasure and self-improvement. The deferral of desire, with its sharp yet delicious pain of longing, is the "refiner's fire" in which a knight is brought to ever greater heights of prowess and perfection. But this is something that a giant finds difficult to fathom. Up to this point, Maudit has reveled in the boundless drive toward violence, satiation, and death; if he never experienced the pleasure of resistance, reciprocal violence, or mutual love, it also never occurred to him to want those things. Only now, in his sudden and unexpected experience of *amors*, does he become aware of the possibility of either the requital or the refusal of desire. Initially submitting to his lady, confronted with the alien notion that power must be renounced as a means of gaining it back in different form, he struggles with the imperative to rein in his boundless energies.

The lady, then, gives Maudit an experience he has never had before: resistance that he cannot overcome. Until now he has led an easy existence of simple, unchallenged domination: having taken the homage of the local men, "Si les mist a servage et prenoit les damoiseles a force; et quant aucuns em parloit, si les occioit" (4:252; He reduced them to servitude and took the damsels by force; and if anyone spoke out, he killed them). He could certainly overpower and rape this lady, and we may well be meant to assume that he does just that; but he cannot command her love. For the first time he discovers limitations to his power and an object of desire that is not simply there to be taken. He now finds himself implicated in a relationship that is not just corporeal, in the sense of one body exploiting or consuming another. The relationship in which the lady enmeshes him has a crucial dimension of subjectivity, in which two singular beings shape, and are shaped by, one another in mutual desire, partial requital, and an inevitable measure of unrequitedness as desire can never be absolutely fulfilled. In some ways his trajectory parallels that of Febus: a figure of peerless masculine prowess, undefeated and undefeatable in battle, finally meets his match in the form of a resistant lady; and his self-refashioning through this new experience of desire will climax in the Absolute of death. But where Febus initially sought to transpose his erotic desire into ever-escalating feats of homosocial violence, Maudit is told from the start that he must effect a different sort of sublimation, in which it is the desire for violence—the orgiastic *jouissance* of pillage and murder—that must be deferred. A knight's love for a lady may impel him into combat with giants; but it does not follow that a giant's love will impel him into combat with knights. Or perhaps, more accurately, the constraining force of love will indeed force him to channel his energies, not into the all-out massacre of helpless, unarmed victims, but precisely into the ordered and regulated format of combat with an armed and worthy opponent.

Importantly, it is in this new context that the giant finally has his first (and only) experience of resistance in battle. Up to now no one could stand against him; by the time he was knighted at the age of fifteen, "cil fu de tel force qu'il ne trouvoit chevalier armé si pesant qu'il ne troussast sor son col si legierement com l'an feist .I. petit anfant" (4:252; he was so strong that he never found an armed knight so heavy that he could not carry him over his shoulder as easily as one would a small child). Bohort, however, is an opponent of exceptional prowess, and he succeeds in knocking the giant's helmet from his head in a deadly replay of the gesture carried out by Yvain in the giant's forest pavilion. Removing the helmet and sword and knocking his shield to the ground was only a symbolic attack on the giant, and as such it was one that carried no actual danger—if anything, it was a welcome opportunity for the giant to unleash his pent-up violence on the pretense of avenging his honor. But Bohort now makes that threat exceedingly real; and "Li jaianz . . . n'a mie petit de paor, car moult est cil preuz a cui il se combat, si com il cuide vraiement" (5:21; The giant . . . feels no small fear, for he truly thinks that the one he is fighting has great prowess). This new experience of fear—an emotion he has so often inspired in others but never received in return—is, in a sense, the gift that the lady has given him, as his efforts to comply with her conditions afford him a kind of passionate transport and bodily extreme hitherto unknown.

The chronic inability of knights to resist adventure ensured from the start that, sooner or later, someone would accept the challenge of dislodging Maudit's exposed shield and thereby release him from his "prison." In this sense, the giant's ploy exploits the very principles of knightly valor, and the perhaps uncomfortable truth that violent conflict is every bit as integral to a knight's way of life as it is to that of a giant. Initially, he seems to have found a way of undermining the chivalric values that the lady struggles to impose. In fact, however, the giant's plan has the unintended consequence of reframing his habitual behavior. The rampage unleashed by Yvain's unwitting challenge is no longer simply an end in itself, the *jouissance* of absolute mayhem that has always characterized the giant's life. Rather, it takes place in the context of an altercation with a specific adversary, and Yvain defines the situation very explicitly as such in the message he sends the giant once he understands what he has done: "Si li diras que Yvain, li filz au roi Urien, a abatu son escu en despit de lui ne ne soit pas si vilains que il a cels de ceanz se preingne ne de cest païs, ainz viengne combatre a lui, s'il ose" (4:256; You will tell him that Yvain, son of King Urien, knocked down his shield in an affront to him, nor should he be so uncouth as to attack his intimates or landspeople, but let him come fight Yvain, if he dares). Needless to say, this concept of limiting one's vengeance to the particular knight responsible for the affront is foreign to a giant. Maudit in fact "ne fine de tuer touz cels que il ataint" (4:259–60; does not desist from killing everyone he finds); intoxicated with the thrill of bloodlust, the giant "se rit del mal qu'il a fait" (4:259; rejoices at the evil he has done). Whether he understands it or not, however, the giant is now embroiled in conflict with a knight of the Round Table whose companions are sworn to support his cause; and combat with Maudit soon becomes a collective object of chivalric desire. Yvain desperately pursues the rampaging giant in the hope of fighting him; as other knights learn of the situation, Bohort tricks Lancelot into granting him the privilege of fighting the giant, while Lancelot attempts to reclaim the mission for himself (5:18–19). And being now implicated in the narrative of chivalric quest and combat, Maudit is forced into the only role possible for a giant: that of being killed by an Arthurian hero. A giant cannot, it seems, achieve the elusive prizes of love and honor, both of which can be sought only indirectly, through the pursuit of other goals temporarily substituted for the real thing. Indeed, a giant's only viable role may be as the means by which these much-prized qualities are won by the knights who target him as the ultimate proving ground for their own chivalric prowess.

There is another dimension to the erotics of this surprisingly complex episode. We have seen that Maudit's final burst of fury is unleashed because of Yvain's symbolic challenge in the forest pavilion. But Yvain does not commit this act on a simple whim. While riding through the forest, he encounters an old woman mistreating a dwarf; when he demands that she stop, she promises to do so on condition that he pledge to do whatever she asks in return. Sizing him up, "Ele le voit bel chevalier et bien fait de vis" (4:243; She sees him to be a handsome knight with a comely face) and asks him to give her a kiss. But seeing her to be "laide et si froncie que nule plus" (4:244; ugly and as wrinkled as anyone could be), Yvain retorts that he cannot possibly do that; it is only when the old woman taunts him for breaking his word, threatening to shame him by spreading the rumor of his disloyalty, that he reluctantly offers to go through with it. At this point the woman offers an alternative. Noting that "del baisier n'avez vos mie trop grant talant" (4:245; you don't have much desire for the kiss), she points out a nearby pavilion and asks him to knock down the shield hanging in front of it, and to give her the sword and helmet inside. Relieved, Yvain brushes off the dwarf's frantic warnings and carries out her request, with the dire consequences that we have just seen. The old woman, in other words, is aroused by Yvain's male charisma; but judging that a kiss extracted by force may not provide much erotic titillation, she settles for a different form of passion and catharsis: the universal destruction meted out by an angry giant. Alternatively—or additionally—she may be exacting vengeance for Yvain's sexual repudiation by imposing a different, more extreme bodily ordeal. Either way, the giant, chafing under the constraints of love imposed by a noble lady, is aided and abetted by a villainous old woman inflamed by desire for a royal knight.

The old woman—an icon of lechery and corruption in medieval literature, and the very antithesis of erotic appeal—is thus the implicit partner of the giant in unleashing an orgy of unspeakable destruction, designed to culminate in the bodily mortification and death of the knight. Yvain and the giant's unfortunate wife are the other couple in this complicated foursome, as members of the courtly world targeted by the unwanted and destructive desire of one who, by definition, is beyond love. This somewhat bizarre framework sets up a parodic reading of the ostensibly serious tale of Maudit. Yvain is pitted against a giant by a lady, not as a means of winning her love, but as a means of avoiding it: conflict with a giant here is quite literally a substitution for sexual contact on his part, and a ploy to send the knight to his death on hers. It is the giant himself who sallies forth in an even darker travesty of love service. Once again the combat is not a sublimation but a substitution for love, as the giant abandons his efforts at courtly gallantry to indulge his lust for violence. Though the giant's love for a courtly lady does ultimately culminate in death, this is not an expression of the absolute quality of his passion, or of its sublimation into bodily mortification, but only the natural result of his impatience with sublimation of any kind and his incomprehension of love as selfless devotion. And for his part, Yvain is not even allowed the satisfaction of killing the giant. First the giant is substituted for the lady as the malevolent other that he must face in bodily conflict; then Yvain himself is replaced by another knight.

The only character who truly touches the Absolute in this tale of misdirected and thwarted desire is Bohort, who comes through the ultimate violence of combat with a giant to bask in its aftermath of universal rejoicing. As the grateful inhabitants tell Bohort: "Si en avez tele honor conquise que jamais hom n'en orra parler qui plus ne vos an redout a touz les jorz de vostre vie" (5:24; You have won such honor that never will anyone hear of it who will not revere you for it all the days of your life). A knight's love for a giantess, a giant's love for a lady, an old woman's lust for a knight: these impossible pairings interact to warp the conventional paradigms of violence, sublimation, and desire beyond all recognition, with results both comic and horrific. The giant does have a sense of unrequited desire, and a wish to be the object of reciprocal desire; but the result is a parodic distortion of courtly subjectivity. A similarly comic treatment of giant love—together with a fairy's demands on her lover, and a skeptical view of the Absolute as a feature of either love or combat—occurs in the *Conte du Papegau*.

Giants, Fairies, and the Comic Distortion of Love Service in the Conte du Papegau

The marriage of a giant and a lady also features in *Papegau*, where the Chevalier Jayant tells Arthur that "son pere estoit ung jayant, qui despucella sa mere a force, et elle le preist a mary pour ce qu'il estoit si preus et si hardis et estoit moult cremus de la gent du païs" (his father was a giant who took his mother's virginity by force, and she married him because he was so bold and so valiant and was greatly feared by the people in that country).[50] Whether this is actually a free choice, motivated by anything other than fear of reprisal, is not clear. But with its comment that the giant was *preus* and *hardis* the text does raise the troubling possibility that, whatever her iconic value as the embodiment of Christian and courtly values, a noble lady may find herself irresistibly drawn to the compelling masculine potency of the giant. In this respect the giant's parents, though mentioned only in passing, contribute to the sardonic and often misogynistic humor that pervades the romance, in which aristocratic ideals of love and chivalry are lauded in some episodes, while being parodied and ironized in others. First of all, this episode is another example of the potential dangers of human-giant miscegenation: though she might perhaps have some civilizing influence on her husband, the lady is nonetheless the mother of giants, whose mimicry of chivalric honor and love service is troublingly coupled with an underlying savagery. Beyond this reminder of the dangers of liaisons across racial or cultural boundaries, the text uses marginal figures—the half-blood giants and a strong-minded fairy—to stage skewed and parodic versions of chivalric exploits and love service, which take on a troubling quality as they are appropriated by characters outside the courtly world.

We saw in chapter 1 that the Chevalier Jayant enters the *Papegau* as a suitor of the Duchess of Estregalles, vowing to prove his mettle by bringing her the right hand of the Chevalier du Papegau. When Arthur kills the giant in the ensuing combat, his brother, Jayant Redoubté de la Roche Secure (Fearsome Giant of the Solid Rock), seeks vengeance by challenging Arthur to combat; but when he sees that Arthur is winning, he surrenders and the two knights arrive at an amicable truce. Nonetheless, Chevalier Redoubté has not gotten over his anger and decides to punish the duchess by pretending to have brought the grisly token and asking her to reach out the window for it, intending to cut off her arm when she does so. When she instead sends one of her ladies, the giant settles for cutting off that woman's arm—as if individual women cannot really be distinguished one from another—with the furious cry: "Ha maulvaise chose . . . que Dieu a faite pour destruire bonté et valeur et pour acroistre mal et jour et nuyt, pour vous ay je perdu le meilleur frere qu'oncques nulx homs peust avoir" (176; Oh wicked creature . . . created by God to destroy goodness and worth and to increase evil night and day, because of you I have lost the best brother that any man could ever have). This act in turn sparks a long and bloody war between his people and hers.

There is more than a hint of giantesque brutality here: not only was the injury inflicted on a lady with no direct connection to the original agreement, but even the duchess had never actually asked for Arthur's severed hand. All she had done was to announce a tournament, with the intention of marrying the knight who proved himself the best; and when she heard that the Chevalier du Papegau was occupied in another adventure, she put the tournament off for a month in the hope that he would be able to participate. The other knights were disappointed but accepted her decision; the Chevalier Jayant, however, took the added step of telling her that he was undefeated and certain of victory, and that she should grant him her love at once without waiting for the tournament—already a breach of custom. The lady replied that she would grant him her love—"Je vous octroy m'amour" (160)—if he could win a joust against the Chevalier du Papegau, reputed to be the best knight in the world. It was the giant who, eagerly accepting this offer, transformed the promise into one of typical giant excess by adding that "vous appourteray sa main destre par congnoissance de bataille" (160; I will bring you his right hand as proof of the battle). The Chevalier Jayant's challenge to Arthur, in turn, reveals a motivation that is more economic than amorous: "Il luy dist qu'il avoit promis a une dame a porter sa main destre, qui luy avoit dit que, s'il le faisoit, elle le prendroit a mary et luy donroit toute sa terre" (164; He told him that he had promised a lady to bring her his right hand, who had said that if he did that, she would marry him and give him all her land). The giant, in his enthusiastic effort to win a bride, has transformed the very concept of love service and chivalric honor. For him, the idea of a symbolic display of prowess and military potential within the strictly codified parameters of a tournament holds no purchase; what he understands is a much more basic notion of violent aggression.[51] Though Arthur has shown no interest in marrying the lady in question, the Chevalier Jayant targets him as a rival who must be eliminated, or at least neutralized, in the quest for fame, glory, and a lucrative marriage. That his goals are material rather than amorous is further underscored at the giant's death. Far from welcoming death as a means of realizing his total devotion to the lady, the Chevalier Jayant regrets it as the result of self-deceiving pride and begs Arthur's forgiveness: "Si vous pry que vous me pardonnés ce que je me suys combatu a vous sans raison et a moult grant tort" (168; I beg you to pardon me for having fought you without reason, and very wrongly).

Chevalier Redoubté's rage at the duchess reflects a misogynistic interpretation of her original challenge as an unacceptable affront to male pride: merely to suggest that another knight could be more powerful is already to provoke deadly combat and to incite vengeance. Giants, it must be noted, are not good losers. One is reminded of Febus's athletic victory over the giant in *Guiron le courtois*. Though the competition was a purely recreational match taking place in the context of court festivities, the giant's brother is so outraged at this stain on the family honor that "il ne pot tant estre amesurés qu'il ne se levast en estant et prist s'espee et courut esroment sus Febus pour metre le a le mort" (132; he could not contain himself from getting to his feet and took his sword and charged at Febus intending to kill him). Here, as in the *Papegau*, giants demonstrate their inability to comprehend a staged or recreational violence—athletic matches and war games as opposed to actual combat and warfare—and their tendency to turn the former into the latter. This kind of absolutism reflects the biblical view of giants as lacking the rational capacity to place limits on violence. And it often figures in medieval literature as a feature that sets giants apart from their human counterparts, underpinning what we might (if anachronistically) think of as "giant culture."[52]

In all, the episode of the Chevalier Jayant explores the darkly comic distortions that result when giants attempt to fit themselves to chivalric and courtly conventions.[53] But it also brings out the potential for social disruption that pervades these same conventions, and the latent misogyny underlying the notion of chivalric love service. A knight may commit acts of violence and mayhem in an effort to win himself an advantageous marriage while disguising his self-serving motives under the cloak of love—a ploy that allows him to blame the woman, or any convenient lady attached to her court, if the plan backfires. And the very act of using a tournament to select a husband—a common romance motif—loses its courtly veneer. As the facade drops, we suddenly glimpse a custom that objectifies women as mere booty, to be won in destructive rivalry between men; one that encourages women to enjoy the spectacle of male violence, in which losers are shamed or even killed. Winners may not even bother to claim their prize: having killed the Chevalier Jayant in what the former viewed as a battle for marriage with the Duchess of Estregalles, Arthur continues on his way, showing no more interest in the lady than he had done before the altercation. The giant, with his incomprehension of symbolic gestures, poisons a well-established chivalric institution by unleashing all the violence and destructive potential that it was designed to contain: a desublimation in which desire fuels not selfless acts of prowess but aggressive acts of acquisition and self-aggrandizement.

If giants serve to comment on the dangerous pitfalls of chivalric masculinity, a fairy allows the author of the *Papegau* to explore excesses on the part of women, in an episode that acts as a pendant to the one described above. The "Fée en qui tout sagesse abonde" (Fairy in Whom All Wisdom Abounds), also known as the Dame aux Cheveux Blons (Blond-Haired Lady), emerges early in the text as the love interest that will engage Arthur for the rest of the narrative. After he has killed the monstrous Poisson Chevalier that was terrorizing her city, the fairy falls in love with him; and having extracted the promise that he will do whatever she commands, she blithely announces: "Je veux que vous soiés demain au tournoyement pour moy, et que vous m'y serviez pour le plus maulvais chevalier d'armes qui soit en tout le monde" (130; I want you to participate in tomorrow's tournament in my name, and for you to serve me as the worst knight there is in the whole world). This, of course, is a ploy familiar from Chrétien's *Chevalier de la charrete*, where Guenevere gives Lancelot a similar directive in the tournament at Noauz.[54] But Arthur is no Lancelot, prepared to obey his lady's commands no matter what the cost, capable of embracing shame if it is suffered in the name of love. And Arthur's dismay at her request lays bare the irrational and destructive potential of the absolute devotion that a figure like Guenevere demands. What already had a dimension of ironic comedy in its twelfth-century manifestation now explodes into disaster in a fully parodic replay of the motif. Arthur accepts that he is forced to make good on his promise, and at the tournament he is duly covered in shame. But that evening, incensed at the affront to his honor, he visits the fairy in her chamber; and when she offers to reward his compliance by giving him free access to her person, he erupts in anger. With a cry of "Maulvaise putain, plaine de toute maulvaistié" (140; wicked whore, full of every evil), he grabs her and "la traine par les tresses par toute la chambre, batant la et defoulant aux piez" (140; drags her around the room by the hair, beating her and kicking her). At her pleas for mercy, he points out that she was the one who wanted him to be the worst of knights, and that she is only reaping what she so richly deserves: "Si vous veux je rendre en ce jour tel service com le plus mauvais chevalier du monde et comme a vous affiert" (140; Thus today I want to serve you as the worst knight in the world, just as you deserve). Fairies are notoriously capricious, toying with their lovers and maintaining a fierce autonomy. But the victim in this case is none other than King Arthur himself—a man less interested in experiencing transcendence or touching the Absolute than in establishing law, order, and courtly civilization throughout Britain. And so he teaches his fairy a lesson, attacking her as one might expect a giant to attack a lady. And after this he finds her manners to have improved so considerably, and her feelings to be so contrite, that the two are able to settle into a love affair after all.

This bizarre episode parodies the empowerment of the lady and the willing self-effacement of the lover, implicitly dialoguing with the episode of the Chevalier Jayant to approach the problem from the perspective of female rather than male transgression. Arthur willingly entered the space of death and horrific monstrosity in fighting the giant Poisson Chevalier on behalf of the lady; and now the lady imposes a different sort of combat-horror as a further sign of the hero's love. But this test now requires not only the sublimation of erotic desire into the aggressive energies of homosocial violence but a further sublimation of the desire for prowess and victory into an aggressive renunciation of honor. If a knight is willing to embrace bodily death in the name of love, surely he will likewise embrace the symbolic death of public shame and ignominy: power, after all, must be renounced completely before it can be regained in the gift of reciprocal love. But in the extreme version demanded by the fairy, the intricate game of love unravels.[55] If the lady tries to appropriate too much power, subverting the courtly construct by reducing the knight to a literal puppet or plaything, there is a risk that her emasculated lover will revert to the sexual violence that the courtly codes were designed to mask.[56] The parodic version of love service demanded by the Blond Fairy perhaps gives us an idea of how the giant Maudit might have understood the ethical behavior that his wife attempted to impose on him. We are no longer in the idealized world of Febus, Lancelot, or Tristan; though Arthur is willing and even eager to fight both monsters and giants, he expects a tangible reward for his efforts—something other than increasingly arduous opportunities to sublimate desire into ever-more rarefied forms. In this fifteenth-century text, coming so late in the Arthurian tradition, the traumas and ideals of earlier Arthurian literature are subjected to ever more skeptical scrutiny. In its amplification and foregrounding of the comic irony that has always characterized Arthurian romance to at least some extent, the *Papegau* offers a wry riposte to the paradigms that we have seen developed in earlier texts.

CHAPTER 4

Giants and Saracens in the Prose *Tristan*

Rival Narratives, Hostile Desires, and the Struggle to (Re)write History

We have seen that some giants are fiercely isolationist, shunning all contact with the chivalric world. Others, however, welcome contact with aristocratic knights and ladies, as long as this contact takes place on the giant's own terms and in service of the narrative and historical trajectories that support his independence and his chosen way of life. In this and the following chapter, we will examine ways that this desire of giant for human—a desire in which deadly hostility, condescending amusement, and affection or even love may be variously mixed—is coupled with a competition to control the common narrative in which knights and giants alike are actors. In this respect the giant world again presents an analogy with medieval European perceptions of the rival culture of Islam, which, as Uebel has noted, "threatens the preservation and renewal of sacred history by setting up an alternative, perverse history."[1] As Uebel argues, the canonical historical narrative propounded by Roman Catholicism—one leading inevitably to the universal spread of Christianity and the transfer of imperial power and learning from East to West—is threatened but also authorized by the rival histories it encounters at its borders: "Islamic history . . . calls imperial history into being, and demands that its narrative be retold. Roman history, in turn, demands that Islam remain outside the frontier separating the two histories to ensure that their narratives do not converge."[2] Individuals or communities marginal to the Arthurian world also operate according to an alternative sense of history and its narrative trajectories, one that conflicts with the "master narrative" of Arthurian and Christian hegemony. Concomitant with this competing construction of history is giants' or Saracens' determination to maintain laws or customs within their own domain, particular to them, without infringement from the universalizing concept of absolute justice and right that emanates from the royal court. James R. Simpson has commented on the clash of authority that unfolds in *Erec et Enide* when Erec challenges two giants who are abducting the knight Cadoc de Cabruel "con s'il fust pris a larrecin" (as if he had been arrested for theft); the giants reply in effect that Erec has no right to intervene in their affairs ("A vos que tient?" [What's it to you?]).[3] The reader has no way of knowing whether Cadoc is guilty of a crime or not, since he has only just entered the narrative at this moment. His presumed innocence, expressed in the subjunctive "con s'il *fust* pris a larrecin," is based entirely on the fact that his abductors are giants; theirs is not a rule of law but one of caprice, in which they are free to vent their wrath on anyone they choose. As Simpson elaborates:

> Their [the giants'] response is in effect a targeting of Erec's perception of the nature of the judicial spectacle they have created where Cadoc is treated "as a thief." . . . Cadoc is an "outlaw" of the law of their land, but this does not mean he can be claimed by any other version of the law that happens along, the giants arguing that Erec's concerns overstep legal bounds into a terrain over which, as far as their will is concerned, Erec has no jurisdiction. . . . This is the vision of a land before the advent of a universalist "Age of Chivalry," a land that still belongs to giants.[4]

This struggle for the shape, dynamics, and direction of history may be cast as one of deadly conflict or as one of friendly—even amorous—persuasion. And its outcome, in setting the contours of the Arthurian world, is one that identifies that world as inevitable: the incarnation of natural, cultural, and spiritual values, a matrix for the glory and the folly of humanity.

The four examples treated in this chapter are drawn from the prose *Tristan* and are innovations beyond anything found in the twelfth-century verse Tristan romances. The first two elaborate points of contact between the Tristan legend and that of the Lancelot-Grail cycle, a central feature of the prose *Tristan* overall. Contact with the Other World of giant or Saracen focuses attention on Tristan's entrance into the larger Arthurian narrative and on his ultimate displacement from its center with the advent of Galahad and the channeling of the various Arthurian story lines into the larger framework of the Grail Quest. As the Quest develops, Tristan's obsession with Iseut ultimately sidelines him to the peripheral space of Cornwall, with its claustrophobic court riven by the jealousies, passions, and rivalries of a different and more purely secular tale. And while his death is certainly a momentous event, mourned by all, it does not mark the end of the romance, which continues without its eponymous hero until the Quest itself has been brought to conclusion. The other two episodes are more purely focused on the Tristan material itself, contributing to the establishment of themes crucial to the legend of the Cornish lovers or to the resolution of particular narrative threads within it. All, however, confirm this grand Arthurian narrative as the only possible path that (legendary) history might have followed. At the same time, this master narrative is shown to be one that contains numerous failed histories, whose purpose seems ultimately to be that of affirming the totality of the Arthurian world as one that can manage historical rupture and halt or dismantle rival narratives.[5] Giant or Saracen lords may attempt to determine the course of history, in isolation from or in opposition to that of Christian and Arthurian hegemony. But such resistance, even if it is successful for a time, is ultimately futile. To the victor goes the privilege of writing history; and the history thus conceived will always be one that could not have turned out any other way.

Isolationist Kingdoms and the Resistance to History

Widely separated episodes of the prose *Tristan* describe two isolated realms in the hinterlands of Arthurian Britain: one ruled by giants, and one by "Saracens," a term referring here not to Muslims but to pagan Britons maintaining the beliefs of their Trojan ancestors. The former—located on the Isle del Jaiant, part of the Loigtiegnes Isles—is the birthplace of Galehot, Son of the Beautiful Giantess, and was ruled by the giant Dyaletes at the time of Joseph of Arimathea's arrival in Britain.[6] The latter, founded by the first Trojan settlers in Britain, is set "en une montaingne si haute et si fort que cil dedens n'eüssent garde de tout le monde" (on a mountain so high and so impregnable that those inside would have felt no threat from the entire world);[7] at the time of the Grail Quest, when the castle is visited by Galahad, Hector, and Meraugis, it is ruled by King Harpion. Though "Harpion" is attested as a Saracen name in other texts, and nothing indicates that the inhabitants of this mountain kingdom are of giant descent, the king's name in this context is nonetheless highly suggestive, associating him with the giant Harpin de la Montagne in Chrétien de Troyes's *Chevalier au lion*. Once again, the distinction between pagan and giant is tenuous, as both hold themselves apart from the Christian chivalric world, and both prey on the ladies and the warriors of Arthurian Britain. The Saracen kingdom has never wavered from its pagan "law," while the Isle del Jaiant has a more complex history of religious conversion and reversion. Both are defined by their aggressive refusal to be incorporated into either the kingdom of Logres or the larger community of Christendom itself. And both, in their extreme isolationism, embody the medieval theological view that true alienation and otherness are defined less by racial difference or geographic distance than by resistance to the all-embracing matrix of Christian faith.[8]

At the time of the first Christianization of Britain, we are told, Joseph of Arimathea sends missionaries to the Distant Isles who convert the entire population to Christianity, including Dyaletes's twelve sons; Dyaletes himself is the only holdout. Faced with a united front of Christian opposition led by the band of brothers, Dyaletes resorts to desperate measures: nothing short of murdering all twelve sons. As the narrator explains: "Il se porpense que mieuz li vient qu'il ocie ses doze fis que il le destruississent et qu'il perdist sa terre, car sanz faille tuit cil des ysles s'acorderent a ce qu'il li todroient terre et le destruiroient entr'eus, ou il recevroit crestianté" (He considered that it would be better for him to kill his twelve sons than for them to destroy him and for him to lose his land, for without exception all the inhabitants of the islands agreed that they would take over his land and destroy him unless he converted to Christianity).[9] The Christian missionaries are also killed, while the local inhabitants are forced to return to their pagan beliefs; the realm is marked as one explicitly and aggressively predicated on eradicating the new religion. Dyaletes then builds a castle—the Chastel de Plour (Castle of Weeping)—on the site of these mass executions, "en tel maniere que li chastiax soit fondez de lor sanc" (2:71 such that the castle was founded on their blood). The giant vows never to leave his castle unless forced to do so in military defense of his lands and establishes an "evil custom" aimed at ensuring an ongoing vengeance on the outside world. Noting that he has suffered unspeakable damage and lost his own sons because of "estranges genz" (2:72; foreigners), Dyaletes decrees that any foreigners who arrive in the kingdom will be imprisoned unto death in the Chastel de Plour. Their only possibility of escaping this fate will be to face the lord in a fight to the death: and if they are victorious, they will be forced to marry the lord's widow and become themselves lord of the island. Moreover, any lady who enters from the outside will be placed in a beauty contest with the lord's wife; whichever is judged the most beautiful will thereby remain as wife of the lord, while the other will be beheaded. In any case, neither the lord nor the lady is to leave the castle, unless it is to fight an invader or engage in a beauty contest respectively.

Not only, then, does the island represent a withdrawal into isolationism and resistance to the new cultural hegemony of Christianity; it exists in a state of permanent antagonism toward any representative of the outside world, treating all visitors as mortal enemies. An interesting aspect of the Chastel de Plour episode is that it features giants who actually do convert to Christianity: the possibility of true assimilation is raised, even as Dyaletes blocks it. The giant does, nonetheless, establish a mechanism for incorporating superlative outsiders into the ruling family: if there is to be assimilation, it will not take the form of giants joining the outside world, but rather of that outside world being absorbed into the giant kingdom. In so doing he also aims to ensure himself a prominent place in history, vowing: "Je m'en vengeré en tel maniere que lonc tens aprés ma mort en iert parlé" (2:71; I will take such vengeance that it will be spoken of long after my death). Dyaletes and his kingdom will be the subject of oral histories; but this history will be one determined by him, and not one by which he is overtaken and subsumed.

Harpion's Castel Felon (Wicked Castle), in turn, is a military stronghold impregnable to siege and impervious to Christian missionary efforts. Mordrain, Nascien, Uterpendragon, and Arthur all launch unsuccessful attacks, finding that "il ne lour porent nul mal faire" (*PT*[M], 9:127; they could do them no harm); neither Joseph of Arimathea nor St. Augustine can turn them away from their *errour* and *mescreance*, and it is the exasperated Augustine who gives the castle its sinister name. For many generations, the kingdom keeps to itself, but it is eventually moved to action by the establishment of the Round Table, which the Saracens see as an intolerable flowering of Christian arrogance and expansionism: "Mais quant il sorent la verité de la Table Reonde, qui par si grant orgueil ot esté establie . . . adont dist cil qui sires estoit d'aus: 'Li rois Artus est li plus poissans des crestiiens. Je ai pensé conment jel porrai destruire!'" (9:127; But when they learned the truth about the Round Table, which had been established with such great pride . . . then the one who ruled over them said: "King Arthur is the most powerful of the Christians. I've thought of a way that I can destroy him!"). In accordance with his plan, Harpion erects a beautifully carved marble pillar, engraved with a message aimed at entrapping knights and ladies:

> Os tu, chevaliers errans qui vas querant aventures! Se tu entres lasus et mes a fin les aventures du castel, ja ne demanderas cose que tu n'aies. . . . Os tu, damoisele qui vas querant cevaliers aventureus! Si tu veus aler el castel lasus, ja n'em partiras que tu ne soies conseillies a ta volenté. (9:127–28)

> [Hear this, knight errant seeking adventures! If you enter this place and put an end to the adventures of the castle, you will get everything you ask for. . . . Hear this, damsel seeking adventurous knights! If you want to go up to the castle, you will never leave without being advised according to your wishes.]

In this way he lures Christian knights and ladies into his trap; the former are thrown in the dungeon to die, while the latter are enslaved as silk workers to enrich their captors.

Both the Isle del Jaiant and the Saracen kingdom are places that travelers cannot visit unscathed or escape from once they go there, a kind of "black hole" at the edges of the Arthurian world. The Saracen stronghold, indeed, is quite unknown throughout the rest of Britain, for there is no way that news of it could ever spread: "Nus cevaliers n'i entroit qui n'i demourast, car tout estoient mort; ne nule damoisele n'en retournoit, cat toutes estoient retenues" (9:128; No knight went in there who did not remain, for they all died; nor did any damsel ever return from there, for they were all kept captive). And in both cases also the antagonism that shapes the culture and customs of the realm is tinged with desire and envy—desire for the rejected other who might in fact turn out to be superior to oneself, and for the power and prestige that he is seen as hoarding. Far from looking down on the knights of the Round Table, Harpion is well aware that it will be the worthiest and most valiant who are least able to resist the lure of adventure in a strange castle, and it is precisely this excellence—maddening in its adherence to a Christian power—that he targets: "En tel maniere quidoit bien Harpion . . . qu'il peüst en la fin destruire le roi Artu, pour ses boins cevaliers qu'il ocioit" (9:128; In this way Harpion was sure . . . that he would, in the end, be able to destroy King Arthur, by killing his good knights). On the Isle del Jaiant it is even clearer that the hated Christian foreigners are also objects of desire, as long as they can be subjected to the giant's founding laws. As Dyaletes explains to his people: "Et savez vos por quoi je ai ensi establie ceste costume? Por ce que je veil que vos avez des ores mes a seignor le meillor chevalier que aventure aportera ceste part, et que vos aiez a dame la plus bele que aventure vos i envoiera" (2:72–73; And do you know why I've established this custom? Because from now on, I want you to have as your lord the best knight that chance may bring this way, and for you to have as your lady the most beautiful one that chance may send you). Both giant and Saracen lords attempt to control the course of history, mounting an aggressive "master narrative" in opposition to that of Christian and Arthurian hegemony and holding out against the inexorable integration of isolated communities into a larger whole. But this effort fails as both kingdoms ultimately take their place as mere curiosities embellishing two of the grand narrative threads of Arthurian history—on the one hand that of the irresistible Tristan and Iseut, and on the other that of the unstoppable Galahad and the Quest for the Holy Grail.

The first blow struck against the giants' hold on power comes when Brunor, future father of Galehot, arrives from Ireland and kills the lord; in accordance with the custom he then enters the Chastel de Plour "et trova laianz la plus bele jaiante dou monde, qui n'avoit pas d'aaige plus de doze anz. Il jut avec la dame, et engendra Galahot" (2:73; and found inside the most beautiful giantess in the world, who was no more than twelve years old. He lay with the lady, and engendered Galehot). The young Galehot, in turn, nurtures dreams of ambitious adventuring and abhors the idea of being either conquered by some outsider, or forever trapped as lord of the island: "Il dist que ja se Dieu plest n'atendra tant qu'il li conviegne estre en servaige" (2:73; He said that if it pleased God, he would not wait around until he was reduced to servitude). He accordingly departs on the series of conquests that will eventually lead to his war with Arthur and his encounter with Lancelot. It is after Galehot's surrender to Arthur, but still during Brunor's lordship, that the decisive event occurs: Tristan and Iseut are blown off course during their fateful journey from Ireland to Cornwall and make landfall at the Isle del Jaiant, where they are accordingly taken prisoner. Needless to say, Iseut is judged more beautiful than the giantess, while Tristan is victorious over Brunor; and the island now falls entirely into human—and Christian—hands.

Initially this seems a Pyrrhic victory for both. Iseut's beauty, though much admired, also occasions mass mourning for the vanquished giantess. Like other giantesses who marry knights—Galotine, the mother of Maudit, the daughter of the Riddler—this one too is fully assimilated to the courtly values of aristocratic society. Faced with the loss of his beloved wife, Brunor exclaims, "Mar veïsmes vostre biauté" (2:75; Woe that ever we saw your beauty), while the people collectively tell her: "Ceste que nos tant amion et qui tant a esté avec nos covient que nos la livriens a mort por vostre sorvenue, et ce nos poise mout durement" (2:76; We have to deliver to death the lady that we love so much, and who has been with us for so long, because of your arrival, and that grieves us greatly). Tristan, who is forced against his will to behead the giantess, bitterly laments the shame that this has brought upon him; the populace, attempting to console their new lord, can only reply: "Le blame metez sor cez qui ceste costume establirent" (2:78; Place the blame on those who established this custom). Tristan initially attempts to reach a truce with Brunor, promising to spare his life if the lord acknowledges defeat; but of course this too is impossible. The final shock comes when Tristan learns that neither he nor Iseut is allowed to leave, a state of affairs to which he can only respond in disbelief: "Coment? dit Tristanz, me cuidiez vos toz jorz tenir en prison?" (2:79; What? said Tristan, do you expect to keep me in prison forever?). Perhaps more disconcerting still, it turns out that none of the people who were traveling with him are allowed to leave either; everyone aboard the ship must remain in prison, and even Tristan, despite now being lord of the island, has no power to release them.

Once the initial shock has subsided, however, the lovers find that life as the lord and lady of the Isle del Jaiant actually suits them very well. Their constrained circumstances in effect relieve them of any need for caution or secrecy, as Tristan discovers:

> Il n'a ores dotance ne paor que nus li blasme, car se li rois Mars savoit bien coment et en quel maniere il sont en prison, il n'i penseroit ja nul mal. Que vos diroie je? Tant lor plest ceste prison et atalante qu'il n'en vodroient jamés issir, car puis qu'il sont ensemble, la bone vie qu'il moinent nuit et jor lor fait tot le monde oblier. (2:85)
>
> ———
>
> [Now he has no anxiety or fear that anyone might blame him, for if King Mark knew just how and in what manner they were imprisoned, he would never think ill of it. What can I tell you? This prison so pleased and delighted them that they did not wish ever to leave, for as long as they were together, the good life that they led night and day caused them to forget the rest of the world.]

Though hitherto portrayed only as a space of blasphemy, death, and dishonor, the giants' realm is more truly one of what we might call countercultural fantasy. Its total isolation from the world nurtures not only paganism and barbaric customs but also the self-indulgent and socially destructive passions of adulterous love.[10] It therefore comes as a second shock when Tristan and Iseut are told that Galehot—alerted by his sister, who longs for vengeance—has returned to avenge the deaths of his parents, triggering a replay of the notorious local custom. Once again Tristan faces mortal combat with an utterly formidable opponent; and if he loses, not only will he die, but Iseut will have no choice other than to marry the half-blood giant.

In the ensuing battle, Tristan gains the upper hand and is on the verge of defeating Galehot when an army suddenly appears in the distance: Galehot's vassal, the King of a Hundred Knights, is ready with two hundred armed men to defend his lord and ensure vengeance against the one who murdered his father and mother. Seeing this treachery—the custom after all stipulates single combat—Tristan accepts defeat, offering Galehot his sword. And here the story takes another twist, for Galehot in fact has no intention of killing Tristan, telling him: "Je ne regarderai pas a ce que tu m'as mesfait, mes a ta bonté, car tu iés sanz faille le meillor chevalier que je onques veïsse; et por ce te rent je t'espee, car je ne te metrai mie a mort" (2:89; I will not look upon your crimes against me, but rather your goodness, for you are without a doubt the best knight I have ever seen; and for that reason I give you back your sword, for I will not kill you). In a replay of his treatment of Lancelot during the battle with Arthur's army, Galehot commands the king to fall back as he is on the point of running Tristan through with his lance, and explains that his near-fatal combat with the young knight has in fact delighted him: "Je ne vodroie por riens dou monde que je ne me fusse acointiez a li en tel maniere. Se je pooie veoir Lancelot et li ensemble je ne demanderai plus" (2:89; I wouldn't for anything in the world want not to have encountered him in this way. If I could see Lancelot and him together, I could ask for nothing more). He then abolishes the ancient custom and sends Tristan and Iseut on their way to Cornwall, with the proviso that Tristan must join him and Lancelot as soon as possible. Invoking his "cortoisie" in forgiving Tristan's (forced) misdeeds, he makes an extravagant promise that is once again typical of Galehot's character as developed in the prose *Lancelot*: "Et je vos creant come chevaliers . . . que je donrai a monseignor Lancelot et a vos totes les terres que je onques conquis por solement avoir la compaignie de vos deus" (2:90; And I pledge to you as a knight . . . that I will give my lord Lancelot and you all the lands that I have ever conquered, just to have you two as companions). Tristan fully intends to maintain relations with Galehot, but the plan is foiled by Galehot's heartbreak and death not long thereafter, at the (false) rumors of Lancelot's demise.

The Castel Felon, for its part, is destroyed by the sheer superiority of its last Arthurian prisoners: Galahad, Boorz, and Meraugis. Unable to resist the lure of adventure, the three enter the castle and are summarily imprisoned in the tower. But whereas Boorz and Meraugis first lament and then fall asleep, Galahad remains single-mindedly unperturbed: "Galaad ne dormoit mie, conme cil qui pensoit a autres coses que cil ne faisoient. Si fu en orisons le plus de la nuit, priant Nostre Signeur que il, par sa pitié, les secoureüst et les jetast de laiens" (PT[M], 9:130; Galahad did not sleep at all, being one who was thinking of quite other matters than they were. But he spent the better part of the night at prayer, imploring Our Lord, in his mercy, to help them and get them out of there). Like the prayers of a saint, those of Galahad do not go unheeded; and the following night, in a terrible storm, the tower in which our heroes are imprisoned splits down the middle and collapses, killing many of the Saracens but leaving the Christians unharmed. Rallying, the three knights recover their arms, free five hundred enslaved silk workers, and set fire to the castle and its town, killing all the inhabitants. After having stood undefeated for centuries, the Saracen kingdom is eradicated in the space of barely twenty-four hours.

At the Chastel de Plour, then, the giant's legacy is abolished and his realm assimilated into the Christian world at large because Tristan and Iseut so perfectly embody the ideals of beauty, courtesy, and chivalry; and faced with this dazzling spectacle of courtly perfection, the ancient order cannot stand. Ironically, the custom once intended to ensure that the fiercely separatist island would always be ruled by the greatest of knights and the most beautiful of ladies—thus remaining an impregnable fortress of masculine virility and feminine allure—has now resulted in the overturning both of giant rule and of the custom itself. The outrage felt by Galehot's sister, in the end, is itself a violation of the spirit in which the custom was originally founded. It was not the bonds of kinship or vassalage that mattered to Dyaletes but the retrenchment of the island under the strongest possible rule, and this principle is accepted—however regretfully—by all of the other participants. Whatever love one might feel for giant family members or rulers, they are not ultimately to be mourned as valued persons in and of themselves. Instead, the initial shock of grief at their death must give way to the joyful acceptance of the superior lady or warrior who has come in their place. Despite their love for the giantess, both Brunor and the local inhabitants readily acknowledge Iseut as the more beautiful lady; and despite the army backing him up, Galehot is vanquished by his admiration for Tristan. He even writes a letter to Guenevere informing her of his exciting discovery:

> En la fin des letres li manda qu'il avoit en cest monde deux chevaliers et deus dames, "ne plus n'en i puis veoir. En ces deus dames est tote la biauté dou monde, et je ne sai la quele est la plus bele. Et es deus chevaliers est tote la chevalerie dou monde, ne ne porroie en nule fin lor parel trover de chevalerie, ne je ne sai li quiex de ces deus est li plus puissanz d'armes." Aprés escrit quatre nons: Lancelot dou Lac; Tristan, le neveu le roi Marc de Cornoaille; la roïne Genevre; Yselt la Bloe. (*PT*[C], 2:90)
>
> ---
>
> [At the end of the letter he told her that in this world there are two knights and two ladies, "and I cannot see any more than that. In those two ladies is all the beauty of the world, and I do not know which is the most beautiful. And in the two knights is all the chivalric prowess in the world, nor could I ever find their equal in chivalry, nor do I know which of those two is the most powerful warrior." After that he wrote four names: Lancelot du Lac; Tristan, nephew of King Mark of Cornwall; Queen Guenevere; Iseut the Blonde.]

Galehot's thirst for vengeance gives way to a longing to bring Tristan and Lancelot together in Sorelois—to a dream of constructing his own minicommunity of impossibly perfect young knights. Relinquishing the last vestiges of his giant heritage, the son of the giantess turns his attention to the new generation of up-and-coming Arthurian heroes.

The Castel Felon, in turn, cannot withstand the virginal purity and militant piety of Galahad. Its strategy of incorporating Christian knights—literally swallowing them up and leaving them to die in the heart of the castle—has foundered on the Grail knight's Christ-like character and his access to divine grace. In a fatal error that parallels that of Satan when he eagerly swallowed the crucified Jesus into hell, thinking thereby to vanquish the Son of God, the Saracens literally bit off more than they could chew; and just as hell was harrowed and the righteous were led into heaven, so the Christian prisoners in the Castel Felon are freed, heading off en masse to Camelot. This Christological allegory, however—so typical of Galahad's career—also recalls another narrative precedent, one proper to Arthurian legend: the ominous portents that strike Sorelois when Galehot first goes there with Lancelot. At the Castel Felon, "Lors vint une grant merveille. . . . Car cele tour meïsmes u li troi compaingnon estoient em prison, fendi en deus parties par milieu d'en haut trusc'a val, si que l'une moitié versa adestre et l'autre a senestre" (*PT*[M], 9:131; Then a great marvel happened. . . . For that very tower where the three companions were in prison split in two down the middle from top to bottom, so that one half collapsed to the right and the other to the left). And in Sorelois, "Lors avint a Galehout une trop grans merveille . . . kar la tor del baille fendi par mi lieu tot a droiture et tuit le kernel d'une partie verserent" (Then there happened to Galehot a very great marvel . . . for the tower of the bailey split right down the middle, and the crenulations on one side completely collapsed).[11] What at first seems a straightforward Crusade-style case of divine intervention against the infidel also adds another thread to the intricate network conjoining and contrasting giant and Saracen in their love-hate relationship with Christian knights. Like the Chastel de Plour episode, though more subtly, the fall of the Castel Felon ultimately reminds us of the conflict of narrative trajectories as giants, Saracens, and Christians compete for control of Britain.

In trying to assert itself as the dominant kingdom into which the best knights are absorbed—to be incarcerated in dungeons or "loved to death" in enforced isolation—the Castel Felon, the Isle del Jaiant, or Sorelois is instead reduced to being an exotic Other World of chivalric adventure.[12] Passing through this Other World, the knight faces and overcomes trials, consolidates his identity, and emerges victorious to resume his role in Arthurian history. The promise of adventure, devised by Harpion as a ploy to capture knights, turns out to have been true after all, as the Castel Felon is subsumed into the larger narrative that it resisted for so long. Galahad will indeed bring the adventure to conclusion and accomplish his every desire, and the damsels he frees are overjoyed to have met the luminous Grail Knight and to follow his direction in going to tell their story at Arthur's court. Indeed, it turns out that the damsels have been awaiting Galahad's arrival for some time. One of their fellow prisoners, daughter of the king of Norgales, prophesied the advent of Galahad, "le tres boin cevalier, cil qui metra a fin les aventures du roiaume de Logres" (*PT*[M], 9:134; the excellent knight, who will bring the adventures of the kingdom of Logres to an end); she assured the other maidens that "vous serés delivrees a sa venue de la prison u vous estes, et chis castiaus demouerra destruis a tous jours" (9:134; you will be delivered, at his coming, from the prison where you are, and this castle will be destroyed forever after). Aware of the eschatological narrative they are living out—again, a chivalric version of the Harrowing of Hell—the prisoners are capable of discerning a truth in Harpion's message that even he could not have known: a deeper truth beyond the lies he thought he was putting forward.

Significantly, then, it is Galahad alone whose Christian knighthood is powerful enough to bring about the destruction of the castle. In an earlier episode, Tristan, Palamedes, and the Chevalier a l'Ecu Vermeil are traveling near the Castel Felon, here described not as Saracen but merely as hostile to Arthurian knights (*PT*[M], 7:233–38).[13] When a damsel warns them of its reputation, Tristan at once insists on investigating, thereby provoking an attack by castle knights. Though the heroes are capable of fending off the attackers and inflicting significant casualties, they do not penetrate the castle grounds. Tristan is eager to pursue the retreating enemy, feeling that his honor depends on defeating this hostile stronghold once and for all; but Palamedes, mindful of the damsel's warning, prevents him from doing so. In a dramatic exchange, he literally restrains Tristan's horse and forcibly leads him away, much to Tristan's fury: "Certes, sire, fait mesire Tristrans, vous me honnissiés tant conme vous poés et me faites faire ma honte" (*PT*[M], 7:237; Certainly, sir, says Sir Tristan, you are shaming me as much as you possibly can and forcing me to shame myself). By this point in the narrative Tristan has already been victorious not only in his battles with Morholt and at the Chastel de Plour but also, as we shall see below, in liberating the Païs de Servaige; he might reasonably believe that he could put an end to the evil customs of the Castel Felon as well. But the text makes very clear that this particular adventure is not for him. Like the rest of the Arthurian world, Tristan too must eventually give way to Galahad, as the grand narrative builds toward its spiritual climax. Victories over giants and Saracens alike require chivalric prowess, but Tristan's success at the Chastel de Plour is due to courtly qualities as well—both his own personal charm and also the generosity of spirit and capacity for forgiveness that he inspires in Galehot. Saracens, who already share in a common culture of aristocratic and chivalric values, are defeated by spiritual fortitude and faith—perhaps the one area in which Tristan cannot be said to excel. And the interplay between these episodes highlights the different ideological uses to which giants and Saracens respectively are put in medieval narratives.

From Païs de Servaige *to* Franchise Tristan*: The Power of the Master Narrative*

The kingdoms in the previous examples are places of no return because all incomers are summarily locked up in castle towers and dungeons. There they may be retained as prisoners, exploited as slave labor, or simply left to starve; but in any case, with the exception of the chosen few who might live to govern the Isle del Jaiant, their conditions will be grim and their life one of permanent incarceration. But while giants often do have the habit of filling their prisons with aristocratic knights and ladies, not all who "collect" human travelers reduce them to quite this level of abject suffering. In some cases a giant's interests, while certainly counter to those of the knights, may not be homicidal but may run more toward a desire to surround himself with human laborers, entertainers, and even companions. Such stories highlight not only the irresolvable conflict between human and giant mentalities but also that fateful desire, at once seductive and lethal, that smolders at the giant-human boundary—a desire most fully explored in the tale of Galehot and Lancelot, subject of the next chapter. As further context for Galehot's story, I turn now to two other episodes from the prose *Tristan*. The most intricate is that of the unnamed riddling giant, who will be examined in the next section; but first, we will look at the episode involving the giant Nabon li Noirs, king of the ominously named Païs de Servaige (Land of Servitude).[14] Like so many giants, Nabon li Noirs detains all those—men and women, nobles and commoners—who find themselves in his kingdom, usually as a result of shipwreck on treacherous rocks offshore. Because of the rocky coastline—heavily guarded to prevent any possible escape—and the impassable mountains that surround the central valley, there is no exit from this land. All incomers immediately become subjects of Nabon, who retains them to populate his kingdom. Though not literally imprisoned—they live and travel freely within the kingdom itself—knights are deprived of horses and arms, treated as commoners, and thereby reduced to a position of servitude that covers them with shame.

In the slightly later *Guiron le courtois*, an episode serving as prequel to that of *Tristan* describes an earlier, failed attempt by Le Bon Chevalier sans paour, king of Estrangorre, to liberate the knights held prisoner in Nabon's Val de Servage, as it is here called.[15] An interesting feature of this account is its depiction of Nabon's own social hierarchy and ethical framework as diametrically opposed to that of the world at large, as represented by his Christian aristocratic prisoners. The point is made almost as soon as the Bon Chevalier arrives in the fateful valley; in response to his questions, one of the knights explains that "Nabon le noir en est seigneur, le plus fort homme de tout cest monde" (fol. 427r; Nabon the Black is its lord, the strongest man in the whole world). The knight thus expresses two facts about Nabon that already hint at the possibility that his aristocratic power may derive more from sheer physical strength than from any kind of legally recognized legitimacy. Perhaps it is for this reason that the Bon Chevalier asks the seemingly odd question of whether the lord of the realm is a knight. In any case, the response sets things straight: "Il se tient pour chevalier, mais il nous est avis qu'il ne le soit pas. . . . Il est jaians tout droitement et seigneur de tout cest païs" (fol. 427r; He considers himself a knight, but he isn't one in our opinion. . . . He is definitely a giant and lord of this land). The designation *jaiant* says it all: both Nabon's chivalric status and his lordship stand outside the principles that define these conditions throughout the Arthurian kingdom—principles implicitly held to be universal. As someone outside the symbolic structures of Christian knighthood, feudal hierarchies, and aristocratic lineage, he promulgates his own personal form of political authority and chivalric privilege, enforced by the audacity of his pretensions and the brute force incarnated in his powerful body.

When Nabon himself appears, his words to the captive king of Norgalles offer further insight into the ethical position he believes himself to occupy. As if abrogating to himself a moral authority that allows him to judge all others, he describes himself as "Nabon le noir qui les orgueilleus set abatre" (fol. 433v; Nabon the Black who lays low the proud) and further reminds his prisoner: "Vous esties moult orgueilleus au commencement quant vous venistes en cestui val. Mais or en estes vous chastiés" (fol. 433v; You were full of arrogance when you came to this valley. But now you are chastened). But Nabon's self-centered concept of "might makes right" is exposed and inscribed within a universalist ethic in the words spoken by a hermit that the Bon Chevalier encounters in the forest outside Nabon's castle. Himself a captive knight who avoided subjugation to Nabon by entering the service of God, the hermit portrays Nabon's behavior as a miscarriage of justice, a violation of aristocratic privilege, and ultimately as contrary to God's law:

> Car certes je croi que a dieu desplaist moult ce qu'il a tant de preudommes el servage de cestui chastel. Cist est le greigneur tort du monde et le greigneur vilenie du siecle que d'emprisonner gent ainsi pour noiant. Il n'i treuve nule autre raison que sa volenté. Ne jamais n'i vendroit si preudomme ne se gentil, neïs s'il fust roys, qu'il ne face tantost serf.... Car je di bien que de cestui fait est le greigneur pechié du monde. (fol. 435v)

> [For certainly I believe that it greatly displeases God that he has reduced so many noblemen to servitude in this castle. It is the greatest wrong in the world, and the most vile, to imprison people like this for nothing. He has no reason other than his own will. Nor would any man ever come here, no matter how noble or worthy, not even if he were a king, but he would immediately make him a serf.... For I say indeed that this behavior is the greatest sin in the world.]

Nabon clearly feels that he alone can judge arrogance, which he defines as including any form of resistance to his own personal will. But just as earlier Nabon's self-styled knighthood is dismissed as mere pretense— mimicry of a condition that cannot simply be assumed but must be earned and received in the prescribed way, according to a universal standard—so here the hermit reminds us of the absolute, transcendent nature of moral authority, which lies in the overarching structure of society and ultimately in God himself. The words that he applies to Nabon's behavior—*tort, vilenie, pechié*—identify the giant as violating natural justice, social values, and divine law, while the concatenation of terms within a single diatribe implies further that these symbolic codes are the components of a single construct: the basis of civilization itself. As so often, the giant is an outsider not merely to a particular court or culture but to what is portrayed as the only legitimate form that culture can assume.

Nabon has become adept at manipulating the customs and institutions of chivalric culture to his own ends. He has redefined knighthood and lordship in such a way as to enhance his personal prestige at the expense of all others: assuming these privileged conditions for himself and his family members, he denies the validity of actual knights and sovereigns, reducing them to the status of serfs. Moreover, even while divesting his prisoners of their aristocratic *franchise*, he simultaneously exploits their sense of chivalric honor by forcing them to swear fealty to him. In answer to the Bon Chevalier's question of how one man can hold 1,500 knights in servitude, the king of Norgalles explains that each one entered the valley individually, at which point he was overpowered and forced to submit to Nabon's authority. As a result, none feel that they can rebel as long as Nabon remains alive: "Ne jamais a nul jour encontre lui ne fourferons, car nous l'avons promis loiaument" (fol. 432v; Nor will we ever commit an act against him at any time, for we gave him our loyal promise). The giant has placed the knights in a double bind, whereby their honor requires them to submit to a servitude that deprives them of all honor. Seemingly, his power is unassailable as he presides over a historical trajectory in which giants will dominate Arthurian knights and lords. But, like King Harpin of the Castel Felon, Nabon fails to realize that all of his maneuvering and his power plays are merely an episode in a larger narrative over which he has no control. In fact, the dissolution of his power and the reincorporation of his realm into Arthurian history are already inscribed at the very heart of his kingdom. The hermit explains that he has seen a stone engraved with the announcement of a liberation yet to come: "Jamais la male coustume de cest val ne faudra devant que la flour de Loenois y venra, et cil le fera remanoir, et tournera le servage en franchise" (fol. 435v; The evil custom of this valley will never end until the flower of Leonois comes there, and he will bring it to an end, and transform the servitude into freedom). The Bon Chevalier assumes that the inscription refers to Meliadus, king of Leonois and the flower of chivalry; but of course the reader knows that it is in fact a retrospectively composed prophecy of an exploit accomplished by Meliadus's son Tristan.

In the *Tristan* episode on which the *Guiron* episode is based, Tristan, Kahedin, and Iseut aux Blanches Mains, having fallen asleep in a boat, drift out to sea and are shipwrecked on the rocky shores of Nabon's realm. Though dismayed to be told that he will never be allowed to leave, Tristan refuses to lose heart; his intentions are instantly focused on finding a way that he can arm himself in order to kill the giant. As it happens, Tristan and his party arrive just in time to participate in a day of festivities organized by Nabon to celebrate the knighting of his son. This event gives an idea of the peculiar attitude that the giant takes to his subjects, all of whom are actually the subjects of neighboring kingdoms—either Logres or Norgalles. As part of the general celebrations in his son's honor, Nabon organizes a fencing competition between the knights of Logres and those of Norgales, greatly enjoying the skill displayed by the Logres champion, Lamorat de Galles. In fact, once Lamorat has successfully defeated all contenders, Nabon chastises the men of Norgales and announces that from there on out the kingdom will be divided by class lines that correspond to the kingdom of origin. Not only will those of Norgales be forbidden to bring charges against anyone of Logres who may have wronged them; but also, Nabon informs them, "Cil del reaume de Logres ont a cesti point gaaigné si grant honor que jamés sers ne les apelerai, mes frans homes, et vos seroiz apeleé serf pardurablement" (*PT*[C], 2:193; Those from the realm of Logres have at this time won such great honor that I will never call them serfs, but freemen, and you will be called serfs forever after). While this gesture suggests respect for at least some of his captives, however, Nabon's next move is to challenge Lamorat to a duel himself, with an arrogant display of bravado: "Il est mestiers que je toz seus vos mostre que je sai plus de l'escremie que tuit cil qui encontre vos sont hui venu por ax essaier" (2:193; I must stand on my own to show you that I know more about fencing than all these others who tested themselves against you today). If the residents provide entertainment and add luster to court festivities through their undeniable talents, nonetheless they are ultimately a means by which the giant can compulsively demonstrate his own superior prowess. Desire for worthy company is matched by anxiety at the implicit challenge that these incomers pose, and only after proving that he could fight Lamorat to the death if he wished to do so does Nabon deign to spare the life of "un si preudome" (2:194; such a worthy man)—no doubt preferring to keep him on hand for future entertainment and repeated self-aggrandizement. It is in this mood of overconfidence that he asks the men of Logres if anyone wishes to step forward now that he has defeated their champion; and this gives Tristan the opportunity to engage the giant in a match that will prove to be anything but recreational. Sure of his own invincibility, Nabon relaxes his guard with Tristan—who feigns a level of expertise well below what is actually the case—giving Tristan the chance to kill him with a sudden blow. Nabon's insatiable desire for British knights as subjects, prized possessions, and outright playthings has, in the end, been his undoing.

The first person that Tristan's party encounters upon arrival in the Païs de Servaige is Seguradés, a knight cuckolded by Tristan when he had not yet become Iseut's lover.[16] Viewing Tristan as an enemy, Seguradés takes a gloomy pleasure in the thought that Tristan, having fallen victim to the same "giant narrative" that he has, will henceforth be reduced to shame and ignominy; but Tristan reminds him that such is not his story. Seguradés characterizes Tristan's position as a reversal of his previous victory over Morholt, taunting him bitterly: "Vos ostastes jadis le servaige d'Yrlande en Cornoaille et l'i tornastes a franchise; or est de vos avenu tot le contraire" (2:182; Long ago you liberated Cornwall from its Irish servitude and set it free; now the opposite has happened to you). Tristan, however, is confident in the upward trajectory of his own story, which is already being told throughout the Arthurian world: "Je sui Tristanz, qui ocist le Morholt et qui tant ai fait par le monde que tant com li siecles durra en sera parlé. . . . Et sachiez tot certenement que onques Tristanz ne mist si grant franchise en Cornoaille com il metra en ceste valee" (2:183; I am Tristan, who killed Morholt and who has done so much that as long as this world continues, it will always be spoken of. . . . And rest assured that Tristan never created such great freedom in Cornwall as he will do in this valley). Later, back in Brittany,

Tristan recounts the entire adventure at court, providing the reader with a condensed summary of the events we have just read about. And the delighted Bretons compose a lai to commemorate it—"li lais de la Franchise Tristan" (2:199; the lai of Tristan's Freedom)—thereby enshrining it as a paradigmatic narrative component of Tristan's growing legend: one that circulated from the beginning as both song and story. The episode is not only a variation on that foundational act of heroism whereby Tristan distinguished himself in the original twelfth-century romances, however; it is also a replay of an episode new to the prose tradition, since it recalls his enforced sojourn on the Isle del Jaiant. An important difference, of course, is that this time Tristan is trapped not with his beloved but with his wife and brother-in-law. If the lovers could not abandon their inevitable story of adultery, intrigue, treason, and sorrow, still less could Tristan allow his story to end like this, severing him forever from Iseut the Blonde and forcing him into the family unit created by his marriage. The momentum of the narrative trajectory—one that can only lead Tristan back to the queen of Cornwall—ensures that Nabon will indeed be killed and that Tristan, Kahedin, Iseut aux Blanches Mains, Seguradés, and Lamorat de Galles will all return to their story lines.

Within *Tristan* as a whole, the passage through Nabon's realm ends up as a means of resolving Tristan's relations with Seguradés. Despite their former conflict, the two knights bond in their shared predicament and plot together to engineer the uprising, agreeing that once Tristan has killed Nabon, Seguradés will rally the other knights in an attack on the giant's family. And once the dust has settled, Tristan refuses to accept kingship of the land for himself but instead gives it to Seguradés, whom the grateful populace accept as their king. From that point on, the two knights are friends; it is Seguradés who proposes renaming the kingdom in honor of its liberator, proclaiming that "por ce que Tristanz i a en sa venue aporté franchise pardurablement sera cist païs apelez des ores mes la Franchise Tristan" (2:198; Since Tristan at his arrival brought everlasting freedom, this land will henceforth be called Tristan's Freedom). Rather than a dead-end space of shame, then, the giant's kingdom has emerged as an opportunity for Tristan to embellish his reputation; the inspiration for another of the growing body of lais that supposedly commemorated his life in musical form before the composition of the written narrative;[17] and a vehicle through which Tristan is able to renegotiate his relationship with a fellow knight, righting a previous wrong and making permanent peace with one who was once a staunch adversary.

It is striking that the episodes in which Tristan finds himself temporarily marooned outside his own story all involve encounters with giants. The Giant's Isle deflects Tristan and Iseut from their ultimately unavoidable collision course with Mark, while Galehot's intervention sets the lovers back on their trajectory to Cornwall. Tristan's period of madness places him in the territory controlled by Taulas de la Montagne, and his successful battle with the giant has the unintended consequence of attracting Mark's attentions and returning him to court, where he is eventually identified and healed. And when he is in danger of being trapped forever in his marriage with the other Iseut, while suffering the schadenfreude of a longtime rival, it is again in a giant's kingdom; and battle with the giant is once more the means by which Tristan resolves a long-standing conflict and escapes a potential dead end to his story. In all three episodes, the possibility is hinted at that Tristan might simply replace the giant and remain in this territory outside his difficult story of a love, disastrous and sublime, that simultaneously enhances and destroys him. The custom of the Giant's Isle might have kept the lovers there forever as lord and lady of a distant realm—their adultery no longer an issue—had Galehot not sprung them and inserted them aggressively into the larger story of Arthurian Britain. Tristan could similarly have assumed lordship of Nabon's kingdom, founding a feudal dynasty with his lawfully wedded wife. And his madness offered a more sinister possibility, that of replacing Taulas as the scourge and terror of the Morois. Medieval romance is characterized by a constant process of revisiting and rewriting earlier texts, a kaleidoscopic reshaping and recombination of narrative motifs. But the free hand taken by medieval authors and *remanieurs* should not blind us to the equally important limits embedded in the textual fabric: the powerful fiction that certain aspects of Arthurian history overall are not subject to change. In particular, we see here that Tristan's story could never be permanently diverted or reinvented by the customs or desires of giants. It is always to his peril that a giant allows his space to be invaded by a story line as powerful as Tristan's. This motif—the giant as unwitting facilitator of a master narrative he cannot understand—is even more elaborately worked out in the episode of the riddling giant, his daughter, and a collection of knights from Cornwall and Leonois.

Narrative Aggression: The Giant and His Riddles

The opening section of the prose *Tristan* covers the period of the Christianization of Britain, beginning with the arrival of Joseph of Arimathea and including the missionary work of St. Augustine.[18] It is a complicated tale, interlacing numerous strands of narrative across two generations, and rich in intrigue: sexual rivalry, fratricide, parricide, incest, divine retribution, religious conversion. Central to this tangled web are the paradigmatic figures with whom we have become familiar: a Saracen princess, a giant, and the giant's daughter.

The Babylonian princess Celinde washes ashore in Britain after being blown off course—somewhat improbably—on her way from Babylon to Persia.[19] She is found by Sador, a nephew of Joseph of Arimathea, who marries her for her great beauty, after first converting her to Christianity. Joseph's brother, however—equally captivated by Celinde's ravishing beauty—becomes "si desvez et si escomeüz de s'amor" (*PT*[C], 1:42; so maddened and so aroused by her love) that he rapes her, prompting Joseph to murder his brother. While fleeing the scene of the crime, Celinde and Sador are separated; she is found by Canor, pagan king of Cornwall. Dazzled by her clearly irresistible beauty, Canor—who "haoit crestiens si merveillement qu'il ne se poïst a eus acorder en nule maniere del monde" (1:45; had such amazing hatred for Christians that he could not reconcile himself to them in any way at all)—attempts to convert Celinde back to a pagan "law." These efforts are in vain, for she is so committed to her newfound faith that "ele vosist ausi tost recevoir la mort, come degerpir la loi crestiene" (1:46; she would rather have died at once than to violate Christian law). Nonetheless the besotted king "la prist a feme a la loi paiene . . . ou cele vosist ou non" (1:46; took her to wife according to pagan law . . . whether she liked it or not). A dream warns him that the son she is soon to bear will one day kill him, so he abandons the child in the forest, where he is adopted by commoners and given the name Apollo li Aventereus. Celinde's next mishap comes when Pelias, the pagan king of Leonois, is enflamed by her beauty while visiting Canor. Sneaking into the royal bedchamber, Pelias pushes Canor out the window and lies with Celinde, who thinks the man beside her is her husband. Canor survives his fall, and more adventures ensue, including a war between Canor and Pelias. Sador, having taken up the Cornish cause, defeats Pelias in single combat, thereby obtaining Canor's release from prison and ending the war. Fearing that Sador may attempt to reclaim his wife, however, Canor banishes him, and he takes refuge in the Leonois. There he is falsely accused of murder; but thinking that the crime for which he is arrested is his earlier defeat of Pelias, Sador acknowledges guilt, and as a result of this confusion he is condemned to death. Pelias longs to free the man whom he now admires as a great chivalric hero, but according to local law he can spare a criminal only if there is more than one awaiting execution. Seeing his father's despair, Pelias's son Luce commits a murder himself; the king is now free to pardon one of the two condemned men and chooses Sador. Before Luce can be executed, however, he is kidnapped by the giant whose daughter has fallen in love with Luce; I will return below to this part of the story.

Unable to forget Celinde, Pelias succumbs to the pains of love, until Sador one day finds him in tears and insists on being told the reason for the king's grief. Little suspecting that the woman in question is his own wife, Sador abducts the Cornish queen and delivers her to Pelias. Once Pelias has married Celinde, however, she and Sador soon recognize each other, and Sador uses the device of the *don contraignant* to force Pelias to let him have the woman to whom he has been married all along—an act that reduces Pelias to tears of rage and grief, so powerful is his love for Celinde. Once again Sador and Celinde flee, this time straight into the Forest au Jaiant (Giant's Forest). After further adventures, Celinde and Sador's son Apollo, now a knight, reenters the narrative; in an altercation in the forest, he kills both Sador (his father) and Canor (his onetime stepfather), unaware of his relationship with either one. Later still, having become king, Apollo inspects the local women and selects the most beautiful to take as wife: none other than Celinde herself, whom he of course does not recognize as his mother. This incestuous marriage lasts until it is unmasked by St. Augustine in a dramatic episode that culminates in the Christian conversion of Apollo and the destruction of Celinde by a divine thunderbolt.

In sum, then, Celinde is deflected from her original intended marriage with the king of Persia to pass through a series of four marriages in Britain—consensual Christian marriage with Sador, then forced pagan marriage with Canor, Pelias, and her own son Apollo—in addition to being raped by Sador's brother. The magnetic allure of her beauty sparks a cascade of desire and violence that results in Sador's act of fratricide; Pelias's attempted murder of Canor and a protracted war between Cornwall and the Leonois; Sador's conflicts with both Canor and Pelias; and ultimately the incestuous marriage with her own son that will be the focus of Augustine's denunciation of the pagan court. Ironically, this lady, who once clung tenaciously to her Christian faith, later shares in—perhaps even contributes to—the apostasy of her one Christian husband. After escaping from the giant, she and Sador "se mentenoient de totes choses a la loi paiene" (*PT*[C], 1:86; lived in all respects according to pagan law), and, in her final role as queen of the Leonois, Celinde resists the missionary saint's claim that she and Apollo are mother and son. Flying into a rage, she fully embodies the stereotype of the vengeful pagan tyrant persecuting the Christian martyr, condemning Augustine to be burnt at the stake. But the fires refuse to touch him and descend instead on her as she is consumed by lightning, while Augustine escapes unscathed to complete his conversion of Apollo. In the end this Babylonian princess, who as a Christian destabilized an entire region of Britain with her potent erotic charge, dies a pagan death, while her pagan husband/son embraces Christianity and ensures its establishment as the official religion throughout the Leonois.

The giant, for his part, enters the narrative when, like some deus ex machina, he carries Pelias's son Luce away from the site of his impending death. As we have already seen in chapter 3, it is because of his daughter's love for Luce that the giant has taken him, and from that point on Luce lives with his giantess wife and her father. For a time he leads a comfortable but isolated existence, in which "riens dou monde ne li faut, fors solement qu'il n'a mie tant de compaignie com il sieust" (1:70; he lacks for nothing at all, excepting only that he does not have as many companions as he had been accustomed to); but that soon changes. This particular giant, we learn, has the habit of waylaying travelers and posing riddles; those who fail to solve the riddles are eaten. Not long after Luce's marriage with the giantess, Sador and Celinde appear on the scene, fleeing from Pelias. Sador readily solves the giant's riddle, at which point the giant declares that he will keep Sador as a companion. Sador complains that the giant is breaking his word in forcibly retaining him, but to little effect: "Ceste force te fais je, dit li jaianz, por ce que je te voi et saige et preu, et te prise plus que je ne prisai pieça home; et por ce requier je ta compaignie" (1:78; I am forcing you like this, said the giant, because I see that you are wise and valiant, and I value you more than I have ever valued any man; and therefore I require your company). Having little choice, Sador and Celinde join Luce in the giants' lair. The next knight forced to engage with the Riddler is Pelias, who solves two riddles and is likewise forcibly adopted into the giant's household. In an effort to escape he poses his own riddle, which baffles the giant; but Sador, fearing that Pelias will reclaim Celinde, gives the giant the solution in exchange for his and Celinde's liberty. Once again the giant retains his knightly visitor, declaring: "Je sai bien que tu iés bons chevaliers et gentis hom, si ne porroie avoir compaignie de plus preudome que tu iés. Et por ce te retendrai je avec moi, dusqu'a tant que aventure amoint ceste part home que je teigne a plus saige de toi" (1:84; I know very well that you are a good knight and a noble man, and I could not have the company of any man worthier than you. And for that reason I will keep you with me, until perchance some man may come this way that I consider wiser than you). Pelias thus joins his son Luce as companion to the giant. The final exchange of riddles is between the giant and Apollo; Apollo solves the giant's riddle, but the giant cannot solve the one posed by Apollo. He appeals for help to Pelias, "en qui il se cuidoit mout fier" (1:92; in whom he thought he could trust greatly); but Pelias, hoping for the giant's death, pretends not to understand the riddle. Victorious, Apollo takes up the giant's sword and slays him, allowing Pelias and Luce, with his giantess wife in tow, to return to their castle.

Of the giant's four riddles, three recount his own heinous crimes in metaphorical language: incest, cannibalism, infanticide, fratricide, and matricide. Interestingly, the giant draws on biblical imagery to construct his riddles. His first riddle recasts the narrative of Original Sin to describe how, in the grip of lust for an object of bodily desire that he valued more highly than the (presumably spiritual) virtues of paradise, he engendered a daughter, whom he then raped—plucking the flower of her virginity—and later ate:

> Un arbre, fait il, oi jadis,
> Que j'amai plus que paradis.
> Tant le gardai que fruit porta;
> La biauté del fruit m'enorta
> A ce que je la flor en pris.
> Aprés le fruit tant en mespris
> Que le fruit manjai sanz refu.
>   (vv. 1–15; 1:76)

[Long ago, he says, I had a tree, which I loved more than paradise. I kept it until it bore fruit; the beauty of the fruit excited me so much that I took its flower. Later I so scorned the fruit that I ate it without hesitation.]

The second continues the biblical narrative in using Cain and Abel as figures for himself and his mother, whom the giant devoured:

> Dui vessel furent jadis bel,
> L'un fu Chaÿm et l'autre Abel,
> L'un fu leal, l'autre trahi,
> L'un ama, et l'autre haï.
> Qui en l'autre ot esté enclos
> Fist tant qu'il ot l'autre en soi clos.
>   (vv. 1–9; 1:79)

[Long ago there were two handsome vessels; one was Cain and the other Abel. One was loyal, the other treacherous; one loved, the other hated. The one who had been enclosed in the other one, caused the other one to be enclosed in himself.]

In the third riddle, which recounts the giant's actual murder of his brother, animal and maternal imagery are combined in a struggle between two fawns, one of which attacks the other and consigns him to his grave in "mother earth": "Tant fait que l'autre a atrapé, / Et de sa mere si le charge, / Qu'a mort le met par cele charge" (vv. 11–13; 1:80; He keeps trying until he's captured the other one, and weighs him down with his mother, thereby putting him to death). In effect, the giant appropriates the language of sacred history—a history common to humans and to giants—and invests it with a meaning that is personal to himself. His riddles are a dramatic revelation of his compulsive reenactment first of the Original Sin committed by the ancestors of giants and humans alike, and then of the sin that, setting Cain apart, distinguished the lineage of giants from that of humans.

The motif of fratricide—explicit in the imagery of the second and implicitly depicted in the third—not only links the giant's two central riddles but also reinforces his spiritual (and most likely also literal) kinship with Cain. His first and last riddles, in turn, underscore his association with Original Sin and sexual culpability through the image of the tree: while the first uses a flowering fruit tree as the vehicle for an allegory of incestuous rape and cannibalism against a daughter, the fourth describes an act of violence against a beautiful and blameless feminine object that turns out to be a tree:

> Une chose voi en cest monde,
> Qui nest sanz pechié net et monde.
> De po vient puis a mout grant chose,
> Mes je le non dire ne t'ose.
> Quant bele est, si ne garde l'ore
> Que maintenant li cort l'en sore;
> Le pié li a l'en tost osté
> Tant gahaigne par sa biauté.
> Mes quant ele est menee au plen,
> Dont la voit l'en corre de plen.
> Mes la trace en est si soutive
> Que ne la sivroit hons qui vive.
> (vv. 1–12, 1:90)

[I see a thing in this world that is born without sin, clean and pure; from something very small it then becomes a very large thing, but I won't tell you its name. When it is beautiful, it is unexpectedly attacked. It is severed from its foot—this is what its beauty gains it. But when it is brought to the plains, one sees it rushing at full speed. But it leaves a trace so subtle that no man alive can follow it.]

As Apollo rightly notes, the riddle describes the destruction of a tree—born without sin because trees reproduce asexually—to build a boat, which races along the "plains" of the sea without leaving a trace. Treating the boat as a kind of riddle within the riddle, Apollo further links its furtive movement to that of an adulterous woman in an unacknowledged adaptation of a biblical commentary on sin (Prov. 30:18–20): "Car quatre choses sont ou monde, que tu sez bien, que l'en ne puet tres bien sivir par trace: colevre sor pierre, oisel volant par l'er, nef corant par mer a force de vent, feme de mal enging, sorprise quant ele vet en son fol deduit, et ele se gaite" (1:91; For as you know, there are four things in the world that one cannot easily trace: a serpent moving over stone, a bird flying through the air, a boat sailing on the sea, a woman of wicked machinations, caught in pursuit of her foolish pleasure, and she dissembles). Apollo's gloss clarifies the link between the giant's first and final riddle, both of which are not only about trees but also about sexual crimes. And if the first three riddles were narratives of personal transgression, the last contains, buried within it, the riddle of sin itself and its ability to persist beneath a cloak of innocence. Apollo's solution explicates the riddle not merely as the artful description of a tree that is killed to construct a boat but also as a narrative of innocence, fall, and corruption: though "born" without sin, the tree ultimately becomes an image for adultery and duplicity. Between them, the giant's riddle and Apollo's gloss recapitulate the biblical narrative that informs the first three riddles.

The acts of which the giant boasts are ones that can barely be spoken of, for they risk corrupting the very language in which they are expressed. The trauma of enunciating such behavior is very clearly stated by the knights themselves when they are forced to solve the riddles. Sador worries that the giant may be displeased at hearing his acts of incest and cannibalism openly stated and has to ask for reassurance before he can continue: "Je te dirai, si com je cuit, la verité de cele devinaille, se je ne cuidasse que tu m'en seüsses mal gré" (1:77; I will tell you, as I see it, the truth of this riddle, as long as I don't think you will hold it against me). Pelias recoils even more violently at being forced to solve the riddle of the eaten mother: "Or oi merveilles, dit rois Pelias, com tu ta desonor et ta honte et ta deleauté me racontes. Se tu tenisses riens des diex, ja n'en parlasses" (1:79; Now I marvel, said King Pelias, how you tell me your dishonor and your shame and your disloyalty. If you cared anything for the gods, you would never speak of it). He reiterates his distaste at having to voice such terrible truths after having expounded the riddle: "Or t'ai devisié ta felonie et ta deleauté, que je ja ne te queïsse avoir dite, se ne fust ce que je en estoie en aventure de morir, se nel deïsse" (1:80; Now I've explained your felony and your disloyalty, which I would never have wanted to tell you; if I had not been in danger of death, I wouldn't have said it). In using figurative language as a means of speaking the unspeakable, the giant's riddling discourse is a parodic debasement of philosophical or theological allegory, which uses coded language to express that which cannot be stated openly because it must be hidden from those who are unworthy, or indeed because it transcends language altogether. Just as sacred mysteries are accessible only to those with sufficient wisdom and insight to penetrate the letter of the text and discover its vivifying spirit, so the excesses of the giant's life can be glimpsed only by those knights who are capable of uncovering the scandalous bodily truths hidden in the seemingly innocent language of fruit and flower, vessels that contain one another, and a fawn sending its brother back to their common mother. Exegetical training admits the scholar to an intellectual and spiritual elite, as reflected in the narrator's playful claim that he is not permitted to repeat spiritual teachings and exegeses in a mere romance:

> S'il fust otroié a chevalier a deviser en livre de deduit e de cortoisie la senefiance des ancienes estoires qui a la devinité apartienent e as choses de Sainte Yglise, ge endroit moi, qui chevalier sui, seüsse bien deviser apertement tous les poins de devinité qui a ce apartienent, tout ensi come Saint Augustin le devisa au roi de Leonois a celui point qu'il le converti . . . mais je ne puis, quar l'arcevesque de Contorbiere le me devea. (1:105–6)

> [If it was permitted to a knight to explain in a book of pleasure and courtly matters the meaning of the ancient stories pertaining to divinity and the matters of Holy Church, I myself, who am a knight, would know very well how to expound openly all the points of divinity that pertain to this, just as St. Augustine expounded it to the king of the Leonois when he converted him . . . but I cannot, because the archbishop of Canterbury forbids me to do so.]

If knights are denied entrance to the lofty heights of theology, however, they do certainly have access to the realm of poetry, with its portrayals of passion both amorous and violent. And the ability to solve the giant's riddles, and to present him with poetic enigmas that elude his understanding, admits the knights (however unwilling) to a different sort of elite: humans who are valued by a giant not as food or sport but as intellectual companions.

The Knights Strike Back: Riddles of Human Identity

The two riddles posed by knights—Pelias and Apollo respectively—make an interesting comparison to those of the giant, as does a similar use of riddling language on the part of St. Augustine. Apollo's riddle about a lamb triumphing over a wolf is a warning to the giant of his own impending death, as well as an assertion of the giant's culpability and Apollo's innocence:

> En une meson mout pluveuse,
> Mout gaste et mout frieleuse,
> Vi ja un leu et un aignel.
> Quant li leus cuide avoir la pel
> De l'ainel a tote la char,
> Li aigniax, qui doute l'eschar,
> Cort a un petit hameçon,
> Sel giete au leu de cel laçon,
> L'endort, et par itant s'en fuit.
> L'un s'en deust, l'autre s'en deduit,
> L'un en chante, et l'autre en pleure.
> (vv. 1–12; 1:91)

[In a rainy, dilapidated and chilly house, I once saw a wolf and a lamb. When the wolf thought to have the lamb's skin and all its flesh, the lamb, fearing destruction, ran for a little hook and threw it to the wolf on a string; he put him to sleep, and thus fled.
The one mourns, the other rejoices; the one sings of it, and the other one weeps.]

Pelias had earlier remarked on the delight the giant takes in obsessively constructing riddles about his own extreme behavior: "Or oi merveilles, fait li rois Pelyas, les greignors que je onques mes oïsse, que raconter en tel maniere ta felonie et ta deleauté ne te targes, enz te plest et enbelist tant que tu ne te puez tenir que tu ne regeïsses ta mauvese vie" (1:80–81; Now I hear a marvel, says King Pelias, the greatest one I have ever heard, that you never tire of recounting in this way your felony and your disloyalty, but it pleases and delights you so much that you can't keep from confessing your wicked life). Apollo's riddle constitutes a similarly boastful declaration of his own prowess and privileged role, differing from those of the giant only insofar as it refers to events located in the near future rather than the more distant past. For the Christian audience, the meek but crafty lamb triumphing over the more powerful and sinister wolf is easily decoded as a metaphorical version of David and Goliath, biblical archetype for Apollo's altercation with the giant. This is the only one of the six riddles to focus on the encounter in which it is first told, defining the relationship between the riddler and his interlocutor, though of course Pelias's riddle did take on that aspect once it had been relayed to Sador. And as such it casts in high relief the very impossibility of shared discourse between knight and giant.

In her analysis of Julia Kristeva's theories of estrangement and subjectivity, Anna Smith comments: "Speech and writing presuppose an interlocutor to whom I address my desires. I constrain my aggression and my need to devour by constructing subjectivity in loving relation to an other.... In so doing, I am subject to constant change and renewal, for as I enter into conversation, 'my' speech, 'my' opinions become 'ours,' and meaning becomes pluralized, enriched."[20] The giant, estranged from human society, uses his riddles as a means of establishing a relationship with his chivalric interlocutors. As they are constrained to repeat the riddle's narrative, this time in literal terms, one could say that speech or meaning once personal to the giant—"his"—has been shared and has become "theirs." Given the giant's anthropophagic habits, this use of language to select companions literally replaces an aggressive "need to devour" with a different sort of incorporation, bringing the knights not into his physical body but into the community of the giant and his daughter. Insofar as this shared discourse incorporates the knights into the giant's "master narrative," making them narrators of his life story, it could be said to constitute a "relation" of sorts. In initiating a dialogue, the giant might seem to be engaging in the kind of community building that Charles Taylor ascribes to linguistic exchange: "Language creates what one might call a public space, or a common vantage point from which we survey the world together.... What is set up is a certain coming together in a common act of focus."[21] For Taylor, this use of language to create a space for shared "focus" is fundamental to the creation of human subjectivity or "personhood": "I become a person and remain one only as an interlocutor."[22]

But although the Riddler repeatedly expresses his delight in the knights and the extent to which he values their companionship, the resulting bonds are not ones that can work to the mutual benefit of both parties; a shared narrative discourse conjoining knight and giant can lead only to the demise of one or the other. From the knights' perspective, the "loving relation" sought by the giant is simply a displacement of violence from bodily to linguistic coercion. Far from establishing an intersubjective dialogue, knight and giant objectify one another; in Kristeva's words, again, each remains for the other the "symptôme qui rend précisément le 'nous' problématique, peut-être impossible."[23] The giant's aggressive use of riddles does not, in fact, create a public space for shared focus between two persons; it is merely a parodic imitation of such a construct. Striking back, Apollo constructs a poetic "hook" that effects its own "change and renewal," redefining the balance of power between knight and giant, and consigning the latter to ignominious death.

From the giant's perspective, the riddle of his own death—and particularly that of his death at the hands of a mere human—is one that he cannot translate into direct speech. Not only is he unable to solve the riddle; he does not even seem to grasp the import of Apollo's statement when the giant admits defeat—in effect, a statement of the riddle's solution: "Puis que tu nou sez . . . a morir te covient par les covenances qui sont entre moi et toi" (1:92; Since you don't know the answer . . . you will have to die in accordance with the agreement between me and you). Despite having acknowledged Apollo's right to kill him—"Tu diz verité" (1:92; You speak the truth)—the giant remains completely unconcerned when the victorious young knight asks to handle his sword: "Il li baille maintenant, car il cuidoit que Apollo n'eüst pas tant de cuer qu'il l'oceïst" (1:92; Now he hands it over to him, for he did not think that

Apollo would be so bold as to kill him). Even as Apollo raises the sword to strike the death blow, "Le jaians ne se remue onques, com cil qui ne peüst croire en nule maniere que cil l'osast envaïr" (1:92; The giant does not move at all, like one who couldn't believe in any way that he would dare attack him). Poetic language mediates but also obstructs communication between human and giant, highlighting rather than bridging the estrangement between the two. What is unspeakable for the knights is the very essence of the giant's being, something he delights in hearing them expound. And what is unthinkable for the giant and devastating for his daughter—his death at the hands of a chivalric hero—is the very stuff of knightly adventure, eagerly anticipated by Pelias the moment he hears the riddle: "Et tot maintenant qu'il ot la devinaille escotee, sot bien a quoi elle pooit torner tot maintenant. . . . Et li rois en lesse atant la parole, qui mout voudroit la mort dou jaiant" (1:92; And as soon as he heard the riddle, he knew very well where it could lead right away. . . . And the king, who greatly desired the death of the giant, fell silent at that point).

It is in the exchange between Apollo and Augustine, finally, that we most clearly see the differences that set the giant apart, in his enjoyment of riddles, from both saint and human sinner. When Augustine arrives at Apollo's court, he confronts the royal couple, exposing Apollo's crimes in a cryptic statement whose imagery recalls that of Apollo's own riddle to the giant. The denunciation is launched in metaphorical language, as the saint exclaims: "Je me sui entre vos deus enbatu ausi con li aigniax qui s'enbat entre le lou e la love" (1:101; I've happened upon you two like the lamb that bursts in on the wolf and the she-wolf). When Apollo asks in astonishment why he and the queen are compared to wolves, Augustine provides the key to his "riddle":

> Ge di, fait il, que vos estes encore peiors e plus nonsachans, quar li lous est de tele maniere qu'il ne vera ja son pere venir de si loing qu'il nel conoisse au flair e au regart. . . . Mais tu, qui as reisonable ame en toi, e sens de conoistre mal e bien, n'as pas ensi fait, quar tu de ta main as ocis ton pere, e aprés as ta mere espousee. (1:101)

> [I'm saying, he said, that you are still worse and more ignorant, for the wolf is such that he will never see his father coming, no matter how far

off, without recognizing him by scent and sight. . . . But you, who have a rational soul and the understanding of good and evil, have not done that, for you killed your father with your own hand, and after that you married your mother.]

Unlike the riddles of the giant, the saint's "riddle" targets sin, not as a means of endlessly reliving the pleasures of transgression, but for the purpose of sparking penance and atonement. And though the queen explodes in anger at these words, calling the saint "deable" (devil) and "enchanteres" (magician), Apollo is eager to learn the truth of his own origins, and "mout se delitoit as paroles de Saint Augustin" (1:102; delighted greatly in St. Augustine's speech). After the drama of the queen's incineration, he questions Augustine further and converts to Christianity. Augustine's challenge and Apollo's reaction explicitly articulate a crucial difference between human and animal that I have invoked in the analysis of other episodes involving giants: though animals adhere to natural law and lack the perversity of human sin, they also lack the human capacity for self-knowledge, contrition, and redemption. The larger narrative context identifies this incapacity for spiritual interrogation and conversion with both the pagan queen and the giant. Impervious to any inner feelings of guilt, and unconcerned with shame in the eyes of others, the Riddler cannot recognize himself in the discourse of an interlocutor. And if it did not occur to the giant that the wolf in the riddle symbolized himself, still less would he have worried about *why* he was represented as a notorious beast of prey.

The giant's behavior is not, after all, entirely dissimilar to that of the human protagonists, who are variously guilty of the rape of a sister-in-law, the murder of a brother, the attempted murder of a stepson, the abduction of another man's wife, the murder of both father and stepfather, and the incestuous marriage of mother and son. Critics have noted that the intrigue and melodrama of this opening section lay thematic groundwork for the masterwork to follow, with its combined stories of Tristan, Lancelot, Galahad, and the changing fortunes of the Arthurian world.[24] But whereas the giant boasts ceaselessly of his misdeeds, the knights are susceptible to feelings of both trauma and guilt. Sador is horrified at the altercation with his brother and resists speaking of it whenever asked about his past; Canor cannot bring himself to kill an innocent baby and simply leaves him in the forest. Apollo's crimes are all unwitting, since he has no idea who his parents are; and when he does learn the truth, far from boasting, he is ready to mend his ways. The concentration of these transgressions in the figure of the giant allows the knights—and by extension, the romance audience—a measure of relief by accentuating their own difference from the ostentatiously unrepentant Riddler. This use of the giant as an expendable, racialized other, offers a striking parallel to the scapegoating of the black or Asian man in modern Western society, as noted by Fanon and many others. As Meili Steele has commented with regard to a scene in Ralph Ellison's *Invisible Man*, in which a white man encounters a black man on whom he can project his own incestuous urges: "'Black' becomes the social place to disguise his own desires and hate them as other. The other is not simply what white society excludes but a safe place for hiding self-referential statements."[25] Similarly, a giant is a man who, in his exclusion from chivalric masculinity, human dignity, and Christian redemption, can serve as embodiment of the sinful nature from which Christian knights believe themselves to have been cleansed.

Illustrations of the Riddler reflect his identity as an image of uncultured, undisciplined masculinity run amok. The manuscript fr. 189 of the Bibliothèque de Genève, copied circa 1470, portrays him as a knight in full armor. The giant's garb does not distinguish him from the other knights in the region, who also sport the exotic, ornate armor frequently associated with pagan or Saracen knights; aside from his size, only his impressive spiked mace—a weapon that giants are often depicted as using—marks him as a giant and not part of the royal guard (fig. 3).

In this image the giant is rescuing Luce from royal knights who have been charged with his execution. In this vision of a Britain as yet barely Christianized, the giant does not stand out as a specifically "pagan" enemy; most of the heroes in this part of the text are pagans themselves, including both Luce and the knight who eventually kills the giant. What does distinguish the Riddler is his lack of respect for the pagan gods and their laws, as manifested in his unrepentant practice of both incest and cannibalism. A blasphemer not only in Christian eyes but even by the standards of his own religion, the Riddler is treated here less as a foreign element than as a figure of aristocratic tyranny and amorality, and a caricature of hypermasculinity, that has spun out of all control. The

Figure 3. The giant rescues Luce from the royal guards. Geneva, Bibliothèque de Genève, fr. 189, fol. 9r.

illustration of this passage in the thirteenth-century manuscript Bnf n.a.fr. 6579 (fol. 17r), though less ornate, similarly depicts the giant with armor and weaponry identical to that of the other knights in the image. The manuscript Bnf fr. 335, copied around 1400, offers yet another version of the standard scene, with the giant taking Luce aside while the huddled group of knights look on helplessly. Here too, the giant's armor is indistinguishable from theirs; the artist has marked him as a knight with a touch of savagery by giving him a sword at his waist, while showing him in the act of brandishing a large, roughly hewn club. Both versions imply that the giant is not entirely an "outsider" element in pagan Britain. He is after all about to marry his daughter to a British prince; and we have seen in texts such as *Les premiers faits* and *Guiron le courtois* that giants could maintain diplomatic and feudal relations with pre-Christian British lords. He is, however, a particularly rapacious element within it, a survival of antediluvian savagery that must be eliminated. Though the giant is portrayed in hostile opposition to the king's knights, he is also a marker of the degenerate character of pagan culture overall and the extent to which it is ripe for both spiritual reform by Christian missionaries and political and cultural renovation by Christian kings.

The Riddler's scandalous life story, revealed in riddles, pits him in opposition to nature, culture, and God. Devouring his mother, in fact, is a crime so heinous that it calls forth divine retribution, an event alluded to in the closing lines of the riddle and glossed by Pelias: "Del grant mesfait que tu feïs de ta mere, si com je t'ai dit, se correcierent a toi li dieu si durement que en leu de la devine venjance cheï sor toi li feus celestiax, qui te brula le vis et le cors" (1:80; For the great crime that you committed against your mother, as I've described to you, the gods were so enraged with you that celestial fire fell upon you as divine vengeance, and burned your face and body). This scourge of celestial fire recalls the fate of the classical giants, struck down by Jovian thunderbolts, as well as the fall of the rebel angels into the fires of hell. It is also in this riddle that the giant identifies himself with Cain. This particular giant lives up to the demonic origins retroactively posited in *Des grantz geanz* and is a prime example of the literary antecedents that inspired the fourteenth-century author of that poem. But if the Riddler is aware of having been punished by the gods for crimes against nature, this warning clearly fails to deter either his ongoing cannibalism or the satisfaction he derives from recounting the stories of his past crimes. The Riddler is trapped in a matrix of self and intimate kin, whom he rapes, kills, and eats, just as his primordial ancestors, as imagined by the Anglo-Norman poet, lived a chaotic existence of incestuous mating and internecine strife. Humans and giants may share a common descent from Adam and a common corruption by Original Sin; but giants are distinguished by their absolute indifference toward the possibility of conversion, penance, and salvation.

That the giant was burnt by "li feus celestiax" (celestial fires) links him to Celinde, who was not merely burnt but entirely reduced to ashes by "li feux dou ciel" (1:104; fires from heaven). These figures, coupled in damnation, are the two foci for the elliptical movements of the narrative. The giant does not understand that he becomes a point of contact for a network of knights already linked through the sexually charged figure of a Babylonian princess: though he incorporates them into his life and forces them to conform to his terms, they also inhabit their own story to which he remains oblivious. Luce's exposure on a rock, which allows the giant to carry him away, comes about in the first place only because he has become a sacrificial victim in the intrigue between Sador, Pelias, and Canor. Marriage into the giants' world offers him an alternative to death, but no sooner has he entered this other world than he is joined by the key players of his near demise: first Sador, then Pelias. And the three knights with whom the giant trades riddles are Sador, Celinde's first husband; Pelias, her third husband; and Apollo, who is both her fourth husband and the son born of her first marriage. The narrative that the giant seeks to impose with his riddles centers on his life of violent libidinous pleasures, but it clashes with the knights' own narrative of male bonding and sexual rivalry. And whereas the giant uses his riddles to form a community of knights capable of understanding his behavior and narrating it in explicit terms, the knights are able to appropriate the riddling game as a way of manipulating their own collective story.

This alternative narrative is the substance of the other riddle that the giant cannot solve—one posed by Pelias in an effort to escape his forced residence with the giant. The riddle combines animal imagery with the language of courtly love poetry, describing a man (Pelias) and a leopard (Sador) to whom the man shows great honor. But having first enriched the man, the leopard then destroys him by stealing the heart and the rib from his body: that is, Sador first gave Pelias the thing he most desired—Celinde—and then robbed him of his beloved. As stated above, it is Sador who gives the giant the solution in exchange for his freedom, since he fears that if they are joined by Pelias he may once more lose Celinde. Sador's explanation of the riddle includes a miniexposition of love and marriage:

> Et ce est ce qu'il apele coste, por ce que selonc la loi del regne et selonc la loi des diex l'avoit a soi retenue et acostee, ausi com Adam acosta a soi Eve, sa feme. A ce qu'il dist vos poez encores aler veoir le cors sanz cuer, doit l'en entendre que encores aime il la dame tant que touz ses cuers et tote s'arme et tote sa pensee est en li. (1:83)
>
> ---
>
> [And this (Celinde) is what he calls "rib," because in accordance with the law of the kingdom and the law of the gods, he had taken her for himself and lain at her side, just as Adam lay beside his wife Eve. Where he says that you can still see the body without a heart, one should understand that he still loves the lady so much that all his heart and all his soul and all his thoughts are in her.]

It is doubtless this allusion to the bonds of love that renders the riddle particularly baffling for the giant, for whom a romantic passion that long outlives any bodily contact would surely be unimaginable—even if, as we have seen, such passion is by no means foreign to the heart of a giantess. The concept of chivalric service to one's lord would also lie outside the experience of a solitary figure like the giant, making the riddle's central conflict—between feudal bonds and the bonds of love and marriage—as incomprehensible to him as his own sources of pleasure are to the knights. Pelias presents himself as a tragic hero: a devoted husband and a beneficent lord overwhelmed by the passions of love, victim of his own faith in the beloved wife and the favored knight who betrayed him. This very image of long-suffering nobility—like Apollo's portrait of the valiant and virtuous "underdog" who uses skill and wits to slay a more powerful predator—is completely alien to the giant's own self-image as one who stops at nothing in the drive toward bodily gratification, and for whom power lies in brute strength.

Nonetheless it is striking that if the giant is unable to solve the knights' riddles, they—however traumatized by the experience—are always able to solve his. Lesser men, it is true, often lacked the mettle to unravel the giant's words, and through his riddling challenges "avoit il mout ocis, et fait mourir a duel et a honte" (1:76; he had killed many men, causing them grievous and shameful death). The chivalric heroes of the story, however, rise easily to the challenge. The darkest recesses of the soul, it would seem, are known to knights as they are to giants. Where the knights have the advantage is in their capacity—should they choose to use it—to master these destructive bodily drives, to exploit a knowledge of good as well as evil in order to achieve both cultural refinement and spiritual absolution. No doubt part of the trauma experienced by the knights in solving the riddles—and perhaps also by the reader—is that very realization of one's own capacity to recognize, understand, and verbalize seemingly unspeakable and unimaginable acts. No wonder Pelias and Apollo rush to construct riddles affirming their own paradoxical fusion of vulnerability, ethical consciousness, and nobility of spirit: an identity that, in opposition to the giant, is further affirmed as fundamentally human. Having just been forced to acknowledge their comprehension of the giant, and facing the implications of their ready ability to identify (with) his behavior, they must now establish their crucial differentiation from him. If the Riddler seeks to construct a shared discourse with knights—a textual community of autobiographical riddles—he is doomed from the start, because his reading of the common history binding him to the knights is fundamentally opposed to theirs. For him, the story of Original Sin and its consequences of fratricide, incest, and cannibalism carries no moral or spiritual value; it is simply a catalog of events that have shaped his life. Apollo's gloss, with its citation of Proverbs, implicitly reinstates the biblical and moral framework that also operates in his own riddle: one that casts the giant as a member of the cursed, divinely marked line of Cain, excluded from human society and destined to extermination. Even when human and giant do have a shared repertoire of imagery and narrative motifs, they remain divided by the ways in which these motifs function to articulate a sense of personal, cultural, and ethical identity.

Once again, desire threads through the tale of violent encounters between giants and humans. Desire for a Saracen princess destabilizes the chivalric world, and Celinde ultimately falls victim to the spread of Christianity; along the way the men most intimately associated with her renegotiate their relationships through a giant. And both the giant and his daughter have an insatiable desire for human knights: on the one hand as food, but on the other hand as companions or as spouse. Their behavior recalls Dyaletes's desire to retain all knights and ladies who visit his island—as rulers if they measure up, otherwise in the dungeon, but either way as permanent residents. Nabon similarly populated his kingdom with human subjects, divided into social strata of serfs and freemen according to their entertainment value on the sporting field. All three episodes offer variations on the common giant practice of collecting and hoarding chivalric prisoners, often in very large numbers. The Riddler seeks to surround himself with knights who understand him and his ways: with their ability to solve all riddles, his human companions act as interpreters between the giant and the chivalric world. He believes, almost touchingly, that he can trust them both as wise men to help him with riddles posed by newcomers and as warriors to whom he can safely hand over his own sword. Desire for human companionship, as is so often the case, is the giants' point of vulnerability; and they ultimately meet their inevitable fate, split along gendered lines. The male giant, for whom language is a lethal weapon, sin a source of obsessive delight, and desire a murderous force, stands outside the bounds of human society; though fascinating, he is also utterly taboo and must ultimately be done to death. As we have seen, the very terms of the marriage that the giant enabled posit the giant's own death as object of desire for both Luce and his father. As Pelias reflects when deciding not to give the giant the solution to Apollo's riddle, it would do him little good to purchase his own freedom when "son fil qu'il tant aime covendra a remenoir aprés li, et estre leanz avec la fille au jaiant tote sa vie" (1:92; his son whom he loves so much will have to stay behind, and remain in there with the giant's daughter for all his life). It is in the giantess that human desire can be focused, responding to and re-forming the powerful yearning of giant for human and of human for exotic other: a love that is—if only just—containable within the bonds of marriage.

CHAPTER 5

Outsiders in the Story

Galehot, Palamedes, and Saladin

I have touched already on both the affinities and the differences between giants and Saracens, whether (pseudo-) Muslim or pagan. Giants are sometimes allied with pagan or Muslim lords and are frequently portrayed in explicit resistance to Christian hegemony; the more comic or sympathetic giants of *chansons de geste*, such as Fierabras and Rainouart, are little more than oversized Saracen princes. The giants of Arthurian romance, however, are distinct from these Saracen heroes; their excesses are particular to them, and they are less easily assimilated through baptism and marriage or military companionship. In this chapter we will examine the parallel, yet never quite similar, use of the giant and the pagan through the detailed analysis of two iconic figures from Arthurian romance: Galehot the half-blood giant and Palamedes the Saracen. In the concluding section, we will see how both of these figures contribute to the literary fantasy of Saladin as the mixed-blood descendant of an Iberian sultan and the French count of Ponthieu.

Galehot: Desire and Assimilation

Two facts of Galehot's life are reiterated throughout Arthurian prose romance: that he is the son of a beautiful giantess and that he had an overwhelming love for Lancelot—so great that he died of grief when he thought that Lancelot had been lost.[1] Though initially presented in *Lancelot* under the guise of femininity and beauty, Galehot's giant ancestry is revisited and elaborated in later texts that posit a genuine ferocity at its origins: the prose *Tristan* gives us the murderous Dyaletes, sworn enemy of the Christian faith, while *Perceforest* establishes an even earlier descent from the Golden-Haired Giant. These texts inscribe Galehot's lineage in a context of violence, identifying his ancestors as rapacious villains: Dyaletes massacred everyone in his kingdom who converted to Christianity, including his own sons, while the Golden-Haired Giant was a serial rapist who intended to murder his wife and marry his own daughter. Together, these episodes additionally depict Galehot as twice descended from a beautiful giantess and the man who either killed or assisted in killing her father. Successive authors, in other words, repeatedly frame Galehot's character in a picture of human-giant relations combining violent homosocial conflict and heterosexual desire—in a sense, a normalization of *Lancelot*'s original depiction of Galehot as one whose relations with other knights are an unorthodox mix of violent aggression and homosocial, even homoerotic, desire. In keeping with his mixed origins, the half-blood giant embodies both absolute military might and a spirit of courtliness and generosity unrivaled in the Arthurian world. He also has another trait that, as we have seen, is sometimes associated with giants: a longing for the companionship of a select group of knights. Though undefeated in battle, he is vulnerable to his desire for two young paragons of knighthood, Lancelot and Tristan. Neither conquers him through force of violence, but both do conquer him through personal charm and an impressive display of military skill. Galehot's inability to resist the attractions of these two figures, both equally famed for chivalry and for love, proves his undoing, bringing about the destruction of his giant heritage, the end to his dreams of conquest, and ultimately his own untimely death.

We have seen how his admiration for Tristan causes Galehot to accept the deaths of his parents and to abolish the custom that linked his island to its giant past. This episode is a replay of Galehot's even more extreme love for Lancelot, which causes him to renounce all earthly honor, to become one of Arthur's knights, and to retreat to Sorelois for a life of increasingly stultifying leisure. The different versions of *Lancelot* provide scant information about Galehot's life before his encounter with Lancelot, though it is clear that he has been a formidable force. Galehot tells his new friend that as a young knight he set out to conquer the world and that he had planned to have himself crowned as a glorious, all-powerful king once he had achieved his goal.[2] Though his vassals criticize his capitulation as shameful, Galehot insists that he has won far more in gaining Lancelot's friendship than he has lost in giving up his plans of conquest. As the narrator comments: "En ceste maniere torna Galhout a savoir et a gaaing ce que li autre tornoient a perte et a folie, ne nus n'osast avoir cuer de tant amer buens chevaliers com il faisoit" (*PLanc*, 1:2; In this way Galehot interpreted as wisdom and profit what the others saw as loss and folly, nor would anyone be so bold as to love good knights the way he did). This half-blood descendant of giants, then, shows no moderation in his dealings with the knights and feudal lords whose ancestors first colonized the giants' homeland. Whether in love or in warfare, he is driven to extremes of behavior that rewrite the very concepts of honor and shame.

Galehot does not manifest the savagery of the full-blooded giants fought by Arthurian heroes. Theirs was an indiscriminate policy of predatory assault; his is a systematic program of feudal expansionism, conducted under the rules and customs of chivalric warfare. In fact, Galehot is renowned for his chivalry. It is the very magnitude of his chivalric splendor and prowess—his human-giant hybridity—that makes Galehot a threat unlike that of any ordinary knight or giant. His extraordinary lineage has produced a formidable physique and a charismatic intensity that make him literally unstoppable: as Galegantis li Galois tells Arthur, "Il est bien plus grans demi piet que chevalier que l'an sache, s'est li homme el monde plus amés de sa gent et qui plus a conquis de son eage" (*PLanc*, 7:440; He is half a foot taller than any knight that is known, and of all men he's the best loved by his people, and has conquered more than anyone else his age). But when he encounters Lancelot, Galehot's desire to subjugate the Arthurian knights is transformed into a desire for intimate love and friendship. His new idea for military adventuring, though it is never put into practice, is that he will conquer Lancelot's ancestral lands and that the two companions could be crowned kings of one another's realms, their friendship reinforced with the bonds of feudal alliance (1:73–77). I will return to this point below.

As a half-blood vestige of monstrous indigenes, Galehot is a sign not of the extermination of the ancient race but of their assimilation and absorption by the incomers—a far more problematic process.[3] Having entered the narrative as a dangerous force that could supplant Arthur as supreme king, Galehot then becomes instrumental in establishing the love relationship between Lancelot and Guenevere: an ambiguous role at best. It is Galehot who, after surrendering to the amazed and delighted Arthur, asks his hosts what each would be willing to do in order to win the companionship of Lancelot, then known only as the Black Knight.[4] Arthur says that he would give that knight anything he wanted except, of course, the queen; Gawain says that he would wish to become a damsel so that he could be the knight's beloved; and Guenevere discreetly comments that Gawain has already said it all. Having pressed Arthur into saying that in order to attract Lancelot he would give him anything *except* Guenevere, then, Galehot proceeds to make sure that it is precisely Guenevere that Lancelot gets. In this respect he does actually make good on the typically giantesque threat with which he had launched the war with Arthur. The messenger sent to deliver the declaration of war announces that Galehot not only intends to conquer Arthur's lands but also "te taudra Genievre, ta feme, qu'il a oïe proisier de biauté et de valor" (7:440; will take away Guenevere, your wife, whom he has heard praised so much for her beauty and valor). Despite his surrender and his stated willingness to give up worldly honor, Galehot is hardly the compliant ally that he may superficially seem. His predatory, expansionist agenda is transferred onto Lancelot, who is now the beneficiary of Galehot's scheming; but Arthur is robbed of honor nonetheless. And as if that is not enough, having brought Lancelot to everyone's attention as the savior of Arthur's kingdom—having pressed both the king and his nephew to admit that they would go to extraordinary lengths to keep Lancelot in their company—Galehot proceeds to spirit Lancelot away to Sorelois, where he makes every effort to keep Arthur's knights at bay. What seems on the surface a relatively straightforward arrangement among men, in which Lancelot mediates between Arthur and Galehot, is in fact a more complicated foursome, consisting of interlocking triangles: one of Arthur, Lancelot, and Galehot; another of Arthur, Lancelot, and Guenevere; and another still of Guenevere, Lancelot, and Galehot. There is even a humorous implication of yet another triangle, made up of Galehot, Lancelot, and Gawain. Having jokingly stated that he would like to be a lady so as to have a love affair with Lancelot, Gawain is also the one who astutely sizes up the erotic overtones of Galehot's own designs on everybody's favorite knight. Warning Arthur that he will need to act quickly if he is to retain Lancelot at court, Gawain points out that "Galahot l'enmenra au plus tost qu'il porra, car il est plus jalous de lui que nuls chevaliers de jouene dame" (8:482; Galehot will take him away as soon as he can, for he is more jealous of him than any knight ever was of a young lady). Galehot may have surrendered to Arthur, but he remains a troublesome presence, queering the amorous and feudal relationships at the heart of the Arthurian kingdom.

Galehot's human ancestry makes him a domesticated, civilized version of a full-blooded giant like Ritho, who also sets out to conquer the kings of the world.[5] In contrast to the barbaric collector of beards, Galehot wants only Arthur's homage. Nonetheless, if he does not literally steal Arthur's body—or at any rate, a bodily sign of his masculinity and royal power—he does for a time steal Arthur's most valuable knight. And by engineering the consummation of Lancelot's love for Guenevere, he invades the intimate, sexual space of Arthur's marriage to make him a cuckold: a literal realization of the metaphoric "unmanning" implied in the threatened confiscation of Arthur's beard. Galehot's treatment of Lancelot himself is also disturbing in its very intensity. Beneath its courtly veneer, Galehot's hospitality in Sorelois, like that of the riddling giant in *Tristan*, verges on imprisonment. Lancelot does not hide his frustration at this life of enforced leisure, expressing a wish for some form of knightly combat whereby he could continue to test his mettle and lamenting that "nous somes chi en prison et a moult grant piece que nos ne vismes joustes ne chevaleries, si perdons no tans et nos eages" (8:418; we're in prison here, and it's been a very long time since we saw any jousts or knightly exploits; we're frittering away our time and our youth). Galehot's reaction to Lancelot's complaint is to take him to an even more isolated retreat, the Isle Perdu, determined that "il le gardera de combatre" (8:418; he will prevent him from fighting). There Lancelot languishes, unable to eat or drink in his misery, desperate for word from Guenevere. Though Galehot's behavior is motivated by love, there is nonetheless something decidedly threatening about this son of a giantess.

Galehot contrasts interestingly with the giant Caradoc, the central figure in a lengthy episode that dominates much of the action during the period of Lancelot's friendship with Galehot.[6] Caradoc also desires one of Arthur's knights, in this case Gawain, but not out of love. He intends to hold Gawain prisoner and inflict such torments on him that he will long to die, but without ever quite killing him. Caradoc, that is, wants literally to possess Gawain and to keep him in a bodily state that will forever remind Gawain of Caradoc's power over him. In his fixation on an Arthurian knight he is a negative version of Galehot, and the contrast brings out all the more clearly just how chivalric Galehot is, how close he does come to assimilating into the Round Table, yet how fraught his identity still is. Like Caradoc, he removes a knight from circulation, endangering the Arthurian kingdom by depriving it of an important warrior, and causing unhappiness to the knight in question. The analogy between these episodes is highlighted by their symmetry. Gawain overcomes all obstacles to "rescue" Lancelot from Galehot's clutches, including near-lethal battles with the knights that Galehot posts as guards in his hopes to keep Lancelot for himself, and succeeds in bringing him back to Camelot—escorted by Galehot, of course—to assist Arthur against the Saxons. And while many knights attempt to rescue Gawain, it is Lancelot who succeeds. This symmetrical structure further contributes to the implicit suggestion of the fourth triangle I alluded to above, that of Lancelot, Galehot, and Gawain: one in which the feudal bonds of chivalric friendship and loyalty to a common lord are tested against those binding a knight to the (half-blood) giant who loves and desires him.

As we have seen, a giant's relations with human knights tend to the extremes. He may imprison or even eat them; he may, like Nabon li Noirs, use them to populate his kingdom; or he may find their company so delightful that he keeps them as treasured companions, albeit against their will. In all cases, however, it is the knights who are absorbed into his world, whether they are literally devoured as food, incarcerated in prisons, put to work as laborers, or sequestered as slaves to his desire for human friendship. Giants show no capacity for reciprocal relationships and do not concern themselves with earning the respect, loyalty, or devotion of the humans they collect. Even if Maudit and the Chevalier Jayant—each, as it happens, raised by one giant and one human parent or stepparent—may have accepted the letter if not the spirit of terms set by the lady they wished to marry, neither they nor any other giant ever exhibits the slightest discomfort with the indifference of a prospective bride or the anguished protests of a female victim. In this respect they differ from the Saracen Palamedes, who, when he carries off Iseut, is so disturbed by her tears and lamentations that he seriously considers setting her free, and who dwells obsessively on his longing to be loved by her.

Galehot's behavior is also shaped by the two impulses of extermination or incarceration, signs of his maternal descent from giants. But in keeping with his status as son of a worthy knight, this behavior is recast in human terms as military conquest, feudal subjugation, and of course the all-consuming friendship that comes to define his being: his longing for a perpetual tête-à-tête with Lancelot deep within his own lands. It is Galehot's hybridity that produces the tragic overtones of his story: a giant's commitment to absolute power and instant gratification, combined with a human need for mutual love and reciprocity—for that elusive but crucial quality of requitedness. Galehot's love for Lancelot is nothing short of passion, and its homoerotic qualities have been noted by numerous scholars.[7] Galehot pleads with Lancelot to return to Sorelois after the Saxon war, unable to face the prospect that Lancelot might stay behind in Camelot: "Biaus douls compains, nous sommes venu la ou vous perdirai.... Et que ferai jou, qui tout ai mis en vous mon cuer et mon cors?" (8:483; Fair sweet companion, we have reached a point where I am going to lose you.... And what will I do, when I have given you my heart and my body?). Guenevere is well aware of the competing claims that she and Galehot have on Lancelot's person, and when she makes her own plea for Lancelot to stay with her, it is not Arthur but Galehot from whom she must conceal her request:

> Et la roine li prie que, se mesire Gawain li prie de remanoir, que il remaigne, que ele est si sosprise de lui et de s'amor, que ele ne voit mie comment ele s'en puisse consievrer. Mais ce dist ele si bas que Galahos ne l'ot mie, car trop en fust dolans. (8:445)
>
> [And the queen implores him, if Sir Gawain asked him to stay, that he would stay, for she is so overwhelmed by him and his love that she doesn't see how she could get along without him. But she said it so softly that Galehot didn't hear her, for it would have greatly upset him.]

And it is when he thinks he has lost Lancelot forever that Galehot himself dies of a broken heart, gazing longingly at Lancelot's shield as he lingers on his deathbed (1:388).

Collectively, prose romance implies that a love marked by human-giant difference can be resolved through translation into gender difference, where it can be stigmatized as monstrous rape or neutralized as exogamous marriage. But if heterosexual lust or intimacy enables both the criminalization of an alien race and their absorption through marriage, same-sex intimacy offers no such solution. In contrast with the crimes of rape and incest conventionally favored by giants, Galehot's love of Lancelot redefines the structures of similarity and difference that enable erotic desire, while also recasting the homosocial friendship of the Round Table. The half-blood giant struggles to reshape the Arthurian world according to his own terms, seeking first to make himself the supreme ruler over Arthur and then to construct a competing model of chivalric life and love. As Jane Gilbert has argued, Galehot's efforts to gratify Lancelot's desires are "excessive," undermine conventional concepts of knightly identity, and disrupt the companionship of the Round Table by attempting to impose a different set of values and behavior patterns: "Lancelot does not want his overgenerous adhesion or his sacrifice-demand, which therefore become themselves acts of protest against knighthood."[8] But he is defeated by Lancelot's commitment to a different trajectory, one defined by his love for the queen, his willing defense of Arthur's kingdom, and his participation in chivalric quests. Galehot's efforts and ultimate failure to recast Arthurian history reflect his roots in the world of giants and bear closer scrutiny.

Lancelot, Tristan, and Galehot: Competing Narratives

Returning with Lancelot to Sorelois after the Saxon defeat, Galehot experiences portents of his imminent death—collapsing castle towers and ominous dreams—and learns from Arthur's clerk that he will indeed live only for so long as he can keep Lancelot at his side. In reaction to this troubling state of affairs, Galehot hatches a plan that he hopes will bind Lancelot even more tightly to himself. He explains to Lancelot that he had intended to be crowned king of all his lands by now but that he does not wish to proceed with that unless Lancelot is crowned first. He therefore makes a startling proposal:

> Je vos dorrai demie la seignorie de tote la terre que je tieng, et si la vos ferai creanter a tos mes barons et si en avrés les sairements et les feautés . . . et vos tendront autretel homage com a moi. Et si serons ensamble coroné a cest Noël la ou li rois Artu mes sires tendra sa cort. (1:74–75)
>
> ———
>
> [I will give you the half of the lordship of all the land that I hold, and I will make all my barons pledge themselves to you, and you will have their oaths and fealty . . . and you will hold just as much homage as I do. And then we will be crowned together this Christmas, where my lord King Arthur holds court.]

Having been crowned, in turn, the two friends will then wage war on Claudas to recapture Lancelot's lands. Galehot's words imply that a similar arrangement will be put in place in Benwic; as he states, "Je conquerrai molt bien le vostre heritage por amor de vos et je l'amerai miels que je ne feroie le mien et tote la terre le roi Artu" (1:75; I will fully conquer your ancestral lands for love of you, and I will prefer them over my own or all the land of King Arthur). Lancelot, in other words, will reign over lands held in fealty from Galehot, while Galehot will reign over lands held in fealty from Lancelot. If enacted, Galehot's plan would have produced both a highly unusual model of kingship and feudal alliance— two kings reigning jointly over one another's lands—and a radically different role for Lancelot in the Arthurian world. Though he could have continued as a companion of the Round Table, Lancelot's feudal center of gravity, as it were, would have shifted away from Logres to fuse with that of Galehot, who would simultaneously be Lancelot's feudal lord and his most important vassal. But it was not to be. Guenevere has forbidden Lancelot to swear fealty to any man, and he has no interest in conquest—least of all without her permission. As he tells the crestfallen Galehot: "J'ameroie miels a estre tos jors ansi com je sui hui que estre rois et avoir honor et la richesce par coi je perdisse ma dame la roine ne ele moi" (1:76; I would rather remain forever just as I am today than to be king and have honor and wealth that might cause me to lose my lady the queen, or for her to lose me).

Galehot's attempt to restructure the Arthurian world and rewrite the romance of Lancelot runs aground on Lancelot's absolute identification as lover of Guenevere—a feature of vernacular Arthurian legend that can be reimagined in various ways by different authors but never lost from view. The closest Lancelot ever comes to excluding Guenevere from his story is in the *Queste del Saint Graal*, when he is persuaded that his love is a mortal sin for which he must do penance. At this point, his concerns for spiritual salvation apparently outweigh his love for Guenevere. And as he moves closer to Galahad, son of Guenevere's rival and grandson of Pelles, keeper of the Grail, it seems as if he might finally be moving away from the temptations of Camelot and into the orbit of the Holy Grail. But of course the story could not end here either; the author of *La mort le roi Artu* ensures that Lancelot's return to Camelot is also a return to Guenevere, and the love story will provide an overarching context within which Arthurian history is finally brought to its end. Neither the warnings of the hermits nor the spectacle of his saintly son could ultimately deflect Lancelot from a lifetime spent as devoted lover and humble servant of the queen; nor, at the outset of Lancelot's chivalric career, could the manipulative friendship of the half-blood giant set him on a different course.

It is not only Lancelot's identity that Galehot seeks to alter, however; it is also his own. On the one hand, having just learned from Arthur's clerk that his life depends on proximity to Lancelot, Galehot is simply trying to ensure that he will never lose contact with his beloved companion. An interesting detail, however, suggests that the half-blood giant may be motivated by a more profound need to redefine himself. Having overheard Arthur's clerk speaking to Galehot about the catastrophic consequences of separation from a beloved friend, Lancelot is deeply troubled that this may apply to himself. And Galehot, wanting to shield Lancelot from the awful truth, invents an alternative explanation, claiming that his grief arose because he had just learned the death of his mother: "Kar je feisse le greignor duel del monde, ne ja ne fuisse liés, se vos ne fuissiés. Mais si tost com il me menbra de vos, si oi le duel oblié; si n'avoie je onques nule rien tant amee com ma mere devant que je fusse acointes de vos" (1:73; For I would have had the greatest grief in the world, and would never have been happy again, if not for you. But as soon as I remembered you, I forgot my grief; I had never loved anything so much as my mother before I met you). Galehot's words imply a substitution of Lancelot for his giantess mother as principal love object in his life—in effect, a disavowal of his giant heritage in an effort to move closer to his Arthurian beloved. It is just after this exchange that Galehot makes his proposal of joint kingship. Symbolically sacrificing his mother, Galehot tries to create a space for himself in the feudal world as king and companion of Lancelot—a giantess's son no longer.

The Chastel de Plour episode in *Tristan* takes its inspiration from Galehot's comment to Lancelot, inventing the story of his mother's actual death and linking it to his abolition of the evil custom, legacy of his giant ancestor. Whereas in *Lancelot* his origins are mysterious—we do not in fact even know if his mother really is dead or alive—in the later text we learn that she did die at about this point in the story. The effect is a retrospective rationalization of Galehot's behavior in *Lancelot*: his new companion is a genuine source of solace, and we might conclude that maternal bereavement only contributes to Galehot's intense need to keep his friend at hand. Even more to the point, Tristan now emerges as the one for whom Galehot really does sacrifice not only his mother—or at least her memory—but his father as well, and the one because of whom he can set aside his grief. Lancelot's presence alone was not enough to deter Galehot from seeking vengeance, even when it meant being separated for a time from his precious companion; but at the sight of Tristan, Galehot abandons that idea, replacing it with the goal of bringing Tristan and Lancelot together, with himself, in Sorelois. Having sacrificed his dreams of future conquest for Lancelot, in other words, he now sacrifices his parentage and the customary law that linked him to an isolationist giant past for Tristan. He will neither extend his reign over the surrounding world nor fortify himself as an invincible island lord who views all other knights as rivals. One might say that the author of *Tristan* completes what he saw as a process beginning in *Lancelot*. There Galehot's future is foreclosed, while his past is unknown; now his ancestral heritage is revealed, only to be discarded in turn. Effectively boxed into a present moment that allows him little room for movement, Galehot catapults Tristan into the Arthurian limelight and identifies him as the equal—or the rival—of Lancelot, then meekly effaces himself in death, leaving the two young knights as the star performers in the Arthurian world. Ultimately, Galehot might be seen as sacrificing his own chivalric career, his giant-centered history and feudal dynasty, while launching the new story of the intertwined adventures of Lancelot and Tristan: peerless knights whose stories are forever complicated by their absolute commitment to an adulterous love. The interactions of Lancelot, Tristan, and Galehot will have the most profound effect on shaping the Arthurian world—both on reforming it and on identifying the limits beyond which it cannot be altered.

As we have seen, Galehot even offers Tristan the same unorthodox feudal arrangement that he has already proposed to Lancelot. The allusion to Lancelot in Galehot's offer—"Je donrai a monseignor Lancelot et a vos totes les terres que je onques conquis" (*PT*[C], 2:90; I will give you and my lord Lancelot all the lands that I ever conquered)—hints at the further possibility that Galehot might have helped Tristan, too, to recover his ancestral lands. The reader knows that even had Galehot lived on, he would never have succeeded permanently in drawing Tristan away from Cornwall and into this proposed triad; for Tristan would not have abandoned the queen of Cornwall any more than Lancelot was prepared to jeopardize his relationship with the queen of Logres. Galehot does, however, successfully implicate Tristan in the Lancelot-Grail narrative. His letter to Guenevere establishes the preeminence of the two famous adulterous couples and ignites the first sparks of desire within the kingdom of Logres for contact with the Cornish lovers: "Quant la roïne vit ces letres, mout li plot et mout li enbeli, et dit qu'ele verroit volentiers Yselt la Bloe, puis qu'ele est si bele, et Tristan, puis qu'il est si bons chevaliers" (*PT*[C], 2:90–91; When the queen saw the letter, it greatly pleased and entertained her, and she said that she would like to see Iseut the Blonde, since she is so beautiful, and Tristan, since he is such a great knight).⁹

Galehot's intuitive understanding of the affinities between Lancelot and Tristan is borne out in later developments that set the prose *Tristan* decisively apart from the earlier verse texts—in particular, the period in which Lancelot provides the Joyous Guard as a haven for Tristan and Iseut after they have fled from Cornwall, in an arrangement that echoes Galehot's own nurturing of Lancelot's love for Guenevere and the haven he provided during the False Guenevere episode. The Tristan narrative merges fully with that of Lancelot at precisely the site in which Galehot himself—author, as it were, of this fusion—is laid to rest in Lancelot's own tomb. But Galehot's death means that it is Lancelot, and not the son of the giantess, who provides the matrix in which this trio of illustrious knights, with their intricate web of adulterous love and passionate friendship, can be brought together. The life led by Tristan and Iseut at the Joyous Guard could even be seen as a realization of fantasies that Galehot entertained about Lancelot and Guenevere but that he was never able to put into practice because of Lancelot's very different approach to love. The Tristan story, as it runs in tandem with that of Lancelot, allows for the juxtaposition of different patterns of love, desire, and passion, such that narrative possibilities hinted at by Galehot can be explored in a different context—one that does not threaten Arthurian hegemony but indeed strengthens it by demeaning that of the king of Cornwall. To see just how this works, we must examine more closely Galehot's various interventions, or proposed interventions, in the story of Lancelot and Guenevere.

Galehot's most spectacular intervention in Arthurian history is surely his instrumental role in bringing Lancelot and Guenevere together: it is he who first perceives their love, and his urging that prompts their first kiss. The resulting love affair is crucial not only to Lancelot's own story but to the Arthurian world as a whole; it is ultimately an important factor in the demise of the kingdom, supplementing the treachery of Mordred that brought about Arthur's downfall in Geoffrey of Monmouth's account. Galehot thus fosters an alternative narrative that runs alongside the one set forth in the *Historia regum Britanniae*, culminating in *La mort le roi Artu*. In this final text of the Lancelot-Grail cycle, the roles of Lancelot, Gawain, and Mordred are intertwined in a multithreaded tale of Arthurian self-destruction that is far more complex than the version given by Geoffrey. Guenevere's adultery with Lancelot complements Arthur's earlier crime of incest with Mordred's mother; a blood feud between Lancelot and Gawain, directly arising from the disruptive effects of the adulterous affair, provides the context that enables the treachery of Gawain's half-brother. Galehot does not succeed in creating his own "master narrative" of three kings reigning over each other's lands in a kind of feudal triumvirate, rivaling Arthur in chivalric and courtly preeminence. Nonetheless, with the advent of the son of the giantess—an innovation introduced in the vernacular adaptation and expansion of Geoffrey's material—the Arthurian master narrative is never the same again.

In keeping with his role as the facilitator of adulterous passion, Galehot's lands provide temporary refuge for both pairs of lovers: Tristan and Iseut experience a few months of bliss on the Isle del Jaiant, while Lancelot and Guenevere live for two years in Sorelois during the queen's displacement by the False Guenevere. Galehot would have been willing to do far more for Lancelot and Guenevere, admitting at one point that he seriously considered invading Arthur's kingdom and abducting the queen so as to give her to Lancelot in Sorelois. While acknowledging the radical nature of this move, Galehot defends his plan as having arisen from "poor de mort et force d'amor" (1:36; the fear of death and the power of love) and explains that he hoped thereby to foreclose any possibility that Lancelot might ever wish to leave Sorelois himself: "Par ce euisse je tos jors mes et vos et vostre cuer en baillie" (1:37; That way I would have both you and your heart forever in my possession). At this eruption of "giantesque" thinking, the horrified Lancelot can only reply: "Sire, par Dieu, mort m'euissés, se ensint fust fet, ne tel chose ne fet pas a emprendre sans son congié" (1:37; Sir, by God, you would have killed me if you had done that, nor is such a thing to be done without her permission). When the False Guenevere causes Arthur to turn against his queen, Galehot cannot understand Lancelot's concern, pointing out that this should be good news: he will give Guenevere lordship over Sorelois, and she and Lancelot can be married (1:34–35). Again, however, Lancelot hesitates to countenance any action not proposed by Guenevere herself; and the drastic measures imagined by Galehot, which would have altered Arthurian legend beyond recognition, never come to pass. Indeed, although Guenevere does take refuge in Sorelois until the crisis has passed, she imposes a vow of chastity on her relations with Lancelot during her stay there, feeling that it is necessary to atone for the sexual sins that brought about her misfortune. Only once this crisis has been resolved will it be possible for the lovers to resume sexual intimacy:

> Si vos requier por la grant amor que vos avés a moi que vos des ore mes ne me querrois nule compaignie, ne mes de baisier et d'acoler . . . et quant j'en avrai lieu et tens et vostre volentés sera, vos avrois volentiers le sorplus. Mais tels est ore ma volentés que il vos en covient a soffrir une piece. (1:152)
>
> ---
>
> [I ask you, for the great love that you have for me, that from now on you do not seek intimacy with me, not even kissing or embracing . . . and when it's the right time and place and accords with your wishes, I will gladly give you the rest. But for now it's my will that you have to do without for a while.]

Needless to say, Lancelot's acceptance is unqualified: "Dame, fet Lancelos, riens ne me grieve qui vos plaise" (1:152; Lady, says Lancelot, nothing can upset me that pleases you). One could hardly imagine an attitude more different from that of Galehot—or from that of any giant. We must wait for the Tristan legend to develop a somewhat different narrative of truly unquenchable passion, in which Lancelot can do for Tristan what he was not prepared to let Galehot do for him.

Even after the False Guenevere is unmasked, the queen could have chosen to remain with Lancelot in Galehot's lands; but this escapism is not what either she or Lancelot wants. When she is offered the possibility of returning to Arthur's court, Lancelot wholeheartedly encourages her to do so, proclaiming that "cil ne vos ameroit pas qui ceste honor vos loeroit a refuser, c'est la seignorie de Bretaigne et le roi Artu qui est vostre sires espos" (1:166–67; anyone who would advise you to refuse this honor—the lordship of Britain and King Arthur who is your wedded husband—would not love you). Though acknowledging that it might gratify his own personal pleasure and that of Galehot to keep

Guenevere at his side, Lancelot cannot countenance any such indulgence: "Si vos amerions nos miels en ceste terre entre moi et mon seignor qui ci est. Mais nos volons miels soffrir paines et mesaises" (1:167; Albeit that we would rather have you in this land, with myself and my lord who is here. But we prefer to suffer pain and sorrow). Guenevere is quick to agree. Rather than living out their fantasy desires in the Other World of Galehot's kingdom, both lovers prefer reintegration into life at court. Similarly, Tristan and Iseut cannot remain on the Isle del Jaiant. Humans can pass through the giants' world; they may even, like Luce, Clamidés, Lyonnel, or Arthur himself, return forever changed, marked by some relic of their experience—a giantess bride, a giant's head, a cloak of royal beards. But return they must, just as Lancelot and Guenevere must always return to Logres, and just as Tristan would certainly have left Sorelois for a return to Cornwall.[10] Galehot can complicate the Arthurian world and alter its narrative lines, but he is powerless to resist its overall forward movement.

Emmanuèle Baumgartner has noted that Lancelot's devotion to Guenevere creates conflicting desires not only with regard to Galehot but also with regard to Morgan, who repeatedly kidnaps Lancelot and holds him prisoner.[11] Morgan initially captures Lancelot in an attempt to punish Guenevere, with whom she has a long-standing feud; but like virtually everyone else in Logres, she soon succumbs to Lancelot's irresistible charisma. During a subsequent imprisonment—the episode in which Lancelot paints the story of his love for Guenevere on the walls of the chamber in Morgan's castle—her love is no longer secret:

> Car ele l'amoit tant conme fame pooit plus amer home pour la grant biauté de lui, si est moult dolante qu'il ne la voloit amer, car ele nel tenoit mie em prison por haïne, mes vaintre le cuidoit par anui, si l'an avoit maintes foiz proié; mais il ne l'an voloit oïr. (5:53)

> [For she loved him as much as any woman could love a man because of his great beauty, and she was very sorrowful that he didn't want to love her; for she wasn't keeping him in prison out of hatred, but thought she could conquer him through boredom and irritation. And she had asked for his love many times, but he didn't want to hear about it.]

Arthur's greatest knight is thus at the apex of yet another pair of interlocking triangles, this time one in which the fascination and hostile or amorous desire of the fairy rivals that of both Galehot and the queen. In fact, it is Morgan who has "disappeared" Lancelot—first in imprisonment, then by driving him into a state of *forsenerie* by imposing a year-long prohibition of contact with Guenevere as the condition of his release—when Galehot believes him to be dead, and dies himself of a broken heart. But unlike earlier heroes of the *matière de Bretagne* who preferred to be sequestered by a fairy lover rather than to stay in court as the lover or husband of a queen—one thinks of Lanval, or of the tortured vacillations of Guinglain, the Fair Unknown—Lancelot unhesitatingly chooses the court and the queen. With this choice, in Baumgartner's words, "La chevalerie affirme . . . son désir d'être au monde et d'y servir."[12] Consistent with this orientation, Lancelot escapes the clutches of both Galehot and Morgan. And according to *Tristan*, at some point after Galehot's death Lancelot liberates the three bridges allowing access to Sorelois, all of which have been guarded by knights who prevented access to the kingdom, as well as freeing a group of Arthurian knights who were held prisoner there.[13] One of these, the Pont au Jaiant, is the same bridge at which Uterpendragon killed the giant Brun, and where Morholt and the Chevalier de l'Ecu Vermeil killed that giant's sons, in *Guiron le courtois*.[14] Lancelot thus eliminates the last vestiges of giantesque isolationism and hostility in Sorelois, ensuring that it will henceforth be a kingdom that travelers and knights errant can enter and leave at will.[15] This exploit can be seen as the final culmination of his protracted interactions with Galehot: in the end both Galehot personally and Sorelois as a kingdom are domesticated and brought into the Arthurian fold.

Galehot dies because he cannot prevent Lancelot from taking part in lengthy quests, sever his ties to Camelot, or protect him from the predations of Morgan. Excluded from Lancelot's adventures as lover of Guenevere and knight of the Round Table, Galehot cannot go on. Yet he is buried not in the Distant Isles or in his remote kingdom of Sorelois but in Lancelot's tomb at the Joyous Guard: the site of Lancelot's first great exploit, in which he learned his own name, lineage, and destiny. The closing pages of the *Mort*—end point of the Lancelot-Grail cycle—describe the entombment of Lancelot's body with that of his devoted friend. The Joyous Guard is a fitting place for the final reintegration of the half-blood giant into the Arthurian world. Once a demonic site of imprisonment and hostile isolation—the Dolorous Guard—it was liberated from its past and, rather like Galehot himself, brought into the Arthurian present through the intervention of Lancelot. A similar pattern is replicated in the sarcophagus itself, originally constructed for "le roi Narbaduc qui trova emprés Mahomet les poins que li Sarrazin tienent" (*PLanc*, 2:253; King Narbaduc, who, after Mohammed, devised the tenets of the Saracen creed). With the arrival of Joseph of Arimathea and the establishment of Christian law, however, the castle ceased to be a "mahomerie as paiens" (2:253; pagan temple), and the bodies were removed from all the tombs, leaving them available for Christian burials. Even if only in death, it is this site of chivalric and spiritual redemption—marking the inexorable conquest but also the renewal of the old order by the new—that allows Galehot and Lancelot finally to be united within the Arthurian world.[16]

A Saracen Knight at King Arthur's Court: Palamedes

At his first appearance, Palamedes is identified as "Palamedes li Sarradins," one of twelve sons of Esclabor li Mesconneü, king of Babylon, and a pagan: "Onques n'avoit esté crestiens, et si cuidoient li preudome entor qui il reperoit qu'il fust crestiens" (*PT*[C], 1:164; He had never been a Christian, but the noblemen with whom he was associated thought that he was Christian).[17] Palamedes does not continue to "pass" as Christian for long, however, and is soon known throughout the Arthurian world as a Saracen knight—admired for his extreme chivalric prowess but set apart by his refusal of Christian baptism. His separatism is stressed in an aside occasioned by the narrator's explanation of his brother's name:

> Estoit apelés Sephar, non de païen, mais il estoit crestïens. Car tout li frere Palamidés estoient crestïen fors Palamidés seulement, qui en nule guise ne s'acordoit as crestïens fors de cevalerie et de compaingnie. A la loi crestïenne ne so pooit il acorder, por quoi si frere charnel en

lessoient sa compaignie, et si faisoient maint autre cevalier. Et nonpourquant mesire Tristrans ne Lanselos ne l'avoient onques laissié pour la haute cevalerie qu'il savoient en lui, ains se tenoient a bien paiié quant il le pooient aucune fois avoir. (*PT*[M], 6:68)

[He was called Sephar, a pagan name, but he was Christian. For all of Palamedes's brothers were Christian, excepting only Palamedes himself, who would have nothing to do with Christians in any way except for chivalry and companionship. He could not reconcile himself with the Christian faith, for which reason his brothers avoided his company, and so did many other knights. And yet my lords Tristan and Lancelot had never avoided him, because of the exalted chivalry they recognized in him, and indeed they considered themselves well rewarded whenever they could have his company.]

Palamedes offers a model, at once subversive and attractive, for chivalric community and homosocial bonding outside the structures of Christianity; and both of the knights who are drawn to him are characterized by a chivalric excellence and an adulterous passion that simultaneously sustain and undermine their respective kingdoms. It seems no accident that, in addition, Palamedes's two companions are the very ones who, at earlier stages of their respective stories, were targeted by Galehot for his own inner circle of knights. This very fact provides an implicit and subtle point of contact between the Saracen and the son of the giantess and is crucial to the particularity of Palamedes's character within Arthurian legend overall.

Most fundamentally, Palamedes's pagan beliefs exclude him from membership in the Round Table, a fact lamented by Arthur and by other knights. Arthur frequently urges Palamedes to accept baptism. In a move mirroring Galehot's effort to draw Lancelot and Tristan into a narrative of his own construction, Arthur even offers to give Palamedes Camelot if he becomes a Christian, but to no avail (*PT*[M], 9:100–101). Galahad attempts to trick the Saracen into conversion through the device of the *don contraignant*, but Palamedes sees through the ruse, replying: "Certes, il n'est riens que je ne feïsse pour vous fors seulement que crestiens devenir" (*PT*[M], 8:78; To be sure, there is nothing I would not do for you, except to become Christian). Unable to countenance collaboration with a non-Christian, Galahad later refuses to allow Palamedes to join a small group of Arthur's knights who are badly outnumbered in the defense of Camelot against King Mark's army, declaring loftily: "Vous n'estes mie de nostre compaingnie, puis que vous n'estes crestiens!" (*PT*[M], 9:93; You are not of our company, since you're not a Christian). But as noted, Lancelot and Tristan form a bond with Palamedes based on elite chivalric companionship; and these three are universally considered the best knights in the world after Galahad. Throughout much of the story, then, Palamedes stands in opposition to Galahad, as each knight—the fervent Saracen and the militant Christian—forms a point around which a chivalric community is structured. In Palamedes's case, the narrative model is one of endless adventure, pitting knight against knight in trials of prowess and focusing on self-contained projects of conquest, rescue, rivalry, or judicial combat. Though inspired and fueled by erotic love and a mix of homosocial competition and companionship, Palamedes's narrative space remains that of individual rather than communal identity.[18] And for Galahad the model is eschatological, working within the ever-widening scope of universal Christian salvation or damnation to effect a systematic fulfillment of prophecies and an abolition of pagan or demonic marvels in a "normalization" of the British landscape, and culminating in the beatific vision of the Grail. While Palamedes is certainly driven by an overarching desire—to vanquish Tristan and to win the love of Iseut—this is one that the reader knows can never be gratified. Galahad, on the other hand, is assured of success as he relentlessly works his way through the successful completion of a series of adventures that are all versions of the same ultimate goal.

Palamedes also stands in contrast with Tristan himself.[19] Tristan too is consumed by passionate desire, but his is a desire that is, for the most part, fulfilled. He is assured of Iseut's love, their affair is common knowledge, and despite their travails they experience little difficulty in consummating their love both in Cornwall and during their sojourn at the Joyous Guard. If Galahad experiences the ecstasy of spiritual fulfillment, Tristan enjoys the endlessly repeated pleasures of erotic gratification. Lancelot similarly, though less flamboyantly, enjoys the undying if occasionally petulant love of Guenevere, drawing both inspiration and consolation from his memory of their many blissful moments together. And all three heroes, each the central figure in a well-defined narrative stream, stand undefeated in jousts and battles alike. Palamedes, with his hopeless love, his inability to topple Tristan, and his spiritual isolation, is the lone figure detached from any real community, ever present and yet peripheral to all three of the major plotlines of Arthurian legend.[20]

Palamedes's special but slightly unorthodox relationship with Lancelot and Tristan places him in a position analogous to that of Galehot; but where Galehot was most powerfully associated with Lancelot, Palamedes is intimately linked to Tristan. Galehot was in love with Lancelot, the masculine object of universal desire in the Arthurian world; Palamedes is in love with Iseut, the feminine object of equally universal desire. Galehot was a potent force in Lancelot's early story, working both to nurture his love for Guenevere and to keep him away from her in a complicated skewing of the classic love triangle. Palamedes, for his part, is Tristan's most important rival for Iseut—and, like Galehot, participant in a triangle that bypasses the lady's husband. Moreover, Palamedes is responsible, albeit inadvertently, for Tristan's initial interest in the Irish princess. During his first visit to Ireland—to be cured of his wound from Morholt's sword—Tristan had noted the young Iseut's beauty in a casual way: "Son cuer n'i avoit pas mis dusqu'a l'amer granment" (*PT*[C], 1:165; He hadn't yet committed his heart to loving her all that much). But when he notices that "Palamedes i entendoit si merveilleusement qu'il dit ou il morra ou il l'avra, Tristanz redit a soi meïsmes que ja Palamedes por pooir qu'il ait ne l'avra.... Ensi entra en orguel et en bobant Tristanz por les amors ma dame Yselt" (*PT*[C], 1:165; Palamedes was so amazingly intent on her that he said that either he would have her or he would die, Tristan said to himself that Palamedes would never have her if he could prevent it.... Thus Tristan, in pride and arrogance, entered into his love for my lady Iseut). If Lancelot is caught between the conflicting desires of the queen, her fairy rival, and the half-blood giant, Iseut is, from the very start, an object of sexual rivalry between Tristan and the as yet unconverted Saracen. And if Galehot distances himself from his giant origins in an effort to draw closer to Lancelot—and, for that matter, Tristan—Palamedes considers that Iseut might be the one thing for which he would be willing to relinquish his religion:

> Et tant li plest et atalente qu'il n'est riens ou monde qu'il ne feïst por li avoir, nes sa loi guerpi. Et ce estoit la riens ou monde que il feïst plus a enviz, mes totevoies la gerpiroit il por avoir Yselt, s'il poïst estre. (*PT*[C], 1:164)

> [And she so pleases and delights him that there is nothing in the world that he wouldn't do to have her, even renounce his faith. And that was the thing he would most hate to do in the whole world, but nonetheless he would renounce it in order to have Iseut, if it could be.]

But Palamedes's willingness to accept Christianity for the sake of marrying Iseut is never put to the test; for Tristan interposes himself, producing the triangle of passionate desire, chivalric esteem, and murderous rivalry that will dominate the story from there on out.

Because Palamedes can never triumph over Tristan in either tournaments or single combat, it need never be specified whether the real obstacle between Palamedes and the woman he loves is his outsider status as a Saracen or his inability to measure up to Tristan's chivalric excellence. The undying and desperate love of the Saracen knight is an innovation of the thirteenth-century prose *Tristan*, distinguishing this version of Tristan's story from that of the twelfth-century verse texts and casting the adulterous lovers in a somewhat different light. Their love is of course both a crime against the king and a sin against God, and the starkly secular quality of their behavior—even on his deathbed Tristan neither asks Mark's forgiveness nor commends his soul to God—is striking.[21] The delight taken by the lovers in their forced sojourn on the Isle del Jaiant associates their love with the pagan and giant prehistory of Britain. Yet Tristan's intervention could also be seen as fortuitous, saving Iseut from a Saracen lover who might in the end not have been willing to accept Christianity and might instead have forcibly imposed his "law" on her. Prior to her involvement with Tristan, the young Iseut had been favorably inclined toward Palamedes—then still passing as a Christian—and commented to Brangain that of the two she would prefer Palamedes "por sa bone chevalerie" (*PT*[C], 1:165; because of his chivalric excellence) but that she might transfer her affections to Tristan if he proved equally valiant, because of his greater beauty. When Palamedes attempts to abduct Iseut, using the device of the *don contraignant* to trick her into promising him that he can have her as the reward for bringing Brangain back to court, it is unclear just what might have happened if Tristan had not been available both to rescue her and to ensure that she wanted to be rescued. As with Lancelot, Tristan's adulterous love for the queen is transgressive, but it lacks the particularly taboo qualities embodied in the alternative: Galehot's love for Lancelot, and Palamedes's love for Iseut. One might even say that Palamedes's presence at the Irish court colors Tristan's actions with a subtle reminiscence of Crusade narrative: in a distant and potentially dangerous land, whose champion he has killed in battle, Tristan wins the love of a beautiful princess that a Saracen knight had hoped to have for himself, and brings her back home to Britain. Though this undercurrent is not enough to legitimize what is still adulterous and, in medieval law, consanguineous love, it does contribute to the reader's sympathy for the lovers and the sense of Tristan as Iseut's only truly rightful partner.

Palamedes, like Galehot, is ultimately unsuccessful in his efforts to shape the narrative trajectory—in effect, to produce a historical narrative compatible with his own values and desires, and one in which he would play the central role. Just as Galehot was reduced to being an accessory in the story of Lancelot and Guenevere, Palamedes remains a side character (albeit an important one) in the tale of Tristan and Iseut. Palamedes is, however, far more capable of accepting his role. Whereas Galehot dies when he thinks he has lost Lancelot, Palamedes survives the deaths of the two people—Tristan and Iseut—who had defined his very existence. It is after their death, in fact, that Palamedes finally bows to the mounting pressure from Arthur and the other knights: "Li roi et li roïne et tout li baron de la court li priierent qu'il devenist crestiens et compains de la Table Reonde, et tant firent qu'il leur otroia" (*PT* [M], 9:248; The king and queen and all the barons at court begged him to become a Christian and a companion of the Round Table, so much so that he agreed to it). As companion of the Round Table, Palamedes takes the further step of joining the Grail Quest. This move should finally have given him the solace of community; as full participant in the pan-Arthurian quest for the Grail he might have experienced a kind of collective fulfillment. But the company of the other questers turns out to be lethal. With his conversion still too recent to have become common knowledge, Palamedes is challenged to combat by Lancelot, for no other reason than because the great paragon of chivalric excellence wishes to test the mettle of the illustrious Saracen.[22] Severely wounded from this altercation, Palamedes is attacked by Gawain and Agravain, who finish him off. Gawain's murder of Palamedes is a treacherous act, motivated purely by the former's inability to countenance a knight greater than himself. And it shocks even Gawain's brother, since Palamedes has told them that he is now a companion of the Round Table; he is disabled by his very recent wounds; and it is, in any case, a matter of two knights against one. But of course Palamedes is far from being the only companion of the Round Table to be killed by the implacable Gawain.[23] In a sense his conversion does afford him a communal fate shared by numerous other Arthurian knights; but it is a tragic one, and not the glorious achievement he had hoped it would bring.

The Giant and the Saracen

Galehot enters the romance of Lancelot with a mission of giant proportions: nothing less than conquering the world. He has so far been successful, and a victory over Arthur—which initially seemed assured—would have brought him that much closer to his glorious coronation. So powerful is his love for Lancelot that it causes him to veer from this path, renouncing honor and conquest just when it lay within his grasp. But his desire for Lancelot is of an entirely different order from his desire for feudal glory: not only does it block his original goal, but it is itself by definition inexhaustible and unattainable. Military conquest proceeds in a series of discrete steps, each of which can be completed with success. Possession of Lancelot proves far more elusive, as the new love object turns out to be prone to melancholic languor, fits of madness, and mysterious disappearances. Galehot's love for the knight in love with Guenevere draws him into the Arthurian orbit whether he likes it or not; and this is a world in which knights frequently devote themselves to searching for the enigmatic Lancelot. Even more generally, the Arthurian world is one characterized by Calogrenant's famous statement in Chrétien's *Chevalier au lion*: "Je sui, çou vois, uns chevaliers / Qui quier che que trouver ne puis" (As you see, I am a knight who seeks what

I cannot find).[24] This state of endlessly deferred desire is one that Galehot simply cannot live with.

Galehot seeks to ensure his own happiness and to bind Lancelot to himself by fulfilling all of Lancelot's desires, but this is an impossible goal. Lancelot's desire for Guenevere is of the kind that will always include an element of deferral: although he does have her love, and the relationship is consummated sexually from time to time, it is also one that entails long periods of separation and that works around obstacles—both her marriage to Arthur and his participation in adventures and battles—rather than trying to eliminate them. For Lancelot, love is a driving force in his spectacular chivalric achievements. For Galehot, however, love provides no inspiration for military exploits: instead, it replaces them. Love demands bodily presence, not just an assurance of reciprocal affection and admiration, or the hope of a future reunion. We have seen something like this in the twelfth-century *Tristan* romances: there too, a promising chivalric hero is derailed by his obsessive need for constant contact with a beloved that can never belong exclusively to him. Even Tristan, however, carried through on his obligation to bring Iseut to Cornwall for marriage to Mark; and when he did finally elope with her, it was to a public life at the Joyous Guard, in which Tristan continued to participate in adventures with other knights, rather than to a secretive and isolationist retreat. Indeed, Béroul invented the stratagem of the expiring potion in order to extract the lovers from an unacceptably isolated existence in the forest. Galehot's insistent need for exclusivity and for constant gratification, and the way in which it brings him into conflict with the chivalric world, is a quality that ultimately links him to the giants of medieval romance. Giants who establish evil customs or collect knights in their prisons actively make themselves vulnerable targets for the next chivalric hero; and they are frequently pawns in the rivalries and alliances between men. Giants thrive on violence and on the immediate gratification of violent bodily desires, whether homicidal, lustful, or cannibalistic; in the end, they meet a violent death from a human avenger. When Galehot hides Lancelot in Sorelois, he unwittingly triggers a quest to "rescue" Lancelot from his "prison." As if on cue, the knights fall into the narrative pattern of "companion held prisoner by a giant"; and in the Arthurian world, this particular quest is one that is always, eventually, successful. The voracity, the fixation on knights as objects of desire or prey, and the instinctive isolationism of the giant collide in Galehot's hybrid nature with the gentility and amorous perfection of the chivalric hero.

The role of desire in Palamedes's life is significantly different. First, it is noteworthy that Galehot does not explicitly seek to be the object of Lancelot's desire, but rather to be the means by which Lancelot can obtain the objects of his desire, or at least what Galehot imagines those objects to be: ready access to or even marriage with Guenevere, lands and vassals, a crown. In contrast, Palamedes derives no pleasure from proximity with Iseut as long as her love remains focused on Tristan. The great rivalry between Tristan and Palamedes is not simply for bodily possession of Iseut. This particular tension is more relevant in the triangle formed by Iseut, Tristan, and Mark—who, as husband, is focused on safeguarding his exclusive right to Iseut's body and can take pleasure in this even when it is obvious that she does not love him in return. After his violent abduction of Iseut from the Joyous Guard, Mark finds that indeed he possesses Iseut in body only, with no access to her heart; but this never causes him to regret his actions or even to join in the general mourning for the loss of men in the bloodbath occasioned by the abduction:

> Tout entendent a faire doeil, fors seulement li rois March. . . . Toutes les fois qu'il resgarde madame Yseut, il oublie toutes ses pertes. . . . Il en a le cors seulement, et que vaut li cors d'une dame morte? . . . Il l'aimme tant que por mauvais samblent qu'ele face, il ne le puet onques amer mains. . . . Cele est tous ses soulas et toute sa vie. (*PT*[M], 9:147–48)

> [Everyone goes into mourning, except King Mark. . . . Every time he looks at Madame Iseut, he forgets all his losses. . . . He has only her body, and what good is the body of a dead woman? . . . He loves her so much that no matter what ill will she shows him, he cannot love her any less. . . . She is his entire solace and his entire life.]

In contrast, Palamedes longs for Iseut's love: "Ha! roïne Yseut . . . Pleüst a Dieu que vous m'amissiés d'aussi grant amour com vous faites monsigneur Tristan!" (*PT*[M], 8:215; Oh! Queen Iseut . . . please God that you would love me with a love as great as you have for Lord Tristan). And unlike Mark, Palamedes recognizes that his attempt to abduct Iseut with the device of the *don contraignant* may have to be abandoned: "De ce qu'il la voit si tres durement iriee est il tant correciez qu'a po qu'il ne la met a chois d'aler ou avant ou arrieres" (*PT*[C], 2:106; Seeing her so terribly distraught, he is so upset that he is on the verge of giving her the choice of carrying on or going back). This desire to be the object of desire, in fact, may be seen as a sign of a knight's nobility of spirit, one that distinguishes him from giants. The latter, even the cultured Galehot, seem invariably content to rely on tactics of force and isolation to sequester their chosen companions and partners—perhaps also what we might think of as bribery, in offering substitute love objects such as a bride or a crown—rather than depending on the principle of reciprocal love and consent so vital to the model of "courtly love." That Mark feels so little concern to possess Iseut's heart underlines the noncourtly nature of his love for her.

The Christian bias of medieval culture held that Saracens, by definition, pursued inappropriate and even destructive objects of desire, hope, and veneration with their worship of demonic or simply nonexistent gods. And there is a sense in which Palamedes does thrive on impossible desire. Though tormented by his love for Iseut, he draws on this passion for inspiration and motivation in his endless adventuring. And while his inability to defeat Tristan is a constant source of pain, Palamedes does not actually want his rival's death either and even saves his life on more than one occasion.[25] Palamedes also devotes himself to another impossible quest, the hunt for the Beste Glatissant, which functions largely as an exotic and equally elusive substitution for Iseut when he is banned from her presence.[26] And he ultimately joins in questing for the Grail, the unattainable object par excellence. Palamedes's long pagan life would doubtless have excluded him (like most knights) from any real success in the Grail Quest. But in dying at the hands of two whose prior chivalric excellence is tainted by sin—Gawain the wrathful and Lancelot the lustful—Palamedes is at least located on the side of virtue. Even as a pagan, Palamedes never falls into treachery against his archrival Tristan, nor does he ever commit adultery or fornication. Human love and prowess brought him endless frustration; but Christianity provides the context in which he can achieve a kind of fulfillment in martyrdom.

Galehot, the half-blood giant, finds to his peril that the Round Table is dedicated to seeking what cannot be found: that chivalric culture is grounded not in the instant gratification of bodily drives but in the manipulation and prolongation of desire. For all his fabled individuality, the Arthurian knight inhabits a collective narrative that exceeds his control. And only in death does the endless drive to love, adventure, and glory find an end, as each knight takes his place in the great narrative sweep of Arthurian history. Palamedes, the Saracen, is already accustomed to seeking what he cannot find and has also long since accepted regulation of his desire. But he finds to his peril that the Round Table is too corrupt to offer a safe haven and that Christianity entails an acceptance of loss and martyrdom in this world. Again, it is only in virtuous death that the soul finally achieves redemption and full integration into the community of the blessed. The respective efforts of these two figures to possess absolutely the absolute object of desire, and to be seamlessly integrated into the ideal community, shape their heroic and tragic contours and offer commentary on the dynamics of the Arthurian kingdom.

Historical Fantasies: Saladin, Galehot, and Palamedes

In closing, I wish to look at the legend of Saladin in medieval French literature, as developed in a fifteenth-century version of the *Fille du comte de Ponthieu* and its sequel, the prose *Saladin*, which forms part of the cycle of the Second Crusade.[27] The *Fille du comte de Ponthieu*, originally written in the thirteenth century, explains the circumstances that led the daughter of a French count to be temporarily married to an Iberian sultan; when she eventually returned home with her French husband, father, and brother, she brought with her the son she had borne the sultan but left behind their daughter. The son, Guillaume d'Aumarie, married the daughter of Raoul de Praiaux, and his son Jean — grandson of the sultan and great-grandson of the earlier Count of Ponthieu — became Count of Ponthieu himself. Back in Spain, the daughter fell into neglect at court because of her father's sorrow and anger at the loss of his beautiful wife; as a result, she was known as "la Belle Chetive." She was married to the Syrian prince Malaquin de Baudas; their daughter, in turn, married the sultan of Damascus and became the mother of Saladin. According to this literary history, then, Saladin is cousin to the Count of Ponthieu, who has as much Saracen blood as Saladin does French. The two men, however, are portrayed in *Saladin* as reacting very differently to their respective mixed-blood ancestry. Jean's response to Saladin's questions about his family shows an awareness of his father's Saracen sister but little interest in learning anything about her: "Mon pere eult jadis une sereur oultre ceste terre, comme aulcuns miens parens m'ont recordé, laquelle je ne vis jamais, et pourtant la voeulle Dieu garder s'encores elle est vivant" (57; My father once had a sister in foreign lands, according to what some of my relatives have told me, whom I never saw; but may God save her, if she is still alive). His journey to the Holy Land is ideologically driven—a pilgrimage to the sites associated with the origins of Christianity, not that of his lineage—and his interactions with Saracens will take the form of Holy War rather than family bonding. Saladin, in contrast, is driven by a desire to know his French relatives, to tour France itself, and to appropriate the trappings of French culture, culminating in an abortive attempt to conquer England and France and an apparent deathbed conversion to Christianity. It is clearly the French blood that exerts a pull on the Saracen, and not the other way around—just as mixed-blood descendants of giants, while displaying behavior patterns that betray their ancestral origins, nonetheless tend to identify with the human world and focus their attentions on engagement with it. The ensuing narrative explores the issues of mixed-blood ancestry and cross-cultural intimacy, drawing on a rich background of medieval literary traditions. In particular, as we will see, the imaginative reconstruction of the great Saracen king owes something to both Galehot and Palamedes.

Saladin is presented explicitly as a medieval Alexander, an implicit model for Galehot when he is first described to Arthur. As noted above, Arthur's informant explains that Galehot is "li homme el monde li plus amés de sa gent et qui plus a conquis de son eage, car il est joines bachelers" (*PLanc*, 7:440–41; of any man in the world the one most beloved by his people, and the one who has conquered the most territory for someone his age, for he is a young bachelor), as well as being "li plus jentix chevaliers et li plus deboinaires del monde et tous li plus larges" (7:440–41; the noblest and most refined knight in the world and certainly the most generous). All of these qualities link Galehot to Alexander, famed precisely for having conquered the known world at an astonishingly young age, for inspirational leadership and chivalric refinement, and for his fabled generosity. Saladin displays similar qualities of compassion, nobility, and generosity, winning thereby the undying loyalty even of conquered peoples: after capturing Babylon and distributing its wealth to his subjects, for example, "Salhadin, par sez grans et largez dons, acquist a son commencement la bienveulant de tant de pueple qu'onquez puis ne fut heure qu'il n'eust a son besoing assés plus de gens que mestier ne luy en fust, si fut bien amé des Babiloniens" (*Saladin*, 29; Saladin, through his great and noble gifts, won from the start the goodwill of so many people that from there on out there was no time that he could not call upon more people than he even needed, and he was well loved by the Babylonians). The French too are so impressed by the beneficence of their mysterious visitor that "disoient aulcuns que Alixandre n'eust sceu plus largement faire" (*Saladin*, 99; some said that Alexander couldn't have been more generous). Though Saladin claims lordship over only a Middle Eastern empire—"Babilonne, Egypte, Damas, Perse et . . . la pluspart de Surye" (38; Babylon, Egypt, Damascus, Persia, and most of Syria)—he is able to call upon vassals and allies on a global scale, covering an area reminiscent of Alexander's empire: "Salhadin fist son mandement a toute haste et envoia en Aufricque, Egypte, Babilonne, Damas, Inde, Perse, Farinde, Morienne, Arragoce et jusquez a l'arbre secq, segnifiant aux princes qu'i, a puissance toute, venissent a luy a ung certain jour" (39; Saladin hastily issued his command and sent it to Africa, Egypt, Babylon, Damascus, India, Persia, Farinde, Mauritania, Aragon, and all the way to the withered tree, telling the princes that they should come to him on a certain day with their full armies). Most interestingly of all, Saladin claims descent from the great Macedonian emperor in asserting his rights to the kingdom of England: "Ce pays et tout le demourant du monde est a moy appartenant a cause du bon roy Alixandre le Grand, duquel lignage mes peres anchiens sont yssus et descendus, et par ce me compette par vraye et directe sucession" (131; This land and all the rest of the world belong to me because of the good King Alexander the Great, from whose lineage my forefathers are descended, and I thereby count myself the true and direct successor). In response to this claim, Andry de

Chavigny retorts that Alexander may have conquered the entire world, but to no good end, "car il ne la tinst q'un jour seulement, par quoy en ceste cy ne povés vous riens avoir" (132; for he held it for but a single day, for which reason you can have nothing here). Needless to say, Saladin's Saracen allies take a more favorable view of his supposed ancestor, in particular Bruyant, the Saracen king of Greece, who compares Saladin's generosity and sense of honor to that of Alexander and notes that "en ce monde n'est plus nouvelle de lui aprés sa mort, sinon du bon renom" (135; since his death his reputation in this world has been nothing but good).

As archetypal global conqueror, Alexander is a figure of ambiguous repute in medieval French literary tradition. He too is of mixed origin, being the son of an adulterous liaison between the Macedonian queen and a sorcerer. And his conquests and explorations, while admirable in some respects, are also tainted by an aura of hubris, as he constantly pushes at the limits of human knowledge and experience. The medieval French Alexander is defined by this dual image: intellectual fortitude, chivalric excellence, courtly manners, and liberal generosity combined with an overbearing and even blasphemous curiosity and drive for power and an inability to respect both natural and supernatural boundaries. His untimely death results from external treachery but is also a reflection of personal excess. In Galehot, the implicit memory of this ambiguous legacy is recast in the mixed-blood feudal lord whose charismatic leadership and military might coexist with the rapacious yet precarious existence of the giant. Saladin offers yet another interpretation of a mixed-blood hero whose overweening pride will lead to a spectacular fall and whose behavior simultaneously thrills, inspires, and repels the medieval Christian reader.

It is in Saladin's initial encounter with Jean de Ponthieu at the battle of Jerusalem that the legacy of Galehot is most clearly discernible. Upon realizing that this exceptionally valiant warrior is his cousin, Saladin forbids any of his men to kill him, insisting that he must have him taken alive: a position that arouses the anger of Corsuble, his uncle, "qui moult blasma son nepveu pour tant qu'il ne se vouloit consentir a la mort du crestien" (55; who greatly blamed his nephew for not consenting to the death of the Christian). When Jean is finally captured and Saladin has agreed to spare his life, Jean asks for a *don contraignant*, which turns out to be the right to return to the thick of battle and aid the heroic Bastard de Bouillon, fighting for his life alongside the equally illustrious Huon Dodequin. Saladin's agreement to this again arouses the anger of his uncle, but to no avail. His divided loyalties, split between blood relatives on both sides of the war, lead Saladin to continue pursuing the battle while also continuing to protect Jean from being killed. This seemingly incomprehensible treatment of a dangerous enemy strongly recalls Galehot's infatuation with Lancelot during the battle with Arthur, in which Galehot similarly offers protection to Lancelot as long as he continues to fight heroically, keeps him supplied with fresh horses, and agrees to a *don contraignant* in exchange for having Lancelot spend the night with him. Galehot's closest allies and counselors are duly shocked when asked to swear that if Galehot breaks his word to Lancelot they must become Lancelot's liege men and declare Galehot their mortal enemy. His cousin, the King of a Hundred Knights, protests that "ce est trop grant chose a faire" (*PLanc*, 8:78; this is going too far). Like Saladin, however, Galehot is not to be dissuaded; and just as Galehot attempts to keep Lancelot forever in the virtual prison of Sorelois, Saladin literally retains both Jean and Huon Dodequin as prisoners, treating them always as companions but also forcing them, on pain of death, to do his bidding.

Saladin's behavior thus calls to mind Galehot's giantesque desire to appropriate and sequester what he perceives as the best of the chivalric world: both the exotic strangeness of the Saracen king and his capacity to be seduced by a Western hero are reinforced. The implicit memory of Galehot subtly supports the fantasy that the great Saracen warrior might, like the son of the giantess, capitulate and surrender to the Christians. In effect, the motif of the Saracen princess who falls in love with a crusader knight fuses with that of the half-blood giant lord who falls in love with his opponent's champion: an extravagant *coup de foudre* that, had it fully realized its literary potential, might have led to a realization of the ultimate crusading dream, that of European Christian rule over the entire Middle East. The narrative possibility opened here is never articulated as such and would place unacceptable pressures on even the semblance of historical accuracy; but it is present nonetheless, discernible as a driving force in the decidedly strange rewriting of history staged in this text. The analogy with Galehot also prepares us both for

Saladin's startling agenda—his request to experience the Christian ceremony of knighthood, his incognito travels in Europe, his abortive invasion of England in preparation for his real goal of conquering France—and for his rapid demise after his Christian companions have turned against him. Like Galehot, Saladin is an insider/outsider figure whose unfulfilled potential for greatness carries a tragic dimension: he is consumed with an impossible desire, inevitably betrayed and disappointed. Though Galehot is not explicitly betrayed by Lancelot, Lancelot's refusal to remain at his side in the seclusion of Sorelois is experienced by Galehot as a kind of betrayal of his enormous sacrifice for Lancelot and all that he did both in surrendering to Arthur and in facilitating the love affair with Guenevere: an abandonment that can only spell his death. Saladin has done less for Jean de Ponthieu and Huon Dodequin, sparing their lives but not surrendering to their armies. But he is certainly betrayed by them, as they knowingly guide his army into a cul-de-sac and warn the English of his coming invasion. Intentionally or unintentionally, the mixed-blood figure is betrayed by those who are simultaneously his natural allies and his mortal enemies. In exploring this paradox, both *Lancelot* and *Saladin* reveal a fascination, an admiration, a compassion for those—giant or Saracen—who are irretrievably beyond the pale, while also affirming in the end that those who cannot adapt, convert, and assimilate must finally be excluded and effaced.

Both Saladin's greatness and his Saracen limitations are foregrounded in the episode in which Huon Dodequin is forced to take him through the ceremony of Christian knighthood. Though Huon initially demurs, protesting that "n'estez pas ydonne ne habille a si noble ordre recepvoir a cause que n'estez pas crestien" (*Saladin*, 73; you are not fitting or suited to receive such a noble order, because you're not a Christian), Saladin refuses to take no for an answer; and Huon complies, finding justification in a formula often applied to Saracen knights in Crusade texts: "Se vous fussiés crestien, bien fust en vous chevalerie assize" (74; If you were a Christian, knighthood would be appropriately conferred upon you). After going through the ceremony, complete with explanation of its allegorical significance at each stage, Saladin is delighted, "comme cellui qui par advant avoit portees lez armez par rude industrie, non sachant que la tres noble ordre de chevalerie segnifioit" (76; as one who had formerly borne arms just to get the job done, without knowing what the very noble order of knighthood signified). Nonetheless, uncertainty clings to the validity of knighthood in a Saracen. When Saladin decides to enter into judicial combat to defend his cousin the Countess of Ponthieu, Huon brushes him aside: "A vous n'est mie chose faisable d'un tel champs faire" (84; It is not possible for you to take the field in such a way). When Saladin protests, "Ne suis je mie chevalier?" (84; Am I not a knight?), Huon is at pains to point out the religious dimension of a battle fought under sacred oath, while also casting doubt on the very question of Saladin's knighthood: "Supposé que chevalier soiés, si convient il que vous soyés crestien" (84; Assuming you were a knight, it's still necessary for you to be Christian). Since Saladin does take the oath and defeat the countess's accuser, there remains a lingering doubt about the validity of the judicial combat: Was he victorious because of divine intervention, or simply because he was the more powerful warrior? Saladin's ambiguous identity as a knight recalls that of Palamedes: renowned for his military prowess and his chivalric honor, he was nonetheless shunned by many of Arthur's knights, excluded from the Round Table, and banned by Galahad from fighting alongside the Christians in defense of Logres.

Much like Palamedes when he first enters the story of Tristan, Saladin can pass as a Christian knight because he is fully endowed with the necessary courtly, moral, and martial qualities; yet he lacks the all-important spiritual faith that underpins those same qualities and gives them their real meaning. Palamedes and Saladin both embody a kind of hybridity, as non-Christian Saracens who are also British or French knights respectively, and as such they raise serious questions about the most crucial identity matrix of aristocratic Christian masculinity: Is knighthood defined by a set of skills and acknowledged in an essentially theatrical ceremony, or does it reside in spiritual adherence to a code combining sacred and secular values? Can ethical and spiritual values be picked apart, such that a different religious faith might equally well inform the institutions of aristocratic culture? The successful mimicry of Christian knighthood by Palamedes and Saladin has the unsettling effect ascribed by Bhabha to colonial hybridity, the effect created by the imposition of the dominant culture onto the colonized: a process whereby "other 'denied' knowledges enter upon the dominant discourse and estrange the basis of its authority—its rules of recognition."[28] Galehot's unorthodox relationship with Lancelot, along with the intimations of what might have transpired between him and Tristan, similarly threaten to destabilize concepts of knighthood and feudal alliance by introducing what Bhabha termed "other knowledges"—other forms of behavior, determined by different cultural priorities—from Galehot's giant past. In the former two cases, the Saracen knight's religious conversion—explicit in the case of Palamedes, somewhat less clear in that of Saladin—ultimately confirms the importance of the Christian faith as a necessary element in both chivalric heroism and aristocratic virtue, dispelling the troubling vision of chivalric alliances marked by religious difference. And all three figures fail in their efforts to rewrite chivalric history: Saladin's desire to assimilate the West into his Saracen empire proves fatal, as does Galehot's effort to assimilate Lancelot into his own private world; and Palamedes ultimately does not survive his contact with the Round Table.

Saladin's love affair with the French queen further recalls Palamedes's lifelong love for Iseut, exploring a different trajectory to the tale of love between a Christian European queen and a Saracen knight who mysteriously turns up at her court. The queen's aggressive pursuit of Saladin hints at what might have happened to Iseut without Tristan's intervention. She could potentially have fallen in love with a Saracen, possibly even run off with him; and she could also have been burnt at the stake for adultery, as is the French queen in *Saladin*, without a superhero like Tristan to rescue her. As again we see a Saracen knight adventuring in Europe at Christian courts and flirting with a queen, we are implicitly reminded of that unwritten, unthinkable narrative trajectory lurking within the Tristan legend: one never allowed to develop but nonetheless glimpsed between the story lines. The queen's treatment of Saladin also points to a potential reversal of the "Saracen princess" motif. First she summons Saladin to her chambers, offers her love, and threatens him with dire consequences if he refuses, thereby setting their affair in motion. Later she extracts permission to visit him in Babylon under pretense of trying to convert him to Christianity; but having joined him, she shows little interest in religious debate, settles in as mistress to the Saracen king, and refuses to return to France. As in *La prise d'Orange*, *Huon de Bordeaux*, and other Crusade texts, an aristocratic lady will fall in love with an exotic foreign warrior, accept or possibly even convert to his religion, assimilate into his culture, and potentially preside over the absorption of her entire kingdom into that culture as well. But this unthinkable trajectory, like that of Iseut falling in love with Palamedes, is nipped in the bud as the queen is summarily abducted by a French knight, sent home to her brother the king of Aragon, and burnt for adultery and treason. This lady's presence as an object of love and erotic desire within the Saracen world will be even shorter than that of Saladin's great-grandmother, daughter of the Count of Ponthieu, and its dénouement extremely different. It is as if the narrative overall needs to drive home the point that a liaison between Christian and unconverted Saracen may be permitted under certain unique circumstances and its damage contained but that it cannot become standard practice.

As portrayed in medieval French tradition, Saladin makes two journeys to the West. When he visits France, he travels as a European knight, fully identifying with his French ancestry and even arranging the marriage of his countess cousin; and when he goes the second time—diverted to England, though intending ultimately to conquer France as well—he acts as a Saracen conqueror, identifying with his pagan ancestor Alexander and calling upon the Saracen gods to favor his mission. In the first instance his secret French identity is used as a public mask cloaking his official identity as Saracen king, while in the second instance his official identity is the public one and his links with France are hidden. Both sides of his character are always present at some level, however. He speaks as a Saracen in critiquing what he sees as Christian hypocrisy and heresy during his first visit—noting the shabby treatment of the poor and professing shock at the idea of confessing one's sins and seeking absolution from a human priest—while the very notion of conquering Christendom is motivated, at least in part, by his sense of a blood connection to these lands. When the all-important divide between "us" and "them" runs right through one's very self, conflict and betrayal are inevitable. From Saladin's perspective, he is betrayed in his invasion of England by what he thought were his most intimate companions and allies: his cousin Jean and Huon, the man who conferred his knighthood. Perhaps Saladin expected them to support him as fellow Saracens, since Jean has as much Saracen blood as Saladin does French, and Huon himself is a Saracen convert to Christianity. Jean, however, clearly acts as a Frenchman whose only conceivable duty is to thwart a Saracen invasion of Christian territory. Trapped in an impossibly narrow mountain pass, facing an immense Christian army, Saladin has no choice but to agree to a combat of champions from either side; and when his champions are both defeated, he is left with no option but ignominious retreat.

The motif of betrayal by a member of one's own army who turns out to be in league with the enemy, and the resulting defeat in a dangerous mountain pass, has overtones of Roland's betrayal and death at Rencesvals.[29] The landscape in which Saladin finds himself is similar to that of Roland's final battle, where "Halt sunt li pui e tenebrus e grant, / Li val parfunt e les ewes curant" (High are the peaks and dark and imposing, the valleys deep and the waters rushing).[30] Saladin, having landed in England at the spot so carefully chosen by Jean and Huon, finds that the trail leading forward is "fort et penible, les montaignez d'environ terriblez a gripper" (*Saladin*, 117; harsh and precarious, the surrounding mountains terribly difficult to scale). First Saladin's scout and then Saladin himself climb to a lookout point and behold "la belle plaine couverte de gens d'armez" (118; the beautiful plain covered with soldiers), leading Saladin to the realization that "les deux crestiens l'avoient trompé" (119; the two Christians had betrayed him), just as Oliver, returning from the lookout point where he has seen the pagan army advancing through "un val herbus" (a grassy valley), realizes that "Guenes le sout, li fel, li traïtur" (Galelon knows this, the criminal, the traitor).[31] The narrative paradigm is of course reversed: this time it is Christians who, in defending their homeland, prepare an ambush for a Saracen army. Just as the Saracen knight cannot seduce and convert a French queen, so also his army cannot overcome internal treason to conquer a Christian kingdom, and no subsequent reinforcements will save the day. The text affirms that crusading warfare cannot be reversed: the powerful narrative patterns work in one direction only.

In Saladin's predicament, the inadvertent betrayal of Galehot by Lancelot is overlaid with the explicit betrayal of Roland by Ganelon, and the dual context thereby created promotes a double reading of Saladin. If he is a Saracen version of Galehot—a dangerous but admirable figure in whom an abundance of virtue and prowess is somehow misplaced or misused, and within whom an incompatible lineage is forever in conflict with itself—his death requires a double reading as tragic, yet necessary to the trajectories of European Christian history. In the more immediate context of Holy War, we might see him as an anti-Roland, whose defeat is the only possible narrative outcome. The episode even acts as a kind of implicit counterbalance to the tragic, though glorious, death of Roland himself under similar circumstances of Holy War and mountain ambush. Yet Saladin is also, on another level, a genuine Roland: a hero betrayed but then (apparently) rewarded with Christian redemption. Though he has long hinted at the possibility of religious conversion without acting upon it, Saladin's final move upon regaining Babylon is to summon a Jew, a Christian, and a "payen" to dispute their religions in a contest reminiscent of St. Catherine's dispute with the pagan philosophers of Alexandria; and he signals his apparent submission to Christian law in his self-baptism at the point of death. Since Saladin in effect sacrifices himself in the retreat from his final, disastrous battle—waiting until all of his men have safely entered the ship before boarding, and thereby exposing himself to the deadly assault of Gerard le Bel Armé—there is a dimension of chivalric martyrdom to his death. Still, ambiguity surrounds his final religious orientation. His words spoken as he poured the water over his head are not discernible, and it is not entirely clear that a self-baptism performed by a Saracen with no formal religious training is legitimate in any case. The narrator can go no further than to state: "Si fait a supposer qu'en celle fin il se converty a nostre seigneur Jhesu Crist, selon la disputoison qu'il entendy des trois clercz" (*Saladin*, 169; Thus one can suppose that in dying this way, he converted to Our Lord Jesus Christ, from having heard the disputation of the three clerics). Indeed, the narrator acknowledges that a different tradition places Saladin's death at the siege of Acre, definitively identifying him with the infidel enemy whom European crusaders were sworn to defeat. In the end, his moral and chivalric identity may have to be separated from his identity as Saracen warrior: "Quoy qu'il fust et ou il fina, ses fais monstrent qu'il doibt estre axaucié, car de grand vaillance, largesse et courtoisie il fut aourné" (169; Whatever he was and wherever he died, his deeds show that he should be honored, for he was endowed with great valiance, generosity, and courtesy).

In the fanciful history of Saladin, the temporary liaison of the daughter of the Count of Ponthieu with a Spanish sultan has ambivalent results for both sides. Their daughter, left behind in the Saracen world, is not only an emblem of the betrayal and loss suffered by the sultan but also the grandmother of a heroic warrior and empire builder who, in a sense, avenges this loss by posing a greater threat to France and to Christendom than any other Saracen leader. Saladin also could be seen as avenging the "theft" of the sultana by attempting to harbor the runaway French queen as his mistress. Yet Saladin is equally an exemplar of just rule, generosity, and mercy, and not only to his own Saracen allies and subjects. At the siege of Crac, he gives food and shelter to the defeated Christian lord and his pregnant wife, as well as supplying food to the starving inhabitants of the castle out of courtesy to the noble lady—behavior that leads the narrator to characterize him as "courtois" and "franc" (31). Later, he is similarly merciful to ladies trapped in the siege of Sur and extends protection to the Princess of Antioch (71). During his visit to France he successfully defends the wrongly accused Countess of Ponthieu and reconciles her with her accuser. He is therefore a profoundly mixed legacy for the compatriots of his French great-grandmother. And the French descendant of the sultan is similarly problematic for the Saracens. The mixed-blood son, spirited away to France, is the ancestor to Jean, Count of Ponthieu. The historical Jean de Ponthieu died at the siege of Acre in 1147, but the fictional Jean is rewarded by Saladin with kingship in Acre (72), thereby linking the liaison between a French lady and a Spanish sultan with the establishment of an important crusader kingdom.[32] And Jean eventually thwarts the plans and contributes to the religious apostasy of the sultan's most celebrated descendant.

As in stories of giants, love across an absolute divide leads to unintended consequences of loss and betrayal within the hybrid individual, couple, or community thereby created. The riddling giant sees his knightly companions turn against him; and his daughter—who initiated the process of absorbing knights into her father's household with her love for Luce—discovers too late that her father's life is the price she pays for her marriage. Galehot similarly allows both his parents and his own personal honor to be sacrificed to his love for young British knights, and ends up a kind of sacrificial victim himself to the eradication of the giant race and the forward march of Arthurian hegemony.

Esclabor found refuge in Britain, but this turned out to be a place where he and his sons were still outsiders. Though his greatest son, Palamedes, accepted Christianity and membership in the Round Table, he was nonetheless destroyed by the very culture he had embraced. Saladin too is portrayed as driven by the conflicting identities and ideologies generated by his hybrid lineage; in the end his efforts to resolve these conflicts lead to military disaster tempered by a possible spiritual salvation, and a deeply ambiguous legacy.

CHAPTER 6

Desire, Subjectivity, and the Humanity of Giants

In *Peau noire, masques blancs*, Frantz Fanon states that "le véritable Autrui du Blanc est et demeure le Noir."[1] In elaborating upon this particular formulation of the other, which he identifies with the Lacanian Imaginary, Fanon explains that "pour le Blanc, Autrui est perçu sur le plan de l'image corporelle, absolument comme le non-moi, c'est-à-dire le non-identifiable, le non-assimilable."[2] Fanon's characterization of the racial Other parallels much of what we have seen in medieval accounts of giants—beings in whom a striking bodily difference translates into behavioral differences antithetical to Christian chivalric culture—and can aid in the analysis of medieval romance as a form of racial or colonial discourse. Giants, of course, differ from the Old and New World natives of modern colonial narratives in being purely fictional beings; there is no question, for example, of addressing their own participation in or reactions to the construction of their literary image. Rather, as we have seen, giants are vivid fantasies of racial and ethnic difference: a way of imagining peoples stigmatized as primitive and barbaric, and variously fought, slaughtered, and absorbed in the expansionist march of European Christian civilization. And even if tales of giants are not immediately grounded in the experience of actual encounters with specific colonized or enslaved races, they are nonetheless vehicles through which medieval writers and their audiences could think through ideologies of racial and cultural difference and the ways that these categories of similarity and opposition inflect individual identity.

The objectification of giants or other subjugated or "hostile" races often has the effect, in Arthurian or colonialist discourse respectively, of edging giants or colonized natives respectively into a category closer to the animal—a type of human that is nonetheless animalistic, or indeed demonic, in various ways. A giant, like a Saracen, is a man, but he is an "inhumain homme" in whom the boundaries between the human, the bestial, and the demonic are redrawn. Fanon's comment regarding the white community's perception of a black man who joins their group would apply equally well to the knight's instant recognition of a giant: "Ce n'est pas un nouvel homme . . . mais un nouveau type d'homme, un nouveau genre. Un nègre, quoi!"[3] The identification of the enemy race as visually aberrant bodies, and their characterization through the qualities associated with the Lacanian Imaginary, constitute a powerful and pernicious area of overlap between the colonial discourse of race and that of species. It has long been taken for granted in Western thought that animals, lacking language and an unconscious, cannot be thought of as participating in a Symbolic Order. In his analysis of Western humanism and its creation of the category of "animal," Derrida notes that both biological and psychoanalytic discourses relegate the animal to a purely Imaginary realm, whereby it is regarded as incapable of true subjectivity. Lacan, in Derrida's words, posits an opposition "between the imaginary and the symbolic, between the specular capture of which the animal is capable and the symbolic order of the signifier to which it does not have access."[4] Thus denied subjecthood, the animal, in Derrida's reading of Lacan, is kept "prisoner within the specularity of the imaginary."[5] A similar process can be observed in the medieval treatment of giants in particular, and sometimes of Saracens or other enemy races in general. But if giants, like animals, with whom they share a dangerous resemblance, are excluded from full subjectivity, they are nonetheless crucial—again, like animals—in the construction and exposition of the fully human subject. As an external other menacing social and political order, they provide a figure against whom Arthurian civilization can define itself, as well as a medium through which the intersubjective network of a culture may operate. And the giant also offers an image of the darker drives and impulses that lurk within the human psyche. In this way—like the allegorized animals of bestiary tradition—the giant in his eternal struggle with the knight may be less a subject in his own right than an objectified representation of that which must be repressed or disavowed in the formation of the chivalric subject.

Imaginary and Symbolic Identification: The Other and the "Other Within"

In her analysis of Lacan's theory of the "mirror stage" and Imaginary identification, Shuli Barzilai has noted certain parallels between the Lacanian model and the Christian allegorical discourse of moral conflict within the soul. While acknowledging that these two discourses remain distinct—the Christian emphasis on eternal salvation or damnation, for example, is not reflected in Lacanian thought—Barzilai identifies three points of contact between the Lacanian and the Christian model, as the latter is developed in the *Psychomachia* of Prudentius.[6] In the first place, both Prudentius and Lacan "envision a scene of interiorized conflict," and second, this conflict is realized in "scenes of intrapsychic battle between twinned rivals."[7] Where Prudentius imagines a conflict between each Virtue and its corresponding Vice, Lacan envisions opposition between the subject or Ego and its double: a relationship in which identity and alterity are simultaneously present, and which thus both confirms and threatens the integrity of the self. And it is this "simultaneity of fatal aggression and attraction, of desirous intent to destroy," that constitutes the third point of contact between Lacan and the Christian allegorical tradition.[8] Prudentius's battle within the soul, in which each Virtue grapples with its mirror-image Vice in mortal embrace, is imagined, in Barzilai's words, as "a nightmare of consummation-in-death," an "intermingling between making love and making war." Barzilai compares the Prudentian allegory with Lacan's description of the emergence of the self as a constant dynamic of seduction and subjugation, identity and alienation, as "the ego defines itself against the specular image, with which it also merges."[9] For Lacan, these processes of identification and alienation, attraction and repulsion, are at work not only within the individual psyche but also externally, in relations between self and other.

We have seen various examples of encounters between knight and giant in which the giant killer comes perilously close to incarnating the very qualities of irrational rage and violence that he is attempting to eradicate in his giant adversary. Arthur's mix of fear, rage, and thrilling pleasure in fighting Ritho or the Giant of Mont-St-Michel, or Tristan's descent into nearly unstoppable mayhem as he fights Taulas, reminds us that the giant can in fact be vanquished only by one capable of equaling—or bettering—his capacity for sheer destructive power. The battle with a giant is indeed a case of fatal attraction between two figures who are at once opposites and yet all too similar—an encounter spurred by both desire and fury, in which the death of one or the other party is nearly always the only possible outcome. And it is but one step from this fatal doubling to the explicit allegorization of giants in biblical and mythographic exegesis as well as moral and philosophical writings. We saw in chapter 1 that Augustine interpreted the biblical giants not as the demonic offspring of women and incubi but as a figure for sinful men consumed with pride and lacking all sense of rational control or moderation. A similar treatment of giants appears in mythographic tradition, with its readings of the classical giants who attempted to scale Mount Olympus and were struck down by Zeus, the almighty king of heaven. In the *Ovide moralisé*, for example, the giants' assault is explained as a pagan version of the same story recounted in Genesis 6. The classical giants are glossed as "les orgueilleus du monde, / Ou toute mauvaistiez habonde" (the prideful of this world, in whom all evil abounds).[10] In attempting to scale Olympus, they allegorically enact the extreme sinfulness of the Old Testament giants, so evil that their deeds sparked divine vengeance:

> Les enfans Dieu les filles virent
> Des homes beles, si les prirent
> Par mariage charnelment.
> De ce vindrent comunement

> Homes qui jaiant orent non,
> Poissant home et de grant renon,
> Qui pour lor force s'orgueillirent
> Et Dieu lor creatour despirent.
> . . . .
> Tant firent de mal, ce m'est vis,
> Que de lor vie honteuse et vilz
> Sont jusqu'au ciel, outre les nues,
> Devant Dieu les clamors venues.[11]

> [The sons of God saw the daughters of men to be beautiful,
> so they took them carnally in marriage. From that came the men
> called giants, powerful men of great renown, who became arrogant
> because of their strength and despised God their creator. . . .
> They did so much evil, as I see it, that word of their shameful and vile
> life reached all the way to heaven, beyond the clouds, before God.]

Explicitly, then, the giants are treated as a moral allegory for human sin. But as Cristina Noacco has pointed out, the description of their cataclysmic fall into hell further associates the demise of the giants with that of Lucifer and the rebel angels:[12]

> Mes Dieus, qui tout orgueil confont,
> Ou feu d'enfer, ou puis parfont
> Fait ceuz confondre et trebuschier
> Qui si se vuelent encruchier.[13]

> [But God, who confounds all pride, confounded those who
> aimed to scale [heaven] and cast them down into the fires of hell,
> in the deep abyss.]

For the *Ovide moralisé* poet, then, the behavior attributed to giants in classical mythology identifies them with the ancient giants—in reality, a race of particularly arrogant and sinful men—whose evil ways brought on the Deluge, while also echoing the earlier rebellion in heaven that corrupted the cosmos with the birth of sin and produced the diabolical spirits who were still sometimes seen as the progenitors of the earthly giants.

The clash of giants and gods offers another instance of paired beings—in this case, paired "races" or collectivities—whose binary opposition masks an underlying potential for similarity and identification. The Olympian gods themselves were seen by medieval exegetes as demonic figures in their guise as pagan deities worshipped by idolatrous infidels. Jupiter, here identified with the Christian God, also appears in medieval texts as a deity revered by Saracens and even by giants themselves.[14] His bodily drives—in particular, his lustful appetite for an endless series of goddesses, nymphs, and mortal women—and his capacity for destructive wrath could potentially identify him with the rapacious giants themselves. It is his role as enemy and destroyer of giants that allows him to be identified instead with the supreme deity. But as in the psychomachian allegory, and as in the battles between Arthurian knights and British giants, the war between the classical giants and the Olympian gods implicitly illustrates a complex process of hostile attraction, of identification through differentiation of the self from its specular image. The giants attempt to put themselves in the place of the gods, as if aspiring to godhead; the gods resist this move to dislodge them from their privileged position of power, dispatching the giants to a subterranean realm. This geographical separation of the gods—or of God and his angels—in a lofty celestial space inaccessible to earth dwellers, and the giants—or Lucifer and his minions—in underground confinement reifies the distinction of privileged and demonized peoples. It parallels the evacuation of giants from the fertile British countryside, their forced confinement in forest thickets, in caves, and on mountaintops, and the process by which they are relentlessly dislodged even from those safe havens in the wilderness.

The demonic giants of classical and biblical tradition were easily adapted by later writers as an allegory for irrational or unnatural behavior of various kinds. For Boethius, the rebellious giants dispatched to their rightful place in hell were an image for the restoration of rational order, applicable to the understanding that dawns in the rational mind when false notions are dispelled. Philosophy invokes the giants when Boethius's persona finally understands that the supreme Good is manifest in all that happens: "'Accepisti,' inquit, 'in fabulis lacessentes caelum Gigantas; sed illos quoque, uti condignum fuit, benigna fortitueo disposuit'" ("You have read in stories," she said, "of the giants challenging heaven; but those too, as was wholly right, a kindly strength put in their proper place").[15] In a similar vein, John of Salisbury, in the *Policraticus*, used the arrogant giants as an image for philosophers who trust more in their own intellect than in the grace of God: "Quasi ergo mole gigantea subuecti et iam non humanis uiribus roborati intumuerunt indixeruntque bellum gratiae Dei de uigore rationis" (As therefore with the bulk of giants, with strength no longer human, they became swollen with pride and proclaimed war against the grace of God with the strength of their reason).[16] Like the giants hurled into the abyss, these overweening philosophers suffer a fall, as "dicentes se esse sapientes stulti facti sunt" (professing themselves to be wise they became fools).[17] John also used the ever-culpable giants in a more lurid vein, as an image for male prostitution and transvestism: "In ipsam naturam, quasi gigantes alii teomachiam nouam exercentes, insurgunt" (They rise against nature herself like a new set of giants waging a new war against heaven).[18] While retaining their biblical status as historical enemies of both God and Nature, the giants of old also take on a timeless quality as figurative embodiments of the carnal and intellectual vices that pervade—have always pervaded—humankind. The traits attributed to giants as representatives of a racial, cultural, or mythical "other"—arrogance, libidinous excess, sexual deviance—are thus reclaimed as "ours": failings that corrupt the very society addressed by the texts in question. Though the combat of knight and giant in Arthurian romance is not presented as allegory, nonetheless the fact that giants so readily lend themselves to this kind of exegetical discourse inflects a reading of these episodes, allowing the processes of cultural imperialism, "ethnic cleansing," and land settlement to take on an implicit dimension of psychomachia.

It is this interplay between intrasubjective and intersubjective conflict, rivalry, and desire that informs a Lacanian analysis of interracial and intercultural encounters. Homi Bhabha has commented on Fanon's location of racial otherness in the realm of the Lacanian Imaginary, in which a sense of selfhood is predicated on "a series of equivalences, samenesses, identities, between the objects of the surrounding world."[19] As Bhabha explains: "This positioning is itself problematic, for the subject finds or recognizes itself through an image which is simultaneously alienating and hence potentially confrontational. This is the basis of the close relation between the two forms of identification complicit with the Imaginary—narcissism and aggressivity. It is precisely these two forms of identification that constitute the dominant strategy of colonial power exercised in relation to the stereotype."[20] In a similar vein, Karl Steel emphasizes the role of Imaginary identification in distinguishing the human from the nonhuman: "Humans attempt to form themselves as human by (mis)recognizing themselves as 'not animal,' and then by subjecting themselves to the impossible demands of living up to this ideal self, one distinctively rational. . . . Faced with a constitutive and irreparable disparity between themselves and their human self-image, humans assert that animals lack what uniquely afflicts humans. To give this assertion strength, they treat animals 'like animals,' as instruments available for labor or slaughter, violence which does not count as morally significant violence and which therefore qualitatively differs from the violence humans suffer."[21] Steel's comments are relevant, not only to the formation of human identity as opposed to animals, but also to that of an identity position in which humanity is equated with a particular set of racial and cultural attributes. The Arthurian knight is human not only because he is not an animal—because he is capable of mastering and employing an animal, with whom he may bond but from whom he always remains distinct—but also (among other reasons) because he is not a giant. I have discussed in previous chapters the ways in which an alien race may be constructed as the embodiment, in stigmatized form, of that which the dominant culture represses and forbids. As Jerry Phillips states regarding perceptions of racial identities in early modern Britain and America: "The alleged profligacy, immorality, childishness, and laziness of 'blacks' . . . asserted to the 'white' proletarian subject that those renunciations he had made—in the realms of desire, communality, and play—were truly worthwhile."[22] Though somewhat differently drawn, the giant occupies an analogous position in texts informed by an ideology of courtliness and chivalry. While the knight might secretly envy the giant his libidinous freedom, it is precisely the knight's capacity for rational self-constraint, emotional vulnerability, and penitential remorse that define his superior human worth: that is, his adherence to the chivalric, courtly, and Christian codes of aristocratic culture. In accepting the pain of unrequitedness and the burden of moral responsibility, the knight distinguishes himself from those—both giant and animal—who, in Steel's words, "lack what uniquely afflicts humans." The "psychomachia" of conflict between good and evil—in which these moral opposites are defined through complex patterns of resemblance and opposition, and operate according to processes of lethal attraction and dominion—plays itself out both within the individual and in the encounters of desire and hostility that take place between the representatives of opposing races and cultures. And the confrontation of knight and giant allows both for articulation of the cultural values that shape the knight and for a quasi-allegorical depiction of the internal struggles through which his character is formed.

We have seen many examples of medieval tales of giants that are characterized by the seemingly paradoxical combination of "narcissism and aggressivity" described by Bhabha, or what Barzilai calls a "desirous intent to destroy." There can be an almost invisible line between what we might call psychological and sociological levels of meaning within these texts; and this is true from the earliest examples of Arthurian romance. When Yvain fights the giant Harpin de la Montagne, for example, in Chrétien's *Chevalier au lion*, he is ridding the world of a barbaric threat to civilization. Harpin's predations nullify the value of daughters as chaste objects of exchange between men in feudal marriage, and that of sons as potential warriors and defenders of law, faith, justice, and territorial integrity; and as such he can have no place in Arthur's kingdom. But as I noted in chapter 3, Yvain is also, and just as importantly, confronting an image of his own dark side.[23] Yvain's sudden emergence from the forest in a deadly attack on Laudine's magic fountain—in which he killed the lord and took the lady as wife, then quickly abandoned her once he had exploited her wealth in lavish entertainment of the royal court—is uncomfortably mirrored in the giant's behavior. The giant is explicitly a representative of a racial and cultural other: a remnant of the savage, aboriginal race whose extermination was itself central to the cultural order established by Brutus, then renewed and continued by Uterpendragon and Arthur. But he is also a stark image of Yvain's recent behavior, stripped of its courtly veneer of honor, prowess, and reciprocal love. The role of the giant in Yvain's reinvention of himself is illuminated by George P. Rawick's comments on early modern English perceptions of Africans as an image of a "primitive" and "barbaric" past from which they wished to distance themselves: "The Englishman met the West African as a reformed sinner meets a comrade of his previous debaucheries. The reformed sinner very often creates a pornography of his former life. He must suppress even his knowledge that he had acted that way or even that he wanted to act that way. . . . But because he still has fantasies that he cannot accept, he must impute these fantasies to the realities of someone else. . . . What the English unconsciously realized about the Africans was not so much that they were different but that they were frighteningly similar."[24] The fear and revulsion that the giant inspires are simultaneously xenophobic— the specter of an alien and inassimilable people—and narcissistic, the trauma of having to face unacceptable revelations about one's own libidinous drives.[25] As such, his eradication fulfills both the agenda of cultural hegemony and that of personal identity formation.

Indeed, the narrative framework of the fight contributes to its function in separating the remorseless violence of the giant from the emotional complex driving Yvain. The knight is torn between competing codes of honor. On the one hand, he is mindful of the need to reciprocate his host family's hospitality by defending them against the giant, an obligation reinforced by their intimate blood relation to Gawain, his closest companion. And on the other, he is acutely aware of his responsibility to rescue Lunete—who, as a direct result of Yvain's own irresponsible behavior, will be burnt at the stake that very day if he does not arrive in time to fight her accusers—and to atone more generally for his crimes against Laudine. The profound anxiety and inner conflict, the fear of innocent deaths and the grief that these inspire, all contrast markedly with the insouciance of the giant, concerned only with venting his rage, reveling in the shame and suffering he can inflict on aristocratic bodies, and with the perfunctory nature of his own death, requiring neither mourning nor funeral rites. One could, of course, argue that the giant's treatment of his victims is no different from the treatment his people receive from knights: he has been shamed in the refusal of his marriage offer and is now staging his comeback by reducing his human persecutors to the status of vermin or casual playthings. Such, however, is not the ideological thrust of the text, which uses outsider figures like the giant, the demon brothers of Pesme Aventure, and the herdsman encountered by Calogrenant as a means of commenting upon, and thereby resolving, anxieties and conflicts within the aristocratic world.[26] The giant is the terrifying, violent, fascinating image of all that is at once alien—to be expelled and destroyed—and intimate, to be suppressed and disavowed.

Two surviving illustrations of Harpin reflect the slightly different ways in which the giant can contribute to the construction of chivalric masculine subjectivity. The depiction of Harpin in MS 125 of the Firestone Library, Princeton, depicts the giant as an uncouth ruffian (fig. 4).[27] His giant stature is highlighted not only in Yvain's exaggerated reach—horse rearing, sword arm extended as he aims for the giant's head—but also in the way that the picture frame itself is seemingly stretched out of normal proportions in order to accommodate his hulking figure.

In contrast, the artist of Bnf fr. 1433 contradicts the text by portraying Harpin not only mounted on a horse but equipped with sword and shield, though still lacking in armor of any kind (fig. 5). Here Harpin emerges clearly as a figure of chivalric arrogance: an armed and mounted knight who, as the narrator explains, "en sa forche se fioit / Tant quë armer ne se deignoit" (had such confidence in his own strength that he did not deign to wear armor).[28]

And indeed the giant does contrast with the knights that Yvain fights in the lower register of the miniature: all of the latter are clothed in full armor, and their horses are covered in protective heraldic drapery as well. In the Garrett manuscript the giant naturalizes the identification of lawless brutality with figures standing outside the privileged class of aristocratic knighthood, a reading that implies a more positive position for Yvain himself: whatever his transgressions, as a knight and the son of a king he will surely be more than capable of redeeming himself and recovering both public honor and the love of his wife. The Paris manuscript supports a reading of Harpin as more directly mirroring Yvain, a knight of overbearing pride who has lapsed into violent and abusive behavior. Thus the Garrett manuscript emphasizes Yvain's service to society in defending the honor of the aristocracy against challenges from outside its own ranks; while the Paris manuscript implies a moral lesson aimed at knights themselves, warning them of the necessity to curb their passions—to recover, as the Lady of the Lake might say, the proper balance of cruelty and mercy, ferocity and humility.

A similar variety characterizes the portrayal of the Giant of Mont-St-Michel across the numerous texts and manuscripts in which he appears.[29] Of particular relevance to the present context are two contrasting

Figure 4. Yvain fights Harpin de la Montagne. Garrett MS 125, fol. 56v, Manuscripts Division, Department of Rare Books and Special Collections, Princeton University Library.

Desire, Subjectivity, and the Humanity of Giants   249

Figure 5. Yvain fights Harpin de la Montagne (upper register); Yvain defends Lunete against the wicked seneschal and his supporters (lower register). Paris, Bibliothèque Nationale de France, fr. 1433, fol. 90r.

images from the Vulgate *Suite du Merlin*. In the manuscript Bonn, Universitäts- und Landesbibliothek 526 (fol. 160r), he appears in the guise of the savage giant, fighting barefoot and bareheaded in a simple tunic, armed only with a rustic club; while in the early fourteenth-century manuscript London, BL Add. 10292 (fol. 205v), he lies prostrate at the point of death, clad in armor indistinguishable from that of Arthur.[30] The image in the London manuscript visually assimilates the Spanish giant to other foreign warriors fought by Arthur—most notably, in *Merlin* and its continuations, Romans and Saxons. Though enemies, such figures still adhere to a familiar code of chivalric honor and rule of law.

As a result, battles with them need not necessarily take the form of all-out carnage but may also be a means of arriving at a negotiated settlement, whereby the invaders are either expelled from Britain or incorporated as vassals and subjects holding their lands in homage to Arthur. At the same time, however, the text makes clear that the giant is not in this category. Not only does the designation *giant* set him apart, but also his behavior is that of a lone predator bent on rape and destruction, not that of an army led by a king with whom one might negotiate. The disjunction between text and image imparts an uncanny quality to the giant, who seems at once a familiar figure and part of the Arthurian world, and also one utterly alien in his savagery. Whether intentionally or accidentally, the London manuscript overall sets the giant up as an image of the terrifying, destructive potential of the masculine drives that are barely, but crucially, contained and held in check by the constraints of Christian knighthood—and of the disastrous consequences should these limitations fail to hold. As such the giant is less an alien monster than an image of the all-too-human failings to which all knights are subject. The Bonn manuscript, on the other hand, visually reinforces the giant's status as an outsider not only to Arthur's court but also to knighthood and nobility of any kind. Like the image of Harpin in the Garrett manuscript, this miniature portrays the giant as a threat to the very fabric of aristocratic government and its hierarchies of power.

Important though the framework of Imaginary narcissism and aggression is, of course, it is not sufficient in itself to account for all of the scenarios and "primal scenes" either in colonial texts or in medieval tales of giants. We must also consider the ways in which the figure of the giant works in tandem with the intersubjective alliances and conflicts between knights, as well as the extent to which the giant himself may occasionally be portrayed as a subjective interlocutor or, in Lacanian terms, a "Symbolic Other." Abdul JanMohamed has proposed a division of modern colonial narratives into "Imaginary" and "Symbolic" modes of depicting relations between colonizer and colonized: while "Imaginary" texts are structured around objectification and aggression, "Symbolic" texts are more willing to consider colonized peoples as "a bridge toward syncretic possibility" and "a mediator of European desires."[31] Parallels to these two narrative modes, which may be found separately or in combination, can be discerned in medieval literary texts as well. Lynn Tarte Ramey has considered the relevance of JanMohamed's model to the portrayal of Saracens in twelfth-century French literature, identifying a vacillation between "Symbolic" and "Imaginary" treatment of the Saracen lord or warrior in early *chansons de geste*.[32] It is intriguing to consider to what extent the same dual process might apply to the depiction of giants. As a subject in his own right, the giant of medieval romance could be seen not only as a traumatic reflection of chivalric guilt, or a rival who threatens to obliterate the hero and the social order that he upholds. On occasion, the giant might also be seen as participating in the subjective identities of chivalric romance, or even as investing the institutions of chivalric culture with new—if inevitably problematic—meaning. And even if, for the most part, he is shown as failing to comprehend the cultural codes that define chivalric identity, it is illuminating to examine the way that this failure is portrayed.

Specular Doubles: Attraction and Aggression

The custom established in the prose *Tristan* by Dyaletes, ancestor of Galehot, offers a clear example in which the giant is portrayed in terms of Imaginary rivalry. Knights who arrive by chance or by design at the Isle del Jaiant are not challenged to an ideologically driven combat or one defined by competition for a common object of desire— despite the fact that the victor will possess both the castle and the giantess wife or daughter of the lord—but more simply because they mirror the giant ruler as lord and warrior. The advent of a rival image of aristocratic masculinity, at once similar yet foreign, threatens the bodily and territorial integrity of the local lord, with his blood ties to the castle and its traumatic history. A doubling of this kind cannot be allowed; the difference between the two warriors—the greater military prowess of one or the other—must be determined, and the weaker man eliminated, in order to protect the singularity of the island lordship. Similarly, a foreign lady who arrives at the island is perceived entirely in terms of her capacity to mirror the local lady. Again the crucial difference, identifying one as more beautiful, must be found, and only the most perfect image of feminine beauty can be allowed to go on existing within the castle confines. Tristan, pleading with Brunor to save his own life by surrendering and later with the local inhabitants to spare him from the shame of beheading Brunor's giantess wife, tries to turn the confrontations into symbolic rivalry: "Par le bien que je voi en vos sai je bien que ce seroit trop granz domaiges se je vos metoie a mort. Por ce vos demant je se nos porriens lessier ceste bataille a l'onor de moi et a la delivrance de mes compaignons" (From the virtue that I see in you, I know that it would be a great pity if I killed you. Therefore I ask if we can end this battle, granting honor to me and liberation to my companions).[33] Merely demonstrating the ability to defeat his opponent is sufficient to establish the symbolic hierarchy of prowess, and prowess itself will have no meaning if it is not underwritten by chivalric honor.

Rather than desiring one another's death, in other words, Tristan feels that he and Brunor should acknowledge their shared desire for honor: one common to all noblemen precisely because the identity of "chevalier" or "preudom" is defined, in part, by that very desire. Sarah Kay has described the Lacanian subject in the following terms: "To speak of desire and subjectivity as positioned relative to language is to say that the 'I' of the text, its first-person subject, is produced within language . . . and that the desires voiced by this 'I' are subject to language rather than springing, in some original and natural way, from the self. This regulating structure of linguistic (and other institutional) codes makes up what Lacan calls the symbolic order."[34] As beings subject to an ideologically determined concept of honor, knights both seek and produce this elusive value through mutual submission to its codes, which require, among other things, that knights display their skill in martial confrontation but do not kill a worthy opponent or seek to be killed by him. Indeed, the cultural norms of the Arthurian world would foster a subsequent friendship or feudal alliance between Brunor and Tristan, as subjects formed by common adherence to the ideology of chivalry.

Tristan's efforts are foreclosed by the custom itself. Brunor has no interest in establishing himself in a symbolically constructed community of other chivalric subjects. His attitude, in fact, corresponds reasonably well to Kay's characterization of the Lacanian Imaginary as "[nurturing] the delusion of being whole and autonomous selves."[35] For Brunor, as for the founding giant whose custom he upholds, a knight is one who exists in isolationist splendor, effacing all rivals until he is finally effaced himself: "Cil qui dusques a la mort se combat et qui en morant garde s'onor a son pooir, cil est chevaliers, cil doit estre tenuz a preudom" (*PT*[C], 2:77; He who fights to the death, and in dying protects his honor as best he can, should be considered a worthy man). Tristan's ideal of chivalric alliance and companionship is eventually endorsed by Galehot, who—perhaps because of his experience in the wider world—is similarly unwilling to kill an obviously exceptional knight. Still, Galehot betrays a grounding in the Imaginary in his letter to Guenevere, where he presents the four idealized paragons of prowess and beauty, not as two couples joined in adulterous love—and thus as a more complex mirroring of culturally coded, transgressive desires, each enmeshed in its own network of rivalries and alliances—but as two men and two ladies:

> "En ces deus dames est tote la biauté dou monde, et je ne sai la quele est la plus bele. Et es deus chevaliers est tote la chevalerie dou monde, ne ne porroie en nule fin lor parel trover de chevalerie, ne je ne sai li quiex de ces deus est li plus puissanz d'armes." Aprés escrit quatre nons: Lancelot dou Lac; Tristan, le neveu le roi Marc de Cornoaille; la roïne Genevre; Yselt la Bloe. (*PT*[C], 2:90)

> ["In those two ladies is all the beauty of the world, and I do not know which is the most beautiful. And in the two knights is all the chivalric prowess in the world, nor could I ever find their equal in chivalry, nor do I know which of those two is the most powerful warrior." After that he wrote four names: Lancelot du Lac; Tristan, nephew of King Mark of Cornwall; Queen Guenevere; Iseut the Blonde.]

Within each of these same-sex pairs, in other words, the members are defined both by the perfect resemblance they bear to one another and by the absence of any other knight or lady who might resemble them. In seeking to surround himself with these individuals, it is as though Galehot hopes to make their excellence his own, to confirm his own chivalric ideals by seeing them reflected back in these figures that he uses as mirrors.

In and of itself, of course, the Imaginary is not unique to the portrayal of giants but also figures prominently in the classic love stories of Arthurian romance. There is, however, a difference in the way that Imaginary mirroring manifests itself in the chivalric and giant worlds respectively. Galehot's humanity is expressed in part through his embrace of similarity as a positive thing, through which he enters into relationships of desire with figures who embody his own ideals of beauty, courtliness, and chivalry. In these liaisons, narcissistic wholeness and perfection are sought through the ever-greater effacement of difference: the more similar Galehot can be to his companions, the truer his reflection in the idealized image that they embody. In this respect Galehot's attachment to Lancelot and Tristan parallels the love that binds Lancelot himself to Guenevere, and Tristan to Iseut. As various critics have noted, all of these crucial relationships are grounded in the Imaginary; trauma and death are associated with the impossibility of effacing difference in order to arrive at a perfect and seamless unity.[36] Indeed, Tristan's plea to Brunor, though invoking their shared subjection to a symbolic code of behavior, does also valorize the affirmation of similarity in two well-matched opponents rather than the drive to establish difference. This attraction to the same—this obsessive love for the specular double—distinguishes the figures at the center of the Arthurian world from the full-blooded giants at its periphery. Though equally defined by the specular relations of the Imaginary, encounters with giants are all too often informed not by narcissistic desire but by a paranoid disavowal of resemblances that do not reflect favorably on the subject. In the meeting of knight and giant, death or dismemberment arises as the necessary means of establishing a difference absolute enough to be safely unbridgeable.

Giant Bodies and Royal Sovereignty in Guiron le courtois

We saw in chapter 3 that pre-Arthurian Britain is imagined in *Guiron le courtois* as a place where lords and giants together form a community, defined by their common adherence both to feudal structures and to "pagan law." In this world, giants not only live in family groups but also rule over territories, earn knighthood through their military service, and participate in a symbolic network of alliance and exchange with human knights and lords. But this vision of human-giant coexistence is no utopian fantasy of interracial harmony. Rather, it is an image of a Britain in dire need of salvation from Christian heroes such as Febus or

Uterpendragon and his retinue. And the manner in which this is addressed serves to differentiate giants from the human inhabitants of Britain. I cited the example in chapter 2 of the giant Brun, who "baaoit a avoir la segnourie toute de la Grant Bretaingne, par la force de son cors et pour ce qu'il ne pooit trover home ki conquester li peüst" (aimed to have lordship over all of Great Britain, through the force of his body and because he could not find any man who could conquer him).[37] The confrontation of Brun and Uterpendragon is one that pits a concept of brute force against the symbolic construct of kingship. The exploits of Febus develop this thematic in even greater detail. Pagan armies are fought in organized battle; giants are individually killed as Febus tracks them down in their homes or challenges them on the sporting field. These explosive encounters, pitting knight against giant in a swift and brutal fight to the death, ignore the giants' symbolic status as aristocratic lords and objectify them as rival bodies: images of masculine prowess whose excellence mirrors that of Febus. And far from acknowledging the merits of their opponent and seeking to establish a relationship of mutual respect—as so often happens in altercations between knights—the giants lose their facade of gentility and erupt into lethal rage, while Febus aggressively demonstrates that if the giants are images of physical strength and chivalric splendor, still they fall short of the idealized model that he incarnates. Like the wrestling match of Corineus and Gogmagog on which it is modeled, Febus's struggle with the giant brothers in Northumbria illustrates a means of generating dominance over another people or race, in Michelle Warren's words, "by forcefully exacting differences from near-resemblances."[38]

Febus's approach to the pagan Britons themselves, however, takes a somewhat different form, splitting along gender lines. Having achieved decisive victories on the battlefield, he then attempts to initiate a love relationship with the Northumbrian princess. Had she accepted marriage, this could have been the means of achieving the religious conversion of the kingdom; if nothing else, it acknowledges the status of the Northumbrian aristocracy as human subjects worthy of being re-formed under Christian law. Meanwhile, the Northumbrian king seeks to activate the symbolic networks at his disposal. He would be willing to use his daughter as an object of exchange with which to establish at least a temporary truce and reconciliation with this indomitable Christian warrior; and he appeals to the giant warriors, whose favor he renews each year with tribute payments, to avenge his losses by assassinating Febus. But neither of these plans succeeds. And whereas the giants are overcome in a body-to-body test of strength, in which the gap separating them from the image of supreme masculine potency proves their downfall, the king is defeated through an erosion of his symbolic identity as father and ruler. As Febus makes his moves, slaying giants and negotiating directly with the princess herself, the king is increasingly marginalized as a figure of impotence and emasculation. Dependent on giants, defeated by Christians, unable to guarantee the safety of his most honored guests or to coerce the will of his daughter, he has failed in the exercise of martial, feudal, royal, and paternal functions. By the end of the story he has become an inconsequential figure who does not even need to die because he no longer poses any threat to Febus's status as supreme hero and, if only in death, beloved of the princess. The outcome is equally somber for all involved, but the presence of the Christian warrior has served to identify categories of persons in pre-Arthurian Britain. Giants may mimic feudal lordship but are really nothing more than specular images of bodily force and violence, eliminated through what Warren has termed "the destruction of near-resemblances."[39] Pagan kings and warriors are symbolically constructed subjects, though no less vulnerable both through the tactics of feudal warfare and through the systematic dismantling of the attributes that constitute their subjecthood. And the pagan princess, though resistant to manipulation or easy appropriation as an object, can in the end be persuaded to give herself freely, as desiring and self-sacrificial subject, in response to a truly absolute love and similarly sacrificial gesture from her suitor. As peerless in beauty as Febus is in prowess, the princess emerges as the singular, subjective counterpart within pagan culture to the conquering Christian hero.[40] As so often, it is the feminine face of the racial or cultural other that can be recuperated, desired, loved.

A similar contrast between the giant and the rival king occurs elsewhere in *Guiron* in an episode where King Meliadus defeats a giant at Arthur's court.[41] Every year at Christmas, we are told, the giants inhabiting a manor owned by Arthur send one of their family members to court, in compliance with their obligation of service to their overlord. The stipulation laid down by the giants, however, is that they will provide that service only if a knight at court succeeds in defeating their emissary in a contest of strength. Since this has never yet been possible, Arthur suffers the ongoing affront of being unable to subdue his arrogant subjects, as well as the humiliation of seeing his best knights fall short year after year. The setup is typical of giants as we have come to know them in the Arthurian world. Though on one level they do acknowledge the symbolic power of kingship, they have subordinated political sovereignty to a narcissistic contest of individual bodily strength. From their perspective, Arthur's authority as anointed king is meaningless unless he can produce a vassal or ally capable of matching and exceeding the giant in his incarnation of sheer muscular prowess. But it happens one year that the giant arrives on a day when Meliadus is present at court, and this heroic king succeeds in matching and indeed surpassing the giant's feat of strength: first the giant carries an enormous rock a certain distance, after which Meliadus carries the rock for a similar distance with the added weight of the giant sitting on it. And having done that, he kills the giant by crushing him with the rock. The delighted knights increase the weight of the boulder by adding an amount of lead equal to the weight of the giant, and leave it in place as a monument to Meliadus's strength—and also as an invitation to any future knight to see if he can match the peerless king by lifting the rock himself. No knight, we are told, was able to move it until Meliadus's son Tristan came to court—and he at last proved even more powerful than his redoubtable father.

Interestingly, this rock that played such a central role in restoring the honor of Arthur's court and affirming his sovereignty as king was one already associated with human-giant rivalry. On an earlier occasion during the reign of Uterpendragon, we learn, when the knights were vying with one another to see if any of them could lift the rock, a giantess suddenly appeared and carried the rock a significant distance, before setting it down and disappearing without a word. Since she refused to give her name or place of origin, she could be identified only by her bodily form—an anonymous *jaiande*—and the rock was duly called "La Perron a la Jaiande" in commemoration of her feat. By the time Meliadus has finished with the giant, this particular piece of stone has become overdetermined with a history of recurring bodily contests between knights and giants, contests in which the giant's identity is limited to that of powerful body and aggressive challenger, with no name or rank to confer a symbolic identity beyond that. Once it has passed from a marker of brute giant force to one of chivalric honor, however, it is associated with a figure whose symbolic identity within feudal society will allow him to compete, from beyond the grave, with his own son—a figure whose greater prowess will not shame the father that it overshadows but only add to his glory as patriarch.

Meliadus's victory, as always with giant killers, is met with the adulation of the court; and the praise that everyone heaps upon him leads the queen of Scotland, whom he has been courting, to fall in love with him. Though his prowess is clearly a factor in sparking her desire, it goes without saying that she would not have fallen in love with the giant had he won the contest. It is not the visual spectacle of a brutishly powerful body that captivates her; her love arises within from within the intersubjective network of the court and its symbolic constructs. Meliadus offers the spectacle of physical might subjected to the discipline of courtly manners and a chivalric code of behavior. But even more importantly, the queen's desire is shaped in mimetic response to the general admiration in which the king is held: "Or l'aimme plus qu'ele ne seut, car ele voit bien tout clerement que tous li mondes en dist bien, et que tous li mondes le loe" (fol. 121r; Now she loves him more than she realized, for she sees very clearly that everyone speaks well of him, and everyone praises him). The love that blossoms between Meliadus and the queen has the obvious consequence of drawing him into rivalry with her husband, the Scottish king. And unlike his confrontation with the giant, this is a rivalry that arises, not from animosity between the two men or from a primal need on their part to establish preeminence, but rather from competing desires for the same love object. In fact, whereas the giant represented a concept of authority based solely on varying degrees of bodily strength, in which one party must inevitably be shown to be inferior to the other, the two kings seem almost indistinguishable in their adherence to feudal, courtly, and chivalric ideals. Gawain, for example, discerns the meaningful glances exchanged by the budding lovers and understands very well what this means, but he elects not to inform the king of Scotland, "car il ne vouroit que entre ces deux preudommes avenist ne ire ne courous" (fol. 121v; for he wouldn't want anger or resentment to come between these two noble men). The rivalry here turns less on the relative merits of the individuals in question than on conflicting feudal and cultural codes—perhaps most fundamentally of all, on the question of how to balance the competing demands of amorous passion and courtly gallantry on the one hand, moral propriety and legal right on the other.

The Imaginary rivalry between giantesque and chivalric bodies, then, is resolved in a spectacle witnessed by all, recorded in a public monument created by the now hypermassive stone, and commemorated in the endless repetition of the story at public gatherings. And a Symbolic rivalry of royal authority, courtly and chivalric perfection, and sexual privilege opens in its wake. This is a rivalry played out through the interpretation or misinterpretation of secret signs, covert conversations, and the stealthy intrigue of plots and counterplots. And it is one that calls into question the fundamental values of Arthurian society, which seem to contradict one another as means by which the central conflict could be judged: Should a lady love the man to whom she is wedded or the one regarded by all as the best knight in the land? Is it better to punish adulterers or to preserve peace and concord between two powerful kings, both icons of chivalric perfection? Does love ennoble a man or debase him? Knights do certainly compete with one another in simple feats of strength or in jousts triggered automatically by the sight of another knight in the forest; but their relations are also, and importantly, shaped by competition for common objects of desire and by the harmonious or conflicting ways that each conforms, or fails to conform, to symbolic codes of behavior. Once again, giants are important players in the Arthurian world; but the limited terms under which they operate distinguish their interventions from the interactions among the knights themselves.

The Riddling Giant and Chivalric Subjectivity in Tristan

An association of the giant with Imaginary rivalry, and its contrast with the differently constructed relationships formed between knights, is even more intricately at play in the episode of the riddling giant at the beginning of the prose *Tristan*. Despite his protracted dialogues with knights and his manipulation of figurative language, the Riddler never really emerges from the Imaginary rivalry ascribed by both Fanon and

Bhabha to the interracial encounter. The giant's riddles focus on himself and his bodily drives, consuming and destroying anything in his path; he is unable to solve riddles that present different sorts of subjective relationships, including one that depicts himself from what to him would be an alien perspective, or that articulate a sense of perpetual desire in the absence of bodily gratification. Despite his apparent attraction to the knights, his attitude toward them is one of aggressive objectification. In forcing them to solve the riddles cataloguing his life story, he literally uses them as mirrors, reflecting back his own invincibility without actually embodying a similar power or voracity themselves. Indeed, he always considers himself the victor in the riddling game, since knights who fail to solve his riddles are eaten, while those who succeed are sequestered in his lair; and even when he is unable to solve the final riddle, he does not foresee that this will result in his death.

The Riddler is clearly one who cannot brook any genuine threat to his sense of self, whether from cultural or linguistic codes regulating bodily drives or from other beings against whom he might be measured. His brother was his most serious rival; as Pelias explains in deciphering the riddle of fratricide, "Tu veïs et aperceüs que tes freres estoit greignour et plus forz et plus legiers et plus puissanz de toutes choses. . . . Por ceste chose porchaças tu sa mort" (*PT*[C], 1:81; You saw and perceived that your brother was larger and stronger and more agile and more powerful in all ways. . . . For that reason, you sought his death). The brother also manifests a capacity for fraternal charity and protective behavior that is foreign to the Riddler; as Pelias further notes, he rescued his smaller sibling when he fell into his own trap, "par pitié et de nature et de norreture" (1:81; out of pity derived both from nature and from upbringing). The brother presents an intolerable image of an alternate self whose superior prowess and antithetical moral orientation can be experienced by the Riddler only as confrontational and alien. He therefore buries him alive in a pit, an act described in the riddle as smothering him within their mother's body—"Et de sa mere si le charge, / Qu'a mort le met" (1:80; and he weighed him down so much with his mother's body that he killed him)—glossed by Pelias as "la terre, que nos apelons mere" (1:81; the earth, which we call "mother"). By burying his brother, the giant removes this threatening image from view; in figuratively sending him back to the womb, he attempts to undo his very existence, as though he had never been born at all. And by eating his actual mother, the giant again obliterates an image of alienating giantesque virtue—his mother having been, as Pelias patiently recounts in his solution to the matricidal riddle, a pious "Abel" to the giant's blasphemous "Cain"—while also aggressively confronting another threat to his sense of bodily integrity: the maternal body that once contained his own. As the mother is devoured, the two bodies are once again merged, but in a way that marks the Riddler himself as the image of supreme bodily integrity, in implicit contrast to his hapless brother, absorbed back into "mother earth." With this act the mother is reduced to a mere fragment to be integrated into the giant's all-encompassing wholeness: "Qui en l'autre ot esté enclos / Fist tant qu'il ot l'autre en soi clos" (1:79; The one who had been enclosed in the other, acted so that he enclosed the other in himself).

Having removed these threats to his sense of bodily supremacy, the Riddler proceeds to surround himself with men capable of parroting back his most extravagant exploits while remaining safely unable to match his achievements, and does away with all those unable to serve this function. For their part, the knights react with aggression toward this man whose unrepentant bravado over acts with which they may be dangerously familiar—fratricide, rape, incest—makes him an image of masculine potency that is similar to their own self-image in all the wrong ways. If the giant mirrors the knights, it is by presenting an image not of human perfection but of the inhuman chaos that is held in check only by their subjection to the laws and constraints of language and chivalric culture. In response to his confidence in the superiority of sheer physical force, the knights take refuge in an intellectual and moral superiority, flaunting both their ability to decode even his most shocking riddles and their righteous indignation at his autobiographical revelations. At the same time, the very premise of the giant's desire for knightly companionship betrays a chivalric fantasy of self-affirmation through the admiring recognition of the other. The twin qualities of narcissism and aggression, identified by Bhabha as lying at the heart of colonial and interracial relations, could not be more clearly embodied in this grotesque caricature of interracial relations.

The real dialogue that takes place in the episode of the Riddler unfolds between the knights themselves, who objectify the giant by using him as an unwitting medium through which to negotiate their own relationships. The knights of the prose *Tristan* are almost comically defined by their intense competition for a common object of desire—Celinde in the opening segment and Iseut in the rest of the story—and by rivalries and loyalties triangulated through that and other shared desires (for honor, for Christian or Arthurian hegemony, for the Grail). The first such instance in the episode of the Riddler turns on the rivalry of Sador and Pelias, each of whom considers himself to be the husband of Celinde. And since Sador's claim is based on Christian marriage and that of Pelias on pagan law, the two men are caught in a triangle of shared desire, itself split between opposing cultural codes. Pelias's riddle is incomprehensible to the giant in its evocation of two subjects bound through their common adherence to feudal codes of honor and loyalty but divided in deadly rivalry through their respective love and marriage to the same woman; but it is correctly read by Sador as a coded message for himself, laying down a challenge. Sador's strategy enables him in turn to ensure that his rival is removed from circulation and incarcerated by the giant, while allowing himself and Celinde to escape. In the second instance, Apollo's riddle obliquely figures something that the Riddler cannot conceptualize—the giant's own death at the hands of a smaller and weaker man—but that is readily grasped by Pelias as the solution to his and his son's enforced isolation. Again, the riddle, relayed through the giant to his prisoner, functions as a communication between the knights, enabling Pelias to plot his course in implicit collusion with this new chivalric visitor: "Et tot maintenant qu'il ot la devinaille escotee, sot bien a quoi elle pooit torner tot maintenant. . . . Mieuz li vient qu'il lest le jaiant metre a mort a cesti point" (*PT*[C], 1:92; And as soon as he had heard the riddle, he knew very well what its immediate outcome could be. . . . It seemed to him better to let the giant be put to death at that point). For the knights, the giant himself is a constant specter of death. Their imprisonment in his lair imposes a symbolic death in removing them from the social and subjective networks that defined them as chivalric warriors and feudal lords, while his anthropophagic habits and generally violent disposition place them under perpetual threat of bodily death as well. The giant's death reduces him to nothing more than an object, now meaningless and—in their eyes, at least—unworthy of mourning or burial: "E il montent adonc e laissent le jaiant tout estendu devant le perron" (1:93; And then they mounted their horses and left the giant all stretched out in front of the stone).

Diana Fuss, in her reading of Fanon's analysis of black-white race relations, notes that colonialism is, in part, a process of "policing the boundaries of cultural intelligibility, legislating and regulating which identities attain full cultural signification and which do not," and that this in turn entails the exclusion of the black man from "the cultural field of symbolization."[42] Medieval tales of knights and giants similarly map the complex and shifting intersubjective rivalries and alliances that arise among the knights themselves, in distinction to the static objectification of the giant. As interlocutors bound by shared symbolic codes, able to conceptualize both their own desires and those of their companion or competitor, the knights are capable not only of cooperation but also of manipulating, deceiving, and exploiting one another. The giant, for all his use of riddling language, seems to lack a capacity either to recognize or to perpetrate duplicity; he understands only the exposition of past actions and the straightforward enunciation of present intentions. And he shows no awareness of the knights as desiring subjects in their own right. Though capable of entering into agreements of exchange, such as granting Sador his freedom in exchange for the solution to Pelias's riddle, the Riddler never seems interested in reading the desires or hidden agendas of his interlocutors. He does not seek to position himself as the object of their desire or to gratify their desires as a way of enticing them to stay with him more willingly but contents himself with his ability to detain them by sheer brute force. One might add that he also remains outside the dynamic of mimetic desire that fuels the chivalric narrative. Though Sador is accompanied by Celinde when he encounters the Riddler, the giant shows no interest whatsoever in the lady, making him virtually the only male character who is not inflamed with desire at the very sight of the Babylonian beauty. In this way medieval tales of giants implicitly enact an ideology of race and culture that identifies the chivalric subjects of Arthurian legend as fully human, with all the complexities and paradoxes that this entails. Giants are relegated to a simpler plane of existence that does still intersect to some extent with aristocratic humanity but tends to fall short of the mark. With their oversized bodies, ferocious appetites, and lack of rational discretion or spiritual complexity, giants illustrate Cohen's comment that in medieval discourses of race or ethnicity, subaltern peoples are depicted as "more *embodied* than their supposed superiors."[43]

It is Apollo who glosses the movement of the ship in the giant's final riddle—an object that moves swiftly and leaves no trace—as the duplicitous behavior of one whose true desires and transgressive actions are cloaked under an external guise of propriety. This reading—so fundamental to human nature with its simultaneous capacity for rationality and irrationality, its skill at reading and exploiting the desires of others for personal gain, and its ability to manipulate linguistic and cultural codes—is not even acknowledged by the giant. Apollo's reading of the "riddle within the riddle," and the giant's indifference toward this entire point, construct the human-giant opposition in a manner that corresponds strikingly to Lacan's opposition of the human and the animal. In his analysis of the philosophical construction of human subjectivity in contradistinction to the animal, Derrida singles out Lacan's insistence on two qualities that define the subjectivity unique to humans: the individual's capacity to "pretend to pretend" and to "erase its traces."[44] Though they may engage in a simple feint, such as playing dead or abruptly switching course when running from a predator, animals are commonly understood as incapable of lying in the human sense, and in particular of "telling the truth in order to lead the other astray"—what Lacan calls a "pretense in the second degree."[45] In Lacan's words, "An animal does not pretend to pretend. He does not make tracks whose deception lies in the fact that they will be taken as false, while being in fact true ones.... Nor does an animal cover up its tracks."[46] Susan Crane has noted that medieval bestiaries do in fact attribute certain kinds of deception to animals, including the lion's supposed use of its tail to erase its tracks and thus elude hunters.[47] But she also readily acknowledges that such claims must be reconciled with centuries of classical and medieval discourse stressing the binary opposition of humans and animals, a distinction typically grounded "in speech, in signification and falsification, in judgment and deduction."[48] And tellingly, this capacity to mislead or even to lie by telling the truth, or to manipulate the perceptions of others in such a way as to render one's own behavior invisible, is precisely what Apollo sees in the metaphor of the ship as a cunningly deceptive woman. It is also, of course, a skill that is fully and repeatedly deployed by both Tristan and Iseut in this same text. Indeed, Apollo himself could be seen as "pretending to pretend" when he reminds the giant that as victor in the riddling contest he has the power to decide whether the giant lives or dies and when he then asks in an offhand manner if he can heft the giant's sword, commenting, "Si verras que je en fera por toe amor" (1:92; And then you'll see what I'll do with it for love of you). Apollo is in fact announcing his intention to kill the giant and requesting permission to use his powerful sword as a means of doing so. But the casual way that he broaches the subject allows the giant to believe that his words are mere bluster or play: "Il cuidoit que Apollo n'eüst pas tant de cuer qu'il l'oceïst" (1:92; He didn't think Apollo would be so bold as to kill him). Not only is he unable to understand the knights' riddles, to comprehend their self-image or the way in which they interact among themselves; he also fails to read the covert intentions hidden in their conversations with him.

Giant Subjectivity?

The Riddler gives us a particularly detailed portrait of a giant as a man whose incapacity for metacommunication, and insensitivity to the internal conflicts caused by incompatible but equally compelling obligations and desires, separates him from the refined subjectivity of aristocratic knights. But however evil and one-dimensional the Riddler is, and however disrespectful of his gods, the fact remains that he does accept some degree of subjection to overarching ethical principles. He honors his oaths not to harm the knights who live with him, including those who have agreed to a day's delay in allowing the giant to ponder their riddle: "Ja par moi ne te vendra mal tant com tu soies en ma compaignie et en mon conduit. . . . Et celi creante sor toz ses diex et sor sa loi" (1:82, 92; No harm will ever come to you as long as you're in my company and under my safe conduct. . . . And he swears to him by all his gods and by his law). He is, moreover, capable of seeing his daughter's great love for Luce; and rather than punishing her for looking beyond himself, or simply ravishing her in direct fulfillment of his own lust, he prefers to solidify his relationship with her by providing her with the object of her desire and attempting to guarantee her happiness by imposing a vow of fidelity onto her husband. In this element of contractual honor with the knights, then, and in this capacity to understand and satisfy the exogamous desires of his daughter, we might glimpse the possibility of a "giant subjectivity," even if it is only hinted at and ultimately disavowed as the narrative unfolds. The giant's daughter, in turn, mourns his death, suggesting a mutually valued relationship. This picture of father-daughter love might seem irreconcilable with the Riddler's own account of his other daughter—itself a paradoxical mix of attraction (rape triggered by his delight in her great beauty) and scorn (whereby she was nothing more to him than food). If the paternal love and behavior of a giant do have a true subjective dimension, formed by symbolic codes and sustained in relationships with other subjects, it is one that is alien indeed to the medieval aristocratic reader. But even as it allows us to entertain this fantasy, the text also permits us to ignore it by splitting the two portraits of the giant as father, not only between two daughters, but also between two narrative planes. Within the frame narrative, the giant can provide a suitably filial and virginal bride for Luce, while also treating his son-in-law and his other chivalric guests with a measure of respect and honor. At the same time, the tale told by the riddles gives us the cartoon villain that we know (or want, or need) giants to be, a picture reinforced by the coercive aspects of the giant's behavior. And the Riddler's death allows these troubling contradictions to be not so much resolved as set aside. Once fully objectified as inert corpse, the giant is no longer of interest, and the chivalric story lines that he had temporarily impeded can simply pick up where they left off.

We have seen the hint of a possible subjective identity for the Golden-Haired Giant as well. He too, despite his voracity, displayed an uncharacteristic willingness to defer desire and wait for his daughter to come of age: when the giantess presents Galotine to Lyonnel, she notes that the giant "ne desire tant chose qu'il puist jesir avecques elle" (desires nothing so much as to lie with her).[49] That he would bide his time suggests that Golden-Hair did accept his subjugation to at least some sort of symbolic law, a prohibition on sexual relations with young children. His affectionate engagement with Galotine, moreover, her refusal to get out of bed until her father's return, and her ebullient response to his greeting would seem to indicate a trusting, loving father-daughter relationship that sits very uneasily with the incestuous desires that the giant is voicing and his cruelly abusive treatment of his wife. Perhaps the fact that he never did actually rape Galotine opens the possibility for her future descendants and in-laws to reconstruct the giant as a worthy lord and patriarch. And of course Golden-Hair's death allows him to become the object of incompatible discourses and story lines that need never be integrated in a portrait of living masculine subjectivity. This construction of competing perspectives and different versions of history is an important, and fascinating, characteristic of *Perceforest* overall.[50] And in keeping with his manipulation of narrative perspectives, the *Perceforest* author also hints at a possible double vision of the giant in the way that he presents the story of Holland.

As we saw in chapter 1, the text makes it abundantly clear that Holland is an evil character. With its extra limbs, all of them useless and paralyzed, his body is a grotesque doubling, a man's body overwritten with a corpse. He is repeatedly characterized as "inhumain," "monstre," "pervers," "cruel," and "tyrans." There is universal rejoicing at his death, and certainly no thought of mourning or funeral rites; his body is left lying in the deep depression hollowed out by his violent death throes, creating a toxic wasteland known forever after as "Le Paradis du terrible Holland" (the Paradise of the terrible Holland).[51] Nonetheless, the text does also allow us to glimpse a different perspective, one that would grant the giant an inner life of sorts and a measure of subjectivity. Holland kills and eats anyone who visits his island, typical giantesque behavior; and one of the reasons for killing him is to open up new avenues for commerce and travel. It is not simple, unmotivated savagery that causes this behavior, however, but the giant's painful awareness of his own inability to match the image of bodily perfection that he sees in all those around him, "la vergoigne qu'il avoit de luy meisme" (1:111; the shame he felt at his own person). This one point—a sense of shame and anxiety caused by bodily flaws—recalls another character in *Perceforest*, a hunchback knight known as Le Bossu de Suave.[52] Originally rejected by his father, who cannot imagine himself as having engendered such a creature, Le Bossu is eventually accepted; but if he is allowed into the male homosocial realm of aristocratic knighthood, he remains intimidated by the prospect of heterosexual love. He fears that he is unworthy of expressing amorous sentiments or of attracting the attention of a lady; and these anxieties are touchingly expressed in a song that he performs at court. This very eloquence, combined with his chivalric excellence, earns Le Bossu the love of a noble maiden, whom he marries. Maintaining our earlier distinction of Imaginary and Symbolic identities, we might conclude that those who fail to measure up in the realm of the Imaginary—those for whom visual mirroring of the ideal is impossible—can nonetheless succeed in the realm of the Symbolic through their perfect adherence to cultural and ideological norms of religion, class, and gender. In the end, of course, the positive example of Le Bossu serves only to accentuate the failures of Holland. Still, this revelation of the giant's sense of shame is our first hint at an inner life and subjective dimension to the "monster," even as the text forecloses any real possibility of sympathy for him.

Our second insight into the giant's behavior comes after his death, when his subjects explain to the victorious Chevalier au Delphin that Hollandin is not the giant's son but his nephew and stepson: some twenty years earlier, Holland killed his (apparently nongiant) brother in order to appropriate the brother's pregnant wife, and when she died he raised her son as his own. This behavior cannot be condoned either, least of all in *Perceforest*, where Gadifer's first law upon becoming king of Scotland is a ban on theft and on the exploitation of the weak by the strong, and where rape stands out as the most wicked of crimes. Established by Perceforest as his first act on ascending the throne, the eradication of rape is said to be responsible for the institution of chivalric culture. Holland manifests the same fraternal rivalry as the Riddler, an inability to tolerate the image of one who is so close and so like him, and yet so unlike him; and he attempts to appropriate his brother's successful identity position by taking over his role as husband and father. His plan is foiled, first by the death of the lady in her horror at a sexual liaison with a "monster," and then by Hollandin's budding love affair with the maiden Marse, heiress to the neighboring island. Still, we are told that Holland loved the lady and was willing to respect her wish not to consummate her forced marriage with him until after the birth of her child; like Golden-Hair, like Maudit even for a time, the giant was capable of modifying his behavior and deferring his desire in the interest of a higher law of love and moral propriety. He also seems to have loved, or at least esteemed, his stepson, and "l'a honnourablement fait garder jusqus a l'eage de vingt ans" (*Perce/IV*, 1:122–23; had him honorably cared for up to the age of twenty)—albeit that he then imprisoned him to prevent him from pursuing his relationship with Marse, which threatened to remove the boy from his exclusive relationship with Holland alone.

Clearly the giant did not desire a son as a means of forging feudal alliances of marriage and chivalric service, but only as an object for his own enjoyment, or indeed as a means of mimicking his brother's infuriating superiority: as a mirror of the bodily perfection that he longed for, as a sign of paternal power and virility. Holland's behavior in this respect is a classic illustration of envy, the emotion attributed by Fanon to the native as he gazes upon the foreign settlers who have taken over his land: "The look that the native turns on the settler's town is a look of lust, a look of envy; it expresses his dreams of possession—all manner of possession: to sit at the settler's table, to sleep in the settler's bed, with his wife if possible. The colonized man is an envious man."[53] Envy, the longing and the torment of the outsider denied access to the pleasures he imagines others to be enjoying, is identified by Lacan with Imaginary identification: an emotion of rivalry, a painful experience of one's own difference from the ideal constantly on display. Envy is also singled out by Augustine, in a passage much discussed by Lacan, as a mark of Original Sin in even the youngest of infants.[54] Augustine identifies envy as having been responsible for Cain's foundational crime of fratricide, which Holland here reenacts.[55] His willingness to wait for the lady's baby to be born associates his act less with unbridled libido than with an envious desire directed at his brother: the desire for that which the other desires, possesses, or enjoys.

Though Holland is clearly evil and a menace to be eliminated, then, the text does also allow us to construct a counternarrative. This is a man taunted and rejected for his physical deformity, of which he is so ashamed that he cannot bear to be seen by anyone who does not already know him; he develops a pathological need to kill any potential witness to his condition. He falls in love with a lady, seduced by her beauty and her fertility, hoping perhaps—like Le Bossu—that heterosexual love and successful procreation may redeem his bodily failings; but the lady chooses death as the preferable alternative to marriage with a man like him. He then transfers his love to his one remaining family member, his nephew and stepson; but he is betrayed when the boy grows up and begins looking to the outside world, and to a relationship that will definitively exclude his stepfather. Holland is thwarted at every turn by the unbridgeable difference that separates him from the human race, even as he continues to manifest emotions—shame, resentment, envy, jealousy, love—that identify him as all too fully human. For all that, of course, I must hasten to acknowledge that *Perceforest* is hardly a Romantic novel in the vein of *Frankenstein*. Mary Shelley took pains to develop the monster's inner life, allowing him to narrate his own story and placing his perspective at the center of her novel, so as to trace his progression from a genuine desire for human knowledge, pleasures, and love to more sinister forms of resentment, envy, and wrath. In contrast, the *Perceforest* author limits his giant's subjectivity to occasional hints, oblique glimpses, and the frankly biased assessments of various third parties, some of whom were not even acquainted with the giant in question. And in the end, Holland's very bodily monstrosity is something that he cannot shed: though in his final battle he loses the limbs that had disfigured and obstructed him, these amputations also cause his death. From a body marked by hideous excess, he goes to one defined by leakage and lack, as blood streams from his wounds, blinding him and sapping his strength. Our painful recognition of the giant's humanity is salved by the reassuring conclusion that—unlike us—he is truly irredeemable, human but also inhuman, a "pervers et inhumain homme" (perverse and inhuman man; *Perce/IV*, 1:113). In its condemnation of giants, with their fiercely independent resistance to exchange networks of commerce, marriage, and feudal alliance, and in its glorification of the equally ferocious (but courtly!) warriors who dismember and kill them, *Perceforest* distinguishes between acceptable and unacceptable forms of law, power, and violence. And in this respect, as I noted at the very beginning of this study, it enacts what Žižek has termed "the highest form of violence": namely, "the imposition of this standard with reference to which some events appear as 'violent.'"[56]

Homosocial Rivalry and the Triangulation of Desire

The interplay of rivalries is explored in numerous other texts depicting murderous clashes between knight and giant, some of which further inscribe the human-giant encounter within the framework of heterosexual love. In the *Conte du Papegau*, for example, the downfall of the Chevalier Jayant derives from his inability to understand the tournament organized by the duchess as a symbolic structure within which knights can vie for a common object of desire; he can see only the necessity of asserting his supremacy above all possible rivals. As soon as the Chevalier du Papegau is identified as the paragon of knighthood, the giant sets out to defeat him—not in the theatrics of the tournament but in actual mortal combat—and seeks to inflict some stigmatizing difference on his rival, who will thus cease to be a mirror of chivalric perfection. Indeed, the giant treats Arthur's body as a commodity—an object that can be fragmented into easily manageable pieces to produce a token for the lady. The lady had agreed to grant the Chevalier Jayant her love if he successfully staged his superior prowess in a joust with the Chevalier du Papegau, but as we saw in chapter 1, the giant turns this into a commercial transaction, whereby the rival knight's hand would be presented to the lady in exchange for a marriage that would endow him with aristocratic lordship and lands.

The Chevalier Jayant here, in effect, treats Arthur as Arthurian knights treat giants—as Lyonnel, for example, treats the Golden-Haired Giant. The latter two men are not rivals for a common object of desire: any trace of direct rivalry with the giant is, as we have seen, displaced onto Clamidés, who (if somewhat inadvertently) supplants the giant as lover and husband of Galotine. Lyonnel's aim in seeking out the giant is to prove his mettle and procure a trophy for his beloved. As was also intimated with the Chevalier Jayant, however, the extraordinarily complex treatment of the Golden-Haired Giant across several episodes allows us to trace ways that a giant can split into Imaginary and Symbolic otherness. In the initial encounter, Lyonnel fights the giant as a means of testing himself against a specular figure that reflects back the qualities of the knight—physical prowess, libidinous drives, a handsome appearance—in an alienating form. Lyonnel's stated mission is to take the giant's head back to Scotland, and his challenge casts the confrontation in the classic model of two knights competing for an object desired by a third party—the lady—to whom it will ultimately be given:

> Or me fut depuis fait a sçavoir que se je faisoie tant que je luy apportasse le chief au Gueant aux Cheveulx Dorez, je avroie lieu de la veoir

et regarder a mon vouloir. . . . Sy vous calenge doresenavant la teste atout les cheveulx, qui sont les plus beaulx que je veisse onques. (*Perce/II*, 1:353–54)

[Then after that I was informed that if I managed to bring her the head of the Golden-Haired Giant, I would have the opportunity to see her and behold her as I desired. . . . Thus hereby I challenge you for possession of the head and all its hair, which is the most beautiful that I have ever seen.]

Dismembering the giant's body, again, objectifies it and robs it of its power as an image of masculinity compared to which the chivalric body may seem weak and powerless. And when the head is finally brought to court, it is kept as a static visual image enshrined and fixed in the museum-like setting of the Temple de la Franche Garde, dedicated to Venus and filled with objects and paintings providing a detailed record of Lyonnel's many accomplishments. This treatment of the giant corresponds very clearly to Fanon's characterization of the objectification of the black man in white colonial culture, as summed up by Fuss: "Forced to occupy, in a white racial phantasm, the static ontological space of the timeless 'primitive,' the black man is disenfranchised of his very subjectivity . . . [and] sealed instead into a 'crushing objecthood.'"[57]

In the isolated setting of the Temple, accessible only to the chivalric elite, the disembodied head presents the contradictory aspects of the giant as Imaginary rival to the knight: his extreme ferocity and his exotic beauty. These two qualities endow him with a hypermasculinity on the one hand and a strangely effeminate quality on the other. The golden hair, luxurious and radiant, might indeed make his head an appropriate gift for a maiden enamored of all things beautiful, and Lyonnel's taunts objectify the giant as nothing more than an object of visual contemplation:

Sachiez que quant la maçue vous cheyt, au reprendre vous en eusse la teste coppee se n'eusse cuidié empirier les cheveulx. Mais la belle a qui les ay promis a plus chier les cheveulx que la teste et pour ceste pitié en joïssiez vous encores. (*Perce/II*, 1:358)

[Know that when you dropped your club, I could have cut off your head when you were picking it up if I had not been afraid of damaging the hair. But the beautiful girl to whom I promised it prizes the hair more than the head, and in deference to her you still have the use of it.]

Male spectators, however, are struck by the savage aggression expressed in the giant's facial features, exclaiming at "ce chevalier que nous veons cy sur ce pilier sy orrible a regarder ou viaire pour la grandeur et la fierté de luy et si esmerveillable de cheveleure" (2:78; this knight that we see here on a pillar, with a face so horrible to behold because of his size and arrogance, and with such marvelous hair). In response to this comment Blanchete's mother, Queen Lydoire, succinctly states the giant's status as Imaginary rival in a confrontation that served to create Lyonnel's identity as paragon of knighthood: "Sire chevalier, dist la dame, au chief pouez vous veoir quel le gueant estoit, et au gueant quelle la proesse et le hardement du chevalier qui le conquist" (2:78; Sir Knight, said the lady, from the head you can see what the giant was, and from the giant, the prowess and audacity of the knight who defeated him).

At the same time, the giant's transgressive desires—violent, homicidal, incestuous—would seem to enmesh him in a symbolic conflict in which Lyonnel becomes the enforcer of a particular code of law, regulating legitimate and illegitimate desires and uses of violence within the realm of sexuality. Golden-Hair's barbaric cruelty is depicted in lurid terms. Returning home after a short absence, he taunts his wife with the possibility that their daughter may have reached the age where he can marry her and throw the giantess into the sea: "Orde vielle mauldicte, mandez vostre fille pour veoir s'elle est assez creue depuis .II. jours" (1:352; Filthy, cursed old woman, summon your daughter so we can see if she's grown enough in the past two days). In consoling the giantess, Lyonnel first cites "Amours" and "Espoir" as the sources of inspiration that motivate his challenge and give him confidence of victory; but he does also frame the battle in ideological terms, commenting that "si ay grant fiance ou Dieu Souverain que, par les maulx qu'il a emprins a faire sans repentance, qu'il sera pour moy et a luy contraire" (1:352; I have great faith that, because of the evil that (the giant) has been doing without repentance, the Sovereign God will be for me, and contrary to him). Remarkably, however, neither the giant's ravaging of local maidens nor his designs on his wife and daughter are addressed in the dialogue between Lyonnel and his adversary, where attention is exclusively focused on acquiring the head as a gift for Lyonnel's beloved. It is only in dialogue with the giantess—and later in the words of the grateful inhabitants who come to honor Lyonnel for liberating them—that the giant's aberrant behavior is articulated. Indeed, Lyonnel never even considers the possibility that the Scottish queen may have targeted the Golden-Haired Giant as a means of ensuring that his violation of sexual norms was punished with death; his explanation of his mission relies solely on Blanchete's presumed fascination with the giant's beautiful hair.

Though Lyonnel's victory over Golden-Hair does have the consequence of punishing criminal behavior, his failure to acknowledge that during the combat itself suggests a refusal to recognize the giant as a subject, defined and constrained by the laws that have shaped Lyonnel's own chivalric identity. In his objectified state, the giant is not worthy of judicial combat, of fighting to justify his own code of behavior, or even of giving up his life in expiation for his sins: like a poisonous but colorful insect he is at once an exotic curiosity to be collected, and a pest to be eliminated.[58] From Lyonnel's perspective, the Golden-Haired Giant is an anthropomorphic version of the primal violence and lawlessness that is also incarnated in his other exotic adversaries: the dragon that terrorized sailors from its lair on the Ylle au Serpent and the ferocious lions that had virtually depopulated the kingdom of the Estrange Marche. And his appropriation of the head is not dissimilar to his triumphant possession of the claws and feet of both the serpent and the lion, embedded in the shield that is later displayed, alongside the giant's head, in the Temple de la Franche Garde. The serpent resembles the giant in that both inhabit distant islands—the Ylle au Serpent is later identified with Orkney, while the giant's home can probably be located in the Shetland Islands—and both eat human flesh.[59] The lions, in turn, parallel the giant's household in that they too form a family unit. And just as the giant's daughter is salvaged as a prize, a sign of victory that can be assimilated into aristocratic court culture, so one of the lion cubs attaches itself to Lyonnel as a living trophy. Seemingly eager to atone for the ravages of its parents, the cub fawns on Lyonnel and becomes a devoted pet for

Blanchete and her companions, while its natural ferocity also enables it to act as indomitable guardian of the Temple housing the giant's head. Like Galotine, the cub represents the potential benefits to be reaped by extracting the potency of giant or beast in an assimilable form; the giant himself, like the adult lions, embodies violence in a form too extreme to be contained or subjected to civilizing codes.

And yet the giant is also different from these purely bestial adversaries. He is human; and the marriage of his daughter, who is not merely a trophy but also the mother of knights and ladies, implicates the giant as well in the codes of aristocratic lineage and lordship. Outside the sealed-off space of the Temple, in the living world of feudal politics and family networks, Golden-Hair is remembered in oral histories: first in his cousin Brancq's tale of the giant's valor and Lyonnel's treachery, and later in the way that he comes to be commemorated as founding head of an illustrious feudal house. The very fact that Clamidés takes Galotine away from the giant imposes a retrospective framework of Symbolic rivalry onto the encounter: a conflict of desires that is resolved antagonistically. The giant's inward-looking endogamy, whereby the daughter is coded as the object of paternal desire and the means of gratifying his lust, is confronted by an outward-looking exogamy, whereby the daughter is coded as an object of exchange between feudal families, serving to generate an ever-expanding network of alliances in successive generations.[60] Although Golden-Hair is defeated and stigmatized, he is still in that same stroke acknowledged as a desiring subject supplanted by another desiring subject, and then redefined yet again as patriarch. The Temple installation fixes him in collective memory as a timeless image of irreducible otherness; but as we saw in chapter 1, the oral traditions passed down within the extended family allow his partial (albeit strictly posthumous) assimilation as he is reshaped in conformance with paradigms of chivalric prowess and lordship.

This Man Which Is Not One: Giants and the Refusal of Exchange

Lyonnel's battle with Golden-Hair is inscribed in the context of chivalric service to Venus: the principle of erotic desire—initially deferred and diverted into male homosocial rivalry, then consummated in marriage as the female love object enters into an exchange between men—that underpins feudal alliances, aristocratic lineage, and civilization itself, at least as these are presented in *Perceforest* and other courtly romances. And the very fact that the giant is waiting for his daughter to come of age means that he, in his own way, submits to a principle of prolonged desire and deferred gratification, albeit that the resulting energies are channeled by him into destructive acts rather than noble exploits. His battle with Lyonnel—explicitly for possession of his golden-haired head, but also implicitly and retrospectively for the right to claim or bestow Galotine as wife—is a distorted version of the battles waged in aristocratic tournaments. The battle was ultimately triggered, after all, when Galotine aroused the giant's wrath by announcing her desire to marry Clamidés instead of him. And *Perceforest* contains numerous examples of the classic model of knights competing directly for a bride whose father or guardian bestows her on the winner, as well as others in which knights stage their prowess in order to win the approval of the family whose daughter or ward they hope to marry.

Much has been written about the Lévi-Straussian theory of kinship and exchange, according to which the incest taboo lies at the origins of patriarchal culture, or even of civilization itself, by instituting the exchange of women between men.[61] This model has been applied to medieval society by historians such as Georges Duby, as well as being used in readings of medieval romance and *chanson de geste*.[62] Feminist critics have focused on the implications of this model for gendered identity, arguing that it objectifies women while granting full subjectivity only to men; and they have questioned its validity both as an account of social realities and as a key to the structures and ideologies of medieval literature.[63] The often powerful and active female characters in medieval texts, as well as the frequent presence of ironic, skeptical, and humorous innuendo in the portrayal of love, courtship, and marriage, offer a counterbalance to any simplistic reading of these narratives as reducing women to the status of objects in cementing social and symbolic relations between men. Nonetheless, a model of women as gifts, prizes, and objects of exchange does operate in many medieval texts, even if it is deployed with ambivalence or partially undermined by narrative developments, and even if female as well as male characters are often portrayed as manipulating this model to their own advantage.

The "exchange of women" model must be nuanced not only with regard to gender, however; there is also a racial dimension. I have touched in chapters 2 and 3 on ways in which the Saracen princess often stands outside a simple model of exchange between families. Not only does she embody an alternative version of femininity, but also Saracen men, being inassimilable enemies, are generally not in a position to enter into relationships of exchange with Christian warriors. If, as Kay argues, the Saracen princess expresses skepticism about feudal and patriarchal values, this skepticism is ultimately more damaging for the Saracen power structures from which she comes than for the French society into which she integrates. And the complex network of rivalry, kinship, and alliance that forms masculine subjectivity is one from which giants are even more definitively excluded. This is not to say that giants never take human women as wives or sexual playthings, or that a knight could never marry a giantess; as we have seen, both of these events do occur across the corpus of medieval French romance. But such liaisons generally arise outside the structures of male exchange that govern aristocratic marriage; at the very least, a giant's attempt to participate in the network of chivalric rivalry and exchange is likely both to distort the operative customs and to result in the giant's demise. And this pattern, repeated consistently in various tales of giants, forms another parallel with the modern discourse of racial stereotyping and subjugation. It has become a truism to note that, in Western societies, black and Asiatic men have traditionally been excluded from the exchange of women: it has been white men who controlled sexual access to women of all colors.[64] If women are in some sense a medium through which men negotiate their relationships, then these structures also allow for the cultural definition of some men as human subjects, while objectifying others as threats to the sexual purity and market value of white women, or as obstacles in the way of white male sexual gratification. Such, at least, are the fantasies elaborated not only in modern discourses of racial difference but also in medieval romance and its tales of giants and giantesses.

We have seen that Maudit, Holland, and the father of the Chevalier Jayant all acquired their wives, not through negotiation with the lady's father, but through violent assault and abduction. In Maudit's case, this liaison with a lady drew him into an impossible position in which he was forced to adapt to the model of aristocratic knighthood, governing his lands in peace and using violence only in controlled, generally nonlethal combat when it was necessary to defend his honor and the integrity of his territory. But whereas the love of a noble lady may have an ameliorating effect on a knight, in the life of a giant it leads only to ignominious emasculation, and ultimately to defeat and death. The lady's efforts to impose chivalric discipline and courtly sensibilities on her giant abductor make no more sense to him than the Blonde Fairy's command to be the worst knight at the tournament did to Arthur in the *Papegau*. We do not know what became of the Chevalier Jayant's father, but the son failed in his effort to attract a lady's love or to prove himself in the high-stakes combat for marriage, while his brother's attempt to avenge his death led only to further defeat and ultimately to protracted conflict with the people of Estregalles. Despite the complexities and nuances with which the brothers are depicted, the end result of a half-blood giant's attempt to marry a duchess is a long and bloody war: "Ainsy commença la guerre mortelle d'entre eulx deux, dont morurent maint chevalier et d'une part et d'autre et dura moult longuement" (Thus began the deadly war between the two parties, in which many a knight on both sides died, and it went on for a very long time).[65] The lady had originally planned the tournament as a ceremonial and symbolic "war" that would allow her to identify a husband; but the war that actually breaks out is very real indeed. Though the war is presumably still fought as organized battles, carried out according to a chivalric code, the aesthetic veneer has been stripped away. In this way, Chevalier Redoubté fulfills the process begun by his brother, who first made the move from tournament joust to deadly battle. All of these examples suggest that giants, even in submitting to the laws and customs of the realm, can never truly be assimilated but will always remain in some sense outsiders and disruptive elements.

In narratives of giantess brides, we have also seen that it required Arthur's validation to legitimize the marriage between Maudit's mother and the knight who loved her and that it was crucial for Clamidés to receive Galotine as a gift from Lyonnel, rather than to feel that he was being given as compensatory payment to her mother. The bridegroom was determined to retain his role as a sovereign subject participating in an economy of exchange with another male subject and not to let himself be objectified by the desires of his bride or by the indignation of his mother-in-law. Similarly, Luce's marriage is fully legitimized when his father Pelias formally accepts the giantess bride into his family, completing the act of exchange between the two fathers and relocating the couple from giant's lair to royal palace. And in all cases this exchange between men takes place after the death of the giant father. The narrator explains that Maudit's mother is the last survivor after Arthur has exterminated the giant population of that region; it is from the victorious king that the knight receives her, not from her own family. The Riddler, in turn, prevents any sense of exchange with Luce's family; indeed, he sequesters Pelias along with Luce. Luce himself is a gift given by the giant to his daughter, and the prohibition on ever leaving the giant's lair further reduces Luce to a kind of bait used by the giant to ensure that the giantess will always remain at his side. Absorbing father and son into his own household, the giant severs their ties with the external world and uses them to further his own isolationist agenda. Pelias presumably provides the giant with some form of entertainment and is clearly also expected to assist in the riddling game with which he hopes to entrap other knights. Again, a relationship that should have inserted the giant into the larger world of feudal politics by establishing an alliance with the royal lineage of Leonois instead serves only to drain the kingdom of knights by incorporating them into the giant's space as either food or prisoners and to tighten the giant's hold on his daughter. As for the Golden-Haired Giant, like Holland he stands outside any kind of exchange whatsoever. Golden-Hair's marriage, running counter to the wishes of his wife's parents, was the result of elopement, while Holland's was one of violent abduction. And both giants hoard their children—daughter and stepson respectively—in a stark refusal either to give or to receive.

In these fictional depictions it is not a question of giants attempting to enter into the aristocratic male network of exchange and being barred; the racial stereotype that the giant embodies is that of beings who resist the very concept of exchange and subjective dialogue, who cannot accept a system of public competition and negotiation, and whose violent sexuality places them at the very limits of female desire. Again, the objectification of giants contributes to a reading of aristocratic feudal society and its gendered identities, not merely as one form of human culture and society, but as the definition of civilization and of humanity itself. The giant is quite literally a man who is not one, or one who is not recognized as having a fully human subjectivity. In the encounter of Lyonnel and Golden-Hair, as we have seen, the giant enters into the exchange economy not as a participating subject—as either giver or recipient—but as a gift object himself; and the Chevalier Jayant attempts a similar objectification of Arthur. This transformation of the rival into an object of exchange between the would-be lover and his lady bears closer scrutiny.

The tournaments of *Perceforest* provide not only a context in which knights can compete for brides but also one in which they may fight for an object that neither will end up possessing, but that will be passed to a lady. This other form of exchange also defines masculine subjectivity. Tournaments, with their aestheticized staging of combat, are elaborate mechanisms for the exchange and circulation of honor, service, treasure, and women. Within *Perceforest*, the most intricate set of battles for objects that the knight in question does not actually want for himself unfolds in the tournament held to celebrate the double coronation of Perceforest and Gadifer. On this occasion, the Chevalier au Delphin pledges to fulfill a wish from each of the twelve granddaughters of Pergamon, who is hosting the tournament. Each maiden selects an item of clothing or jewelry being worn by another knight in the tournament— often something given to the knight by another lady—which the Chevalier au Delphin duly captures and presents to its new feminine owner.[66] While it would be dishonorable for a knight to challenge another knight in order to rob him of goods, the act is permissible with the triangulation produced by the presence of the lady as beneficiary. Indeed, this principle is explicitly articulated by Lydoire when she gives Gadifer the intricate gold circlet that will soon be captured by the Chevalier au Delphin and passed on to the maiden Blanche, who—unbeknownst to Lydoire or Gadifer—has selected that as the prize she wishes to claim. When Gadifer expresses fear that the beautiful object may be hacked from his helmet in the heat of battle, Lydoire assures him that he will only gain, rather than lose, honor through that act: "Et s'il est despiecé sur vostre heaume au trenchant de l'espee par bras de preu chevalier, plus noblement ne puet estre departy . . . et vous en avrez la louenge et l'onneur" (And if it is cut to bits on your helmet by a sword blade in the hand of a worthy knight, it could not be more nobly dismantled . . . and you will have praise and honor from that).[67] The ideal outcome, in fact, is for the circlet to be won and given to a lady, since in this way it supports the process of love service essential to knightly honor and fame: "Et s'aucun preux chevalier le gaigne, ce n'est pas joyel a homme: il sera presenté a aucune pucelle gentille et de valeur, dont mainte proesse sera encore faicte a l'occasion de luy et du cercle" (2:861; And if some worthy knight wins it, it is not a jewel for a man: it will be given to some noble aristocratic maiden, whereby many an act of prowess will yet be performed because of her and because of the circlet). As I have already noted, the rivalry and violent combat of the tournament are purely theatrical, as Gadifer and his assailant work together in a joint performance to enhance their own honor while granting the lady's wish. Chivalric combat, staged for female spectators, is also a means by which precious and beautiful objects are transferred, through men, from one female owner to another. This circulation of both honor and treasure is an important means of constituting the symbolic community to which all knights and ladies belong. Knights can be ranked in a shared hierarchy of prowess and acclaim, while ladies are similarly ranked as greater or lesser instigators and beneficiaries of chivalric service. And of course the use of decorative objects at this early stage of the text masks the actual, underlying desire that fuels both male and female competition: that of the knights and ladies respectively for one another as lovers and spouses. Lyonnel's battle for Golden-Hair's head, however, like the Chevalier Jayant's battle for Arthur's hand, short-circuits this model. In these cases it is not an object possessed by the adversary—still less, an object that originated with another lady—but a part of the adversary's own body that is identified as the object of feminine desire. In these battles there can be no question of a reciprocal exchange of honor but only a violent collision leading to the death of one or the other party.

In this view, it is illuminating to return to Lyonnel's insistence on Blanchete's desire for the giant's head. In fact, the text does not portray Blanchete herself as showing any interest in the giant's head either before or after its arrival at court. Not that Blanchete remains passive in the courtship process; on the contrary, she expresses desires and makes requests of her own, presents Lyonnel with carefully chosen gifts, and composes poetry that is instrumental in affecting the course of the narrative.[68] One thing that she does not do, however, is to demand the giant's head. Although Lyonnel claims to be acting on her request, this request actually appears in the wake of a series of effects magically produced by the queen Lydoire as a means of both enticing and distracting Lyonnel when he sees Blanchete for the first time. Lydoire's magic spells partially block Lyonnel's vision of Blanchete when she is picnicking with her mother and companions in the forest, by surrounding the group with a wall of light as bright as the sun, and then conjure up a ferocious bull that the knight is forced to fight. When the bull suddenly disappears, Lyonnel finds that the ladies have vanished as well but that pinned to the oak is "ung rolle ou il y avoit dedens escript en telle maniere: 'Damp chevalier, se faisiez tant que vous eussiez le chief du Gayant aux Crins Dorez, vous verriez a plain ce que tant desirez'" (*Perce/II*, 1:194; a scroll on which was written as follows: "Sir Knight, if you managed to acquire the head of the Golden-Haired Giant, you would see freely what you so desire"). It is clearly Lydoire who sets this condition, just as it is later she who installs the head in the Temple, and she who shows it off to various knightly visitors. And in so doing, she focuses on the head as an icon of ferocity and savagery proving the marvelous prowess of her future son-in-law, not as a beautiful object enjoyed by her daughter. One can logically assume that what Lydoire really wants is the giant's death—since he represents a menace to the civilization that she is committed to upholding—as well as evidence of superlative prowess in her daughter's suitor. The head is simply a sign that both of these have been achieved.

It is Lyonnel himself who interprets the head as a love gift to Blanchete, and he who expresses the most fascination with the long golden hair. We have seen that he exclaims over the beauty of the golden locks when he first meets the giant and that he is careful to kill and behead him in a manner that will not damage the hair. The text emphasizes Lyonnel's ongoing pleasure in the beauty of his prize, describing how he admires it on rest stops during his journey back to court, and how he tends the hair to keep it from becoming tangled or broken:

> Quant Lyonnel eut mis ainsi son chief au soleil, il commença a pignier les cheveulx et a redrecer de ses mains, qui estoient si beaux, si clers et sy luisans que ce sembloit fin or a veoir la ou ilz flambioient ou ray du soleil. Sy ne porriez croire comment Lyonnel fut lié en ce maniement. (*Perce/II*, 2:24)

[When Lyonnel had thus placed his head in the sun, he began to comb the hair and arrange it with his hands, which was so beautiful, so bright and so lustrous that it looked like pure gold as it sparkled in the sunlight. And you could not imagine how happy Lyonnel was in doing this.]

Lyonnel's experience of the giant is divided between aggression and desire, repulsion and delight, and in his identification with Blanchete he attributes similar feelings to her. He imagines, in other words, that Blanchete does desire the giant's body, but only in fragmentary form, and only as an object of beauty to gaze upon. The obsessive focus on the giant's hair—the feature that names and defines him—displaces any possible erotic interest in the rest of his body. In Lyonnel's conversation with the giantess, moreover, it is rapidly and unambiguously clarified that no lady could ever desire the giant as a sexual partner: in fact, sexual contact with him is lethal, "car elles ne sont pas de grandeur pour le recepvoir" (*Perce/II*, 1:348; for they are not big enough to receive him). The possibility of the giant as rival for Blanchete's love or erotic desire is momentarily glimpsed, but only to be disavowed before it can even take form. The dual context in which Lyonnel fights Golden-Hair further allows the giant to be the object of sexual fantasies, while dissociating the erotic element from both Lyonnel and Blanchete. It is Galotine that the giant desires, not Blanchete; and it is Clamidés who desires Galotine, not Lyonnel. In effect, the giant's death is the gift that Lyonnel gives the giantess, and the currency with which he purchases Clamidés's life; while the head is the gift he brings Blanchete. Galotine, the other prize won by Lyonnel in his battle, can be used as a means of recompensing his squire and settling him into a feudal estate.

Far from participating in this intersubjective network of exchange, the giant is reduced to nothing more than an object within it. His death removes him as the obstacle blocking Galotine's marriage; and his head becomes a surrogate that mediates between Blanchete and Lyonnel, allowing for a displaced expression of their mutual love and desire. If Lyonnel takes such pleasure in the giant's hair, after all, this is surely not only because of the hair's intrinsic beauty but also—and more importantly—because the hair is a fetishized substitution for an erotic relationship with Blanchete herself. Within the elaborate fantasy he has constructed, taking possession of the giant's head allows Lyonnel to refocus Blanchete's desire from the giant's body to his own; while the association of the hair with Blanchete makes it a site of erotic pleasure for Lyonnel himself as well. The giant's head, with its savage features, its status as trophy of a spectacularly ferocious battle, and its seductively radiant hair, simultaneously conjures up masculine virility and feminine beauty; it becomes an object that retrospectively configures and conjoins both male and female fantasy and desire. Though Lyonnel is allowed to see Blanchete after killing the giant, he is strictly forbidden to touch her in any way throughout the period of courtship; but the hair is a ready source of both visual and tactile delight. For a time, the giant's head becomes the object onto which Lyonnel can project desires that he dares not yet articulate openly, and around which he can fantasize a reciprocal desire from his beloved.

The Chevalier Jayant's interest in Arthur's hand is not of the same order; he shows no sign of believing that the hand is a marvelous or desirable object in and of itself. In *Papegau*, the severed hand would have functioned more simply as a token of prowess, proving the giant's victory over the latest chivalric hero. Still, the giant is clearly distressed by the duchess's interest in the Chevalier du Papegau, whom she hopes to win as husband: "Quant la duchesse ot oÿ dire qu'il avoit mort le Chevalier Poisson et en avoit delivree la terre de la Dame aux Cheveulx Blons, il luy entra si en cueur qu'elle cuide bien mourir s'elle ne l'a" (*Papegau*, 158; When the duchess had heard that he had killed the Knight Fish and liberated the land of the Lady with the Blond Hair, he so entered into her heart that she really felt she would die if she did not have him). By aggressively substituting the Chevalier du Papegau's hand as the object of the lady's desire, rather than the man himself, the giant both acknowledges and disavows the duchess's amorous designs on the rival knight, just as Lyonnel both imagined and disavowed Blanchete's possible desire for the Golden-Haired Giant. As with Lyonnel and Golden-Hair, the adversary is rendered impotent through objectification and fragmentation; the designated body part is detached and fetishized, producing a medium through which the desired sexual and marital relationship can be established. What the knight can do with the giant, the giant tries to do with the knight. And yet in his failure to neutralize his rival, the Chevalier Jayant undergoes what for a giant seems an utterly remarkable transformation, one that sharply distinguishes him from Maudit, Golden-Hair, the Riddler, or any of the other giants slain by knights in Arthurian romance. Perhaps because they are only half-blood giants, and perhaps also in keeping with the emphasis on Arthur's civilizing influence throughout the *Papegau* as a whole, both the Chevalier Jayant and his brother display a human dimension that moves them closer to Galehot—another half-blood giant—than to the full-blooded giants we have seen. This humanity lies in a capacity for introspection, remorse, and an acknowledgment of one's own limitations: in the subjectivity born of self-knowledge, and the opportunity that this affords to know and to be known by another subject.

Remorse, Penance, and Redemption: Can the Giant Know Himself?

The *Conte du Papegau* pits the young Arthur against a wide range of adversaries, both human and inhuman. Some of the renegade lords that he encounters simply fight, unrepentant, to the death; they are beyond rehabilitation or remorse. Others, however, do have a capacity for reform that is brought out when they encounter, in Arthur, their first experience of a more powerful knight—one who makes them suddenly aware of their own limitations. In his confrontation of Lion sans Mercy, for example, Arthur finds an entire territory that has become the parody of a feudal estate. Instead of receiving land, wives, and other gifts from the lord in exchange for military service, these knights willingly give up their land, pay tribute, and perform a humiliating homage to Lion every month in exchange for being left in peace. Those who resist are killed, and their possessions and family members are confiscated. Moreover, the lord stages an annual competition of the sort that is common in romance: the knight with the most beautiful *amie*, capable of defending her beauty in jousts against all other competitors, is rewarded with a parrot endowed with the power of human speech and song. Needless to say, it is Lion who wins this competition every year, even though his lady is "la plus laide creature que vous oncques mais veissiez" (82; the ugliest creature you ever saw). A tyrannical, rapacious lord and a band of cowardly, inept knights make a dangerous combination: in their interactions, each reinforces the other's flaws. Together they construct a code of behavior in which the knights are both victimized and complicitous in the lord's arrogant abuse of power.

Arthur is duly shocked to discover this state of affairs. His solution does, however, recognize all players as human subjects who are ultimately to be judged under the same moral and legal codes that he upholds throughout his kingdom. Lion is deprived of his ill-gotten gains and forced to construct the prison where he will await final judgment: his energies and wealth must now be dedicated to self-constraint, as he takes on the painful but necessary task of depriving himself of liberty and power. When eventually summoned to Arthur's court, he must go there riding in a cart, since he is no longer deemed worthy of mounting a horse. The knights who submitted to his rule, in turn, must act as beasts of burden in pulling this cart. In this way they stage their own failure to live up to their full human potential, doing penance for their "coardie" (92; cowardice) and "vitance" (92; debasement). It is striking that all involved accept this judgment without question: "Les chevaliers et toute la baronie se merveillent comment si jeune chevalier com estoit le roy sot prenre tel vengence de Lion sans Mercy. Et moult leur plaist et octroyent tous a faire son vouloir et son commandement" (92; The knights and the lords marveled that a knight as young as the king was could be capable of passing such a sentence on Lion sans Mercy. And it pleased them greatly, and they all pledged to do as he commanded and bid them). Lion has proved himself capable of recognizing a more powerful warrior, and of subjecting himself to the judgment of the king: "Je ne trouvay mais chevalier qui contre moy peust durer, sans vous qui avez conquis moy et eulx tout a vostre commandement" (90; I never encountered a knight who could withstand me, aside from you, who have conquered both me and them and made us subject to your command). He has made his confession, narrating the entire story of his misdeeds to the man who defeated him. His knights, chastised by Arthur immediately before the battle, likewise acknowledged their own complicity in the affair: "Les chevaliers, quant ilz oÿrent ce qu'il leur dist, si ont grant honte" (86; The knights, when they heard what he said to them, felt greatly ashamed). Having experienced the genuine remorse born of self-knowledge, aware of the gap between their respective behaviors and the cultural norms defining both chivalry and lordship, both Lion and his knights will not merely suffer their punishment but, one senses, benefit from it. The terms imposed by Arthur can have a penitential, rehabilitational function, so that in the end knights and lord alike can be reformed as proper subjects of the king. This hope is fulfilled at the end of the story when Arthur finally summons Lion and his men to Windsor:

> Si entra en la sale Lion sans Mercy, il et ses chevaliers moult richement vestuz, ainsi comme le roy l'ot commandé. Et si conta devant la baronnie l'aventure et se mist en la mercy au roy, et on les honnora moult et les feist on assoir tous au mengier d'une part. (248–50)

> [Then Lion sans Mercy entered the room, he and his knights very richly dressed, just as the king had commanded. And he recounted the entire adventure before the assembled barons and submitted to the king's mercy, and he and his men were greatly honored and seated to one side at the banquet.]

The narrative resolution at once acknowledges the full human potential of the players and identifies the courtly and chivalric codes of the Arthurian world as the only cultural constructs capable of producing viable human subjects.

The Poisson Chevalier lies at the other extreme: there can be no possible thought of punishing or reforming this creature but only of killing him. At no point does Arthur attempt a dialogue with the Poisson Chevalier, nor does he accuse him of criminal or deviant behavior: his attentions are focused solely on mortal combat. The monster's association with the tempestuous sea and the roar of the wind and waves identifies him as a primal force of nature, destructive in his very essence, and lying outside the power of legal, moral, social, or spiritual codes. The narrator, in fact, makes a telling comment in describing the creature's death throes after it has been mortally wounded. So violently does it thrash about at the point of death that it poses an even greater threat of bodily harm than it did in combat, and this situation requires Arthur to make a prudent decision:

> Et se combatoit si fort a la mort que, se le Chevalier du Papegau ne se fust trait ariere, cest derreniere guerre luy eust esté pire que la premiere. Mais sens valu mieulx a celle heure que proesse, et pour ce

se trayt le Chevalier du Papegau ariere tant qu'il voit qu'il ne se puet relever. (104)

[And he fought against death so powerfully that, if the Knight of the Parrot had not pulled back, this final war would have gone worse for him than the first one. But sense was worth more than prowess at that moment, and so the Knight of the Parrot pulled back until he saw that he could no longer get up.]

It is this capacity for "sens" as well as "proesse" that defines the human warrior: an ability to assess a situation rationally, to know when it is important to press the attack against an opponent and when it is necessary to stand back from the lethal shock waves of a monster struggling internally against its own death. A similar comment, in fact, highlights the combat tactics of the Chevalier au Delphin, who, in his battle with the monstrous giant Holland, "vey bien que force sans advis et habilleté n'y avoit point de lieu" (*Perce/IV*, 1:112; sees that this was not the place for force without skill and forethought).

Within the spectrum defined by the many adversaries that Arthur fights as the Chevalier du Papegau, the Chevalier Jayant can only be seen as human rather than monstrous. His behavior is deviant, a misunderstanding or abuse of cultural institutions, and it is marked by clear signs of "giant culture" or mentality; but it is not that of an inhuman beast. The Chevalier Jayant is problematic, yet in the end he acquires a redemptive insight into his own behavior. His death at Arthur's hands is not simply the elimination of a menace to society: it also takes on aspects of judicial chastisement, penitential cleansing, and the dawn of a more perfectly formed subjectivity. As I noted in chapter 1, the Chevalier Jayant recites to Arthur the three forms of knowledge his father had taught him were essential for a *preudons*: of one's Savior, of good and evil, and of oneself. One striking feature of this exchange is that the giant has a father at all—though giants often are fathers, the fathers of male giants are rarely mentioned in medieval romance accounts—and that his father, although a giant himself with a history of rapacious behavior, has been capable of imposing an ethical law onto his sons. This fundamental concept of good and evil, moreover, is defined in terms of an ability to judge and regulate one's own behavior, both the actions of the body and the symbolic effects of speech: "le mal et le bien que on puet faire de mains et parler de bouche" (*Papegau*, 168; the evil and the good that one can do with one's hands and speak with one's mouth). Like Lion sans Mercy, the Chevalier Jayant becomes aware of his own limitations and takes responsibility for his behavior and its consequences. He is able to see himself not only in terms of failure to measure up to an Imaginary rival but also in terms of failure to conform to a Symbolic code of behavior that was imparted to him in the form of a paternal law: "Se je me fusse congneu avant que je me fusse combatu a vous, par aventure je feusse plus longuement vif que je ne seray. . . . Si vous pry que vous me pardonnés ce que je me suys combatu a vous sans raison et a moult grant tort" (168; If I had known myself before I fought you, perhaps I would have lived longer than I now will. . . . And I pray you to forgive me for fighting you without reason, and very wrongly). In another striking departure from the normal pattern of giant killing, Arthur then listens to the Chevalier Jayant's confession and treats his death with all the respect accorded a human subject: "Le Chevalier du Papegau . . . pria Dieu qu'il eust mercy de s'ame, et le couvri de branches et d'erbes pour le souloil, et moult voulentiers l'eust enterré s'il peust oncques, tant pesoit il" (168; The Knight of the Parrot . . . prayed God to have mercy on his soul, and he covered him with branches and grass to keep the sun off, and would have greatly liked to have buried him if he could somehow have done so, but his body was too heavy). As was illustrated in Arthur's punishment of those who capitulated to Lion sans Mercy, a knight must know when to fight; but he must also know when not to do so. This rational capacity to judge individual encounters according to an overarching code of legal and moral principles is what distinguishes the human knight from the giant combatant; and like Galehot, the half-blood Chevalier Jayant proves himself, in the end, a human subject, enacting a pious and dignified death and calling forth mourning and commemoration from his erstwhile adversary.

When the Chevalier Jayant's brother, Jayant Redoubté de la Roche Secure, attempts to avenge his death but is also defeated by Arthur, he too illustrates the capacity for human subjectivity and dignity in a half-blood giant. Jayant Redoubté's challenge stands in telling contrast to the giant Brancq's attempt at the posthumous defense of his cousin Golden-Hair, which we saw in chapter 1. Brancq is slain by Blanchete's brother

Nestor, and before he dies he is forced both to admit the illegitimacy of his challenge to Nestor's lord and to recant his accusation that Lyonnel killed the Golden-Haired Giant in treachery. Even this much, of course, is more than one generally gets from giants; Brancq himself is probably also meant to be understood as mixed-blood rather than full-blood, since the narrator describes him as "grant et membru" (large and sturdily built) because of being "extrait de geants" (descended from giants).[69] But he shows no sign of any genuine change of heart, and his death is certainly not mourned or commemorated in any way. Jayant Redoubté, however, freely acknowledges defeat and submits himself to Arthur's mercy: "Il voit qu'il ne se pot plus deffendre, si luy cria mercy au mieulx qu'il pot, et luy pria qu'il ne l'ocist pas" (*Papegau*, 174; He saw that he could no longer defend himself, so he cried for mercy as best he could, and begged not to be killed). And when Arthur learns why this knight has attacked him, he considers the qualities of the brother and deems it to have been a worthy reason: "Quant le Chevalier du Papegau a entendu qu'il estoit frere au Chevalier Jayant qui si doulcement se estoit a luy confessé, si en ot moult grant pitié, si luy pardonna tout son forfait pour son frere qu'il luy avoit mort" (174; When the Knight of the Parrot heard that he was the brother of the Giant Knight, who has confessed to him so meekly, he took great pity on him, and pardoned him his misdeed because of his brother, whom he had killed). Jayant Redoubté invites Arthur to stay at his castle until his wounds have healed and gives him such a warm welcome that "ne fu onc mais nul homs mieulx receu" (174; never was any man better received). Clearly the two knights have bonded in mutual understanding and have sealed their friendship through the ritualistic codes of chivalric combat and surrender, mercy, and hospitality.

And then, as we saw, Jayant Redoubté carries his vendetta to the Duchess of Estregalles, claiming to have brought the hand of the Chevalier du Papegau, and cutting off the hand of the countess who reaches out the window to accept this gift for the duchess. He thus sparks a war that will allow his vengeance to be played out in full as a collective endeavor between his people and hers. It is as though the giant's ability to bond with Arthur as chivalric subject also entails participation in the cultural code of misogyny that is both perpetuated and disavowed in courtly society. Although as I have already noted, the lady had never asked for the severed hand, the countess could be seen as retrospectively approving the arrangement by agreeing to accept it on her behalf; as the narrator comments, she is not "si sage qu'elle la feist monstrer" (176; as prudent as she had seemed to be). The symbolic codes to which Jayant Redoubté is subject include not only adherence to such values as honor, prowess, and the etiquette of chivalric conflict but also the circulation and manipulation of women as objects of desire, mediation, and exchange between men. And perhaps it is no surprise if a half-blood giant takes a particularly misogynistic view of these customs. Thus objectified, a woman who fails to mediate between men to their mutual advantage has herself assumed a deviant position, blocking the production of honor. Like the Blond Fairy with her unreasonable demands on Arthur, she becomes a scapegoat for male dishonor and loss.

As Wolfe notes, "The full transcendence of the 'human' requires the sacrifice of the 'animal' and the animalistic"; this symbolic sacrifice "structures intersubjectivity" and "is foundational for social and cultural self-definition."[70] While the symbolic sacrifice of animals is the most fundamental in defining a basic human identity, similar processes are at work in the more nuanced definition of subjectivity as both raced and gendered. The giant as well is a kind of sacrificial victim whose exclusion and death contribute to the "transcendence" of the aristocratic, and usually Christian, subject. If through intermarriage and acculturation the giant is assimilated into the chivalric world, attention shifts to the role of the woman in the definition of aristocratic masculinity. A discourse of racial and cultural difference—courtly aristocratic Christians as opposed to giants—gives way to one grounded in gender difference. Arthur confronts a new challenge in the form of an erotic but willful fairy; the Jayant Redoubté inaugurates a war whose opposing sides are defined by their respective association with the male and female parties to a courtship gone wrong, and their dispute as to which was the victim of the other. I do not, of course, mean to imply that these various forms of "sacrifice" or scapegoating are in any way mutually exclusive. They operate in tandem, together with other ways of defining difference—class, religion, sexuality—in generating the categories of identity through which subjectivity is defined, perfected, or obscured. Giants, a powerful and troubling presence throughout Arthurian literature, are integral to the process by which the tropes of human identity, culture, and civilization are deployed.

Conclusion

As might be expected in a study of giants, violence has been a recurring theme in this book. I have had cause more than once to refer to Žižek's statement that "the highest form of violence is the imposition of this standard with reference to which some events appear as 'violent'"; and I have touched on ways that this ideological coding of violence is expressed in literary depictions of combat with Saracens and giants respectively.[1] Holy War against Saracens as depicted in *chansons de geste* is explicitly cast as a struggle between, or on behalf of, rival deities. The prayers, religious taunts, and theological debates that take place on the battlefield mask the powerful economic and political motivations for the Crusades by depicting them as a sacred obligation, indeed as a mortification of the flesh for the greater glory of God. The warrior heroes of *chansons de geste* may allude to the atrocities they have committed in fighting other Europeans, sinful acts that have tarnished their soul; but in fighting the infidel comparable acts of destruction, no matter how horrific, are not atrocities but acts of religious devotion. If victory is a manifest sign of divine favor while defeat bestows the sanctity of martyrdom, the Christian warrior literally cannot lose. In contrast, Saracens sometimes turn against their gods in the face of defeat, denouncing them as incompetent or even abandoning them altogether; and of course they are portrayed as denigrating Christ's own death, which they can see only as the ignominious failure of his mission. In blissful or willful ignorance of actual Islamic beliefs, *chanson de geste* poets often depict Saracens as lacking any concept of sacrificial death. And since their gods are false idols, a Saracen warrior who does die for his gods has only sacrificed himself to demons anyway. The construction of Saracens as unable either to comprehend or to achieve martyrdom highlights the sacrificial dimension attributed to Christian Holy War. The motif is echoed in the death of the recently Christianized Palamedes, whose father Esclabor commits suicide in his grief at his son's apparently meaningless death. As Harf-Lancner points out, Esclabor thereby rejects not only the chivalric world with its cruelties and injustices but also "le monde céleste qui a imposé le martyre au nouveau converti. Sa mort . . . est caractérisée par l'indifférence à l'au-delà."[2] Despite everything, Palamedes shows with his pious acceptance of death that he has indeed become a true Christian; Esclabor, in contrast, remains a Saracen at heart.

Giants are highly unlikely to be Christians and are certainly not portrayed as attending Mass before combat or calling upon the Christian god to aid them; as we have seen, they may even invoke "Saracen" deities and are sometimes portrayed in Saracen garb in the miniatures illustrating Arthurian romance. But religious faith is never given as the reason for fighting them. And we have also seen that the sacrificial element of knightly combat with giants is different from that of the crusader, in that death at the hands of a giant brings with it neither honor nor spiritual absolution. We might, however, see a sacrificial element in the double movement made by the victorious knight. First he must shed his courtly bearing to measure himself against a figure of absolute violence, whose lethal force he must now match and indeed surpass through whatever means necessary—even if it means using his horse to trample his opponent's body into the dust, or crushing him beneath a boulder. He must know when to press forward, when to invite unguarded attack by feigning clumsiness or fatigue, and when to stand back and allow his adversary to wear himself out in futile thrashing and flailing; he must unleash a superhuman force that transforms him into a deadly killer every bit the equal of a giant. And he must also know how to curtail that explosion of violent energy so as to subject himself once again to the constraints of chivalric culture. Some knights enact this process effortlessly, felling giants with a single blow—or at least in a quick and decisive battle from which they apparently emerge unscathed—and continuing on their way as though nothing had happened. Still, defeating a giant is not necessarily a simple affair, and a knight who does so with ease may need to stage an explicit refusal to insert himself into the giant's place. As befits a descendant of the peerless Febus, for example, Guiron le Courtois dispatches giants with relative ease. One giant that he attacks is so overcome by the hitherto unknown experience of lethal resistance that (unusually for a giant) he cries for mercy; and while Guiron would have preferred to kill this marauding menace to society, he is compelled to acquiesce and leave the wounded giant where he lies. To have killed an opponent who has fully acknowledged defeat would have placed him on a par with the giant himself, who is certainly deaf to the pleas of his own victims. Moreover, when Guiron arrives at the giant's cave to free his prisoner, the terrified knight mistakes Guiron himself for a giant and requires repeated reassurance before finally accepting that the formidable figure standing before him is his savior and not his executioner. This exchange articulates not only Guiron's personal resistance to the libidinous freedom of giants but also the fundamental distinction between a knight of giantesque proportions and an actual giant. As he reassures the frightened victim: "Or sachiez . . . que tout soie je grans je ne sui pas jaians, ains sui uns chevaliers esrans" (Know now that however big I may be, I am not a giant, but a knight errant).[3]

Though this is a remarkably explicit enactment of the hero's subtle but crucial difference from the giant, the motif exists in numerous other texts. We have seen that Tristan consistently avoids taking the position of giants he has killed. When Gaheriet kills Aupatris in the *Suite du roman de Merlin*, releasing the local inhabitants from their annual payment of human tribute to the giant, the grateful townspeople offer to promise him whatever he wishes: "Il n'est riens que nous puissions avoir que vous n'eussiez, et corpz et avoir et femmes et enfans" (There is nothing we might have that you would not have, be it our persons, belongings, wives, or children).[4] A possibility opens up that Gaheriet could have demanded his own human tribute or exacted some other form of lucrative compensation; but taking on the giant's custom for himself is so unthinkable that it cannot even be explicitly refused. Instead, Gaheriet demands an oath that damsels and knights errant will nevermore be hindered in their travels, thereby implicitly renouncing his own potential rights and abolishing the barbaric practice altogether, as well as extracting a further promise that knights in need of lodging will always be shown hospitality. His encounter with a giant will restore social and political order, benefiting the chivalric class as a whole and not himself as an individual. The motif of the hero's renunciation is present even in the earliest Arthurian texts; when Erec frees the knight Cadoc from two giants in *Erec et Enide*, he is beset by offers of service and unnamed favors from both the knight and his *amie*, who seem to feel that in killing their tormentors Erec has somehow become their new lord and master. The damsel exclaims that "bien nos devez avoir / andeus conquis et moi et lui; / vostre devons estre anbedui" (you have rightfully won both him and me; we should both belong to you), while Cadoc proclaims, "Toz jorz mes avoec vos irai / con mon seignor vos servirai" (I will always go with you and serve you as my lord).[5] But Erec is not interested in capturing human booty from giants. He instructs his fawning admirers to go instead to Arthur's court and publicly announce his exploit: any benefits to himself will be political, not personal. In his reading of this passage, Simpson notes the possible sadomasochistic implications of Cadoc's offer and the unspoken—indeed, for Chrétien and his audience, unspeakable—sexual overtones of the entire exchange, commenting that "such is the debasement to which the system of chivalric masculinity and its various metaphors (love, service) has been subjected that what need to be asserted at this point are the limits and the boundaries that shape society."[6]

In many cases, the battle is an arduous one and may require a transitional phase at its end in which the victorious combatant rejoins his companions, speaking of the enormity of the fear he experienced, or the formidable power of an opponent outstripping any other he has ever faced. He may take the giant's head as a trophy to be displayed, thereby staging his own human distance from his objectified victim, now nothing more than a lurid spectacle reflecting the glory of the hero who killed him. He may give thanks to God in a gesture of humility and reverence; sometimes he needs time to convalesce from wounds, as processes of rupture and containment are written on the body itself. Both the ability to step outside the ordinary bounds of knightly combat and the willingness to renounce the heady freedom thereby discovered are as vital in fighting giants as are the knight's skills in jousting or swordplay in and of themselves. And in these moves, the knight enacts not spiritual sacrifice to God but the sacrifice of libidinous drives and *jouissance* demanded by human society. The hero's simultaneous ability to exercise and to renounce absolute violence entails a sacrifice comparable to that which lies at the heart of Derrida's characterization of Kantian ethics: "le sacrifice des passions, des affections, des intérêts dits 'pathologiques.' . . . L'inconditionnalité de la loi moral, selon Kant, dicte la violence exercée dans la contrainte contre soi-même (*Selbstzwang*) et contre ses propres désirs."[7]

In his work on sacrificial death and European subjectivity, Derrida stresses the singularity bestowed by death. One's death is one's own and cannot be appropriated, shared, or transferred to another; and the loss of the individual through death marks that person as unique and irreplaceable.[8] It is certainly true that the crusader who dies a martyr's death has confirmed his singularity as a spiritual being. But if only the individual penitent or martyr can offer his own death as a gift to God, it is equally true that only the truly exceptional hero can give the giant's death as a gift to the individual or community on whom the giant preys; and the giant killer who does not die in combat achieves a singularity every bit as real as that of the holy martyr. This holds in the obvious sense that the giant can be killed only once. Equally important, however, is the fact that surviving combat with a particular giant in itself confers singularity on the only individual ever to achieve that feat. The giant killer, in measuring himself against the giant, acquires a fundamental knowledge of giantesque force and violence and of what it means to unleash that force in one's own body. He may speak in general terms of the ordeal that he has just been through; but in essence this is a bodily knowledge, beyond quantification or symbolization, and thus one that cannot be passed to anyone else. To state that the giant filled him with fear, or to compare that fear as greater or lesser than the fear occasioned by a different giant; to remark that the giant is the most formidable opponent he has ever faced; to give thanks to God for granting him a seemingly impossible victory over the giant through the force of his own body alone: these statements merely gesture toward the hyperbolic and ultimately inexpressible shock and thrill of contact with giants. In this sense the knight's experience also partakes of the aura of secrecy identified by Derrida with singularity and sacrificial death or renunciation. As Derrida states, "Je ne suis plus jamais moi-même, seul et unique, dès que je parle."[9] Contrary to a more intuitive sense of responsibility as implying some kind of public accountability for one's actions, then, Derrida concludes that "la responsabilité absolue de mes actes, en tant qu'elle doit être la mienne, toute singulière, pour ce que personne ne peut faire à ma place, implique . . . le secret."[10]

That sense of absolute responsibility is another element in Derrida's meditation on death: as he states, "Depuis la mort comme lieu de mon irremplaçabilité, c'est-à-dire de ma singularité, je me sens appelé à ma responsabilité."[11] And certainly the Christian martyr or penitent of medieval literature offers his or her soul to God as a responsible entity, with the self-scrutiny of confession and contrition. Passing from the mutability of life in this world to the eternity of the afterlife, the soul meets a fate determined by its spiritual sickness or health at the moment of death; and the individual's behavior throughout life is permanently colored by the knowledge that its most important consequences will be experienced after death, in the realm of eternity. But the hero's ability to enter the giant's space, to match him in violence, and then to survive and renounce that violence also stages his profound responsibility, not so much to explicitly spiritual ideals, but to cultural norms. That unspeakable experience of absolute force and violence, existing in the hero's body like a secret knowledge, is also bound up with the sacrificial act of self-discipline. Paradoxically, the staging of giantesque force in the body of the knight can be permitted only as a means of eradicating that very same force in a specular rival, whose fatal difference from the knight is simultaneously his lack of discipline—the fully unbridled nature of his libidinous aggression—and his inability in the end to match the combative skills and strength of his opponent. Sometimes the former is predominant, as when a knight triumphs over a giant through his ability to feign weakness, his crafty use of ambush or duplicity, or his agility in dodging blows: it may be in knowing how to manipulate or rein in his martial performance that he ultimately achieves victory. And of course other times it is the latter, as the chivalric hero unwinds into battle with a fury that even a giant cannot withstand.

In all of these ways, the configuration of knight and giant comprises the elements that Derrida associates with the formation of Christian subjectivity around the mystery of sacrificial death: the singularity conferred by the experience, the responsibility that it creates, and the transcendent secret to which it gives access. I argued earlier that combat with giants—an object of intense chivalric desire and a virtually obligatory rite of passage, but also one ringed round with anxiety and prohibition—is analogous with erotic love as it is so often depicted in medieval lyric and romance.[12] The nexus of desire and death, of singularity, responsibility, and the secret knowledge of bodily passion, exists in both of these domains. To some extent, the points I have made regarding giants would apply to any form of knightly combat. Violence is, after all, essential to a knight's way of life, as is the reconciliation of that violence with the ideals of Christian piety and courtly gentility. Giants, however, are an opponent like none other, and this excessive and absolute battle to the death is a particularly potent matrix for the formation of chivalric subjectivity. And while an Arthurian knight can achieve heroic status without necessarily having to fight giants, there is no question that combat with giants is a key motif in any knightly career.

Michael Uebel has noted that "the nucleus of ideology, the center around which cultural and psychic affects orbit, is constituted by trauma, the shock of the real as the everyday confronts . . . the unexpected, the incongruous, the alien, and the manifold ways these threaten or harm."[13] The narratives that we have examined in this study use the trauma of the giant in support of interrelated ideological strands. One of these is the affirmation of European aristocratic identity: of class structures and privileges, of a racial purity that—unlike the heritage of infidel Saracens—is free of contamination from the lines of Cain and Ham. Accounts of Crusade battles allow Christian warriors to be contrasted with a foreign race: a vision of aristocratic culture and aesthetic refinement as it might develop in the absence of spiritual illumination, a *chevalerie* unsupported by Christian *clergie* and contaminated by monstrous and demonic bloodlines. But confrontations with the giants still inhabiting Britain focus attention on the purification of European bloodlines themselves: the heroic lineage of Troy is fused with the sacred lineage of Joseph of Arimathea, while the aboriginal giants are eliminated. If just occasionally a giantess bride may be appropriated into this noble world, the outcome works largely in the direction of purifying the giant lineage of its savagery while retaining its capacity for superlative physical prowess, thereby enhancing the European aristocracy with a touch of the exotic. Though complications or further trauma may arise from the racially hybrid descendants of these unions, in the end they can always be contained within the matrix of Arthurian culture: one capable not only of courtly refinement, justice, and aristocratic gentility but also of martial prowess and lethal force whenever this is necessary for the defense of law, order, and cultural values.[14] Giants perpetrate a range of alternative—at the risk of anachronism, one might say countercultural—models of social behavior and pursue historical trajectories incompatible with the master narrative of Arthurian legend. A giant's incapacity to defer desire, to benefit from the ennobling effects of love, to comprehend a sense of honor as something other than the supremacy born of indiscriminate brutality, to pay homage to a power higher than himself: these features of giant "culture" are depicted as arising ultimately from the constitution of the giant race as a skewed, defective, or contaminated version of the humanity that finds its ideal incarnation in the Arthurian aristocracy.

A second ideological strand to these narratives, related to the first, is the distinction of chivalric violence from that of the giant—a distinction coded into language itself with its careful distinction between *chevalier* and *jaiant*. Giants are not, of course, the only enemies fought by knights, and it is generally true that knightly combat of any kind sanitizes chivalric violence through its opposition to other forms of violence that are explicitly coded as perverse and destructive. Erec's foray into the forest with Enide, for example, might reasonably be seen as something of a killing spree, in which any benefits to society are a fortuitous side effect of Erec's obsessive need to expose his wife to mortal danger so that he can "win" her through feats of prowess over and over again. But since it is devoted entirely to fighting unambiguously villainous figures—brigands, giants, a tyrannical count whose abusive treatment of a damsel in distress is clearly designed to shock the reader—Erec's descent into violence can be seen, not as murder or irresponsible machismo, but as a demonstration of his ability to incarnate the chivalric ideal of upholding the social order by placing his own life on the line. The violent acts committed by crusading heroes are similarly coded not merely as justified but as having an expiatory quality that enables the warrior to atone for sins or atrocities he may have committed in other contexts. And with giants, the unlimited force of violence will invariably be not only permitted but required.

The spectacle of combat with giants is often staged as a communal event: it may be observed by the giant's prisoners, by a few companions of the knight himself, or even by the entire population of a castle or town. As such it fulfills some of the criteria that Girard associates with the sacrificial violence of religion. The concentration of collective rivalry and violence into a single point allows the identification of a scapegoat figure, whose sacrificial death not only allows for communal catharsis but also appeases—and therefore calls into being—a sacred and transcendent Other. In combat with giants, however, the Other to which this sort of violence gives access is not, or not only, God but human culture, shown at one and the same moment to be both arbitrary and transcendent. The knight can, if he needs to, let himself go and match the lethal power of the giant: his discipline and his courtly refinement are in that sense artificial, self-imposed constructions that can be shed as easily as they can be assumed. But the encounter with the giant also confirms cultural order as natural and beyond question, in that the knight inevitably does reassume his social role and his gentility; if he has unbridled himself for a time, we are meant to see that it is only in the interests of preserving the ideals of cultural refinement and self-discipline. Žižek's psychoanalytic interpretation of sacrifice is relevant here: "*Sacrifice is the guarantee that 'the Other exists.'* . . . The trick of the sacrifice consists therefore in what the speech-act theorists would call its 'pragmatic presupposition': *by the very act of sacrifice, we (presup)pose the existence of its addressee* that guarantees the consistency and meaningfulness of our experience."[15] The knight's sacrifice of violent *jouissance* and unconstrained libido, as he slays the giant and reconfirms his own identity as *chevalier*, is ultimately an affirmation of the transcendence, the absolute reality, of cultural norms and prohibitions. Old French may not have had a word for "culture" or "civilization" as we understand it today, any more than they had a word for "subjectivity."[16] But tales of giants nonetheless allowed for the exploration of these concepts, and of their interaction as the masculine warrior shaped, and was shaped by, the values and ideologies of his Christian European society.

Throughout this study, I have noted the phenomenon of giants as a fantasy race, whose elaboration can be linked to the medieval penchant for inventing fantasy histories: a means of exploring ideas about potential interethnic and cross-cultural encounters and considering how these interactions might affect the trajectories of British and European history. The imaginary court chronicle posited as the source for *Perceforest*, for example, lays out the historical developments of pre-Arthurian Britain: the exchanges and interactions between peoples, the cultural blossoming, upheaval, and decline, that might plausibly result in the world described in such texts as the *Tristan* and the *Lancelot-Grail* cycle.[17] The Arthurian world, with its rich and complex layers of history and its many narrative strands, has always been open to adaptation and reinterpretation by successive authors; but there are also limits beyond which this experimentation cannot go. The large body of Arthurian texts reflects a fascination with mapping real or imagined historical changes, racial and cultural identities, and interactions both within and between communities and kingdoms, within a vital if loosely defined framework of Christian, feudal, and chivalric ideologies. The cultural myths thereby formulated implicitly lay out what civilization enables and what it forecloses; which traits enable a people to adapt, survive, and advance, and which traits result in their extinction. The aboriginal race of giants occupies a unique position in this larger picture, helping to identify important boundaries and to support a concept of racial and cultural otherness that—unlike the otherness of Saracens—is not, or not primarily, grounded in religious difference. As we have seen, the very existence of giants showcases Britain as a Promised Land, parallel to the Promised Land of biblical history: the chosen site not only for the flowering of classical learning and imperial might but also for the Grail—the ultimate holy relic. The status of giants varies, of course, across the large body of Arthurian texts, so that some are nearly bestial in their barren existence, while others are disturbingly successful at penetrating the feudal world and aping its structures. Overall, however, giants offer, not the decadent or godless version of opulence, luxury, scientific knowledge, and military skill represented by Saracens, but a different sort of savagery, a vision of human life bereft of the blessings of culture and morality. Since giants did not exist, we might conclude, they had to be invented: a perfect foil for a chivalric culture that viewed itself as the fusion of military might, Christian piety, and the most impeccable courtly refinement.

NOTES

Introduction

The section epigraphs can be located in Cazenave, "Monstres et merveilles," 235; *Suite du roman de Merlin*, ed. Gilles Roussineau, 2:551; and *Tristan en prose*, ed. Curtis, 1:79.

    1. Francis Dubost distinguishes between "grands chevaliers," "colosses," and "géants": ordinary knights who happen to be of large stature; truly giant-sized but otherwise normal knights (typically Saracen), who may be highly civilized and may even convert to Christianity; and the more savage, monstrous, or fantastic giants. See *Aspects fantastiques*, 1:578–80, and, more generally, 568–627.
    2. Mercer, "Busy in the Ruins," 208.
    3. Regino of Prüm, *Epistula ad Hathonem*, xix–xx. For an analysis of the sociological, legal, and political aspects of medieval concepts of race and ethnicity, see Bartlett, *Making of Europe*, especially 197–242, 292–314. Bartlett further explores the medieval politics of race and ethnicity, as well as touching on the importance of geography and climate in medieval racial theory, in "Medieval and Modern Concepts." Cohen offers a counterargument, stressing the importance of bodily characteristics in medieval concepts of race, in "On Saracen Enjoyment." See also Lampert, "Race, Periodicity"; Girbea, *Bon Sarrasin*.
    4. Bartlett, for example, states: "Of the four criteria listed here, only one is biological. Customs, language, and law are the outcome of socialization and hence are changeable" ("Medieval and Modern Concepts," 47).
    5. On the importance of geography and climate in medieval theories of race and ethnicity, see Akbari, "Diversity of Mankind"; Akbari, *Idols in the East*, 36–49, 140–50, 160–64; Cohen, "On Saracen Enjoyment," 117–20.

6. *Aliscans*, vv. 3579, 3582, ed. Régnier. Subsequent citations to line numbers are given parenthetically in the text. Rainouart first appears in *Aliscans*, where he plays a major role in helping Guillaume defeat the Saracen armies attempting to recapture Orange; although the text never explicitly calls him a giant, we are told that "Grant ot le cors et regart de sengler, / En tote France n'ot si grant bacheler, / Ne si fort home por un grant fés lever" [he had a large body and the counenance of a boar; in all of France there was no man so large, nor any man as strong at lifting heavy weights] (vv. 3529–31).

7. Ramey, *Christian, Saracen*, 3.

8. For reflections on the considerable variation in the depiction of Saracen cultures and peoples in *chansons de geste*, and the changes that took place during the twelfth, thirteenth, and fourteenth centuries, see Ramey, *Christian, Saracen*.

9. JanMohamed, "Economy of Manichean Allegory," 80.

10. Goldenberg, "Development of the Idea." Cohen briefly discusses medieval European depictions of Africans in "On Saracen Enjoyment," 117–19. Cohen also comments more generally on the medieval moralization of race and ethnicity in *Hybridity*, 16–22, 32–34.

11. Kruger, "Conversion," 170. On the ways that the conceptualization of racial difference continued to be inflected by perceptions of sexual propriety or impropriety during the early modern period, see Nocentelli, *Empires of Love*.

12. Kruger, "Conversion," 164.

13. On Norman propaganda concerning both the Celts and the English, see Cohen, *Hybridity*. Cohen argues that since the Normans "were a mongrel concatenation of peoples, to imagine their own unity they routinely dehumanized other peoples, especially when they wanted to seize their lands" (35). See also, more generally, Strickland, "Monstrosity and Race" and *Saracens, Demons*. As Strickland notes: "The medieval monstrous races tradition provided a foundational forum for the expression of Christian fears and fantasies about cultural outsiders, notions that were inevitably overlaid onto actual, human groups, to which the cases of Christian-constructed Jews, Muslims, Mongols, and black Africans clearly attest" ("Monstrosity and Race," 385).

14. See, for example, Gaunt's analysis of Marco Polo's sympathetic portrayal both of Kublai Khan and of Indian ascetics, in *Marco Polo's "Le Devisement du Monde,"* 126–31, 135–38.

15. For a succinct summary of the ongoing debate, its scientific and cultural implications, and the kinds of evidence drawn into play, see Lewis-Williams, "Of People."

16. Dubost articulates a similar view of giants: "Le géant apparaît ainsi comme *l'autrefois* de l'homme, un homme que chacun pouvait reconnaître à la rigueur comme son ancêtre lointain, comme une ébauche 'préhistorique' de l'homme d'aujourd'hui, tout en repoussant l'idée qu'il pourrait être son *sem-*

blable" (*Aspects fantastiques*, 1:569; The giant thus appears as the *long ago* of humanity, a man that everyone can recognize, ultimately, as his distant ancestor, as a "prehistoric" forerunner of modern man, while disavowing the notion that he could be his *fellow man*).

17. Lewis-Williams, "Of People," 136.

18. Even within the relatively narrow parameters of eighteenth- and nineteenth-century American society, for example, one can discern significant differences in the stereotypes attached to Indians and blacks respectively, as well as changes that took place during that period; for an overview of race relations in that context, see Roediger, *Wages of Whiteness*, 19–40. On the shifts in European attitudes toward the relationship between race and sexuality throughout the sixteenth and seventeenth centuries, and the related changes in policies regarding interracial love and marriage in Asian and African colonies, see Nocentelli, *Empires of Love*.

19. Brown, "Subjects of Tolerance," 301, emphasis hers.

20. Brown offers a succinct survey of Freud's thought and its relevance for modern political discourse of liberalism and cultural tolerance, in ibid.

21. On this point, see Kawash, "Terrorists and Vampires," 254.

22. Žižek, *Violence*, 23.

23. Kawash, "Terrorists and Vampires," 254.

24. Ibid., 240.

25. Roediger, *Wages of Whiteness*, 22.

26. Steel, *How to Make a Human*, 126.

27. See Geoffrey of Monmouth, *History*, ed. Reeve, trans. Wright, 28. Subsequent citations of the *History* in this chapter are to this edition and translation. Cohen analyzes the pleasure of combat with giants in *Of Giants*.

28. Geoffrey of Monmouth, *History*, 227.

29. *Perceforest: Deuxième partie*, ed. Roussineau, 1:356.

30. Steele, *Theorizing Textual Subjects*, 202.

31. Kaeuper, *Chivalry and Violence*, 143.

32. Žižek, *Violence*, 55.

33. *Tristan en prose*, ed. Curtis (hereafter *PT*[C]), 1:76; subsequently cited parenthetically in the text.

34. Said, *Orientalism*, 58–59.

35. Bhabha, *Location of Culture*, 70.

36. Cohen, *Of Giants*, xii.

37. Ibid., xiii.

38. See Trachsler's excellent analysis of "warring narratives" in the *Lancelot-Grail*, the prose *Tristan*, and other related texts in *Clôtures*, 149–237. This notion of competing narrative trajectories, as associated with different cultural backgrounds (Saracen, Greek, Trojan, etc.), is further explored by Girbea, *Bon Sarrasin*, 59–126.

CHAPTER 1. *Inhuman Men and Knightly Fiends*

1. "The differences repudiated as inhuman are, however, inscribed on a background of resemblance with human nature" (Dubost, *Aspects fantastiques*, 1:569).
2. Cohen, *Of Giants*, 167.
3. Chrétien de Troyes, *Erec et Enide*, vv. 5851–55, ed. Roques.
4. Ibid., v. 5950.
5. Simpson notes that Maboagrain's concern with chivalric customs and formalities distinguishes him from the giants, in *Troubling Arthurian Histories*, 414.
6. On this figure, see my *Postcolonial Fictions*, 107, 137–39.
7. *Perceforest: Quatrième partie*, ed. Roussineau, 1:102; subsequently cited parenthetically in the text.
8. Gen. 6:1–2, 4–6; trans. RSV.
9. On this point, see Stephens, *Giants in Those Days*, 76–84; Cohen, *Of Giants*, 53–54; Dean, "World Grown Old," 560–62.
10. Augustine, *De civitate Dei*, XV.23, gen. ed. Green et al., *City of God* [bilingual ed.], 4:548–50, vol. 4 trans. Levine, 549–51. Subsequent citations are to this edition and translation.
11. Ibid., XV.23, 4:554, trans. 4:555.
12. Ibid., XV.23, 4:558–60. In Stephens's words, Augustine saw giants as "a kind of living allegory, in which God represented the vanity of natural endowments uninformed by Judaeo-Christian religious culture" (*Giants in Those Days*, 75).
13. Bar. 3:26–28; trans. Jerusalem Bible.
14. Peter Comestor, *Historia scholastica*, cap. 37, Patrologia Latina 198:1081.
15. Augustine, *De civitate Dei*, XV.viii, 4:450, trans. 4:451.
16. Ibid.
17. Williams, *Deformed Discourse*, 113, 117.
18. Gen. 10:8, 9; trans. RSV. On the figure of Nimrod in medieval thought as a focal point linking giantism, sacrilege, and tyranny, see Dean, "World Grown Old," 564–68; Roberts, *Alterity and Narrative*, 78–84.
19. Augustine, *De civitate Dei*, XVI.iii, 4:16. I have emended the translation, which reads "mighty" rather than "giant," perhaps in an attempt to move Augustine's text closer to the Vulgate, and to echo the Revised Standard Edition familiar to anglophone readers. Green points out the "Old Latin mistranslation" (XVI.iii, 4:16 n. 1).
20. Ibid., XVI.iii, 4:28, trans. 4:29.
21. For a summary of these arguments, see Stephens, *Giants in Those Days*, 84–92.

22. Num. 13:32–34, trans. RSV. The Vulgate text literally says, "There we saw certain monsters of the race of giants, of the sons of Anak."

23. Cohen, *Of Giants*, 34.

24. Nayar, *Posthumanism*, 5.

25. "The settler makes history and is conscious of making it. And because he constantly refers to the history of his mother country, he clearly indicates that he himself is the extension of that mother country. Thus the history which he writes is not the history of the country which he plunders but the history of his own nation. . . . The immobility to which the native is condemned can only be called into question if the native decides to put an end to the history of colonization . . . and to bring into existence the history of the nation." Fanon, *Damnés de la terre*, 82, trans. Farrington, *Wretched of the Earth*, 40.

26. Said, *Culture and Imperialism*, 327.

27. *Des grantz geanz*, ed. Brereton; subsequently cited parenthetically in the text. I cite the longer version. On this text, see Cohen, *Of Giants*, 47–61; Johnson, "Return to Albion."

28. Regnier-Bohler terms the giants of *Des grantz geanz* "une lignée avortée," confused by incest and resulting in a "Terre Gaste" that must be refounded by Brutus, in "Figures féminines," 89.

29. Cohen, *Of Giants*, 56.

30. On this point see Warren, "Making Contact," 124.

31. Geoffrey of Monmouth, *History*, ed. Reeve, 21, trans. Wright, 20. Subsequent citations to the *History* in this chapter are to this edition and translation.

32. Ibid.

33. Wace, *Roman de Brut*, v. 686, ed. Weiss, trans. Weiss, 19. Subsequent citations to the *Roman de Brut* in this chapter are to this edition and translation.

34. *Perceforest: Première partie*, ed. Roussineau (hereafter *Perce/I*), vv. 6–9, 1:18; subsequently cited parenthetically in the text.

35. Kawash, "Terrorists and Vampires," 253.

36. Ibid.

37. Johnson, "Return to Albion," 30–31.

38. Bhabha, *Location of Culture*, 99–100 (emphasis his).

39. *Conte du Papegau*, ed. Charpentier and Victorin, 100; subsequently cited parenthetically in the text.

40. The complex relationship of knight and horse, and the role of the horse in defining chivalric and aristocratic identity, are discussed at length in Crane, *Animal Encounters*, 137–68; and Cohen, *Medieval Identity Machines*, 35–77. For N. Smith, the Poisson Chevalier represents "the noble who has become imprisoned as if in his own unwieldy armor . . . unable even to dismount from a horse" ("Man on a Horse," 246). V. Greene notes that "knights who forget that their species is 'human' and not 'knight' are in danger of becoming

monsters without species," in "Humanimals," 136. The Poisson Chevalier is clearly related to the *chevaliers de mer* in *Perceforest*—a race of fish whose combat skills, chivalric ethos, and ability to emerge temporarily from the sea in order to engage in jousts and warfare give them a quasi-human feel, but whose armor and weaponry are again part of their bodies. On the latter, and the way that they reflect on the distinction between human and animal, see my *Postcolonial Fictions*, 59–63. For examples of medieval writers who depicted the ability to domesticate animals as a quintessentially human characteristic, see Steel, "Centaurs," 267–69. On the social context of horsemanship in the life and public image of the medieval knight, see Kaeuper, *Chivalry and Violence*, 171–76.

41. For an example of animal imagery as applied to both knights and ladies at an early point in the Arthurian tradition, see Bruckner, "Lady and the Dragon."

42. Chrétien de Troyes, *Chevalier au lion*, vv. 4084–4250, ed. Hult.

43. *Valentin et Orson*, ed. Baird, 48, trans. Baird, 49. Subsequent citations are to this edition and translation.

44. Ibid.

45. Ibid., 228, trans. 229.

46. *Suite du roman de Merlin*, ed. Roussineau, 2:550.

47. Ibid.

48. *Lancelot*, ed. Micha (hereafter *PLanc*), 1:177; subsequently cited parenthetically in the text.

49. Cohen, *Hybridity*, 41.

50. Wolfe, *Animal Rites*, 43.

51. Dubost cites additional examples of anthropophagic giants in both romance and *chanson de geste*; see *Aspects fantastiques*, 1:621–22.

52. See Steel, *How to Make a Human*, 118–35, quote on 124. As Steel notes, narratives of anthropophagy "fabricate the uniquely significant vulnerability of human lives while obliterating the lives and deaths of animals" (127).

53. "Fundamental, dominant . . . essential to the structure of subjectivity, which is also to say to the founding of the intentional subject." (Derrida, "Force de la loi," 952, trans. Quaintance, "Force of Law," 953).

54. Peter Comestor, *Historia scholastica*, cap. 37, *PL* 198:1088. See Dean, "World Grown Old," 565.

55. Gen. 4:3 and 4:4, trans. RSV.

56. "The murderer is the one who does not have the violence-outlet of animal sacrifice at his disposal" (Girard, *Violence et le sacré*, 17; trans. Gregory, *Violence and the Sacred*, 4).

57. Gen. 8:20, trans. RSV.

58. Gen. 9:2–3, trans. RSV.

59. I have amended the translation as given in the RSV in order to remain closer to the Vulgate, since this is the version of the Bible that would have been known to medieval authors and their readers.

60. *Tristan en prose*, ed. Curtis (hereafter *PT*[C]), 1:69–70; subsequently cited parenthetically in the text.

61. For examples of saints who brought about either the death or the domestication of carnivores preying on livestock, see Steel, *How to Make a Human*, 63–64.

62. *Tristan en prose*, ed. Ménard, 1:258–61, 267–69. I will discuss this episode in more detail in chapter 3.

63. Butler, *Bodies That Matter*, 72.

64. See Chambers, "'When We Do Nothing Wrong,'" 411–14, 418. On this point see also Crane, *Animal Encounters*, 79–80; Clark, "Fathers and the Animals."

65. Boethius, *Consolation of Philosophy*, ed. Rand, 204, trans. Tester, 205.

66. On the distinctions in medieval theological discourse between a fundamental nature common to humans and animals and a rational nature unique to humans, as well as a uniquely human capacity for unnatural behavior and sin, see White, *Nature, Sex*. For an overview of these arguments focusing on attitudes toward homosexuality, see Boswell, *Christianity*, 303–32. I am grateful to Richard Newhauser of Arizona State University for advice on this point.

67. Alexander of Hales, *Summa theologica*, prima pars secundi libri, inq. 4, tr. 2, sect. 2, q. 1, t.1, c.3, ad. 5, ed. Fathers of the College, 2:576.

68. Crane, *Animal Encounters*, 36.

69. Kilgour, "Function of Cannibalism," 240.

70. See Freud, *Totem and Taboo*, trans. Strachey, 141–43, for his myth of the horde of brothers who kill and eat their father: envy of paternal authority, incestuous desire for the mother, and cannibalism are united in Freud's vision of the traumatic crime that supposedly lies at the origins of civilization. On the role of cannibalism in Freud's mythic history, see Kilgour, "Function of Cannibalism," 244–45. On Freud's view of the incest taboo as a constitutive element of human civilization, see Girard, *Violence et le sacré*, 265–304, trans. Gregory, *Violence and the Sacred*, 204–34; Girard also discusses ritual cannibalism in *Violence et le sacré*, 379–88, trans. Gregory, *Violence and the Sacred*, 289–95. Girard sees the rituals and prohibitions surrounding both incest and cannibalism as crucial to the establishment of boundaries that define personal identity and control the spread of violence.

71. Albertus Magnus took for granted an animal aversion to incest, citing examples of a camel and a stallion who discovered that they had been tricked by their handlers into mating with their mothers: the camel turned on the handler

and killed him, while the stallion committed suicide by jumping off a cliff. See *De animalibus*, 8.5.2, ed. Stadtler, 1:659. He also notes that the vast majority of animals will refuse to eat the flesh of their own species (8.1.2, 1:574).

72. Gaunt, *Marco Polo's "Le Devisement du Monde,"* 161–71. For a survey of cannibalism as a motif in both Crusade literature and texts depicting the exotic East, see Tattersall, "Anthropophagi." On the motif of cannibalism as attributed to giants and enemy races, and its implications for the ideological symbolism of the giant, see Heng, *Empire of Magic*, 19–21, 37–39, 117–28. Though Heng's argument is somewhat reductive, it is an interesting exploration of possible associations that cannibalism might have for medieval authors and their audience.

73. On St. Christopher as a giant, as well as legends in certain languages that identified him as Cynecephalos, see Williams, *Deformed Discourse*, 286–97. Examples of assimilable giants in Arthurian romance include Galotine, daughter of the Golden-Haired Giant in *Perceforest*, who marries a British knight; and in *Tristan*, the sons of the giant Dyaletes, who convert to Christianity, and an unnamed giantess who marries Prince Luce of the Leonois. These figures will be discussed in subsequent chapters of this book.

74. Jean d'Arras, *Mélusine*, ed. Vincensini, 138; Coudrette, *Roman du Mélusine*, vv. 4973–76, ed. Roach.

75. Stewart, *On Longing*, 74.

76. Renaut de Beaujeu, *Bel Inconnu*, vv. 732–34, ed. Williams.

77. Cohen, *Of Giants*, xv.

78. Geoffrey of Monmouth, *History*, 29, trans. 28.

79. Ibid. Cohen comments on the "obscene enjoyment" afforded by contact with giants in *Of Giants*, 70; see also 152–78. On the encounter of Corineus and Gogmagog, as well as that of Arthur and Ritho, see also Warren, "Making Contact," 124–28.

80. Geoffrey of Monmouth, *History*, 227, trans. 226.

81. Ibid., 227–29, trans. 226–28.

82. Ibid., 227, 226.

83. Geoffrey of Monmouth states simply that Arthur never met another giant as strong as Ritho (ibid., 227–29, 226), a detail expanded on by Wace: "Unches puis Artur ne truva / Gaiant ki fust de tel vigur / Ne dunt il eüst tel poür" (never since had he found a giant of such strength or who frightened him so much). Wace, *Brut*, vv. 11590–92, trans. 291.

84. Cohen, *Of Giants*, 179.

85. Roediger, *Wages of Whiteness*, 95.

86. Phillips, "Cannibalism qua Capitalism," 193.

87. Bhabha, *Location of Culture*, 72.

88. Kawash, "Terrorists and Vampires," 239.

CHAPTER 2. *An Alien Presence*

1. *Estoire del Saint Graal*, ed. Ponceau, 2:332.
2. On this figure, see Dubost, *Aspects fantastiques*, 1:610–13.
3. Geoffrey of Monmouth, *History*, ed. Reeve, 227, trans. Wright, 226.
4. Wace, *Roman de Brut*, vv. 11561–92, ed. Weiss. Subsequent citations of *Brut* in this chapter are to this edition.
5. Ibid., vv. 11579–82, trans. Weiss, 291.
6. *Premiers faits du roi Arthur*, ed. Poirion. Poirion places the composition of this text in the period ca. 1235–45; see the discussion in his notes on the text, 1804–5. Subsequent citations to this work are to this edition and volume and are given parenthetically in the text.
7. *Suite du roman de Merlin*, ed. Roussineau, 1:55–56, 87–119. This text is not to be confused with the contemporary Vulgate *Suite du Merlin* or the *Premiers faits du roi Arthur*. Roussineau tentatively assigns this text the date 1235–40, placing it after the composition of the Vulgate Cycle and the prose *Tristan*, and just prior to that of *Guiron le courtois*; see his Introduction, 1:xxxix–xl. In his note on the passage, Roussineau acknowledges its roots in the tradition leading back through Wace to Geoffrey of Monmouth but suggests that this particular version of Rion is more directly inspired by the account in the *Chevalier aux deux épées* (2:645).
8. Ibid., 1:56.
9. Thomas d'Angleterre, *Tristan*, vv. 715–804, ed. Payen.
10. "Géants en cascade," ed. Albert, 56.
11. Ibid., 60.
12. Ibid.
13. "Visions de l'autre," ed. Albert, 140.
14. Albert, in *"Ensemble ou par pieces,"* notes that in both *Tristan* and *Guiron* the vengeance sought by giants "est un acte éminemment culturel et humain, et non une manifestation de barbarie ou de sauvagerie. Par leurs désirs vengeurs, les géants se rapprochent des chevaliers errants bien plus qu'ils ne s'en éloignent" (452; is an eminently cultural and human act, and not a manifestation of barbarity or savagery. In their desire for vengeance, giants are not distanced from knights errant, but brought closer to them).
15. This episode appears in *Tristan en prose*, ed. Ménard (hereafter *PT*[M]), 1:148–50; quote on 148; subsequently cited parenthetically in the text.
16. *Des grantz geanz*, vv. 469–72, ed. Brereton.
17. Jean d'Arras, *Mélusine*, ed. Vincensini, 718; subsequent citations in the chapter are to this edition. In Coudrette's *Mélusine* the giant's castle is similarly described: "S'apperçoit une tour quarree, / Grande et grosse et moult fort barree; / La porte voit ouverte arriere / Et deffermee la barriere" (He spied a square

tower, large and massive and fully barred; he sees the door open in back, and the barrier raised). Coudrette, *Roman de Mélusine*, vv. 5063–66, ed. Roach; subsequent citations in the chapter are to this edition.

18. Jean d'Arras, *Mélusine*, 666, 668.

19. Lyonnel's quest for the Golden-Haired Giant, and the battle in which he kills him, are described in *Perceforest: Deuxième partie*, ed. Roussineau (hereafter *Perce/II*), 1:279–300, 333–65; subsequently cited parenthetically in the text. On this episode, see my *Postcolonial Fictions*, 122–26, 199–202.

20. *Perceforest: Troisième partie*, ed. Roussineau (hereafter *Perce/III*), 2:257–61; subsequently cited parenthetically in the text.

21. *Perceforest: Cinquième partie*, ed. Roussineau (hereafter *Perce/V*), 1:166; subsequently cited parenthetically in the text.

22. Of Galotine's son Galehau, the narrator states: "Il fut ave au preu roy Galehot des Estranges Isles. Et en celle isle mesmes le preu Tristran occist le pere et la mere du preu Galehot, ce que faire lui convenoit, comme il appert es histoires du preu chevalier Tristran" [*Perce/V*, 1:171; He was the grandfather of the worthy king Galehot of the Foreign Isles. And in this very island the worthy Tristan killed the father and mother of the worthy Galehot, which he was forced to do, as can be seen in the story of the worthy knight Tristan). The episode in which Tristan kills Galehot's parents and meets the famous half-blood giant will be discussed in chapter 3. The descent of Gawain and his brothers from Galotine's daughter Clamidette is described in *Perce/V*, 1:217–18.

23. *Mort le roi Artu*, ed. Frappier, 2. The full exchange between Gawain and Arthur appears on 2–3. The same passage also appears at the very end of the prose *Tristan*; see *PT*[M], 9:283–85. On Gawain's reputation for violence, which develops increasingly through the *Lancelot-Grail* and the prose *Tristan*, see Harf-Lancner, "Gauvain l'assassin."

24. In *Le Bel Inconnu*, for example, Guinglain and his party are happy to help themselves to the supplies that they find in the cellar belonging to the giants he has just killed: "trente pains / Et blances napes et hanas, / Janbes salees, oissals cras, / Tos rotis et tos atornés; / De bon vin ont trovés asés" (thirty loaves of bread and white napkins and flagons, salted hams, rich fowl, all roasted and prepared; they found plenty of good wine). Renaut de Beaujeu, *Le Bel Inconnu*, vv. 902–6, ed. Williams. In this case, at least, giants share the culinary habits of the aristocracy, even down to napkins and tableware.

25. *Lancelot*, ed. Micha (hereafter *PLanc*), 7:449; subsequently cited parenthetically in the text.

26. For a general survey of gigantic knights and monstrous giants in *chansons de geste*, see Dubost, *Aspects fantastiques*, 1:580–604.

27. See Gallois, *Idéal héroïque*, 369–82.

28. Pseudo-Turpin, *Pseudo-Turpin Chronicle*, ed. Walpole, *Anonymous Old French Translation*, 60–61, subsequently cited parenthetically in the text. On

Fernagut's battle with Roland, see Cohen, "On Saracen Enjoyment," 122–23. It is not clear whether this Fernagut, who is killed by Roland, is related to the Ferragu killed by the Duke of Aquitaine in *Valentin et Orson*.

29. *Huon de Bordeaux*, vv. 5140–44, ed. Kibler; subsequently cited parenthetically in the text.

30. Sunderland, "Genre, Ideology."

31. Jean d'Arras, *Mélusine*, 712.

32. Coudrette, *Roman de Mélusine*, vv. 4693–96.

33. See *Estoire del Saint Graal*, ed. Ponceau, 2:495, 497; *PLanc*, 2:330–34. Other medieval texts feature the Saracen "trinity" of Mahomet, Apollin, and Tervagant.

34. Jean d'Arras, *Mélusine*, 654.

35. Baumgartner notes that knightly combat with giants indicates not only "le triomphe de la civilisation" but also "le triomphe de la loi chrétienne," in "Géants et chevaliers," 11–12.

36. "Géants en cascade," 58–60.

37. This miniature, cut from its manuscript, appeared in a sale at Christie's on June 4, 2008 (sale 7590, lot 27). It is shown on their website at www.christies.com/lotfinder/books-manuscripts/lancelot-with-the-slain-giants-miniature-cut-5080721-details.aspx (accessed August 17, 2014). For a similar use of ornate, fanciful armor, turbaned headdresses, and exotic moustaches as a means of assimilating Trojan heroes to Turkish warriors in a set of fifteenth-century tapestries depicting the Trojan War, see Harper, "Turks as Trojans," 158–66. Harper specifies the motif of the half-moustache as "an attempt to convey Turkish Otherness" (164). Kosta-Théfaine notes the use of the belted robe, turban, and double-pointed beard as signs of Eastern exoticism in an early fifteenth-century manuscript, in "Pierpont Morgan Library Manuscript M.723." For illustrations showing both Tartars and examples of various "monstrous races" with double-pointed beards—and sometimes long, drooping moustaches as well—in manuscripts of Marco Polo's *Devisement du monde*, see Strickland, "Text, Image."

38. For examples of Saracen headdress in medieval French manuscript illuminations, see Strickland, *Saracens, Demons*, 174–86.

39. Kaeuper notes the fascination exerted by this question across the spectrum of medieval literature, commenting that "complex figures in chivalric literature, such as Roland himself, or even darker figures, such as Raoul in *Raoul de Cambrai*, Claudas in the *Lancelot do Lac*, or Caradoc in *Lancelot*, were so interesting to their contemporaries in medieval society because of the tension between their admirable prowess and other qualities warped or missing in them" (*Chivalry and Violence*, 159).

40. Bnf fr. 338, fol. 424r. The passage is unedited; see Lathuillère, *Guiron le courtois*, §120, 322. MS Bnf fr. 338 can be consulted on the Gallica website at

http://gallica.bnf.fr/ark:/12148/btv1b8514424m.r=%C2%AB+Cy+commence+le+livre+de+Guiron+le+Courtois.langEN (accessed September 19, 2013).

41. Ibid.

42. Bhabha, *Location of Culture*, 87, emphasis his.

43. A similar point emerges from an episode in a later version of *Guiron le courtois*, in which the king of Sorelois wrongs the knight Melianus by granting land rightfully his to the giant Nabor in exchange for the latter's services in guarding a bridge. Albert points out that Nabor here takes on "l'image du vilain parvenu" (the image of the upstart serf). *"Ensemble ou par pieces,"* ed. Albert, 530).

44. Maudit's background is explained in *PLanc*, 4:251–63; his final battle with Boorz takes place in *PLanc*, 5:17–24. I will discuss this episode in more detail in chapter 3. An interpolated passage in a sixteenth-century copy of *Guiron le courtois* (London, BL Add. MS 36673) narrates the story of Maudit's ancestors, a group of giants who ruled over a Scottish kingdom. When Christian knights invaded the kingdom many of the giants were killed, including Maudit's father; the survivors, among them Maudit's mother, fled into the mountains. See Lathuillère, *Guiron le courtois*, § 257, 484.

45. See Blackman, "Pictorial Synopsis," 3–5.

46. See Kay, *Chansons de Geste*, 29–48, 99–103, 130–32; Kinoshita, *Medieval Boundaries*, 46–73; Akbari, *Idols in the East*, 173–89; Girbea, "Double romanesque," especially 258–61.

47. Kinoshita, *Medieval Boundaries*, 72, 73. On the related motif of the "Saracen prince," see Kay, *Chansons de Geste*, 178, 189–92.

48. The desire of giants for knights or ladies can be seen as a variation on what Schultz has termed "aristophilia"; see his *Courtly Love*, 79–98. In Schultz's formulation, "Visible nobility provokes love" (80). That the aura of European nobility inspires love not only in other Christian or Saracen aristocrats but also in giants further underscores the extent to which this quality is cast as one of universal value.

49. *Prise d'Orange*, ed. Lachet, vv. 287–90.

50. Bhabha, *Location of Culture*, 70–71.

51. See Huot, *Postcolonial Fictions*, 122–24. The episode appears in *Perce/II*, 1:346–64.

52. *Perceforest: Quatrième partie*, ed. Roussineau (hereafter *Perce/IV*), 1:8; subsequently cited parenthetically in the text.

53. Nocentelli, *Empires of Love*, 52.

54. Ibid., 88.

55. Ibid., 76.

56. An air of comedy can adhere even to the more grisly giants; is there not something darkly comic about a cloak of beards, or a giant who—as we shall see in chapter 3—waylays passing knights by posing riddles about himself? Some, such as Rainouart in the *Guillaume d'Orange* cycle, are even more clearly

comic figures. In this regard Cohen notes that "giants are figures of sublime dread, but also of boundless comedy and complex enjoyment" (*Of Giants*, 177).

57. On the "naturalization" of rape as seduction in the Old French *pastourelle*, see Gravdal, *Ravishing Maidens*, 104–21.

58. Akbari, *Idols in the East*, 175.

59. Uebel, *Ecstatic Transformation*, 18–19.

CHAPTER 3. *Touching the Absolute*

1. Spivak's original sentence was "White men are saving brown women from brown men"; see "Can the Subaltern Speak?," 296–308.

2. "In one way or another violence is always mingled with desire." Girard, *Violence et le sacré*, 203; trans. Gregory, *Violence and the Sacred*, 154.

3. Conon de Béthune, "Ahi! Amours, con dure departie," vv. 1–3, and Châtelain de Couci, "A vous, Amant, plus k'a nulle autre gent," v. 20, both in *Poèmes d'amour*, ed. Baumgartner and Ferrand.

4. Conon de Béthune, "Ahi! Amours," vv. 14–16.

5. *Prise d'Orange*, ed. Lachet, vv. 56–57.

6. Ibid., vv. 264–65.

7. I do not, of course, mean to imply that the tale told by the *vida* has any historical veracity; I cite it only as an example of medieval treatment of absolute love and death. On Jaufre Rudel and the irresolvable *amour de loin*, see Gaunt, *Love and Death*, 1–2, 163–67. For a reading of Jaufre and other troubadours more specifically focused on the problematics of love for a woman of a different language, culture, and faith, see Ramey, *Christian, Saracen*, 19–34.

8. Gaunt, *Love and Death*, 208.

9. *Perceforest: Quatrième partie*, ed. Roussineau (hereafter *Perce/IV*), 1:121; subsequently cited parenthetically in text.

10. *Perceforest: Deuxième partie*, ed. Roussineau (hereafter *Perce/II*), 1:359; subsequently cited parenthetically in text.

11. *Suite du roman de Merlin*, ed. Roussineau, 2:551.

12. Ibid., 2:549.

13. *Tristan en prose*, ed. Ménard (hereafter *PT*[M], 1:258–59; subsequently cited parenthetically in the text.

14. On Tristan's madness, see my discussion in *Madness*, 159–71.

15. *Tristan en prose*, ed. Ménard (*PT*[M], 1:262; subsequently cited parenthetically in the text.

16. Crusade literature sometimes indicates a similar anxiety that Christian knights might be drawn into greater depths of depravity or cruelty through contact with the Saracen enemies of Christendom. Haugeard, in his reading of Jean de Joinville's account of the Seventh Crusade in his *Vie de Saint Louis*, sees

"une crainte très particulière—non pas tant celle de l'altérité en elle-même que de son pouvoir d'attraction et de captation. Il faut rester loin de l'autre, parce que son inhumanité est contagieuse" ("Expérience de l'altérité," 135). Baumgartner, in a similar reading of the account of the First Crusade in the *Chanson d'Antioche*, suggests that this latter text portrays the Near Eastern setting of the Crusade as "le lieu et le moment où céder, au nom de la foi, à des pulsions de violence et de cruauté, à se livrer impunément à des actes contre nature" ("Exotisme à rebours," 28).

17. Jean d'Arras, *Mélusine*, ed. Vincensini, 654; subsequently cited parenthetically in the text.

18. On the ambivalence surrounding Gieffroy's character, see Gaullier-Bougassas, *Tentation de l'Orient*, 355–47.

19. Fradenburg, *Sacrifice Your Love*, 8.

20. Châtelain de Couci, "Mout m'est bele la douce commençance," vv. 7–8, in *Poèmes d'amour*, ed. Baumgartner and Ferrand, 76–80.

21. Conon de Béthune, "Ahi! Amours," vv. 35–38.

22. The idea of the "gift of death" as the foundation of the ethical subject derives of course from Derrida, "Donner la mort," translated by Wills as *Gift of Death*.

23. "Visions de l'autre," ed. Albert. Albert discusses Febus's character and his interactions with both pagans and giants in *"Ensemble ou par pieces,"* 275–90, 346–53.

24. *Giron le courtois*, ed. Albert et al., 100; subsequently cited parenthetically in the text.

25. On Pesme Aventure, see Krueger, "Love, Honor," 311–13; Kay, *Chansons de Geste*, 204–7.

26. Geoffrey of Monmouth, *History*, ed. Reeve, 29, trans. Wright, 28.

27. Simpson, *Troubling Arthurian Histories*, 53.

28. As Albert comments: "Le Northumberland que découvre Febus est en effet marqué par une double altérité, géographique et culturelle. Et Febus manifeste, par son comportement, qu'il n'en a pas saisi les lois" (The Northumberland that Febus comes upon is, in effect, marked by a double alterity, geographic and cultural. And Febus shows through his behavior that he has not grasped its laws). *"Ensemble ou par pieces,"* 352.

29. *Estoire del Saint Graal*, ed. Ponceau, 2:332.

30. It is not unheard of for other knights to kill giants with relative ease. Febus's descendant Guiron is also capable of defeating giants in rapid succession, emerging unscathed even after taking on five or six at one time; Lancelot also generally experiences little difficulty in facing giants. Commonly, however, battle with a giant is a more protracted affair, with descriptions of the many blows exchanged and the difficulty with which the knight withstands the giant's attack and finally, at length, manages to defeat him; descriptions of the

knight's wounds and the period of convalescence he must undergo are also sometimes included.

31. Kay, *Chansons de Geste*, 36, 47.

32. R. Greene, *Unrequited Conquests*.

33. "Violent opposition, then, is the signifier of ultimate desire, of divine self-sufficiency, of that 'beautiful totality' whose beauty depends on its being inaccessible and impenetrable. The victim of this violence both adores and detests it. He strives to master it by means of a mimetic counterviolence. . . . If by chance, however, he actually succeeds in asserting his mastery over the model, the latter's prestige vanishes. He must then turn to an even greater violence and seek out an obstacle that promises to be truly insurmountable." Girard, *Violence et le sacré*, 208; trans. Gregory, *Violence and the Sacred*, 157.

34. Kay, *Chansons de Geste*, 41–48.

35. Ibid., 47.

36. Ibid., 42.

37. Nocentelli, *Empires of Love*, 88–89.

38. Kay notes a similar pattern in *Fierebras*, when Gui de Bourgogne initially attempts to refuse marriage to the Saracen Floripas unless she is given to him by Charles; in the event, however, it is Gui who is given to Floripas, first by Roland, and then later by Charles when he confirms the arrangement (*Chansons de Geste*, 44–45). As Kay comments, the mystification of power and the confusion of persons and things are "further heightened by the swapping over of roles between 'gifts,' 'givers,' and 'recipients'" (45).

39. *Huon de Bordeaux*, vv. 6732–38, ed. Kibler; subsequently cited parenthetically in the text.

40. On this point, see Kay, *Chansons de Geste*, 45–48.

41. Ibid., 45, 47.

42. R. Greene, *Unrequited Conquests*, 14.

43. Uebel, *Ecstatic Transformation*, 74.

44. For a reading of the changing face of the "Saracen princess" motif as a reflection of shifting attitudes within Western culture toward interfaith and cross-cultural marriage, see Ramey, *Christian, Saracen*. On the mixture of pleasure and anxiety associated with cross-cultural marriages variously linking Roman Catholic, Saracen, and Byzantine lovers, see Moore, *Exchanges in Exoticism*.

45. *Lancelot*, ed. Micha (hereafter *PLanc*), 4:252; subsequently cited parenthetically in the text.

46. On this figure, see Dubost, *Aspects fantastiques*, 1:625–26.

47. That particular pattern does not always hold; the riddling giant of *Tristan*, who boasts of eating both his daughter and his mother, did not eat his brother but merely buried him alive. Whether cannibalism is imbued with sexual overtones, however, or with those of masculine combat, it is interesting to see that it is given a consistent gender orientation in both cases.

48. Geoffrey of Monmouth, *History*, ed. Reeve, 225, trans. Wright, 224.

49. Ibid.

50. *Conte du Papegau*, ed. Charpentier and Victorin, 168; subsequently cited parenthetically in the text.

51. On the ritualized violence of the tournament, and the incapacity of certain kinds of characters to grasp its distinction from the very different violence of warfare, see Girbea, *Bon Sarrasin*, 337–73.

52. An interesting, and rare, exception to this pattern occurs in *Perceforest*, where a giant (or possibly half-blood giant) accepts defeat in a joust with Nero, son of Nestor, a Scottish prince famed for his peerless ability in both tournaments and battles. The text as edited by Gilles Roussineau identifies the giant as the cousin of Galehout, grandson of the Golden-Haired Giant and ancestor of Lancelot's companion Galehot; though surprised at being defeated, the giant accepts it with grace: "Puis vint remercier Nero de sa jouste" (*Perce/IV*, 1:170; Then he went to thank Nero for the joust). The variant version given by Roussineau comments further that after his defeat the giant "si fist tresbonne chiere, aussi il estoit aourné de gentillesse et de courtoisie" (*Perce/IV*, 2:750; nonetheless maintained a cheerful demeanor, for he was also graced with nobility and courtesy).

53. In a similar vein, Cohen comments in *Of Giants* on the "burlesque humor" generated in the Old French *Aliscans* and the Middle English *Bevis of Hampton* by the "incongruity of a giant as a proper knight," 166–74 (170).

54. On this episode, its relationship to Chrétien's text, and its ethical implications, see J. Taylor, "Parrot"; Walters, "Parody and the Parrot."

55. V. Greene notes that the fairy "did not understand that the absolute power courtly love attributes to the lady works only in a subjunctive mode, in the realm of 'as if,'" in "Humanimals," 129. Jane Gilbert notes the paradoxical aspect of the "courtly love" construct in the prose *Lancelot*, where Guenevere can be seen to shift from a predominantly empathetic attitude toward Lancelot to one increasingly designed to test his love and his endurance, as though this form of clandestine love inevitably shapes men into great heroes and women into capricious, even cruel tormentors; see *Living Death*, 75–85.

56. In *Perceforest*, Queen Ydorus similarly notes that while a maiden may develop a knight's prowess by forcing him to earn her favors, the system will break down and revert to animalistic mating if she does not eventually reward his efforts with love and marriage (*Perce/IV*, 1:149).

CHAPTER 4. *Giants and Saracens in the Prose* Tristan

1. Uebel, *Ecstatic Transformation*, 28.
2. Ibid.
3. *Erec et Enide*, vv. 4360, 4391, ed. Roques.

4. Simpson, *Troubling Arthurian Histories*, 334.

5. For a somewhat analogous reading of medieval genealogical narratives as containing or even requiring moments of rupture such as incest, see Stahuljak, *Bloodless Genealogies*. Citing the example of Charlemagne's supposed incestuous fathering of Roland and the expiatory function of his Crusade efforts, Stahuljak states: "If the sin disrupts by breaking down the crusade narrative and then reconstituting it as a means of 'salvation,' then the 'total statement' can be 'total' only if there has been a (moral) failure" (9). The episode is thus "an exemplary representation of sins that disrupt narratives and their linearity, only to find themselves recuperated by and assimilated into the very narrative they disrupted" (10).

6. On this episode, see my "Love, Race, and Gender," 378–82, 84–85.

7. *Tristan en prose*, ed. Ménard (hereafter *PT*[M]), 9:126; subsequently cited parenthetically in the text.

8. This tenet was first formulated in Paul's famous statement that "non est Iudaeus, neque Graecus: non est servus, neque liber: non est masculus, neque femina. Omnes enim vos unum estis in Christo Iesu" (There is neither Jew nor Greek, there is neither slave nor free, there is neither male nor female; for you are all one in Christ Jesus). Gal. 3:28, trans. RSV. On this view in the early church, see Brottier, "Images de l'étranger." For a close reading of Paul's epistle and a survey of its role in modern and postmodern discourses of race, alterity, and universalism, see Roberts, *Alterity and Narrative*, 41–68.

9. *Tristan en prose*, ed. Curtis (hereafter *PT*[C]), 2:71; subsequently cited parenthetically in the text.

10. The *Chastel de Plour* episode may have been inspired in part by the *Salle aux Images* episode in Thomas d'Angleterre's *Tristan*. The fragment of this episode that survives does not allow for any real evaluation of the passage; see "Fragment du manuscrit de Turin," ed. Payen, vv. 941–96. The Old Norse translation of Thomas's text, however, gives an idea of what Thomas's text may have contained; according to it, Tristan subjugates a giant whose lands abut those of his wife's family and forces him to allow the construction of the grotto containing lifelike statues of Iseut and Brangein. Since Tristan is the only human who can enter the giant's territory without being attacked, the arrangement affords him the secrecy and isolation from the court necessary for his ongoing communion with Iseut, through the medium of the statues. See *Saga of Tristram and Ísönd*, trans. Schach, 115–23, 127–30. The episode thus establishes a precedent for seeing the world of giants, like that of the forest, as one that might provide a kind of safe haven for an adulterous love incompatible with the strictures and scrutiny of the court. In the prose *Tristan*, of course, the Joyous Guard will also serve this purpose, allowing the lovers a period of respite in which to establish their own court in opposition to that of Cornwall, but in a way that does not sever them from the chivalric world. The insertion of the *Chastel de Plour*

episode at such an early point in the story emphasizes the fact that total escape into an alternate world will not be possible for the lovers; their story will form an integral part of the legendary history of the Arthurian kingdom.

11. *Lancelot*, ed. Micha (hereafter *PLanc*), 1:11; subsequently cited parenthetically in the text.

12. Cohen makes a similar point with regard to the giants of the *Historia regum Britanniae*. In his discussion of the Giant of Mont-St-Michel, Cohen states: "Like Gogmagog, this giant's fate is to see his monstrous excess contained within a heroic story about the progress of a nation" (*Of Giants*, 39).

13. Two manuscripts have extended versions of this episode, including a prior battle between the knights of the castle and a different group of Arthurian knights; these are given in *PT*[M], 7:411–41. In the different versions of this episode, the founder of the castle is identified as Galanazar and the current lord as Harpins li Roux. The castle is always defined as militantly isolationist, but it emerges as a Saracen stronghold only in the context of the Grail Quest.

14. The Païs de Servaige appears in *PT*[C], 2:174–99.

15. This episode is unedited; my discussion is based on the text in Bnf fr. 338, fol. 425v–445r. Subsequent folio citations are to this MS and are given parenthetically in the text. See Lathuillère, *Guiron le courtois*, §§ 121–24, pp. 322–27.

16. On Tristan's liaison with the lady and Seguradés's failed attempt at vengeance, see *PT*[C], 1:178–85.

17. No lai meeting this description exists in any of the surviving *Tristan* manuscripts, and it is impossible to know if there ever was one alluding to this episode. Still, the text identifies Tristan's adventure in the giant's land as one that met with general acclaim and was deemed worthy of commemoration in a lai.

18. I have discussed this material in "Unspeakable Horror." See also Van Coolput, "'Préhistoire arthurienne'"; Mickel, "Tristan's Ancestry"; Traxler, "Observations on the Importance."

19. On this figure, see Caulkins, "Chelinde."

20. A. Smith, *Julia Kristeva*, 6–7.

21. C. Taylor, "Person," 273.

22. Ibid., 276.

23. "Symptom that precisely turns 'we' into a problem, perhaps makes it impossible." Kristeva, *Étrangers*, 1, trans. Roudiez, *Strangers*, 1.

24. Mickel notes that the opening section of the *Tristan* prepares for the story that follows, illustrating ways that "man's self-centered nature leads to a life of internecine strife and chaos, ultimately to parricide and incest," in "Tristan's Ancestry," 81. Traxler points out that the giant's riddles and revelations about his own behavior "constitute a metaphor for an important aspect of the romance: the giant's family literally destroys itself from within, as do Arthur's and Mark's families," in "Observations on the Importance," 542.

25. Steele, *Theorizing Textual Subjects*, 187. On a similar scapegoating of colonized Indian subjects as the perpetrators, rather than the victims, of violence in British colonial discourse, see Sharpe, "Unspeakable Limits of Rape."

CHAPTER 5. *Outsiders in the Story*

1. Portions of the following discussion of Galehot and Lancelot are taken from my article "Love, Race, and Gender." I will focus on the version of the story that appears in the Vulgate *Lancelot-Grail* cycle.

2. Galehot's precise ambitions, and the number of kingdoms conquered, vary. In the noncyclic *Lancelot du Lac*, Galehot states that he has already conquered thirty kingdoms and that he intended to be crowned after defeating Arthur and adding Logres to his possessions (ed. Kennedy, 2:588). In the *Lancelot-Grail* the narrator states that Galehot has already conquered twenty-eight kingdoms, and Galehot tells Lancelot that he had intended to be crowned once he had brought the number to 150. *Lancelot*, ed. Micha (hereafter *PLanc*, 1:2, 9–10; subsequently cited parenthetically in the text.

3. Boivin characterises Galehot as "hyperbole du monde courtois *et* chevalier de l'Autre Monde, intégré sans jamais l'être vraiment au monde arthurien," in "Dame du Lac," 23. On the politics and discourses surrounding assimilation and intermarriage of Celtic, Anglo-Saxon, and Norman peoples in medieval Britain, with particular reference to Gerald of Wales and the Welsh Marchers, see Cohen, *Hybridity*, 77–108.

4. On this passage, see Burns, "Which Queen"; Gilbert, *Living Death*, 98–102.

5. Baumgartner notes that although he is not a full-blooded giant, Galehot is nonetheless a formidable figure "de l'Autre Monde," challenging not only Arthur but, with the extravagant structure of the Orgueilleuse Garde, God himself, in *"Tristan en prose,"* 12–13. Gilbert comments that Galehot's initial appearance in *Lancelot* "recalls the giants of the chronicle tradition," while at the same time his brutality and arrogance are "partially assimilated to approved chivalric virtues," in *Living Death*, 86.

6. The Caradoc episode is told at intervals in *PLanc*, vol. 1. Caradoc abducts Gawain in section 10 and is finally defeated by Lancelot in section 28. In *Lancelot* Caradoc is not explicitly called a giant, but he rides "un des plus grans chevals del monde" (1:177; one of the largest horses in the world) and is "li plus grans et li plus corsus que il onques mes euissent veu" (1:177; the biggest and most ferocious man that they had ever seen). He is characterized in the same terms as giants, being "li plus cruels et li plus desloials de tos cels qui onques portaissent armes" (1:182; the cruelest and most perfidious of any who ever bore arms). The *Suite du roman de Merlin* identifies Caradoc as son of the giant Aupatris, who was killed by Gawain's brother Gaheriet (ed. Roussineau,

2:550). And in its summary of this episode, *Tristan* refers to "uns jaianz qui avoit non Caradox li Grans" (*PT*[C], 1:80; a giant named Caradoc the Large).

7. On the homoerotic aspects of Galehot's love for Lancelot, see Gaunt, *Love and Death*, 191–203; Baumgartner, "*Tristan en prose*," 13; Zeikowitz, *Homoeroticism and Chivalry*, 37–43. For a nuanced reading of Galehot as a figure who redefines both sexual and social bonds within the Arthurian world, see Gilbert, *Living Death*, 60–102.

8. Gilbert, *Living Death*, 219–20.

9. On this point, see Trachsler, *Clôtures*, 158.

10. When Tristan and Iseut do flee Cornwall, it is to live at the Joyous Guard in Logres, where they are fully integrated into the public life of Arthur's kingdom; by this point in the story, one might even say that Cornwall itself has taken on the qualities of a negative, antichivalric and anticourtly Other World.

11. Baumgartner, "*Tristan en prose*," 13–14. See also Boivin, "Dame du Lac."

12. "The knight affirms . . . his desire to be in the world and to serve there." Baumgartner, "*Tristan en prose*," 14.

13. See *PT*[M], 1:125–42.

14. "Géants en cascade," in *Guiron le courtois*, ed. Trachsler, 60–66. These adventures are alluded to above in chapter 1.

15. As Boivin states, Galehot's death "scelle la victoire du monde courtois sur l'Autre Monde," in "Dame du Lac," 23.

16. On the significance of the Joyous Guard as the site of Lancelot's burial, see Trachsler, *Clôtures*, 129–30. Cohen reads Galehot's presence in an extravagant pagan tomb within the Joyous Guard as a final, enduring sign of the half-blood giant's "intimate alterity"; see *Of Giants*, 182–83.

17. On Palamedes, see Baumgartner, "*Tristan en prose*," 246–52; Girbea, *Bon Sarrasin*, 102–3. I have briefly discussed Palamedes, and his parallels with Galehot, in "Others and Alterity."

18. On this point see Trachsler, *Clôtures*, 175–78.

19. On the ways that Palamedes and his father stand in counterpoint both to the Grail heroes and to Tristan and Iseut, see Albert, "*Ensemble ou par pieces*," 202–8.

20. Trachsler notes that each of these three major heroes is central to a narrative of teleological nature: spiritual in the case of Galahad, who completes the adventures of the Grail; "historic" in the case of Lancelot, whose story culminates in the Battle of Salisbury Plain and the collapse of the Arthurian kingdom; and erotic in the case of Tristan, whom Trachsler sees as "destiné à faire découvrir aux hommes l'amour passionnel qui peut se passer de l'union sacré de mariage" (*Clôtures*, 191).

21. In her introduction to vol. 9 of *Tristan*, Harf-Lancner discusses the death scene, noting "l'indifférence du héros pour le salût de son âme" (*PT*[M], 9:40–41; the hero's indifference concerning the salvation of his soul).

22. After the battle, Lancelot is forthright in explaining his motivation: "Je n'empris mie ceste bataille pour haine que je eüsse a vous, ains l'empris seulement pour connoistre se vous estes si boins cevaliers a l'espee con vous estes au glaive" (*PT*[M], 9:262; I didn't undertake this battle out of any hatred that I might have for you, but only to find out if you're as good a knight with the sword as you are with the spear). At this the badly wounded Palamedes is simply nonplussed: "Conment, ce dist Palamidés, si ne conmenchastes la bataille pour autre cose? . . . Par Dieu, c'est merveille!" (9:262; What, said Palamedes, you didn't begin the battle for any other reason? . . . For God's sake, that's amazing!).

23. See Harf-Lancner, "Gauvain l'assassin."

24. Chrétien de Troyes, *Chevalier au lion*, vv. 356–57, ed. Hult.

25. On Palamedes's relationship with Tristan, see my *Madness*, 120–25.

26. See Traxler, "Observations on the Beste."

27. *Fille du comte de Pontieu*, ed. Brunel; *Saladin*, ed. Crist (hereafter *Saladin*), subsequently cited parenthetically in the text. On these texts, see Jubb, *Legend of Saladin*; Gaullier-Bougassas, *Tentation*, 355–405; Suard, "*Fille du comte de Ponthieu*."

28. Bhabha, *Location of Culture*, 114.

29. Jubb discusses Saladin's invasion of England, noting parallels with the battle at Rencesvals, in *Legend of Saladin*, 139–41.

30. *Chanson de Roland*, vv. 1830–31, ed. Bédier.

31. Ibid., vv. 1018, 1024.

32. The narrator holds back from crediting Jean with the establishment of Christianity in Acre, while nonetheless implying that, if nothing else, he was responsible for preserving its Christian status: "Ne dit point l'istoire s'elle fu crestienne ou sarrasine a cest fois, mais toutesvoies—comme on treuve en pluseurs histoirez—depuis ce qu'il en eust pris la saisine elle fut crestienne" [*Saladin*, 72; The story doesn't say if it was Christian or Saracen at that time, but in any case—as one finds in many historical accounts—ever since he became the ruler, it was Christian).

CHAPTER 6. *Desire, Subjectivity, and the Humanity of Giants*

1. "The real Other for the white man is and will continue to be the black man." Fanon, *Peau noire*, 131 n. 25, trans. Markmann, *Black Skins*, 161 n. 25.

2. "For the white man the Other is perceived on the level of the body image, absolutely as the not-self—that is, the unidentifiable, the unassimilable." Ibid.

3. "It is not a new man who has come in, but a new kind of man, a new genus. Why, it's a Negro!" Fanon, *Peau noire*, 93, trans. Markmann, *Black Skins*, 116.

4. Derrida, "And Say the Animal Responded," 129. Lacan's ideas about animal as opposed to human consciousness are scattered through different essays. See, for example, "Mirror Stage," 3; "Function and Field," 84–86; "Subversion of the Subject," 305.

5. Derrida, "And Say the Animal Responded," 130.

6. Barzilai, *Lacan*, 101–6.

7. Ibid., 102.

8. Ibid., 103.

9. All these quotes are from ibid., 104.

10. *Ovide moralisé*, bk. 1, vv. 1189–90, ed. de Boer.

11. Ibid., bk. 1, vv. 1471–78, 1485–88.

12. Noacco, "Orgueil," 110–11.

13. *Ovide moralisé*, bk. 1, vv. 1199–1202, ed. de Boer.

14. In the *Estoire del Saint Graal*, a "Saracen" king converted by Joseph of Arimathea worships four gods: Mahomet, Tervagan, Apollin, and Jupiter (ed. Ponceau, 495, 497). The same deities are enumerated when the story is retold in *Lancelot* (ed. Micha, 2:330, 334). In Coudrette's *Melusine*, these four deities are invoked by the giant Grimault (vv. 4695–96, ed. Roach).

15. Boethius, *Consolation*, III, para. 12, ed. Rand, 302, trans. Tester, 303.

16. *Policraticus* VII, 1, ed. Webb, *Policratici*, 2:94, trans. Pike, *Frivolities*, 217.

17. *Policraticus* VII, 1, ed. Webb, *Policratici*, 2:94, trans. Pike, *Frivolities*, 217.

18. *Policraticus* III, 13, ed. Webb, *Policratici*, 1:219, trans. Pike, *Frivolities*, 200.

19. Bhabha, *Location of Culture*, 77.

20. Bhabha, ibid.

21. Steel, *How to Make a Human*, 5.

22. Phillips, "Cannibalism qua Capitalism," 193. In a similar vein, Fanon comments that "le Blanc civilisé garde la nostalgie irrationnelle d'époques extraordinaires de licence sexuelle. . . . Projetant ses intentions chez le nègre, le Blanc se comporte 'comme si' le nègre les avait réellement" (the civilized white man retains an irrational longing for unusual eras of sexual license. . . . Projecting his own desires onto the Negro, the white man behaves "as if" the Negro really had them.) *Peau noir*, 133–34; trans. Markmann, *Black Skins*, 165.

23. On this episode and its importance in Yvain's own identity formation, see Cohen, *Of Giants*, 77–80.

24. Rawick, *From Sundown to Sunup*, 132–33.

25. Simpson notes that confrontations with giants are "libidinally haunted by the obscenity of a scenario that presents the Arthurian world with the sum of all its fears and disavowed enjoyments," in *Troubling Arthurian Histories*, 342.

26. Steel analyzes the figure of the herdsman, with comments on the Harpin episode as well, in *How to Make a Human*, 151–62. Krueger comments on the relevance of the Pesme Aventure episode in "Love, Honor."

27. On this image see Carroll, "Text and Image," 67–68, fig. 2.11. Carroll concurs that the text strongly implies that Harpin is on foot.

28. Chrétien de Troyes, *Chevalier au lion*, ed. Hult, vv. 4203–4. Simpson notes that the giants fought by Erec in Chrétien's *Erec et Enide*, though described as being without armor, sword, or lance, are depicted as armored knights in Bnf fr. 24403 (fol. 155r), in *Troubling Arthurian Histories*, 338–39. This miniature may reflect a similar reading of giants as rogue knights or tyrannical lords, rather than as low-class ruffians or wildmen.

29. On this figure as he is portrayed in the Vulgate *Merlin*, see Dubost, *Aspects fantastiques*, 1:475–76.

30. See Stones, "Egerton *Brut*." Stones reproduces the Bonn miniature as fig. 12, and the London miniature as fig. 13. Cohen reproduces three images of Arthur fighting the Giant of Mont-St-Michel in different texts. In one, the giant is a grotesquely ugly figure without helmet or armor, holding a rough club, while in the other two he is clad in armor very similar to that of Arthur; see *Of Giants*, 42–44, 67.

31. JanMohamed, "Economy of Manichean Allegory," 84, 85. Gates offers a critique both of Fanon and of JanMohamed's argument in "Critical Fanonism." On Imaginary and Symbolic otherness as categories in modern colonial and postcolonial discourses of race, see also Fuss, "Interior Colonies"; Vergès, "Creole Skin," 585–90; Mercer, "Busy in the Ruins."

32. Ramey, *Christian, Saracen*, 11–16.

33. *Tristan en prose*, ed. Curtis, (hereafter *PT*[C]), 2:77; subsequently cited parenthetically in the text.

34. Kay, "Desire and Subjectivity," 213. For a more extended discussion of Lacan's views on subject formation, see Barzilai, *Lacan*.

35. Kay, "Desire and Subjectivity," 213.

36. See Moi, "'She Died'"; Griffin, *Object and the Cause*, 110–11, 135–36; Gilbert, *Living Death*, 83, 87.

37. "Géants en cascade," ed. Albert, 56.

38. Warren, "Making Contact," 124.

39. Ibid., 126.

40. The respective peerlessness of the princess and her suitor is explicitly articulated in an exchange between Febus—then incognito—and the pagan knight Arsahan. Arsahan readily acknowledges that the conquering hero Febus is "si parfeit que l'en ne porroit orendroit trouver en tout le monde nul autre qui fust si bon chevaliers com est celui" (so perfect that one could never find another knight in all the world as good as he is). To this Febus replies: "Quant ensint est avenu que vous avés trouvé en chevalerie chevalier sans per, poés bien seürement dire de ceste damoisele: n'a nule pareille en biauté" (Since it happens that you've found a knight peerless in chivalry, you can certainly say of this damsel: she has no peer in beauty). "Visions de l'autre," ed. Albert, 118.

41. This episode is unedited. My analysis is based on the text in Bnf fr. 338 (hereafter cited parenthetically in the text by folio number), where the contest with the giant is described on fols. 119v–121r; see Lathuillère, *Guiron le courtois*, § 37, p. 219. I am grateful to Timothy Atkin of Cambridge University for bringing this episode to my attention.

42. Fuss, "Interior Colonies," 21.

43. Cohen, *Hybridity*, 26.

44. Derrida, "And Say the Animal Responded," 122.

45. Ibid., 130. For a discussion of Lacan's views on the question of animal duplicity, see also Oliver, *Animal Lessons*, 179–89.

46. Lacan, "Subversion of the Subject," 305.

47. Crane, *Animal Encounters*, 97.

48. Ibid., 98. See also Resnick and Kitchell, "Albert the Great."

49. *Perceforest: Deuxième partie*, ed. Roussineau (hereafter *Perce/II*), 1:350; subsequently cited parenthetically in the text.

50. See my *Postcolonial Fictions*, 183–206.

51. *Perceforest: Quatrième partie*, ed. Roussineau (hereafter *Perce/IV*), 1:125; subsequently cited parenthetically in the text.

52. I have discussed this figure in *Postcolonial Fictions*, 63–69.

53. Fanon, *Wretched of the Earth*, trans. Farrington, 30.

54. The passage appears in Augustine, *Confessions* I.7. See Barzilai, *Lacan*, 144–65.

55. Augustine, *City of God*, XV.vii, 442, 444.

56. Žižek, *Violence*, 55.

57. Fuss, "Interior Colonies," 21.

58. Simpson's comment with regard to the giants in *Erec et Enide* is also relevant here: "The giants' intentions are both *unseeable* in their shaming, debasing intent and *unthinkable* for the unsettling ambiguities they open up. . . . As Maximilien Robespierre was to comment later on the rights and wrongs of trying Louis, 'We do not execute kings: we drop them back into the void.' So here it is with giants" (*Troubling Arthurian Histories*, 338).

59. On the identification of the Serpent and Giant Isles, see my *Postcolonial Fictions*, 130, 201.

60. On the tales of incest in *Perceforest*, and their importance within the grand narrative of royal hegemony, see my *Postcolonial Fictions*, 119–30.

61. The classic formulation of this theory is Lévi-Strauss, *Elementary Structures of Kinship*.

62. See, for example, Duby, *Medieval Marriage*.

63. For a survey of the social and anthropological issues, see MacCormack, "Nature, Culture"; Rubin, "Traffic in Women," 171–83, 204–10. For comments on the exchange of women in the context of medieval literature, see Krueger, "Love, Honor"; Kay, *Chansons de geste*, 15–16, 31–48, 147–52, 200–231.

64. In Bergner's concise formulation: "In the colonial context, the operative 'law' determining the circulation of women among white men and black men is the miscegenation taboo, which ordains that white men have access to black women but that black men be denied access to white women" ("Who Is That Masked Woman?," 81).

65. *Conte du Papegau* (hereafter *Papegau*), ed. Charpentier and Victorin, 178; subsequently cited parenthetically in the text.

66. On this point, see Findley, *Poet Heroines*, 156–59. As Findley notes, with his systematic program of defeating his fellow knights in order to present an article of clothing or jewelry to the maiden who has requested it, the Delphin is "the facilitator of the exchange of finely crafted objects between women" (156).

67. *Perceforest: Première partie*, ed. Roussineau, 2:860; subsequently cited parenthetically in the text.

68. Blanchete composes the "Lai de confort" in response to Lyonnel's "Lai de la complainte." She also contributes a stanza to the "Lai secret" coauthored by herself and her two companions Priande and Lyriope. See my "Chronicle, Lai, and Romance"; Findley, *Poet Heroines*, 139–66.

69. *Perceforest: Troixième partie*, ed. Roussineau, 2:257.

70. Wolfe, *Animal Rites*, 43, 100.

Conclusion

1. Žižek, *Violence*, 55.

2. "The celestial world which has imposed martyrdom on the new convert. His death . . . is characterized by indifference to the afterlife." Harf-Lancner, introduction to vol. 9 of *Tristan en prose* (hereafter *PT*[M]), 9:43.

3. Bibl. Nat. fr. 338, fol. 425r. On this episode, see Lathuillère, "*Guiron le courtois*," § 120, 321–22.

4. *Suite du roman de Merlin*, ed. Roussineau, 551.

5. *Erec et Enide*, ed. Roques, 4526–28, 4467–68.

6. Simpson, *Troubling Arthurian Histories*, 342. Simpson's detailed analysis of this passage (332–45) is relevant to my own argument about the temptations offered by giants and the need to resist them.

7. "The sacrifice of the passions, of the affections, of so-called 'pathological' interests. . . . According to Kant the unconditionality of moral law dictates the violence that is exercised in self-restraint (*Selbstzwang*) and against one's own desires." Derrida, *Donner la mort*, 88, trans. Wills, *Gift of Death*, 93.

8. In Derrida's words: "La mort est bien ce que personne ne peut ni endurer ni affronter à ma place. Mon irremplaçabilité est bien conférée, livrée, on pourrait dire donnée par la mort" (Death is very much that which nobody else

can undergo or confront in my place. My irreplaceability is therefore conferred, delivered, 'given', one can say, by death). Derrida, *Donner la mort*, 45, trans. Wills, *Gift of Death*, 41.

9. "As soon as one speaks, as soon as one enters the medium of language, one loses that very singularity." Derrida, *Donner la mort*, 61, trans. Wills, *Gift of Death*, 60.

10. "The absolute responsibility of my actions, to the extent that such a responsibility remains mine, singularly so, something no one else can perform in my place, instead implies secrecy." Derrida, *Donner la mort*, 61–62, trans. Wills, *Gift of Death*, 60.

11. "It is from the site of death as the place of my irreplaceability, that is, of my singularity, that I feel called to responsibility." Derrida, *Donner la mort*, 45, trans. Wills, *Gift of Death*, 41.

12. On the relevance of Derrida's arguments for the treatment of love in medieval literature, see Gaunt, *Love and Death*, 25–26, 37–38, 79–83, 143–44.

13. Uebel, *Ecstatic Transformation*, 140.

14. One might argue that Gawain is an exception, in that his bloodthirsty wrath and need for vengeance play a decisive role in the destruction of the Arthurian world. It must be remembered, however, that his descent from giants is a feature of the much later *Perceforest* and had not yet been imagined when *La mort le roi Artu* was written.

15. Žižek, *Enjoy Your Symptom*, 56, emphasis his.

16. On the range of meanings attributed to the words *culture* and *civilization* and their historical development in Western thought, see Young, *Colonial Desire*, 29–54.

17. On the fictional oral and written sources cited by the *Perceforest* author, see my "Chronicle, Lai"; Ferlampin-Acher, "Géographie"; J. Taylor, "Fourteenth Century."

BIBLIOGRAPHY

Primary Sources

Albertus Magnus. *De animalibus libri XXVI.* Edited by Hermann Stadtler. 2 vols. Beiträge zur Geschichte des Philosophie des Mittelalters: Texte und Untersuchungen 15. Munster: Aschendorffsche Verlagesbuchhandlung, 1916–20.
Alexander of Hales. *Summa theologica.* Edited by the Fathers of the College of St. Bonaventure. 4 vols. Quaracchi: Collegii S. Bonaventurae ad Claras Aquas, 1924–48.
Aliscans. Edited by Claude Régnier. Classiques français du Moyen Âge. 2 vols. Paris: Champion, 1990.
Augustine. *Confessions.* Edited by P. Knöll and W. H. D. Rouse. Translated by William Watts. 2 vols. Loeb Classical Library. Cambridge, MA: Harvard University Press, 2006.
———. *De civitate Dei contra paganos / The City of God against the Pagans.* Edited and translated by George E. McCracken, William McAllen Green, David Wiesen, Philip Levine, Eva Matthews Sanford, and William Chase Greene. 7 vols. Loeb Classical Library. Cambridge, MA: Harvard University Press, 1965–68.
Bibliothèque Nationale de France. Digital facsimile of Bibl. Nat. fr. 338. Retrieved September 19, 2014. http://gallica.bnf.fr/ark:/12148/btv1b8514424 m.r=%C2%AB+Cy+commence+le+livre+de+Guiron+le+Courtois.langEN.
Boethius. *The Consolation of Philosophy.* Edited by E. K. Rand. Translated by S. J. Tester. Loeb Classical Library. Cambridge, MA: Harvard University Press, 1973.
Chanson de Roland. Edited by Joseph Bédier. Paris: Piazza, 1937.
Chrétien de Troyes. *Le Chevalier au lion.* Edited by David F. Hult. Lettres gothiques. Paris: Livre de Poche, 1994.

———. *Erec et Enide*. Edited by Mario Roques. Classiques français du Moyen Âge. Paris: Champion, 1981.
Christie's. Image of giants killed by Lancelot. Retrieved August 17, 2014. www.christies.com/lotfinder/books-manuscripts/lancelot-with-the-slain-giants-miniature-cut-5080721-details.aspx.
Conte du Papegau. Edited by Hélène Charpentier and Patricia Victorin. Champion classiques: Moyen Âge. Paris: Champion, 2004.
Coudrette. *Le roman de Mélusine ou histoire de Lusignan*. Edited by Eleanor Roach. Paris: Klincksieck, 1982.
Des grantz geanz: An Anglo-Norman Poem. Edited by Georgine E. Brereton. Medium Aevum Monographs 2. Oxford: Blackwell, 1937.
Estoire del Saint Graal. Edited by Jean-Paul Ponceau. 2 vols. Classiques français du Moyen Âge. Paris: Champion, 1997.
La fille du comte de Pontieu: Conte en prose, versions du XIIIe et du XVe siècle. Edited by Clovis Brunel. Société des anciens textes français. Paris: Champion, 1923.
"Géants en cascade." Edited by Sophie Albert. In *Guiron le courtois: Une anthologie*, 51–67.
Geoffrey of Monmouth. *The History of the Kings of Britain: An Edition and Translation of "De gestis Britonum" [Historia regum Britanniae]*. Edited by Michael D. Reeve. Translated by Neil Wright. Arthurian Studies 69. Woodbridge: Boydell Press, 2007.
Guiron le courtois: Une anthologie. Edited by Sophie Albert, Mathilde Plaut, and Frédéric Plumet, under the direction of Richard Trachsler. Gli Orsatti: Texti per un Altro Medioevo 22. Alessandria: Edizioni dell'Orso, 2004.
Huon de Bordeaux. Edited by William W. Kibler. Champion classiques: Moyen Âge. Paris: Champion, 2003.
Jean d'Arras. *Mélusine, ou La noble histoire de Lusignan*. Edited by Jean-Jacques Vincensini. Lettres gothiques. Paris: Livre de Poche, 2003.
John of Salisbury. *Frivolities of Courtiers and Footprints of Philosophers: Being a Translation of the First, Second, and Third Books and Selections from the Seventh and Eighth Books of the Policraticus of John of Salisbury*. Translated by Joseph B. Pike. Minneapolis: University of Minnesota Press, 1938.
———[Ioannis Saresberiensis]. *Policratici, sive De nugis curialium et vestigiis philosophorum, Libri VIII*. Edited by Clemens C. I. Webb. 2 vols. Oxford: Clarendon Press, 1909.
Lancelot du Lac. Edited by Elspeth Kennedy. Presented, annotated, and translated by François Mosès and Marie-Luce Chênerie. 2 vols. Lettres gothiques. Paris: Livre de Poche, 1991–93.
Lancelot: Roman en prose du XIIIe siècle. Edited by Alexandre Micha. 9 vols. Textes littéraires français. Geneva: Droz, 1978–83.

La mort le roi Artu. Edited by Jean Frappier. Textes littéraires français. Geneva: Droz, 1964.

Ovid. *Metamorphoses*. Edited and translated by Frank Justus Miller. 2 vols. Loeb Classical Library. Cambridge, MA: Harvard University Press; London: William Heinemann, 1971.

Ovide moralisé. Edited by Cornelis de Boer. *Verhandelingen der Koninklijke Akademie van Wetenschapen te Amsterdam: Afdeeling Letterkunde*. Vols. 15, 21, 30, 36–37, and 43. Amsterdam, 1915–38.

Perceforest: Première partie. Edited by Gilles Roussineau. 2 vols. Textes littéraires français. Geneva: Droz, 2007.

Perceforest: Deuxième partie. Edited by Gilles Roussineau. 2 vols. Textes littéraires français. Geneva: Droz, 1999–2001.

Perceforest: Troisième partie. Edited by Gilles Roussineau. 3 vols. Textes littéraires français. Geneva: Droz, 1988–93.

Perceforest: Quatrième partie. Edited by Gilles Roussineau. 2 vols. Textes littéraires français. Geneva: Droz, 1987.

Perceforest: Cinquième partie. Edited by Gilles Roussineau. 2 vols. Textes littéraires français. Geneva: Droz, 2012.

Peter Comestor. *Historia scholastica*. Patrologia Latina 198:1053–722.

Poèmes d'amour des XIIe et XIIIe siècles. Edited by Emmanuèle Baumgartner and Françoise Ferrand. Paris: Editions 10/18, 1983.

Premiers faits du roi Arthur. In *Le livre du Graal*, edited by Daniel Poirion, 1:1082–139, 1531–54. Paris: Gallimard, 2001.

La prise d'Orange. Edited by Claude Lachet. Champion classiques: Moyen Âge. Paris: Champion, 2010.

Pseudo-Turpin. *An Anonymous Old French Translation of the Pseudo-Turpin "Chronicle."* Edited by Ronald N. Walpole. Cambridge, MA: Mediaeval Academy of America, 1979.

La queste del Saint Graal. Edited by Albert Pauphilet. Classiques français du Moyen Âge. Paris: Champion, 1967.

Regino of Prüm. *Epistula ad Hathonem archiepiscopum missa*. Edited by Friedrich Kurze. *Reginonis Abbatis Prumiensis Chronicon*, Monumenta Germaniae historica, Scriptores rerum Germanicarum in usum scholarum separatim editi. Hanover, 1890.

Renaut de Beaujeu. *Le Bel Inconnu*. Edited by G. Perrie Williams. Classiques français du Moyen Âge. Paris: Champion, 1983.

Saga of Tristram and Ísönd. Translated by Paul Schach. Lincoln: University of Nebraska Press, 1973.

Saladin. Edited by Larry Crist. Textes littéraires français. Geneva: Droz, 1972.

Suite du roman de Merlin. Edited by Gilles Roussineau. 2 vols. Textes littéraires français. Geneva: Droz, 1996.

Thomas d'Angleterre. *Tristan.* In *Les Tristan en vers.* Edited by J. C. Payen, 145–244. Paris: Garnier, 1974.
Tristan en prose. Edited by Renée L. Curtis. 3 vols. Vol. 1: Munich: Max Hüber, 1963. Vol. 2: Leiden: E. J. Brill, 1976. Vol. 3: Cambridge: Boydell and Brewer, 1985.
Tristan en prose. Edited under the direction of Philippe Ménard. 9 vols. Textes littéraires français. Geneva: Droz, 1987–97. Vol. 1: Edited by Philippe Ménard. Vol. 2: Edited by Marie-Luce Chênerie and Thierry Delcourt. Vol. 3: Edited by Gilles Roussineau. Vol. 4: Edited by Jean-Claude Faucon. Vol. 5: Edited by Denis Lalande and Jean-Claude Faucon. Vol. 6: Edited by Michèle Szkilnik and Emmanuèle Baumgartner. Vol. 7: Edited by Danielle Queruel and Monique Santucci. Vol. 8: Edited by Bernard Guidot and Jean Subrenat. Vol. 9: Edited by Laurence Harf-Lancner.
Valentin et Orson: An Edition and Translation of the Fifteenth-Century Romance Epic. Edited and translated by Shira Schwam-Baird. Tempe: Arizona Center for Medieval and Renaissance Studies, 2011.
"Visions de l'autre: Le païen, le géant, et la femme." Edited by Sophie Albert. In *Guiron le courtois: Une anthologie,* 87–149.
Wace. *Roman de Brut: A History of the British.* Edited and translated by Judith Weiss. Rev. ed. Exeter: University of Exeter Press, 2002.

Secondary Sources

Akbari, Suzanne Conklin. "The Diversity of Mankind in *The Book of John Mandeville.*" In *Eastward Bound: Travels and Travellers, 1050–1550.* Edited by Rosamund Allen, 156–76. Manchester: Manchester University Press, 2004.
———. *Idols in the East: European Representations of Islam and the Orient, 1100–1450.* Ithaca, NY: Cornell University Press, 2009.
Albert, Sophie. *"Ensemble ou par pieces": "Guiron le Courtois" (XIIIe–XVe siècles): La cohérence en question.* Nouvelle bibliothèque du Moyen Age 98. Paris: Champion, 2010.
Bartlett, Robert. *The Making of Europe: Conquest, Colonization and Cultural Change, 950–1350.* London: Penguin Books, 1994.
———. "Medieval and Modern Concepts of Race and Ethnicity." *Journal of Medieval and Early Modern Studies* 31 (2001): 39–56.
Barzilai, Shuli. *Lacan and the Matter of Origins.* Stanford, CA: Stanford University Press, 1999.
Baumgartner, Emmanuèle. "L'exotisme à rebours de la *Chanson d'Antioche.*" In *L'exotisme dans la poésie épique française: In memoriam Klára Csürös,* edited by Anikó Kalmár, 13–28. Paris: Harmattan, 2003.

———. "Géants et chevaliers." In *The Spirit of the Court*, edited by Glyn S. Burgess and Robert A. Taylor, 9–22. Cambridge: D. S. Brewer, 1985.
———. *Le "Tristan en prose": Essai d'interprétation d'un roman médiéval*. Publications romanes et françaises 133. Geneva: Droz, 1975.
Bergner, Gwen. "Who Is That Masked Woman? or, The Role of Gender in Fanon's *Black Skin, White Masks*." *PMLA* 110 (1995): 75–88.
Bhabha, Homi. *The Location of Culture*. London: Routledge, 1994.
Blackman, Susan A. "A Pictorial Synopsis of Arthurian Episodes for Jacques d'Armagnac, Duke of Nemours." In *Word and Image in Arthurian Literature*, edited by Keith Busby, 3–57. New York: Garland, 1996.
Boivin, Jeanne-Marie. "La Dame du Lac, Morgane et Galehaut: Symbolique de trois figures emblématiques de l'Autre Monde dans le 'Lancelot.'" *Médiévales* 6 (1984): 18–25.
Boswell, John. *Christianity, Social Tolerance, and Homosexuality: Gay People in Western Europe from the Beginning of the Christian Era to the Fourteenth Century*. Chicago: University of Chicago Press, 1980.
Brottier, Laurence. "Images de l'étranger chez un prédicateur du IVe siècle, Jean Chrysostome: Idéalisation et diabolisation." In *Images de l'étranger*, edited by Bernadette Lemoine, 317–31. Limoges: Presses universitaires de Limoges, 2006.
Brown, Wendy. "Subjects of Tolerance: Why We Are Civilized and They Are the Barbarians." In *Political Theologies: Public Religions in a Post-secular World*, edited by Hent De Vries and Lawrence E. Sullivan, 298–317. New York: Fordham University Press, 2006.
Bruckner, Matilda. "The Lady and the Dragon in Chrétien's *Le Chevalier au lion*." In *From Beasts to Souls: Gender and Embodiment in Medieval Europe*, edited by E. Jane Burns and Peggy McCracken, 65–86. Notre Dame, IN: University of Notre Dame Press, 2013.
Burns, E. Jane. "Which Queen? Guinevere's Transvestism in the French Prose *Lancelot*." In *Lancelot and Guinevere: A Casebook*, edited by Lori Walters, 247–65. New York: Garland, 1996.
Butler, Judith. *Bodies That Matter: On the Discursive Limits of "Sex."* New York: Routledge, 1993.
Carroll, Carleton W. "Text and Image: The Case of *Erec et Enide*." In *Word and Image in Arthurian Literature*, edited by Keith Busby, 58–78. New York: Garland, 1996.
Caulkins, Janet H. "Chelinde et la naissance du *Tristan en prose*." *Moyen Age* 93 (1987): 41–50.
Cazenave, Annie. "Monstres et merveilles." *Ethnologie française* 9 (1979): 235–56.
Chambers, Katherine. "'When We Do Nothing Wrong, We Are Peers': Peter the Chanter and Twelfth-Century Political Thought." *Speculum* 88 (2013): 405–26.

Clark, Gillian. "The Fathers and the Animals: The Rule of Reason?" In *Animals on the Agenda: Questions about Animals for Theology and Ethics*, edited by Andrew Linzey and Dorothy Yamamoto, 67–79. London: SCM Press, 1998.
Cohen, Jeffrey Jerome. *Hybridity, Identity, and Monstrosity in Medieval Britain: On Difficult Middles*. New York: Palgrave Macmillan, 2006.
———. *Medieval Identity Machines*. Medieval Cultures 35. Minneapolis: University of Minnesota Press, 2003.
———. *Of Giants: Sex, Monsters, and the Middle Ages*. Minneapolis: University of Minnesota Press, 1999.
———. "On Saracen Enjoyment: Some Fantasies of Race in Late Medieval France and England." *Journal of Medieval and Early Modern Studies* 31 (2001): 113–46.
Crane, Susan. *Animal Encounters: Contacts and Concepts in Medieval Britain*. Philadelphia: University of Pennsylvania Press, 2013.
Dean, James. "The World Grown Old and Genesis in Middle English Historical Writings." *Speculum* 57 (1982): 548–68.
Derrida, Jacques. "And Say the Animal Responded." Translated by David Wills. In *Zoontologies: The Question of the Animal*, edited by Cary Wolfe, 121–46. Minneapolis: University of Minnesota Press, 2003.
———. "Donner la mort." In *Donner la mort / L'ethique du don: Jacques Derrida et la pensée du don*, edited by Jean-Michel Rabaté and Michael Wetzel, 11–108. Paris: Métailié-Transition, 1992.
———. "Force de la loi: Le fondement mystique de l'autorité." With translation by Mary Quaintance as "Force of Law: The 'Mystical Foundation of Authority.'" *Cardozo Law Review* 11 (1990): 920–1045.
———. *The Gift of Death*. Translated by David Wills. Chicago: University of Chicago Press, 1995.
Dubost, Francis. *Aspects fantastiques de la littérature narrative médiévale (XIIème–XIIIème siècles): L'Autre, l'ailleurs, l'autrefois*. 2 vols. Nouvelle bibliothèque du Moyen Âge 15. Paris: Champion, 1991.
Duby, Georges. *Medieval Marriage: Two Models from Twelfth-Century France*. Translated by Elborg Foster. Baltimore: Johns Hopkins University Press, 1978.
Fanon, Frantz. *Black Skin, White Masks*. Translated by Charles Lam Markmann. London: Pluto Press, 1986.
———. *Les damnés de la terre*. Preface by Jean-Paul Sartre. Introduced by Gérard Chaliand. Paris: Gallimard, 1991.
———. *Peau noire, masques blancs*. Paris: Editions du Seuil, 1952.
———. *The Wretched of the Earth*. Preface by Jean-Paul Sartre. Translated by Constance Farrington. London: Penguin Classics, 2001.

Ferlampin-Acher, Christine. "La géographie et les progrès de la civilisation dans *Perceforest*." In *Provinces, régions, terroirs au Moyen Age: De la réalité à l'imaginaire*, edited by B. Guidot, 275–90. Nancy: Presses universitaires de Nancy, 1993.

Findley, Brooke Heidenreich. *Poet Heroines in Medieval French Narrative: Gender and Fictions of Literary Creation*. The New Middle Ages. New York: Palgrave Macmillan, 2012.

Fradenburg, L. O. Aranye. *Sacrifice Your Love: Psychoanalysis, Historicism, Chaucer*. Medieval Cultures 31. Minneapolis: University of Minnesota Press, 2002.

Freud, Sigmund. *Totem and Taboo: Some Points of Agreement between the Mental Lives of Savages and Neurotics*. Translated by James Strachey. London: Routledge and Kegan Paul, 1950.

Fuss, Diana. "Interior Colonies: Frantz Fanon and the Politics of Identification." *Diacritics* 24, nos. 2–3 (1994): 20–42.

Gallois, Martine. *L'idéal héroïque dans "Lion de Bourges," poème épique du XIVe siècle*. Paris: Champion, 2012.

Gates, Henry Louis, Jr. "Critical Fanonism." *Critical Inquiry* 17 (1991): 457–70.

Gaullier-Bougassas, Catherine. *La tentation de l'Orient dans le roman médiéval: Sur l'imaginaire médiévale de l'Autre*. Nouvelle bibliothèque du Moyen Âge 67. Paris: Champion, 2003.

Gaunt, Simon. *Love and Death in Medieval French and Occitan Courtly Literature: Martyrs to Love*. Oxford: Oxford University Press, 2006.

———. *Marco Polo's "Le Devisement du Monde": Narrative Voice, Language and Diversity*. Cambridge: D. S. Brewer, 2013.

Gilbert, Jane. *Living Death in Medieval French and English Literature*. Cambridge Studies in Medieval Literature 84. Cambridge: Cambridge University Press, 2011.

Girard, René. *Violence and the Sacred*. Translated by Patrick Gregory. London: Continuum, 2005.

———. *La violence et le sacré*. Paris: Bernard Grasset, 1972.

Girbea, Catalina. *Le Bon Sarrasin dans le roman médiéval (1100–1225)*. Bibliothèque de l'histoire médiévale 10. Paris: Classiques Garnier, 2014.

———. "Le double romanesque et la conversion: Le Sarrasin, le Juif, et le Grec dans les romans allemands (XIIe–XIIIe siècles)." *Cahiers de civilisation médiévale* 54 (2011): 243–86.

Goldenberg, David M. "The Development of the Idea of Race: Classical Paradigms and Medieval Elaborations." *International Journal of the Classical Tradition* 5 (1999): 561–70.

Gravdal, Kathryn. *Ravishing Maidens: Writing Rape in Medieval French Literature and Law*. Philadelphia: University of Pennsylvania Press, 1991.

Greene, Roland. *Unrequited Conquests: Love and Empire in Colonial America.* Chicago: University of Chicago Press, 1999.
Greene, Virginie. "Humanimals: The Future of Courtliness in the *Conte du Papegau*." In *Shaping Courtliness in Medieval France*, edited by D. E. O'Sullivan and L. Shepard, 123–38. Gallica. Cambridge: D. S. Brewer, 2013.
Griffin, Miranda. *The Object and the Cause in the Vulgate Cycle.* Oxford: Legenda, 2005.
Harf-Lancner, Laurence. "Gauvain l'assassin: La récurrence d'un schéma narratif dans le *Tristan* en prose." In *Tristan-Tristrant: Mélanges en l'honneur de Danielle Buschinger*, edited by André Crépin and Wolfgang Spiewok, 219–30. Greifswald: Reineke-Verlag, 1996.
Harper, James. "Turks as Trojans; Trojans as Turks: Visual Imagery of the Trojan War and the Politics of Cultural Identity in Fifteenth-Century Europe." In *Postcolonial Approaches to the European Middle Ages: Translating Cultures*, edited by Ananya Jahanara Kabir and Deanne Williams, 151–79. Cambridge: Cambridge University Press, 2005.
Haugeard, Philippe. "L'expérience de l'altérité dans *La vie de saint Louis* de Joinville: L'Orient, l'ailleurs et la contagion possible de la barbarie." *Bien dire et bien aprandre* 26 (2008): 121–35.
Heng, Geraldine. *Empire of Magic: Medieval Romance and the Politics of Cultural Fantasy.* New York: Columbia University Press, 2003.
Huot, Sylvia. "Chronicle, Lai, and Romance: Orality and Writing in the *Roman de Perceforest*." In *Vox Intexta: Orality and Textuality in the Middle Ages*, edited by A. Nick Doane and Carol Braun Pasternak, 203–23. Madison: University of Wisconsin Press, 1991.

———. "Love, Race, and Gender in Medieval Romance: Lancelot and the Son of the Giantess." *Journal of Medieval and Early Modern Studies* 37 (2007): 373–91.

———. *Madness in Medieval French Literature: Identities Found and Lost.* Oxford: Oxford University Press, 2003.

———. "Others and Alterity." In *The Cambridge Companion to Medieval French Literature*, edited by Simon Gaunt and Sarah Kay, 238–50. Cambridge: Cambridge University Press, 2008.

———. *Postcolonial Fictions in the "Roman de Perceforest": Cultural Identities and Hybridities.* Gallica 1. Cambridge: D. S. Brewer, 2007.

———. "Unspeakable Horror, Ineffable Bliss: Riddles and Marvels in the Prose *Tristan.*" *Medium Aevum* 71 (2002): 47–65.
JanMohamed, Abdul R. "The Economy of Manichean Allegory: The Function of Racial Difference in Colonialist Literature." In *"Race," Writing, and Difference*, edited by Henry Louis Gates Jr., 78–106. Chicago: University of Chicago Press, 1985.

Johnson, Lesley. "Return to Albion." *Arthurian Literature* 13 (1995): 19–40.
Jubb, Margaret. *The Legend of Saladin in Western Literature and Historiography*. Lewiston, NY: Edwin Mellen, 2000.
Kaeuper, Richard W. *Chivalry and Violence in Medieval Europe*. Oxford: Oxford University Press, 1999.
Kawash, Samira. "Terrorists and Vampires: Fanon's Spectral Violence." In *Frantz Fanon: Critical Perspectives*, edited by Anthony C. Alessandrini, 235–57. London: Routledge, 1999.
Kay, Sarah. *The Chansons de Geste in the Age of Romance*. Oxford: Clarendon Press, 1995.
———. "Desire and Subjectivity." In *The Troubadours: An Introduction*, edited by Simon Gaunt and Sarah Kay, 212–27. Cambridge: Cambridge University Press, 1999.
Kilgour, Maggie. "The Function of Cannibalism at the Present Time." In *Cannibalism and the Colonial World*, edited by Francis Barker, Peter Hulms, and Margaret Iversen, 238–59. Cambridge: Cambridge University Press, 1998.
Kinoshita, Sharon. *Medieval Boundaries: Rethinking Difference in Old French Literature*. Philadelphia: University of Pennsylvania Press, 2006.
Kosta-Théfaine, Jean François. "The Pierpont Morgan Library Manuscript M.723: Illustrations of Hayton's *La Fleur des histoires d'Orient*." In *Travels and Travelogues in the Middle Ages*, edited by Jean-François Kosta-Théfaine, 135–54. New York: AMS Press, 2009.
Kristeva, Julia. *Étrangers à nous-mêmes*. Paris: Fayard, 1988.
———. *Strangers to Ourselves*. Translated by Leon S. Roudiez. New York: Harvester Wheatsheaf, 1991.
Krueger, Roberta. "Love, Honor, and the Exchange of Women in *Yvain*: Some Remarks on the Female Reader." *Romance Notes* 25 (1985): 302–17.
Kruger, Steven F. "Conversion and Medieval Sexual, Religious, and Racial Categories." In *Constructing Medieval Sexuality*, edited by Karma Lochrie, Peggy McCracken, and James A. Schultz, 158–79. Medieval Cultures 11. Minneapolis: University of Minnesota Press, 1997.
Lacan, Jacques. "The Function and Field of Speech and Language in Psychoanalysis." In *Écrits: A Selection*. Translated by Alan Sheridan, 30–113. London: Routledge, 1977.
———. "The Mirror Stage as Formative of the Function of the I as Revealed in Psychoanalytic Experience." In *Écrits: A Selection*, translated by Alan Sheridan, 1–7. London: Routledge, 1977.
———. "The Subversion of the Subject and the Dialectic of Desire in the Freudian Unconscious." In *Écrits: A Selection*, translated by Alan Sheridan, 292–325. London: Routledge, 1977.

Lampert, Lisa. "Race, Periodicity, and the (Neo-) Middle Ages." *MLQ* 65 (2004): 391–421.
Lathuillère, Roger. *Guiron le courtois: Étude de la tradition manuscrite et analyse critique*. Publications romanes et françaises 86. Geneva: Droz, 1966.
Lévi-Strauss, Claude. *The Elementary Structures of Kinship*. Translated by James Hare Bell, John Richard von Sturmer, and Rodney Needham. Rev. ed. Boston: Beacon Press, 1969.
Lewis-Williams, David. "Of People and Pictures: The Nexus of Upper Paleolithic Religion, Social Discrimination, and Art." In *Becoming Human: Innovation in Prehistoric Material and Spiritual Culture*, edited by Colin Renfrew and Iain Morley, 135–58. Cambridge: Cambridge University Press, 2009.
MacCormack, Carol P. "Nature, Culture and Gender: A Critique." In *Nature, Culture and Gender*, edited by Carol MacCormack and Marilyn Strathern, 1–24. Cambridge: Cambridge University Press, 1980.
Mercer, Kobena. "Busy in the Ruins of a Wretched Phantasia." In *Frantz Fanon: Critical Perspectives*, edited by Anthony C. Alessandrini, 195–218. London: Routledge, 1999.
Mickel, Emanuel J. "Tristan's Ancestry in the *Tristan en prose*." *Romania* 109 (1988): 68–89.
Moi, Toril. "'She Died because She Came Too Late . . .': Knowledge, Doubles and Death in Thomas's *Tristan*." *Exemplaria* 4 (1992): 105–33.
Moore, Megan. *Exchanges in Exoticism: Cross-cultural Marriage and the Making of the Mediterranean in Old French Romance*. Toronto: University of Toronto Press, 2014.
Nayar, Pramod K. *Posthumanism*. Cambridge: Polity Press, 2014.
Noacco, Cristina. "L'orgueil et la métamorphose dans l'*Ovide moralisé*: Enjeux narratifs, poétiques et pédagogiques." In *Nouvelles études sur l'Ovide moralisé*, edited by Marylène Possamaï-Pérez, 99–119. Paris: Champion, 2009.
Nocentelli, Carmen. *Empires of Love: Europe, Asia, and the Making of Early Modern Identity*. Philadelphia: University of Pennsylvania Press, 2013.
Oliver, Kelly. *Animal Lessons: How They Teach Us to Be Human*. New York: Columbia University Press, 2009.
Phillips, Jerry. "Cannibalism qua Capitalism: The Metaphorics of Accumulation in Marx, Conrad, Shakespeare, and Marlow." In *Cannibalism and the Colonial World*, edited by Francis Barker, Peter Hulme, and Margaret Iversen, 183–203. Cambridge: Cambridge University Press, 1998.
Ramey, Lynne Tarte. *Christian, Saracen, and Genre in Medieval French Literature*. New York: Routledge, 2001.
Rawick, George P. *From Sundown to Sunup: The Making of the Black Community*. The American Slave: A Composite Autobiography, 1. Westport, CT: Greenwood, 1972.

Regnier-Bohler, Danielle. "Figures féminines et imaginaire généalogique: Étude comparée de quelques récits brefs." In *Le récit bref au moyen âge: Actes du colloque des 27, 28, et 29 avril 1979*, edited by Danielle Buschinger, 73–95. Amiens: Centre d'études médiévales, 1980.

Resnick, Irven M., and Kenneth F. Kitchell Jr. "Albert the Great on the 'Language' of Animals." *American Catholic Philosophical Quarterly* 70 (1996): 41–61.

Roberts, Kathleen Glenister. *Alterity and Narrative: Stories and the Negotiation of Western Identities*. Albany: SUNY Press, 2007.

Roediger, David R. *The Wages of Whiteness: Race and the Making of the American Working Class*. Rev. ed. London: Verso, 2007.

Rubin, Gayle. "The Traffic in Women: Notes on the 'Political Economy' of Sex." In *Toward an Anthropology of Women*, edited by Rayna R. Reiter, 157–210. New York: Monthly Review Press, 1975.

Said, Edward W. *Culture and Imperialism*. London: Vintage, 1994.

———. *Orientalism*. London: Penguin Books, 1985.

Schultz, James A. *Courtly Love, the Love of Courtliness, and the History of Sexuality*. Chicago: University of Chicago Press, 2006.

Sharpe, Jenny. "The Unspeakable Limits of Rape: Colonial Violence and Counter-insurgency." *Genders* 10 (1991): 25–46.

Simpson, James R. *Troubling Arthurian Histories: Court Culture, Performance and Scandal in Chrétien de Troyes's "Erec et Enide."* Medieval and Early Modern French Studies 5. Oxford: Peter Lang, 2007.

Smith, Anna. *Julia Kristeva: Readings of Exile and Estrangement*. Basingstoke: Macmillan, 1996.

Smith, Nathaniel. "The Man on a Horse and the Horse-Man: Constructions of Human and Animal in the *Knight of the Parrot*." In *Literary Aspects of Courtly Culture*, edited by Donald Maddox and Sara Sturm-Maddox, 241–48. Woodbridge: D. S. Brewer, 1994.

Spivak, Gayatri. "Can the Subaltern Speak? Speculations on Widow Sacrifice." In *Marxism and the Interpretation of Culture*, edited by Cary Nelson and Laurence Grossberg, 271–313. Basingstoke: Macmillan, 1988.

Stahuljak, Zrinka. *Bloodless Genealogies of the French Middle Ages: Translatio, Kinship, and Metaphor*. Gainesville: University Press of Florida, 2005.

Steel, Karl. "Centaurs, Satyrs, and Cynocephali: Medieval Scholarly Teratology and the Question of the Human." In *The Ashgate Research Companion to Monsters and the Monstrous*, edited by Asa Simon Mittman and Peter J. Dendle, 257–74. Lewiston, UK: Ashgate, 2012.

———. *How to Make a Human: Animals and Violence in the Middle Ages*. Columbus: Ohio State University Press, 2011.

Steele, Meili. *Theorizing Textual Subjects: Agency and Oppression*. Cambridge: Cambridge University Press, 1997.

Stephens, Walter. *Giants in Those Days: Folklore, Ancient History, and Nationalism*. Regents Studies in Medieval Culture. Lincoln: University of Nebraska Press, 1989.

Stewart, Susan. *On Longing: Narratives of the Miniature, the Gigantic, the Souvenir, the Collection*. Baltimore: Johns Hopkins University Press, 1984.

Stones, M. Alison. "The Egerton *Brut* and Its Illustrations." In *Maistre Wace: A Celebration*, edited by Glyn S. Burgess and Judith Weiss, 167–76. Jersey: Société Jersiale, 2006.

Strickland, Debra Higgs. "Monstrosity and Race in the Late Middle Ages." In *The Ashgate Research Companion to Monsters and the Monstrous*, edited by Asa Simon Mittman and Peter J. Dendle, 365–86. Farnham, UK: Ashgate, 2012.

———. *Saracens, Demons, and Jews: Making Monsters in Medieval Art*. Princeton, NJ: Princeton University Press, 2003.

———. "Text, Image, and Contradiction in the *Devisement dou monde*." In *Marco Polo and the Encounter of East and West*, edited by Suzanne Conklin Akbari and Amilcare Iannucci, 23–59. Toronto: University of Toronto Press, 2008.

Suard, François. "*La fille du comte de Ponthieu*: Transgression, parole et silence." In *"Moult a sans et vallour": Studies in Medieval French Literature in Honor of William W. Kibler*, edited by Monica L. Wright, Norris J. Lacy, and Rupert T. Pickens, 357–70. Amsterdam: Rodopi, 2012.

Sunderland, Luke. "Genre, Ideology, and Utopia in *Huon de Bordeaux*." *Medium Aevum* 81 (2012): 289–302.

Tattersall, Jill. "Anthropophagi and Eaters of Raw Flesh in French Literature of the Crusade Period: Myth, Tradition and Reality." *Medium Aevum* 57 (1988): 240–53.

Taylor, Charles. "The Person." In *The Category of the Person: Anthropology, Philosophy, History*, edited by Michael Carrithers, Steven Collins, and Steven Lukes, 257–81. Cambridge: Cambridge University Press, 1985.

Taylor, Jane H. M. "The Fourteenth Century: Context, Text, and Intertext." In *The Legacy of Chréetien de Troyes*, edited by Norris J. Lacy, Douglas Kelly, and Keith Busby, 1:267–332. Amsterdam: Rodopi, 1987.

———. "The Parrot, the Knight and the Decline of Chivalry." In *Conjunctures: Medieval Studies in Honor of Douglas Kelly*, edited by Keith Busby and Norris J. Lacy, 529–44. Faux Titre 83. Amsterdam: Rodopi, 1994.

Trachsler, Richard. *Clôtures du cycle Arthurien: Étude et textes*. Publications romanes et françaises 215. Geneva: Droz, 1996.

Traxler, Janina P. "Observations on the Beste Glatissant in the *Tristan en prose*." *Neophilologus* 74 (1990): 499–509.

———. "Observations on the Importance of the Prehistory in the *Tristan en prose*." *Romania* 108 (1987): 539–48.

Uebel, Michael. *Ecstatic Transformation: On the Uses of Alterity in the Middle Ages*. New York: Palgrave Macmillan, 2005.
Van Coolput, Colette-Anne. "La 'Préhistoire arthurienne': Quelques réflexions à propos de la première partie du *Tristan en prose*." *Lettres romanes* 38 (1984): 275–82.
Vergès, Françoise. "Creole Skin, Black Mask: Fanon and Disavowal." *Critical Inquiry* 23 (1997): 578–95.
Walters, Lori. "Parody and the Parrot: Lancelot References in the *Chevalier du Papegau*." In *Translatio Studii: Essays by His Students in Honor of Karl D. Uitti for His Sixty-Fifth Birthday*, edited by Kevin Brownlee, Renate Blumenfeld-Kosinski, Mary Speer, and Lori Walters, 331–44. Faux titre 179. Amsterdam: Rodopi, 2000.
Warren, Michelle R. "Making Contact: Postcolonial Perspectives through Geoffrey of Monmouth's *Historia regum Britannie*." *Arthuriana* 8, no. 4 (1998): 115–34.
White, Hugh. *Nature, Sex, and Goodness in a Medieval Literary Tradition*. Oxford: Oxford University Press, 2000.
Williams, David. *Deformed Discourse: The Function of the Monster in Medieval Thought and Literature*. Exeter: University of Exeter Press, 1996.
Wolfe, Cary. *Animal Rites: American Culture, the Discourse of Species, and Posthumanist Theory*. Chicago: University of Chicago Press, 2003.
Young, Robert J. C. *Colonial Desire: Hybridity in Theory, Culture and Race*. London: Routledge, 1995.
Zeikowitz, Richard E. *Homoeroticism and Chivalry: Discourses of Male Same-Sex Desire in the Fourteenth Century*. New York: Palgrave Macmillan, 2003.
Žižek, Slavoj. *Enjoy Your Symptom! Jacques Lacan in Hollywood and Out*. New York: Routledge, 1992.
———. *Violence: Six Sideways Reflections*. London: Profile Books, 2008.

INDEX

Akbari, Suzanne Conklin, 102
Alexander of Hales, 59
Arthur, 44–46, 65–66, 71–72, 151–53
Augustine, Saint (bishop of Hippo), 33–36
Augustine, Saint (missionary to England), 188–89

Bartlett, Robert, 3
Barzilai, Shuli, 239–40
Baumgartner, Emmanuèle, 212
Bel Inconnu, 64
Bhabha, Homi, 19, 43, 67, 93, 98, 230–31, 243–44
Bible
  Baruch, 34–35
  Genesis, 32–34, 36, 53–54, 240–41
  Numbers, 37
  Proverbs, 183
Boethius, 59, 242–43
Brown, Wendy, 11–12
Butler, Judith, 57–58

Cain, 33–35, 40, 53–55, 181–82, 192
cannibalism. *See* giants: anthropophagy
Châtelain de Couci, 107, 118

Chrétien de Troyes
  Chevalier au lion, 47, 123, 220–21, 245–48
  Erec et Enide, 28–29, 125, 156, 296, 300–301
Christopher, Saint, 62
Cohen, Jeffrey Jerome, 19, 20, 27, 37, 41, 50, 64, 66, 263–64
Conon de Béthune, 107, 118
Conte du Papegau, 44–47, 50–52, 148–53, 285–91. *See also* giants (individual characters): Chevalier Jayant, Jayant Redoubté de la Roche Secure, Jayant sans Nom
Crane, Susan, 59, 264

Derrida, Jacques, 52, 238, 264, 297–99
Des grantz geanz, 19, 39–41, 67, 75–76
Dubost, Francis, 27

Estoire del Saint Graal, 69, 126

fairies, 62–63, 87–88, 151–53, 212–13
Fanon, Frantz, 38, 237, 238, 269

345

Fille du comte de Ponthieu, 224–25
Fradenburg, L. O. Aranye, 115
Fuss, Diana, 263

Galahad, 165, 167–68, 215–16
Gaunt, Simon, 61, 109
Gawain, 79
Geoffrey of Monmouth, 37, 42.
  See also giants (individual
  characters): Giant of
  Mont-St-Michel, Gogmagog,
  Rion (Ritho/Rithon)
giantess bride, 96–97
  Galotine, 97, 99–102, 134–36,
  278
  Huon de Bordeaux, 136–37
  Isle del Jaiant, 162
  Maudit's mother, 139–40, 279
  Riddler's daughter, 132–37, 279
giants
  as aboriginals, 9–11, 37, 67
  animality, 46, 50–52, 55–59,
  238–39, 264–65, 274–75
  anthropophagy, 16, 52–62, 141,
  180–81, 192–93
  classical mythology, 240–43
  demonic, 33, 35
  desire for knights, 169, 180,
  195–96, 201–4
  as feudal lords, 70–80, 91–96,
  122–23, 170–72, 275
  humanity, 1, 16, 20, 23, 27–32,
  38–42, 55–63, 68, 288–91
  isolationism, 69, 159
  as lovers, 142–43, 149–50
  monstrosity, 5–6, 29–32, 40–41,
  44–46
  origins, 33–34, 39–41
  See also giants (individual
  characters); incest; Saracens;
  subjectivity; terrorism; violence

giants (individual characters)
  Agrapart, 83–85, 136–37
  Aupatris, 49, 110, 123
  Caradoc, 202
  Chevalier Jayant, 20, 46–47,
  148–51, 271, 278, 284–85,
  288–91
  Dyaletes, 158–60, 161
  Fernagut, 81–83
  Ferragu, 47–49
  Galehot
  —in *Lancelot*, 198–207, 209–14,
  220–22, 225–29
  —in *Tristan*, 162, 164–66, 207–9,
  253–54
  Giant of Mont-St-Michel, 15,
  65–66, 141–42, 247–50
  Gogmagog, 19, 43, 65, 124
  Golden-Haired Giant, 6, 16,
  77–79, 141, 266–67, 271–76,
  282–85
  Harpin de la Montagne, 47,
  247–48
  Holland, 29–32, 109–10,
  267–70
  Jayant Redoubté de la Roche
  Secure, 149, 150, 287–90
  Jayant sans Nom, 50–52, 57
  Maudit, 50, 93–94, 95fig.2,
  139–40, 142–47
  Nabon li Noirs, 169–74
  Nimrod, 36, 53
  l'Orgueilleux, 83–84
  Rainouart, 5–6, 81
  Riddler, 18–19, 55, 60–61,
  177–95, 259–66
  Rion (Ritho/Rithon), 66, 70–73
  Taulas de la Montagne, 57,
  111–12
gift of death, 119, 127–30, 134,
  297–99

Gilbert, Jane, 204
Girard, René, 53, 106, 130–31
Greene, Roland, 130, 138
Guiron le Courtois, 74–75, 89, 90–92, 120–31, 150, 170–73, 254–59, 295

Harf-Lancner, Laurence, 294
historical trajectory. *See* narrative trajectory
Holy War, 72, 81–89, 107–9, 118–19, 293–94
horse, and chivalric identity, 45–51
humanity, 14, 50–54, 115.
See also giants: humanity
Huon de Bordeaux, 83–85, 136–37

incest, 40–41, 60–62, 180–81, 188–89

JanMohamed, Abdul, 7, 250–51
Jaufre Rudel, 108
John of Salisbury, 243
Johnson, Lesley, 43

Kaueper, Richard, 17
Kawash, Samira, 13, 42–43, 68
Kay, Sarah, 128, 133, 137–38, 252
Kilgour, Maggie, 61
Kinoshita, Sharon, 96
Kristeva, Julia, 186, 187
Kruger, Steven F., 7

Lacan, Jacques, 238–40, 243–44, 250–61, 268–69, 271–75, 289
Lancelot: Roman en prose du XIIIe siècle, 50, 92–94. *See also* giants (individual characters): Galehot, Maudit
Lewis-Williams, David, 10

manuscripts
Bonn, Universitäts- und Landesbibliothek 526, 249
Geneva, Bibl. de Génève, fr. 189, 190, 191fig.3
London, British Library Add. MS 10292, 249–50
Paris, Bibl. de l'Arsenal, MS 3477, 90fig.1, 90–91
Paris, Bnf, fr. 119, 94, 95fig.2
Paris, Bnf, fr. 335, 192
Paris, Bnf, fr. 1433, 247, 249fig.5
Paris, Bnf, n.a.fr. 6579, 192
Princeton, Firestone Library, Garrett MS 125, 247, 248fig.4
Mélusine, 62, 76–77, 86–88, 114–16
Mercer, Kobena, 2

narrative trajectory, 12–13, 17–22, 38–39, 155–57, 172–76, 193–95, 205–12, 231–33
Nayer, Pramod K., 38
Neanderthals, 8–11
Noacco, Cristina, 241
Nocentelli, Carmen, 100, 134

Original Sin, 10, 34, 62, 180–81, 195
Ovide moralisé, 240–41

Palamedes, 203, 214–20, 222–24, 230–31, 294
Perceforest, 65, 116–20, 267–68, 280–84. *See also* giantess bride: Galotine; giants (individual characters): Golden-Haired Giant, Holland

Peter Comestor, 35, 53
Phillips, Jerry, 67, 244
Premiers faits du roi Arthur (Suite du Merlin), 71–72, 249–50
Prise d'Orange, 97–98, 107–8
Prudentius, 239–40
Pseudo-Turpin Chronicle, 81–82

race, 3–12, 38–39, 43–44, 66–67, 263–64, 299–300
Ramey, Lynn Tarte, 6, 251
Rawick, George P., 245–46
requitedness, 130, 143–44, 203–4
Roland, 81–82, 233–34
Roediger, David R., 13, 67

sacrifice. *See* gift of death; violence: sacrificial
Said, Edward, 19
Saladin, 224–35
Saracens, 4–6, 293–94
　British, 160–61
　giants, 2, 47–49, 80–87, 89–91
　princess, 100, 128, 133
　—*Fierabras*, 102–3
　—*Guiron le courtois*, 121–22, 255–56
　—*Huon de Bordeaux*, 137–38
　—*Prise d'Orange*, 96–98
　—*Saladin*, 231–32
　—*Tristan*, 177–79
　See also Palamedes; Saladin
Simpson, James R., 125, 156, 296
Smith, Anna, 186
Steel, Karl, 14, 52, 244
Steele, Meili, 16–17, 190
Stewart, Susan, 63
subjectivity, 186–87, 252, 263, 265–70, 279–80, 299

Suite du Merlin. See *Premiers Faits du roi Arthur*
Suite du Roman de Merlin, 49, 73, 110, 123, 295–96

Taylor, Charles, 187
terrorism, 11–13, 68
Trachsler, Richard, 21
Tristan en prose, 54–57, 64, 75, 89, 126
　Castel Felon, 160–61, 165, 166–68
　Isle del Jaiant, 158–66, 207–9, 251–53
　Païs de Servaige, 169–76
　See also giantess bride: Riddler's daughter; giants (individual characters): Galehot, Nabon li Noirs, Riddler, Taulas de la Montagne

Uebel, Michael, 139, 155–56, 299

Valentin et Orson, 47–49
violence, 13–17, 53, 58–60, 270
　and love, 116–19, 123–38
　object of desire, 15, 65–66, 108–11, 119, 130–31, 239–40
　sacrificial, 129–31, 293–95, 297–99, 300–301 (*see also* gift of death)
　sexual, 141–42

Wace, 42, 70
Warren, Michelle, 255, 256
Williams, David, 35–36
Wolfe, Cary, 50, 291

Žižek, Slavoj, 12, 17, 301

SYLVIA HUOT

is professor of medieval French literature and
a Fellow of Pembroke College, University of Cambridge.

www.ingramcontent.com/pod-product-compliance
Lightning Source LLC
Chambersburg PA
CBHW061424300426
44114CB00014B/1524